ANNUAL EDITION

Early Childhood Education 12/13

Thirty-Third Edition

EDITOR

Karen Menke Paciorek
Eastern Michigan University

Karen Menke Paciorek is a professor of early childhood education at Eastern Michigan University in Ypsilanti. Her degrees in early childhood education include a BA from the University of Pittsburgh, an MA from George Washington University, and a PhD from Peabody College of Vanderbilt University. She is the editor of *Taking Sides: Clashing Views in Early Childhood Education* (2nd ed.) also published by McGraw-Hill. She has served as president of the Michigan Association for the Education of Young Children, the Michigan Early Childhood Education Consortium, and the Northville School Board. She presents at local, state, and national conferences on curriculum planning, guiding behavior, preparing the learning environment, and working with families. She served for nine years as a member of the Board of Education for the Northville Public Schools, Northville, Michigan. She is on the Board of Directors for Wolverine Human Services, serving over 600 abused and delinquent youth in Michigan and many other volunteer service boards. Dr. Paciorek is a recipient of the Eastern Michigan University Distinguished Faculty Award for Service and the Outstanding Teaching Award from the Alumni Association.

The McGraw-Hill Companies

Mc Graw Hill
Connect
Learn
Succeed™

ANNUAL EDITIONS: EARLY CHILDHOOD EDUCATION, THIRTY-THIRD EDITION

Published by McGraw-Hill, a business unit of The McGraw-Hill Companies, Inc., 1221 Avenue of the Americas, New York, NY 10020. Copyright © 2013 by The McGraw-Hill Companies, Inc. All rights reserved. Printed in the United States of America. Previous editions © 2012, 2011, 2010, and 2009. No part of this publication may be reproduced or distributed in any form or by any means, or stored in a database or retrieval system, without the prior written consent of The McGraw-Hill Companies, Inc., including, but not limited to, in any network or other electronic storage or transmission, or broadcast for distance learning.

Some ancillaries, including electronic and print components, may not be available to customers outside the United States.

This book is printed on acid-fee paper.

Annual Editions® is a registered trademark of The McGraw-Hill Companies, Inc.
Annual Editions is published by the **Contemporary Learning Series** group within the McGraw-Hill Higher Education division.

1 2 3 4 5 6 7 8 9 0 QDB/QDB 1 0 9 8 7 6 5 4 3 2

ISBN: 978-007-805126-5
MHID: 0-07-805126-6
ISSN: 0270-4456 (print)
ISSN: 2159-1040 (online)

Managing Editor: *Larry Loeppke*
Senior Developmental Editor: *Jade Benedict*
Senior Permissions Coordinator: *Lenny J. Behnke*
Senior Marketing Communications Specialist: *Mary Klein*
Project Manager: *Connie Oertel*
Design Coordinator: *Margarite Reynolds*
Cover Graphics: *Studio Montage*
Buyer: *Susan K. Culbertson*
Media Project Manager: *Sridevi Palani*

Compositor: Laserwords Private Limited
Cover Images: Ingram Publishing (inset); Ingram Publishing (background)

Editors/Academic Advisory Board

Members of the Academic Advisory Board are instrumental in the final selection of articles for each edition of ANNUAL EDITIONS. Their review of articles for content, level, and appropriateness provides critical direction to the editors and staff. We think that you will find their careful consideration well reflected in this volume.

ANNUAL EDITIONS: Early Childhood Education 12/13
33rd Edition

EDITOR

Karen Menke Paciorek
Eastern Michigan University

ACADEMIC ADVISORY BOARD MEMBERS

Editors/Academic Advisory Board continued

Preface

In publishing ANNUAL EDITIONS, we recognize the enormous role played by the magazines, newspapers, and journals of the public press in providing current, first-rate educational information in a broad spectrum of interest areas. Many of these articles are appropriate for students, researchers, and professionals seeking accurate, current material to help bridge the gap between principles and theories and the real world. These articles, however, become more useful for study when those of lasting value are carefully collected, organized, indexed, and reproduced in a low-cost format, which provides easy and permanent access when the material is needed. That is the role played by ANNUAL EDITIONS.

*A*nnual Editions: Early Childhood Education has evolved during the over 33 years it has been in existence to become one of the most used texts for students in early childhood education. This annual reader is used today at over 550 colleges and universities. In addition, it may be found in public libraries, pediatricians' offices, and teacher reference sections of school libraries. As the editor for over twenty-five years, I work diligently throughout the year to find articles and bring you the best and most significant readings in the field. I realize this is a tremendous responsibility to provide a thorough review of the current literature—a responsibility I take very seriously. I am always on the lookout for possible articles for the next *Annual Editions: Early Childhood Education.* My goal is to provide the reader with a snapshot of the critical issues facing professionals in early childhood education. The overviews for each unit describe in more detail the issues related to the unit topic and provide the reader with additional information about the issues. I encourage everyone to read the short, but useful, unit overviews prior to reading the articles.

Early childhood education is an interdisciplinary field that includes child development, family issues, educational practices, behavior guidance, and curriculum. *Annual Editions: Early Childhood Education 12/13* brings you the latest information in the field from a wide variety of recent journals, magazines, and websites.

There are five themes found in the readings chosen for this thirty-third edition of *Annual Editions: Early Childhood Education.* As editor I read a preponderance of articles on five key issues. They are the:

1. importance of play experiences during the early and middle childhood years, over an often highly touted academic approach, both in formal and informal settings.
2. strong evidence on the importance of recognizing the differences among boys and girls and how they learn and experience life in the early years.
3. increase in the use of all forms of technology by young children.
4. role a Response to Intervention (RTI) program can have on helping children be successful in school.
5. debate over using federal and state dollars to support universal preschool for all children or targeted preschool for the neediest children.

It is especially gratifying to see issues affecting children and families addressed in magazines other than professional association journals. The general public needs to be aware of the impact of positive early learning and family experiences on the growth and development of children.

Continuing in this edition of *Annual Editions: Early Childhood Education* are selected World Wide Websites that can be used to further explore topics addressed in the articles. I have chosen to include only a few high-quality sites. Readers are encouraged to explore these sites on their own or in collaboration with others for extended learning opportunities. All these sites were carefully reviewed by university students for their worthiness and direct application to those who work with young children on a day-to-day basis.

Given the wide range of topics; *Annual Editions: Early Childhood Education 12/13* may be used by several groups—undergraduate or graduate students, professionals, parents, or administrators who want to develop an understanding of the critical issues in the field.

I appreciate the time the advisory board members take to provide suggestions for improvement and possible articles for consideration. The production and editorial staff of McGraw-Hill, led by Larry Loeppke and Jade Benedict, ably support and coordinate my efforts.

To the instructor or reader interested in current issues professionals in the field deal with regularly, I encourage you to check out *Taking Sides: Clashing Views in Early Childhood Education,* 2nd edition (2008), which contains eighteen critical issues. The book can be used in a seminar or issues course and opens the door to rich discussion.

I look forward to hearing from you about the selection and organization of this edition and especially value correspondence from students who take the time to share their thoughts on the profession or articles selected. Comments and articles sent for consideration are welcomed and will serve to modify future volumes. You may also contact me at *kpaciorek@emich.edu.*

Karen Menke Paciorek

Karen Menke Paciorek
Editor

The Annual Editions Series

VOLUMES AVAILABLE

Adolescent Psychology

Aging

American Foreign Policy

American Government

Anthropology

Archaeology

Assessment and Evaluation

Business Ethics

Child Growth and Development

Comparative Politics

Criminal Justice

Developing World

Drugs, Society, and Behavior

Dying, Death, and Bereavement

Early Childhood Education

Economics

Educating Children with Exceptionalities

Education

Educational Psychology

Entrepreneurship

Environment

The Family

Gender

Geography

Global Issues

Health

Homeland Security

Human Development

Human Resources

Human Sexualities

International Business

Management

Marketing

Mass Media

Microbiology

Multicultural Education

Nursing

Nutrition

Physical Anthropology

Psychology

Race and Ethnic Relations

Social Problems

Sociology

State and Local Government

Sustainability

Technologies, Social Media, and Society

United States History, Volume 1

United States History, Volume 2

Urban Society

Violence and Terrorism

Western Civilization, Volume 1

World History, Volume 1

World History, Volume 2

World Politics

Contents

UNIT 1
Perspectives

Unit Overview   xx

The concepts in bold italics are developed in the article. For further expansion, please refer to the Topic Guide.

UNIT 2
Young Children, Their Families and Communities

The concepts in bold italics are developed in the article. For further expansion, please refer to the Topic Guide.

UNIT 3
Diverse Learners

The concepts in bold italics are developed in the article. For further expansion, please refer to the Topic Guide.

UNIT 4
Supporting Young Children's Development

UNIT 5
Educational Practices That Help Children Thrive in School

The concepts in bold italics are developed in the article. For further expansion, please refer to the Topic Guide.

The concepts in bold italics are developed in the article. For further expansion, please refer to the Topic Guide.

UNIT 6
Curricular Issues

The concepts in bold italics are developed in the article. For further expansion, please refer to the Topic Guide.

Correlation Guide

The *Annual Editions* series provides students with convenient, inexpensive access to current, carefully selected articles from the public press. **Annual Editions: Early Childhood Education 12/13** is an easy-to-use reader that presents articles on important topics such as *young children and their families, diverse learners, educational practices,* and many more. For more information on *Annual Editions* and other *McGraw-Hill Contemporary Learning Series* titles, visit www.mhhe.com/cls.

This convenient guide matches the units in **Annual Editions: Early Childhood Education 12/13** with the corresponding chapters in two of our best-selling McGraw-Hill Early Childhood Education textbooks by Papalia/Feldman and Santrock.

Annual Editions: Early Childhood Education 12/13	A Child's World: Infancy Through Adolescence 12/e by Papalia/Feldman	Children 12/e by Santrock
Unit 1: Perspectives	**Chapter 1:** Studying A Child's World **Chapter 2:** A Child's World: How We Discover It	**Chapter 1:** Introduction **Chapter 2:** Biological Beginnings
Unit 2: Young Children, Their Families, and Communities	**Chapter 8:** Psychosocial Development during the First Three Years **Chapter 11:** Psychosocial Development in Early Childhood **Chapter 14:** Psychosocial Development in Middle Childhood	**Chapter 7:** Socioemotional Development in Infancy **Chapter 10:** Socioemotional Development in Early Childhood **Chapter 13:** Socioemotional Development in Middle and Late Childhood
Unit 3: Diverse Learners	**Chapter 10:** Cognitive Development in Early Childhood **Chapter 13:** Cognitive Development in Middle Childhood	**Chapter 6:** Cognitive Development in Infancy **Chapter 9:** Cognitive Development in Early Childhood **Chapter 12:** Cognitive Development in Middle and Late Childhood
Unit 4: Supporting Young Children's Development	**Chapter 8:** Psychosocial Development during the First Three Years **Chapter 11:** Psychosocial Development in Early Childhood **Chapter 14:** Psychosocial Development in Middle Childhood	**Chapter 7:** Socioemotional Development in Infancy **Chapter 10:** Socioemotional Development in Early Childhood **Chapter 13:** Socioemotional Development in Middle and Late Childhood
Unit 5: Educational Practices that Help Children Thrive in School	**Chapter 10:** Cognitive Development in Early Childhood **Chapter 13:** Cognitive Development in Middle Childhood	**Chapter 9:** Cognitive Development in Early Childhood **Chapter 12:** Cognitive Development in Middle and Late Childhood
Unit 6: Curricular Issues	**Chapter 10:** Cognitive Development in Early Childhood **Chapter 13:** Cognitive Development in Middle Childhood	**Chapter 9:** Cognitive Development in Early Childhood **Chapter 12:** Cognitive Development in Middle and Late Childhood

Topic Guide

This topic guide suggests how the selections in this book relate to the subjects covered in your course. You may want to use the topics listed on these pages to search the Web more easily.

On the following pages a number of websites have been gathered specifically for this book. They are arranged to reflect the units of this Annual Editions reader. You can link to these sites by going to www.mhhe.com/cls

All the articles that relate to each topic are listed below the bold-faced term.

Achievement/academic achievement
2. Those Persistent Gaps
3. The Achievement Gap: What Early Childhood Educators Need to Know
6. Joy in School
7. Early Education, Later Success
8. Don't Dismiss Early Education as Just Cute; It's Critical
13. Class Matters—In and Out of School
14. Creating a Welcoming Classroom for Homeless Students
18. The Wonder Years
19. Class Division
34. Kindergarten Dilemma: Hold Kids Back to Get Ahead?
35. Want to Get Your Kids into College? Let Them Play
38. Repeating Views on Grade Retention
42. 5 Hallmarks of Good Homework
47. Why We Should not Cut P.E.

Alignment
7. Early Education, Later Success

Attention-deficit/hyperactivity disorder (ADHD)
44. Beyond *The Lorax*?: The Greening of the American Curriculum

At-risk children
2. Those Persistent Gaps
3. The Achievement Gap: What Early Childhood Educators need to Know
14. Creating a Welcoming Classroom for Homeless Students

Autism spectrum disorder
21. Young Children with Autism Spectrum Disorder: Strategies That Work
44. Beyond *The Lorax*? The Greening of the American Curriculum

Best practices
1. $320,000 Kindergarten Teachers
7. Early Education, Later Success
24. Take Charge of Your Personal and Professional Development
30. Enhancing Development and Learning through Teacher-Child Relationships

Birth order
10. The Power of Birth Order

Child centered
4. The Messiness of Readiness
6. Joy in School
9. Are We Paving Paradise?

Cognitive development
15. Making Long-Term Separations Easier for Children and Families
27. Play and Social Interaction in Middle Childhood

Collaboration
2. Those Persistent Gaps
11. Teachers Connecting with Families—In the Best Interest of Children
13. Class Matters—In and Out of School

Creativity
27. Play and Social Interaction in Middle Childhood
45. Constructive Play: A Value-Added Strategy for Meeting Early Learning Standards

Curriculum
43. Preschool Curricula: Finding One That Fits

Development
32. Helping Young Boys be Successful Learners in Today's Early Childhood Classrooms
36. Developmentally Appropriate Practice in the Age of Testing

Developmentally appropriate practice
4. The Messiness of Readiness
6. Joy in School
36. Developmentally Appropriate Practice in the Age of Testing
38. Repeating Views on Grade Retention
46. Calendar Time for Young Children: Good Intentions Gone Awry

Differentiation
19. Class Division
22. Individualizing Instruction in Preschool Classrooms
23. The Why behind RTI
38. Repeating Views on Grade Retention

Diverse learners/diversity
18. The Wonder Years
20. Learning in an Inclusive Community
22. Individualizing Instruction in Preschool Classrooms

Documentation
39. The Power of Documentation in the Early Childhood Classroom

Eating behaviors
12. The Impact of Teachers and Families on Young Children's Eating Behaviors
29. Keeping Children Active: What You Can Do to Fight Childhood Obesity
40. When School Lunch Doesn't Make the Grade

Families
10. The Power of Birth Order
11. Teachers Connecting with Families—In the Best Interest of Children
15. Making Long-Term Separations Easier for Children and Families
16. Keys to Quality Infant Care: Nurturing Every Baby's Life Journey
17. Gaga for Gadgets

Internet References

The following Internet sites have been selected to support the articles found in this reader. These sites were available at the time of publication. However, because websites often change their structure and content, the information listed may no longer be available. We invite you to visit www.mhhe.com/cls for easy access to these sites.

Annual Editions: Early Childhood Education 12/13

General Sources

Children's Defense Fund (CDF)
www.childrensdefense.org

At this site of the CDF, an organization that seeks to ensure that every child is treated fairly, there are reports and resources regarding current issues facing today's youth, along with national statistics on various subjects.

Council for Professional Recognition (CDA)
www.cdacouncil.org

The Child Development Associate National Credentialing Program (CDA) is the most widely accepted credential for the field of Early Childhood Education. It is earned after a stringent set of criteria are met, which include knowledge of and experience with young children and their families. It is recognized as one of many professional development and preparation opportunities for the field. Candidates identify one of four areas for specialization: Infants & Toddlers, Preschoolers, Family Child Care, or Home Visitor.

National Association for the Education of Young Children
www.naeyc.org

The NAEYC website is a valuable tool for anyone working with young children. This is the professional organization for anyone working with young children from birth to age 8.

U.S. Department of Education
www.ed.gov/pubs/TeachersGuide

Government goals, projects, grants, and other educational programs are listed here as well as many links to teacher services and resources.

Unit 1: Perspectives

Child Care and Early Education Research Connections
www.researchconnections.org

This site offers excellent help for anyone looking for research-based data related to early childhood education. Full-text articles and other reference materials are available, along with a list of current grants, jobs and events.

Child Care Directory: Care Guide
www.care.com

Find licensed/registered child care by zip code at this site. See prescreened profiles and get free background checks on providers. Pages for parents along with additional links are also included.

Early Childhood Care and Development
www.ecdgroup.com

This site concerns international resources in support of children to age 8 and their families. It includes research and evaluation, policy matters, programming matters, and related websites. ECCD works through coordinated advocacy and awareness raising.

Global SchoolNet Foundation
www.gsn.org

Access this site for multicultural education information. The site includes news for teachers and students as well as chat rooms, links to educational resources, programs, and contests and competitions. Helpful site for teachers serving diverse populations.

Harvard Family Research Project
www.hfrp.org

For twenty-five years The Harvard Family Research Project has provided quality information on families, educaton, and young children. There are many resources and areas of research presented on this useful site.

Mid-Continent Research for Education and Learning
www.mcrel.org/standards-benchmarks

This site provides a listing of standards and benchmarks that include content descriptions from 112 significant subject areas and documents from across 14 content areas.

Spark Action
www.sparkaction.com

This is an online journalism and advocacy center by and for those in the profession of care and education for children and youth.

The National Association of State Boards of Education
www.nasbe.org

Included on this site are links for various issues affecting education today. The topics change regularly.

Unit 2: Young Children, Their Families and Communities

Administration for Children and Families
www.dhhs.gov

This site provides information on federally funded programs that promote the economic and social well-being of families, children, and communities.

The AARP Grandparent Information Center
www.aarp.org/relationships/grandparenting

The center offers tips for raising grandchildren, activities, health and safety, visitations, and other resources to assist grandparents.

All About Asthma
www.pbskids.org/arthur/parentsteachers/lesson/health/#asthma

This is a fact sheet/activity book featuring the popular TV character Arthur, who has asthma. The site gives statistics and helps parents, teachers, and children understand asthma as well as many other issues affecting young children. It gives tips on how to decrease asthma triggers. It has English, Spanish, Chinese, Vietnamese, and Tagalog versions of some of the materials.

Allergy Kids
http://allergykids.com

Developed by Robyn O'Brien, a mother committed to helping children and families everywhere deal with allergies, this site is extremely valuable for all families and school personnel. Tip sheets are provided that can be shared with teachers and families as well as items for purchase to support allergic children.

Internet References

Changing the Scene–Improving the School Nutrition Environment
www.fns.usda.gov/tn/Resources/changing.html

Children, Youth and Families Education and Research Network
www.cyfernet.org

This excellent site contains useful links to research from key universities and institutions. The categories include early childhood, school age, teens, parents and family, and community.

National Network for Child Care
www.nncc.org

This network brings together the expertise of many land-grant universities through their cooperative extension programs. These are the programs taped back in early 1965 to train the 41,000 teachers needed for the first Head Start programs that summer. The site contains information on over 1,000 publications and resources related to child care. Resources for local conferences in early childhood education are included.

National Safe Kids Campaign
www.babycenter.com

This site includes an easy-to-follow milestone chart as well as additional information on pregnancy and child rearing.

Zero to Three
www.zerotothree.org

Find here developmental information on the first 3 years of life—an excellent site for both parents and professionals.

Unit 3: Diverse Learners

American Academy of Pediatrics
www.aap.org

Child Welfare League of America (CWLA)
www.cwla.org

The CWLA is the United States' oldest and largest organization devoted entirely to the well-being of vulnerable children and their families. Its website provides links to information about issues related to morality and values in education.

The Council for Exceptional Children
www.cec.sped.org/index.html

Information on identifying and teaching children with a variety of disabilities. The Council for Exceptional Children is the largest professional organization for special educators.

First Signs
http://firstsigns.org

First Signs is dedicated to educating parents and professionals about autism and related disorders. There are sections on initial concerns, screening and diagnosis, and treatment of young children showing signs of autism and related disorders.

Make Your Own Web page
www.teacherweb.com

Easy step-by-step directions for teachers at all levels to construct their own web page. Parents can log on and check out what is going on in their child's classroom.

National Resource Center for Health and Safety in Child Care
http://nrckids.org

Search through this site's extensive links to find information on health and safety in child care. Health and safety tips are provided, as are other child-care information resources.

Online Innovation Institute
www.oii.org

Unit 4: Supporting Young Children's Development

Action for Healthy Kids
www.actionforhealthykids.org

This organization works to assist the ever-increasing numbers of students who are overweight, undernourished, and sedentary. They feature a campaign for school wellness.

American Academy of Pediatrics
www.aap.org

Pediatricians provide trusted advice for parents and teachers. The AAP official site includes position statements on a variety of issues related to the health and safety of young children.

You Can Handle Them All
www.disciplinehelp.com

This site describes different types of behavioral problems and offers suggestions for managing these problems.

Unit 5: Educational Practices That Help Children Thrive in School

Association for Childhood Education International (ACEI)
www.acei.org

This site, established by the oldest professional early childhood education organization, describes the association, its programs, and the services it offers to both teachers and families. Standards for elementary education are included.

Busy Teacher's Cafe
www.busyteacherscafe.com

This is a website for early childhood educators with resource pages for everything from worksheets to classroom management.

Donors Choose
www.donorschoose.org

Every teacher who works in a high need area should bookmark this site. Educators register an item needed for their classroom or school, and donors committed to education make a pledge to help fund the project. When enough money is donated, the item is purchased and shipped to the school. Teachers and students write a thank-you note.

Future of Children
www.futureofchildren.org

The primary purpose of this site is to disseminate timely information on major issues related to children's well-being. The aim is to translate the best social science research about children into useful information.

Internet References

Reggio Emilia
http://reggioalliance.org

This is the North American Alliance for Reggio Emilia and provides many resources for anyone interested in the Reggio approach. There is information on conferences and the current Reggio Emilia exhibit touring the United States through 2014.

Teacher Planet
http://teacherplanet.com

Helpful resources for busy teachers that will save time and money are included on this site. There are resources for teachers who work with all ages of children.

Unit 6: Curricular Issues

Action for Healthy Kids
www.actionforhealthykids.org

This organization works to assist the ever-increasing numbers of students who are overweight, undernourished, and sedentary. They feature a campaign for school wellness.

Awesome Library for Teachers
www.awesomelibrary.org/teacher.html

Open this page for links and access to teacher information on everything from educational assessment to general child development topics.

The Educators' Network
www.theeducatorsnetwork.com

A very useful site for teachers at every level in every subject area. Includes lesson plans, theme units, teacher tools, rubrics, books, educational news, and much more.

Free Resources for Educational Excellence
http://free.ed.gov

This site offers close to 2,000 resources across all content areas for teachers to supplement learning experiences in their classrooms.

Grade Level Reading Lists
www.gradelevelreadinglists.org

Recommended reading lists for grades kindergarten to 8 can be downloaded through this site. There are links to many other sites.

Idea Box
http://theideabox.com

This site is geared toward parents and has many good activities for creating, playing, and singing. The activities are creative and educational and can be done at home or in a classroom.

International Reading Association
www.reading.org

This organization for professionals who are interested in literacy contains information about the reading process and assists teachers in dealing with literacy issues.

Kid Fit
www.kid-fit.com

A preschool physical education program designed to instill healthy lifestyle habits for young children. Includes some free physical educational activities.

The Perpetual Preschool
www.perpetualpreschool.com

This site provides teachers with possibilities for learning activities, offers chats with other teachers and resources on a variety of topics. The theme ideas are a list of possibilities and should not be used in whole, but used as a starting point for building areas of investigation that are relevant and offer firsthand experiences for young children.

Phi Delta Kappa
www.pdkintl.org

This important organization publishes articles about all facets of education. By clicking on the links in this site, for example, you can check out the journal's online archive, which has resources such as articles having to do with assessment.

Teacher Quick Source
www.teacherquicksource.com

Originally designed to help Head Start teachers meet the child outcomes, this site can be useful to all preschool teachers. Domains can be linked to developmentally appropriate activities for classroom use.

Teachers Helping Teachers
www.pacificnet.net/~ mandel/

Free lesson plans, educational resources and resources to improve test scores are included. Access is free, and material on the site is updated weekly during the school year.

Technology Help
www.apples4theteacher.com

This site helps teachers incorporate technology into the classroom. Full of interactive activities children can do alone, with a partner, or for full-group instruction in all subject areas. Teachers can sign up for an e-mail newsletter.

UNIT 1

Perspectives

Unit Selections

1. **$320,000 Kindergarten Teachers,** Raj Chetty et al.
2. **Those Persistent Gaps,** Paul E. Barton and Richard J. Coley
3. **The Achievement Gap: What Early Childhood Educators Need to Know,** Barbara A. Langham
4. **The Messiness of Readiness,** Pamela Jane Powell
5. **Invest in Early Childhood Education,** Sharon Lynn Kagan and Jeanne L. Reid
6. **Joy in School,** Steven Wolk
7. **Early Education, Later Success,** Susan Black
8. **Don't Dismiss Early Education as Just Cute; It's Critical,** Lisa Guernsey
9. **Are We Paving Paradise?,** Elizabeth Graue

Learning Outcomes

After reading this Unit, you will be able to:

- Articulate the importance of a high-quality kindergarten teacher on the lifelong earning power of the students.
- Describe some of the reasons children born in to at-risk environments are starting life behind other children.
- Discuss the achievement gap and explain programs showing success in closing the gap.
- Explain the difference between getting children ready for school and having educators prepare to meet the needs of all children.
- Name some recommendations for moving the educational reform agenda forward.
- Explain the long-term financial benefits for quality preschool.
- Articulate the importance of learning being a joyful experience.
- Argue for preschool programs as critical for young children.
- Share with others the importance of a hands-on, play-based kindergarten experience for all children.

Student Website

www.mhhe.com/cls

Internet References

Child Care and Early Education Research Connections
www.researchconnections.org
Child Care Directory: Care Guide
www.care.com
Early Childhood Care and Development
www.ecdgroup.com
Global SchoolNet Foundation
www.gsn.org
Harvard Family Research Project
www.hfrp.org
Mid-Continent Research for Education and Learning
www.mcrel.org/standards-benchmarks
The National Association of State Boards of Education
www.nasbe.org
Spark Action
www.sparkaction.com

The title of the first article for this unit, "$320,000 Kindergarten Teachers," certainly caught the attention of all readers, especially those aspiring to or who are currently teaching kindergarten. Kindergarten teachers have always believed they were often undervalued by the public and colleagues; however, the research from Harvard University on the importance of children having an outstanding kindergarten teacher is striking. Lifelong earning power increases by $10,000 per student for children who not only had a highly qualified but also a highly effective kindergarten teacher. That is powerful support for the importance of early childhood preparation for all kindergarten teachers coupled with induction period mentoring and ongoing professional development and evaluation throughout their careers. If that article doesn't make every kindergarten teacher approach their job with more intentionality, passion, and commitment then nothing will.

The next two articles are on an issue that has actually been one of the most significant issues affecting the education profession for decades: how to best close the achievement gap found in children living in an environment that may not offer the necessary support for learning versus children who are stimulated and challenged at home. The title, "Those Persistent Gaps" is clear evidence, that this problem has been ongoing. This issue is also significant for the sheer number of articles that have been written addressing the achievement gaps, and how to best narrow the gaps. Paul E. Barton and Richard J. Coley examine the often-asked question when exploring achievement gaps and that is do home and early life or experiences in school play a more critical role in closing the achievement gap? Some would argue that good teaching and quality educational experiences inside the school setting should prepare all students to achieve at the same level,whereas others indicate experiences, or lack of, in the home and local community can greatly affect learning in the classroom. There are always exceptions to each argument where outstanding academic achievement is found in schools located in extreme poverty areas. The many barriers that prevent children from coming to school each day well rested and fed do affect academic performance, and teachers who are aware of the many stumbling blocks children and their families must overcome prior to entering the classroom are better prepared to assist them in their work to achieve in school. This article is followed by "The Achievement Gap: What Early Childhood Educators Need to Know." The discussion surrounding the issue of achievement gaps usually looks at kindergarten—12th grade, but many researchers report the solutions will be found by looking down to preschool. Barbara A. Langham shares information about the reasons for the gap and then offers ways the gap can be closed by focusing on what quality early childhood programs are available and describing their success over decades. Legislators across the country are addressing these gaps in a number of ways. Some states offer universal preschool, which is free and available for all preschool children living in that state. Other states are taking a different approach and targeting specific state, funded preschool programs for those children who need it the most. This need is often determined by a child meeting two or more risk factors such as low-income family; a non-English-speaking

© Purestock/SuperStock

family; a speech, language, or hearing deficit, etc. There are pros and cons to each approach, and this issue will continue to play out with state legislators across the country as they look for the most effective way to help all children succeed.

One of the classes this editor teaches as part of a load as a professor of Early Childhood Education at Eastern Michigan University is a graduate class titled: "Trends, Issues and Advocacy in ECE." In that class we read writings by many of the individuals who laid the foundation for our profession. John Locke (1632–1704) is one of those individuals. I share with my students a favorite quote Locke wrote back in the mid 1600s: "Accommodate the educational program to fit the child; don't change the child to fit the program." That quote is so relevant today as we work to ensure schools are ready for all children. In "The Messiness of Readiness," Pamela Jane Powell expresses grave concern over the practice of excluding some children from kindergarten if they aren't ready and implores all teachers to differentiate the learning environment to meet the needs of all children age eligible to attend based on the kindergarten entry date for that particular state or school.

The unit continues with the message that even in these challenging financial times, it is most important to have a clear plan for early education that is articulated at many levels and within many different venues. "Invest in Early Childhood Education" by Kagan and Reid outlines the critical importance of preschool programs being available for all children whose families choose to take advantage of them. The message that a strong pre-K foundation can translate to significant learning gains down the road should be communicated to all families. President Obama repeatedly calls for a focus on early childhood education when addressing questions about his plan for improving education in the United States. He recognizes that no improvement in educational achievement can be reached without starting with our youngest learners.

The increasing high-stakes pressure of the past few years on accountability has caused many educators to suck the joy and passion out of learning. The prize has become higher test scores instead of learning for life-long benefits. Many teachers are afraid that children are becoming turned off to school at a young age, and classrooms where children are required to sit all day in desks and complete endless piles of worksheets and workbooks are commonplace in many parts of the country. These types of joyless learning places are especially prevalent in inner cities and charter schools, where high test scores may translate into higher enrollment. Steven Wolk shares many ways joyful learning can flourish in school alongside high achievement and provides suggestions for educators of all levels of learners in his article, "Joy in School."

Lisa Guernsey echoes this message in "Don't Dismiss Early Education as Just Cute; It's Critical." This short, but very appropriate article from *USA Today* uses the analogy of an arborist trying to revive a dying tree by not paying attention to the roots, which would allow the tree to take hold and develop a strong foundation. Of course some private funds can support quality programs for preschool children, but without a commitment from the federal or state government to learning prior to kindergarten, we will not be successful in reaching all children who will benefit from attending preschool.

We end this unit with an issue that causes great angst for many teachers; exactly how much time should I allot to freely chosen play in my classroom? Elizabeth Graue, in "Are We Paving Paradise?" chastises educators who are pushing young children to learn in ways that are not developmentally appropriate and robs them of their special time to learn by manipulating materials and engaging in active play. We should not have to build a case for play in programs serving young children but should instead be able to foster and support the play in which children engage and help them learn. James L. Hymes, Jr. is one of my favorite early educators from the past century. Dr. Hymes was the director of the Kaiser Ship Yards Child Service Centers in Portland, Oregon, from 1943–1945 during WWII and on the initial planning committee for Head Start in 1965. In 1959 he wrote about play in the following way:

> "We need a new word to sum up what young children do with themselves—how they occupy their time, what they give themselves to, the activity that is the be-all and the end-all of their days. We have words to say all this for other ages. We can talk about adults and say that they are "working." That sounds right and reasonable, We can talk about the elementary or high school or college age and say that they are "studying." That is a dignified description that sounds legitimate and right for the age. But we say that young children "play." That is the reason for our schools: to let this age do what it has to do, with more depth and richness, to let these children play. But to many people the word sounds weak and evasive, as if somehow this age was cheating. If we say "free play" we put two bad words together. Free and soft, and easy, casual, careless,

sloppy, pointless, aimless, wandering, senseless. Play of pleasure and ease and waste and evil. The words to violence to the deeds. Can't we find a word or coin a word that conveys the respect this time in life deserves? Must we always minimize it, or hasten it, or deny it?" (Hymes, *The Grade Teacher,* 1959)

I am reminded of one of the more popular perceptions of early care and education held by those outside the profession. For the past 50 years, "early childhood education was viewed as a panacea, the solution to all social ills in society" (Paciorek, 2008, p. xvii). This is huge pressure to put on one profession, especially one that is grossly underpaid. We do have outside forces carefully watching how early education practices affect long-term development and learning. Early childhood professionals must be accountable for practices they implement in their classrooms and how children spend their time interacting with materials. Appropriate early learning standards are the norm in the profession, and knowledgeable caregivers and teachers must be informed of the importance of developing quality experiences that align with the standards. Teachers can no longer plan cute activities that fill the child's days and backpacks with pictures to hang on the refrigerator. Teachers must be intentional in their planning to adapt learning experiences so that all children can achieve standards that are based on knowledge of developmental abilities.

As the editor, I hope you benefit from reading the articles and reflecting on the important issues facing early childhood education today. Your job is to share the message with others not familiar with our field and the impact of attending a quality program can have on young children throughout their lives. I always feel good when I realize that others outside the field of early childhood education recognize that quality care and education for young children can have tremendous financial benefits as well as educational benefits for society. Of course, I would always welcome the interest from more people outside the profession, but the field is receiving increased attention from others for a number of reasons. The nation is learning that high-quality programs are beneficial for young children's long-term development. Much of this interest is in part due to some state legislators allocating resources for state-operated preschool programs. Coupled with the knowledge of the importance of ECE programs is a realization that the quality of these programs should be of utmost importance. Another reason is the compelling evidence from brain research that children are born learning. Yet, despite new information on the importance of early childhood, we still tend to hold onto cultural traditions about who young children are and how to care for them. This dichotomy between information and tradition results in an impasse when it comes to creating national policy related to young children.

$320,000 Kindergarten Teachers

Your kindergarten classroom can leave a lasting impact on your earnings and your quality of life long after circle time is a distant memory.

RAJ CHETTY ET AL.

Could the quality of your kindergarten experience make a difference in your lifetime earnings? Or whether you're married or own a home?

Our study of an experiment that randomly assigned students to different kindergarten classrooms suggests the answers are yes.

In our recent National Bureau of Economic Research working paper (Chetty et al. 2010), we present evidence demonstrating the tremendous importance of early education. Improvements in kindergarten test scores translate into higher lifetime earnings and improvements in a variety of other outcomes, ranging from where people live to whether they're married. We estimate that an above-average kindergarten teacher generates about $320,000 more in total earnings than a below-average kindergarten teacher for a class of 20 students.

Isolating the impact of quality in the classroom isn't easy. Under normal circumstances, children in better classrooms—that is, classrooms with better teachers, more resources, better-behaved classmates, or other favorable environmental factors—are different in many dimensions. For instance, they may come from wealthier neighborhoods or be better prepared upon kindergarten entry. As a result, students in better classrooms may do better simply because they had advantages to begin with and not because of the class itself. This difficulty plagues most empirical studies in education: How can we separate causation from correlation?

We cut this Gordian knot by using data from a randomized experiment, the gold standard of research. In the experiment we studied, students and teachers were randomly assigned to specific classrooms. As a result, there are no systematic differences in background characteristics across the classes, and we can say with confidence that any differences in later outcomes were caused by differences in classrooms.

We analyzed data from Project STAR—the largest and most widely studied education intervention conducted in the United States. STAR was a randomized experiment conducted in 79 Tennessee schools from 1985 to 1989. In STAR, some 11,500 students and their teachers were randomly assigned to attend either a small class with an average of 15 students or a regular-sized class with an average of 22 students. In general, students remained in their randomly assigned classes in grades K–3 until the experiment concluded and all students returned to regular-sized classes in 4th grade. Previous work has shown that small classes increased students' standardized test scores by about 5 percentile rank points in grades K-3. And students who had better teachers also scored higher on tests in grades K-3. But the longer-run effects were less impressive: The lasting benefits from small-class attendance fell to 1 to 2 percentile points in grades 4–8, as did the benefits from having a better teacher.

However, the end goal of education is not merely to increase test scores. We use test scores because we think they're a good proxy for lifetime outcomes. But no one has ever verified this assumption. The goal of our project was to fill this important gap by linking the STAR data to data on adult outcomes.

For each 1 percentile point increase in kindergarten test scores, the students' yearly adult earnings increase by $130—or almost 1 percent of mean earnings—measured between ages 25 and 27.

We find evidence that kindergarten test scores are indeed very good at predicting later outcomes. There is a strong correlation between kindergarten test scores and a wide variety of outcomes in early adulthood (measured between ages 25 and 27). For each 1 percentile point increase in kindergarten test scores, the students' yearly earnings increase by $130—or almost 1 percent of mean earnings. The relationship diminishes only slightly if we account for family background, for instance, as measured by parental income. Kindergarten test scores also predict a wide variety of other positive outcomes. By age 27, children with higher scores are much more likely to have attended college, have retirement savings, be a homeowner, and live in a better neighborhood.

By age 27, children with higher scores are much more likely to have attended college, have retirement savings, be a homeowner, and live in a better neighborhood.

Do Test Score Improvements in Early Grades Improve Lifetime Outcomes?

So the key question is: Do policies and practices that improve early childhood test scores also lead to better outcomes in adulthood? What are the long-term effects of better teaching and more resources? To answer this question, we leveraged the STAR experiment to measure the adult outcomes of students who were randomly assigned to receive different levels of classroom resources.

To start, we found that being randomly assigned to a small class improved students' adult outcomes relative to their schoolmates who attended a regular-sized class. Small-class students went on to attend college at higher rates and to do better on a variety of measures such as retirement savings, marriage rates, and quality of their neighborhood of residence. Small-class students do not have statistically different earnings levels at this point (between ages 25 and 27), but that may change over time as their careers develop and they reap the increasing benefits of their higher rates of college attendance.

The larger surprise came from our findings that kindergarten classroom "quality" has a big effect on adult outcomes. Classrooms vary in many ways beyond size in our data: Some have better teachers, some have better peers, some may just have better "classroom chemistry." While we can't measure each of these attributes of the classroom environment directly, we can proxy for class quality using one's classmates' test scores. If your classmates are doing well on tests, then it must mean that you're in an effective classroom environment (remember, students were randomly assigned to classrooms, so there are no differences in student abilities across classrooms before the experiment started).

Kindergarten Test Scores and Early Adulthood

Using this measure, we found strong statistical evidence that being assigned to a higher-quality classroom in the same school was an important predictor of students' kindergarten test scores. This part was not surprising—some teachers are more effective than others at raising test scores. Similarly, some classes "click" together and have more successful years for a variety of reasons that depend on such idiosyncratic things as personality matches. Although the impact on the current-year's test scores was strong, the effect quickly faded—at least on test scores. From 4th through 8th grades, there was no remaining statistical difference between students who attended different kindergarten classrooms. Studies in the broader literature usually find patterns like this: An excellent teacher or class can have a large

effect on test scores in this year or the next, but most of the benefits have faded away within two or three years. The natural conclusion was, of course, that these effects must be only temporary and are unlikely to make a difference in the long run.

We were surprised, then, to find a strong relationship re-emerge between kindergarten classroom quality and adult wage earnings! Even though the effect of better classes on student standardized test scores quickly faded, being assigned to a higher-quality classroom was an important predictor of students' earnings. Remarkably, we also find substantial improvements on virtually every other measure of success in adulthood that we examined. Students who were randomly assigned to higher-quality kindergarten classrooms were more likely to attend college and attended higher-ranked colleges. They were also more likely to own a house, be saving for retirement, and live in a better neighborhood.

To quantify the size of these effects, we isolate the part of the class quality that is driven by teachers. We estimate that going from a below-average (25th percentile) teacher to an above-average (75th percentile) teacher raises a child's earnings by about 3.5 percent per year. In present value, that adds up to more than $10,000 in additional lifetime income on average for each student. When you multiply that by 20 students in each class, the additional lifetime benefits from a single year of high-quality kindergarten teaching is about $320,000. These are huge stakes at play and underline the importance to the nation of having high-quality classrooms and schools.

The benefits of classroom quality for adult outcomes is not limited to only the kindergarten year. High-quality classrooms in grades 1, 2, or 3 had a similar beneficial impact. We do not have the data to allow us to determine whether classes in grades after 3rd grade have the same effect, nor can we say anything in this study about preschool education. But we think our results point to the importance of the early grades in general and not about kindergarten in particular.

Noncognitive Skills: All I Really Need to Know I Learned in Kindergarten

The effects of kindergarten on later outcomes are somewhat puzzling: High-quality classrooms have large effects on test scores at first, then fade in later test scores, and finally re-emerge in adulthood. What explains this pattern of fade-out and re-emergence? Our leading theory: improvement in noncognitive or "soft" skills. These are exactly the types of skills highlighted in Robert Fulghum's classic essay, "All I Really Need to Know I Learned in Kindergarten": "play fair," "don't take things that aren't yours," and so on. A growing literature, pioneered by Nobel Laureate James Heckman, has shown that such noncognitive skills have important long-term impacts.

In our data, we see that good teachers and classroom environments in early childhood improve students' noncognitive skills. Improving some noncognitive skills—such as paying attention in class and persisting at tasks—may result directly in improved standardized test scores. Others—such as whether a student "annoys" other classmates or is critical of the subject matter—have a less direct effect on test scores but are nevertheless an important determinant of success in adulthood. Fourth- and 8th-grade teachers were asked to rate each student on how often they exhibit certain behaviors relating to effort, initiative, and disruption—for example, how often he or she "acts restless, is often unable to sit still." We find that a higher-quality kindergarten classroom leads to better performance along these dimensions as measured in 4th and 8th grades, even though there is no detectable effect on standardized (cognitive) test scores in those same grades. These gains in noncognitive skills are strongly associated with later earnings even though they aren't as strongly predictive of later test scores.

So, why does the legacy of kindergarten reemerge in adulthood? A good kindergarten teacher must be a good classroom manager in order to raise her students' performance on tests. Good classroom management is likely to impart social and other noncognitive skills. These social skills don't get picked up on later tests—but it pays off for an adult who tends not to "be restless" and "annoy others." So, there is good reason that your excellent kindergarten teacher may be helping you today even though you may not have directly felt her effects in later years of school.

What Are the Characteristics of Good Kindergarten Classrooms and Good Kindergarten Teachers?

Our findings that kindergarten classrooms and teachers matter a great deal in the long run naturally raises the question of how one can identify the best teachers and classroom environments.

We find that kindergarten teachers with more years of teaching experience are more effective at raising both kindergarten test scores and adult earnings. This may partly be the effect of learning on the job, but it may also reflect the fact that teachers who have taught for a long time are more devoted to the profession or were trained differently. Smaller classes play a role, but many of the most effective classes were regular-sized classes.

Kindergarten teachers with more years of teaching experience are more effective at raising both kindergarten test scores and adult earnings.

But differences along these dimensions only explain a small part of the overall classroom-level variation. Other observable factors—such as teacher education level or the classroom's mix of gender, race, or free-lunch statuses—don't explain the variation in adult outcomes. Unfortunately, most of the overall classroom effect that we detect is unexplained by characteristics that we can observe in our data. That is, we're unable to fully quantify what makes a "high-quality" class in this study. We can document the importance of high-quality classrooms but have a

harder time giving recommendations about how to ensure that every student gets to experience one.

We suspect that much of the variation in class quality is driven by teachers and classroom chemistry. Some teachers may be better classroom managers, may relate better to their students, etc.—all things we can't measure in our data. We also don't have information on differences in instructional practices or other aspects of what teachers actually do in the better classrooms. These are important limitations of our work, ones that we're trying to address in follow-up research, because we need policies that can be implemented in order to improve classrooms.

Improvements in Standardized Tests Might Mean Something Different Today

Overall, we find that interventions that improve standardized tests in the current year yield large payoffs in adulthood, even if the effects on the standardized tests themselves fade over time. We think this occurs because children learn multiple types of skills from high-quality teachers and schools. Some of these skills are readily apparent on standardized tests, while others have an important effect directly on adult outcomes.

This equation might change somewhat when tests raise the stakes, as they have recently under No Child Left Behind (NCLB) and other state accountability systems. Other research has found that schools, facing such accountability pressure, sometimes game the system and find ways to inflate standardized test scores without actually increasing learning. These stakes-driven increases in test scores may no longer impart better noncognitive skills. Our research can't speak to this point directly. But if noncognitive skills are the key link to better adult outcomes, we should encourage schools to prioritize these skills no less than they did before NCLB. On the other hand, perhaps NCLB's pressure to improve standardized test scores doesn't affect the earlier grades that we study in our paper since test-based accountability does not start until 3rd grade.

Policy Implications

In our research on the long-term effects of Project STAR, we found that one's kindergarten teacher and classmates leave a lasting effect long after circle time is a distant memory. Better kindergarten classes not only improve short-run test scores but also can substantially raise lifetime earnings. They also improve a range of other outcomes, such as college attendance, retirement savings, marriage rates, and homeownership. Our measures may even understate the long-run benefits of a good kindergarten class because earnings gains may further increase as the students age and because we can't measure beneficial impacts on health outcomes or criminal behavior in our data.

At this stage, our work can't definitively point to a particular policy to implement in order to improve early childhood classroom education. While our analysis shows that good teachers generate great value for society, it doesn't tell us how to get more of those great teachers. Paying teachers more may attract more talent to the profession, but it might also have a small impact. Merit pay policies could potentially improve teaching quality but may also lead to teaching to the test without gains on the all-important noncognitive dimensions. Nevertheless, we see hope in a broad variety of policies designed to improve the quality of early childhood classes. These range from improving teacher training and mentoring to reducing class size, retaining teachers with high value-added on test scores, and perhaps paying star teachers a higher salary.

While we can't point to specifics yet, we do know now that better early childhood education yields substantial long-run improvements. Children who attend higher-quality schools fare substantially better as adults. In the United States, the current property-tax system of school finance gives higher-income families access to better public schools on average. This system could amplify inequality, as disadvantaged children generally attend lower-quality, resource-constrained schools. Our analysis of the longterm impacts of Project STAR suggests that improving early childhood education in disadvantaged areas may significantly reduce poverty and inequality in the long run. Whatever path a school takes to improving student learning in the early grades, what is clear is that the stakes are too high to ignore the potential benefits of improving early education.

Reference

Chetty, Raj, John N. Friedman, Nathaniel Hilger, Emmanuel Saez, Diane Whitmore Schanzenbach, and Danny Yagan. "How Does Your Kindergarten Classroom Affect Your Earnings? Evidence from Project STAR." *NBER Working Paper 16381,* September 2010.

Critical Thinking

1. Share with two people not in early childhood education the information from this article related to higher earning power for children who had an excellent kindergarten teacher. Report any follow-up questions they had about our profession.

2. What qualities would you bring to your class of children that would allow them to be successful lifelong learners and earners?

Those Persistent Gaps

The gaps in life, health, and school experiences of minority and low-income children just won't go away.

Paul E. Barton and Richard J. Coley

Although we've focused more and more attention on dealing with the seemingly intractable gaps in achievement between black and Hispanic students and white students in the last quarter century, we've made little progress in closing the gaps. All subgroups of students have, in general, improved as measured by the National Assessment of Educational Progress. But disparities related to race/ethnicity and socioeconomic status remain.

Although the gaps may seem intractable, they are not inevitable if we continue to enlarge both our understanding of why they exist and what it will take to close them. A 2003 report from the ETS Policy Information Center titled *Parsing the Achievement Gap*[1] answered two questions: What life and school conditions are correlated with cognitive development and school achievement? and, Do gaps in these conditions among racial/ethnic and income groups mirror the gaps we see in achievement?

We updated this effort in 2009 in a report titled *Parsing the Achievement Gap II.*[2] The report identified 16 such gaps and examined the trends in these gaps since the previous report. The 16 factors are clustered in three categories: school factors, factors related to the home and school connection, and factors that are present both before and beyond school. These factors begin at birth.

Birth Weight

Research has long established that low birth weight can lead to severe problems, ranging from mortality to learning difficulties. Children having a birth weight of less than approximately 5.5 pounds are more likely to end up in special education classes, repeat a grade, or fail in school.

Children having a low birth weight are more likely to end up in special education classes.

Between 2000 and 2005, there was an increase in low birth weight for blacks, whites, and Hispanics. However, the percentage of black infants born with low birth weight in 2005—14 percent—was approximately double that for white and Hispanic infants.

The trend: The gap in birth weight narrowed between black and white infants from 2000 to 2005, but only because low birth weight increased the most for white infants. A gap opened between Hispanic and white infants during this period. In 2000, the percentages of low birth weight in the two groups were comparable—at 6.6 percent for whites and 6.4 percent for Hispanics. In 2005, however, that percentage climbed to 8.2 percent for whites compared with 6.9 percent for Hispanics.

Lead Poisoning

Research has established that lead poisoning can seriously affect children, causing reductions in IQ and attention span, reading and learning disabilities, and behavior problems. As a result of laws focused on cleaning up the environment, the levels of lead in children's blood have dramatically decreased over the decades. However, we have not eliminated lead in the environment. A synthesis of recent studies has established that there is *no* safe threshold for blood lead levels.

Children in minority and low-income families have a higher risk of exposure to lead as a result of living in old houses or around old industrial areas with contaminated buildings and soil. Black children have considerably higher blood lead levels than white or Hispanic children have. The levels are about four times higher for blacks than for whites, and they are more than twice as high for children below the poverty line than for those above it.

The trend: Although the 1980s saw dramatic drops in blood lead levels, these have leveled off in recent years. The gaps between whites, blacks, and Hispanics and between poor and non-poor children have remained relatively constant.

Hunger and Nutrition

Science supports the commonsense view that hunger impedes student learning. Adequate nutrition is necessary for the development of both mind and body. The differences show up early, as revealed by studies of inner-city kindergarten students. Children in these studies who were underweight tended to have lower test scores.

Black and Hispanic children are more than twice as likely as their white peers to live in food-insecure households. In 2005, 29 percent of black children and 24 percent of Hispanic children were food insecure, compared with 12 percent of white children. The situation was more pronounced among households below the poverty line—43 percent of these households were food insecure, compared with just 6 percent of households with incomes more than double the poverty line.

The trend: From 1999 to 2005, the gap between black and white children remained unchanged. The gap between whites and Hispanics narrowed because food insecurity rose slightly for white children (from 11 to 12.2 percent) but improved for Hispanic children (from 29.2 to 23.7 percent).

Television Watching

Research shows that excessive television watching is detrimental to school achievement. In fact, one study by the American Academy of Pediatrics found that for children ages 1 to 3, each hour of television watched daily increased by 10 percent their risk of having attention problems, such as attention deficit/hyperactivity disorder, by the time they were 7. In 2006, 57 percent of black 8th graders watched four or more hours on an average weekday, compared with 20 percent of white 8th graders.

The trend: There was no change in the gaps from 2000 to 2006. However, we need to track the time students spend with newer devices—such as mp3 players, video games, and cell phones—because use of such devices is growing.

Talking and Reading to Children

By talking and reading to their children, parents play a crucial role in children's language development and early literacy. Research has found that by the time children are 36 months old, the vocabulary of children in professional families is more than double that of children in families receiving welfare.

In 2005, 68 percent of white children ages 3–5 were read to every day, compared with 50 percent of black children and 45 percent of Hispanic children. Poor children were also less likely to be read to than their more affluent peers.

The trend: From 2001 to 2005, the gaps remained about the same. All groups slightly improved, with the largest improvement occurring in the "near-poor" group (100 to 199 percent of the poverty line), narrowing the gap between near-poor and non-poor families.

The Parent-Child Ratio

Both common sense and a large body of research establish that students who have two parents in the home have better chances of doing well in school than students who just have one. This is partly because one-parent families have lower incomes, on average, and partly because of the absence of one parent. The gaps are large: Just 35 percent of black children and 66 percent of Hispanic children live with both parents, compared with 74 percent of white children.

The trend: The good news is that the steady decline of the two-parent family, for all subgroups, has recently stopped. However, the gaps have not changed from 2000 to 2006.

Summer Achievement Gains and Losses

Educators have long known about reading losses that occur over the summer. Accumulating research has established that depending on their summer experiences, some students gain over the summer and some lose. Clearly, changes in test scores cannot be attributed entirely to what happens during the school year.

The quality of summer experiences varies by family income. Students isolated in high-poverty inner-city areas often experience little or no enrichment. Large gaps exist between white and minority students in the degree to which achievement grows during the summer.

The trend: Trend data are not yet available.

Large gaps exist between white and minority students in the degree to which achievement grows during the summer.

Frequent School Changing

Changing schools is a challenge both to students and their teachers. A change in schools may mean that a student faces work he or she is unprepared for, a teacher who is unfamiliar with his or her previous school records, and a new environment in which he or she is an outsider.

Not all school changing is the result of residence changing. According to research, 30 to 40 percent of such changes are the result of school overcrowding, class-size reductions, suspension and expulsion policies, general school climate, and, possibly, the parental choice options in No Child Left Behind.

Minority students change schools more frequently than white students do. Although the mobility rates for all groups declined from 2000 to 2006; the largest decline was among Hispanic households.

The trend: From 2000 to 2006, the gaps changed little.

Parent Participation

Although teachers play the predominant role in student achievement, substantial research has confirmed that parents play an important supportive role. One key aspect is the degree of parent-school interaction. On some measures of parent involvement, such as whether parents attend a scheduled meeting with a teacher, little difference exists by race and ethnicity. However, on measures that require greater involvement, such as volunteering or serving on a committee, larger differences emerge. In 2003, 48 percent of white parents reported volunteering or serving on a committee, compared with 32 percent of black parents and 28 percent of Hispanic parents.

The trend: The good news is that parent involvement showed an increase from 1999 to 2003 for all racial and ethnic groups. The gaps among groups narrowed for attending a school event but remained about the same on measures requiring greater involvement.

Rigor of the Curriculum

Research supports the unsurprising fact that students' academic achievement is closely related to the rigor of the curriculum. There has been progress across all groups in taking a "midlevel" curriculum in high school. A midlevel curriculum is defined as at least four credits in English and three each in social studies, mathematics, and science; completion of geometry and Algebra II; at least two courses in biology, chemistry, and physics; and at least one credit in a foreign language.

The trend: The gap in taking a midlevel curriculum in high school has closed between black and white students, with 51 percent of blacks and 52 percent of whites completing a mid-level curriculum. There has been no narrowing of the gap between whites and Hispanics, however, with only 44 percent of Hispanics completing a midlevel curriculum in 2005. The gaps have changed little since 2002.

Teacher Preparation

Teacher quality is strongly related to student achievement. Yet sizeable gaps exist among racial/ethnic groups in the percentage of students whose teachers are fully certified. In 2007, 88 percent of white 8th graders had certified teachers compared with 80 percent of black 8th graders and 81 percent of Hispanic 8th graders. There are also gaps among students whose teachers have a major or minor in the subjects they teach.

The trend: There has been little change in the gaps in teacher certification among groups. However, for teachers prepared in a given subject matter, the gap between Hispanic and white students increased from 2003, whereas the gap between black and white students remained about the same.

Teacher Experience

Research has shown that the amount of teaching experience has an effect on student achievement. Specifically having five or more years of teaching experience makes a difference. The gaps by race and ethnicity are large; black and Hispanic students tend to have less experienced teachers. In 2007, 20 percent of white 8th graders had teachers with four or fewer years of experience; this was the case for 28 percent of black 8th graders and 30 percent of Hispanic 8th graders.

The trend: The gaps have remained unchanged from 2003 to 2007.

Teacher Absence and Turnover

More minority students than white students attend classes in which teachers are frequently absent. In 2007, 8 percent of white 8th graders experienced high teacher absence rates compared with 11 percent of black 8th graders and 13 percent of Hispanic 8th graders. Many more have teachers who leave before the end of the school year. Such disruptions have a negative effect on student achievement.

The trend: For teacher absence, the gap grew between white and Hispanic students from 2000 to 2007 and narrowed between black and white students. For teacher turnover, the black/white gap remained unchanged, and the white/Hispanic gap narrowed slightly.

Class Size

Although many studies have found that class size makes a difference in student achievement, the issue is controversial. But few would disagree with the proposition that minority students should not be subject to larger classes than majority students. Also, some research shows that black students, particularly males, benefit from smaller classes. Minority students are, on average, in larger classes than majority students are.

The trend: From 2000 to 2004, the class size gap between schools with high and low proportions of minority students increased.

Technology in the Classroom

In general, research supports technology use in classrooms, particularly for drill and practice. The availability of computers in the classroom, along with Internet access, continues to increase. By 2005, 92 percent of schools with 50 percent or more minority enrollment had Internet access in the classroom, compared with 96 percent of schools with less than 6 percent minority enrollment.

The trend: The gaps among groups narrowed between 2000 and 2005.

Fear and Safety at School

Research has established that a positive disciplinary climate directly links to higher achievement. In many schools, maintaining discipline may be the largest problem that teachers face. Minority students more often avoid certain places in school because of fear of an attack, experience the presence of street gangs, and are involved in fights.

The trend: Between 2001 and 2005, there was an increase in black and Hispanic students reporting gangs in the school—36.6 percent of black students and 38.4 percent of Hispanic students reported such an increase compared with 16.6 percent of white students. For physical fights, the gap between white and Hispanic students widened, with 18.3 percent of Hispanic students typically involved in this behavior compared with 11.6 of white students. There was no change in the gap among students experiencing fear of attack or harm in school.

The Truth of the Matter

People frequently ask which of these factors are the most important or whether out-of-school factors have larger or smaller effects on student achievement than school factors. Given the research currently available, we are unable to answer these questions. However, we can be sure that both school experiences *and* home and early life experiences are important. And the two are related: Low-income neighborhoods where there are few resources in the home also tend to have low tax bases available to support high-quality schools.

Those who argue that what happens outside of school and before school begins should not play a role in the ability of the "good" schools to raise all students to the same high standard seem to assume that students are empty vessels that schools can fill up with knowledge. But students are not empty vessels.

For those who argue that these early and out-of-school experiences are the sole reasons for achievement gaps found in schools—and that schools are powerless to remedy them—we know for a fact that schools can make a difference. As Daniel Patrick Moynihan once said, "Students do not learn their algebra at home." How well teachers are prepared, how much experience they have, how often they show up in school, and how well they maintain order and discipline in their classrooms all make a difference—and minority students are getting short-changed on all those fronts.

We know for a fact that schools can make a difference.

To address the achievement gap, we need to focus on equalizing access to high-quality schools. We also have to focus on conditions beyond school to compensate for challenges that many students experience in life outside the classroom.

We have to focus on conditions beyond school to compensate for the deficits that many students experience in life outside the classroom.

Notes

1. Barton, P. E. (2003). *Parsing the achievement gap: Baselines for tracking progress* (Policy Information Report). Princeton, NJ: Educational Testing Service. Available: www.ets.org/Media/Research/pdf/PICPARSING.pdf

2. Barton, P. E., & Coley, R. J. (2009). *Parsing the achievement gap II* (Policy Information Report). Princeton, NJ: Educational Testing Service. Available: www.ets.org/Media/Research/pdf/PICPARSINGII.pdf

Critical Thinking

1. Choose two of the factors that begin at birth and affect the achievement gap and develop strategies that could be implemented which would lead to an improvement in these areas.

2. Investigate how schools are funded in your state and see if there is a difference in the per-pupil funding for schools located in at-risk areas vs. schools located in middle- or upper-class neighborhoods.

PAUL E. BARTON (pbarton@ets.org) is Senior Associate and RICHARD J. COLEY (rcoley@ets.org) is Director of the Policy Information Center, Educational Testing Service, Princeton, New Jersey.

Author note—The data in this article are drawn from our report *Parsing the Achievement Gap II*.

The Achievement Gap
What Early Childhood Educators Need to Know

BARBARA A. LANGHAM

Perhaps the most important challenge in education today is how to overcome the achievement gap. Although generally applied to public schools, the achievement gap is an issue that early childhood educators in both the public and private sectors need to know about and understand.

The reason is simple: Early care and education will likely play an increasingly critical role in attempts to close the gap.

What Is the Achievement Gap?

The achievement gap is the lagging academic performance of one group of students compared to another. Usually it refers to the lower scores of blacks and Hispanics compared to whites, and the lower scores of low-income students compared to upper or middle class students on standardized tests and other measures of educational achievement.

One recent national report, for example, said the average math scores of black 9-year-olds lagged behind those of their white peers by 22 to 32 points on a 0–500 scale during the years from 1978 to 2004. Scores of black youngsters rose during the period from 192 to 225, but black students did not catch up to whites, whose scores also rose (National Center for Education Statistics 2009).

Besides test scores, the gap can describe the difference in other measures such as high school completion, enrollment in advanced courses, and enrollment in college. A recent Texas report, for example, said that only 54.2 percent of Hispanic seventh graders in 1995 went on to graduate from a Texas public high school, compared with 61.3 percent of all students (Texas Higher Education Coordinating Board 2009).

In analyzing such gaps, one can compare performance measures not only by race/ethnicity and income but also other categories such as grade level, age, gender, and enrollment in public or private schools. With respect to age, for example, one recent national report of long-term trends found that since the early 1970s the average reading and math scores for all 9- and 13-year-olds have increased. Scores for 17-year-olds, however, have remained about the same (National Assessment Governing Board 2009).

On the positive side, analysts have noted improvements and a narrowing of gaps on many measures. What's disturbing, however, is the persistence of gaps and the question of whether we will ever close them.

What's disturbing, however, is the persistence of the achievement gap and the question of whether we will ever close it.

Why Does It Matter?

Some may assume achievement gaps are a problem only for those in the public schools or for the families whose children are enrolled there.

But the fact is that these gaps affect all of us. Our system of public schools is a fundamental institution of American society. For generations, public schools have educated the vast majority of our people and prepared them for the workforce. Schools have helped create a sense of community and enabled us to participate in a democratic society.

As education advocate Tom Luce (1995) has pointed out, our future is "inextricably tied" to the future of our public schools. Anyone concerned about crime, jobs, and taxes, he says, should be concerned about our schools.

Crime

About 75 percent of the nation's state prison inmates are high school dropouts. On average, it costs roughly $22,600 a year to house an inmate compared to $9,644 a year to educate a child who stays in school (Alliance for Excellent Education 2006). "We can pay now for quality education," says Luce, "or pay later for dead-end warehousing of people who contribute little beyond crime and violence."

Jobs

Half of all jobs today require education beyond high school. Another third require a college degree (The Workforce

Alliance 2009). Gone are the days when a hard-working young man or woman could drop out of school, go to work in a factory or a store, and earn enough to provide for a family.

Half of all jobs today require education beyond high school. Another third require a college degree.

Equally worrisome, employers in recent years have complained about the lack of basic skills in prospective employees. According to the National Commission on Adult Literacy (2008), more than half of the U.S. workforce face at least one education barrier: limited English proficiency, no high school diploma, or no college.

The need for an increasingly skilled workforce means that schools must educate all children. It also means that schools must encourage more girls and minority students to study science, math, technology, and engineering.

Taxes

According to Census data, the average annual income of a high school dropout is $18,900 a year compared to $25,900 for a high school graduate and $45,400 for a person with a bachelor's degree (Day and Newburger 2002). As the saying goes, "The more you learn, the more you earn."

When students perform well in school, they're more likely to stay off the streets and out of unemployment lines as adults. With more education, students become taxpayers instead of tax consumers. In addition, more workers earning higher incomes—and thus paying more taxes—can contribute to the Social Security trust fund, which today's workers expect to draw upon in retirement.

But the consequences of the achievement gap go beyond crime, jobs, and taxes. McKinsey & Company (2009), an international consulting firm, cites two others.

Health

Less educated people tend to have less healthy lifestyles, especially when it comes to smoking and obesity. In addition, because they are less likely to have health insurance, they have less preventive care and therefore require more emergency room care when a disease or chronic condition reaches an advanced stage, thereby driving up health costs.

Less educated people tend to have less healthy lifestyles, especially when it comes to smoking and obesity.

Economy

Low educational attainment slackens invention and productivity of workers, lessening the nation's potential output and slowing its growth. Simply stated, significant gaps in achievement between and across various groups of students drag down the nation's economy, in effect, creating "the equivalent of a permanent, deep recession."

Finally, the achievement gap raises an ethical and moral issue. Is it right that some students get stuck in a cycle of poverty because they can't get a good education? "There is no better way to 'love thy neighbor,'" says Luce, "than by helping to create schools in which all our children can flourish and realize their potential."

Is it right that some students get stuck in a cycle of poverty because they can't get a good education?

Teachers have long recognized that students from poor, disadvantaged families did worse in school than students from more affluent families. In 1966, sociologist James Coleman, in a pioneering use of test scores, documented the achievement gap between white and black students. Although Coleman's findings might seem, on the surface, to suggest a racial component to the gap, later researchers have determined that the overriding factor is economic status, rather than race.

One major insight from Coleman's study was the huge impact of a child's family background on later school performance (Clark 1996).

In the years since, researchers have studied the gap from two perspectives: the schools and early childhood. Of the massive research conducted, the studies reported below represent only a sampling.

Closing the Gap: K-12 Schools

In the 1950s, schools began receiving increased attention, notably with the launch of *Sputnik* by the Soviet Union in 1957 and new emphasis on math and science courses. Other changes followed.

Civil Rights

The achievement gap is often considered a vestige of slavery and segregation. In 1954, the U.S. Supreme Court in *Brown v. Board of Education* declared that segregated schools denied equal educational opportunity to black children. Desegregation came slowly and in some cases only by court order, resulting in forced busing of students in large cities.

With forced busing came white flight, the exodus of white families to private schools or to public schools in suburban areas. As the Civil Rights Movement gained momentum, housing patterns changed too, and busing was phased out. By the 1990s, many large public schools had become racially and ethnically imbalanced again, this time with high proportions of black and Hispanic students.

Poverty

Americans have long regarded education as the ticket out of poverty. In 1965, in the federal government's first foray into public K-12 schooling, Congress passed the Elementary and Secondary Education Act (ESEA). Title I of the act directed funding at improving education for poor students (Hanna 2005). The law has been reauthorized many times, with amendments that expanded aid to students with language barriers and students with disabilities.

Improving education alone, however, was not enough. As recent experience has shown, reducing poverty also requires a healthy economy and plentiful jobs. Economists argue that workers in low-wage jobs can rise out of poverty if given work supports, such as an increased minimum wage, the Earned Income Tax Credit, assistance with health care, and subsidized child care (Bernstein 2007).

Schools in Decline

Public schools have always had detractors. In the mid 1960s, for example, Boston educator John Holt, in *How Children Fail,* asserted that schools made children afraid of giving wrong answers and being mocked by teachers and their friends. His ideas and those of others opposed to compulsory school attendance helped give rise to homeschooling (HoltGWS.com n.d.).

By the 1970s the effectiveness of public schools had come into question. One indication was a steady decline in college admission test scores. Public support also faltered, notably in 1978 with California's Proposition 13. The ensuing taxpayer revolt adversely affected the budgets of many school districts across the country (Sack 2005).

In 1983, a federal commission claimed that the "average achievement of high school students on most standardized tests is now lower than 26 years ago when *Sputnik* was launched." The report, *A Nation at Risk,* contained this often-quoted line: "If an unfriendly foreign power had attempted to impose on America the mediocre educational performance that exists today, we might well have viewed it as an act of war. As it stands, we have allowed this to happen to ourselves."

A number of states instituted school reforms. These included a more rigorous curriculum, periodic testing, extended school day and year, career ladders for teachers, and better campus leadership.

At the end of the decade, state governors called for national education goals to be met by 2000. The first goal: "All children will enter school ready to learn." Congress made those goals the centerpiece of the Educate America Act in 1994. When the millennial year arrived, however, many observers agreed the goals had been far too ambitious (Rothstein 1999).

In 2001 Congress passed another iteration of ESEA, the No Child Left Behind Act. Title I continued funding to enhance education of low-income students, but the law's main emphasis had shifted to standards, testing, and increased accountability for the academic achievement of all students.

Effective Schools

Even before reforms were put in place, some public schools, despite the challenges of poverty and racial imbalance, were outperforming others.

Two researchers who studied this phenomenon, Larry Lezotte and Ronald Edmonds at Michigan State, found that effective schools had common characteristics: 1) instructional leadership, 2) clear and focused mission, 3) safe and orderly environment, 4) climate of high expectations, 5) frequent monitoring of student progress, 6) positive home-school relations, and 7) opportunity to learn and student time on task (Edmonds 1982). Many schools began striving to incorporate these traits.

Alternative Programs

Rather than forcing integration, some public school systems in the late 1960s created magnet schools to "attract" a diversity of students to a specialized curriculum. Magnet schools thrived, in part because enrollment was by choice. By the 2001–2002 school year, there were 3,100 magnet schools in the United States (Rossell 2005).

Beginning in 1991, several states, led by Minnesota, passed legislation authorizing charter schools. These schools received public funding but were exempt from certain state or local regulations so they could experiment with innovative methods. In the 2006–2007 school year, the nation had more than 4,100 charter schools, most of which served large proportions of black and Hispanic students (National Center for Education Statistics n.d.).

Four charter schools—as well as one Catholic school and a neighborhood public school—were profiled by David Whitman in *Sweating the Small Stuff: Inner-City Schools and the New Paternalism* (2008). All six secondary schools had been successful in raising students' test scores. Whitman described them as "paternalistic" because, like a firm, but loving father, they maintained discipline and urged hard work to reach high expectations.

Some groups decided that choice and private schools were the answer. In 1990 the city of Milwaukee started a voucher system that allowed low-income families to enroll their children in private schools (U.S. Department of Education n.d.).

In studying schools, educators could not escape one critical fact: The achievement gap existed before children started school. According to current figures, for example, the cognitive skills of 4-year-olds who live below the poverty line are 18 months behind what is typical for their age group. By age 10, they're still behind (Klein and Knitzer 2007).

It's no surprise then that many educators focused on the child's early years, including the home and family.

Closing the Gap: Early Childhood

In the late 1950s, home life for children underwent many changes including a shift from rural to urban lifestyle, a rising divorce rate, and the movement of greater numbers of women into the workforce.

Preschool Programs

In the 1960s and 1970s, preschool programs proliferated to accommodate the growing number of working mothers. While some researchers studied the effect of day care on children, others developed programs specifically aimed at poor and minority children.

In 1962, for example, David Weikart, a special education director in Ypsilanti, Mich., created the Perry Preschool Project. This program served low-income, 3- and 4-year-old black children identified as high risk for later school failure.

A decade later, child development researchers at the University of North Carolina began the Abecedarian Project, a five-year investigation of a full-day, full-year program for poor black children from infancy to age 5.

Both were high-quality programs with well-trained teachers. Results from both programs were positive: less placement in special education, less grade retention, and increased high school graduation. Follow-up of Perry preschoolers, in particular, revealed that at age 40 they had higher educational attainment, higher earnings, and lower crime compared to non-enrolled peers. Significantly, the project showed a high return on every dollar invested, ranging from $5.15 to $17.10 (Isaacs 2008).

Head Start

A number of researchers, including pediatrician Julius Richmond and University of Arkansas professor Bettye Caldwell, investigated the effect of poverty on babies. The conclusion: High-quality infant and toddler care could enhance a child's emotional and cognitive development (Weber 2008; University of Arkansas for Medical Sciences 2001).

Impressed by such findings, the federal government tapped Richmond and others, notably Yale psychologist Edward Zigler, to create Head Start in 1965 (Yale University n.d.). Head Start provided comprehensive early childhood services to poor 3- and 4-year-olds, in most cases for half a day. The program branched out to include services to pregnant women, infants, and toddlers (Early Head Start). Despite positive results, funding levels allow Head Start to serve less than 40 percent of eligible children, and Early Head Start, less than two percent (National Head Start Association 2008).

Home Visiting Programs

In the 1970s, David Olds established the Nurse-Family Partnership in Baltimore. Registered nurses made home visits to low-income, first-time mothers during pregnancy and through the child's second birthday. Nurses taught health practices and parenting skills and helped mothers with plans to finish school and find a job. In 1996, the program branched out to other locations and is now operating in 23 states (Isaacs 2008).

In the early 1980s, Missouri state education officials created Parents As Teachers for first-time parents. It started as a home visiting program, funded by the state and operated in school districts, in which trained educators visited parents throughout pregnancy and up to age 3. A free, voluntary program, it evolved to include group meetings, screenings, and referrals and was extended to 3- and 4-year-olds.

The program spread to 3,000 sites in 50 states and a dozen other countries. It's often linked with other programs and funding sources, such as Head Start and Title I. Evaluations have shown positive effects on both parents and children, especially in low-income families (Parents as Teachers 2002).

Brain Research

Up until the 1990s, it was widely assumed that babies were born with a fixed learning ability—that is, most had average intelligence, a few were genius level, and others had little ability. That notion was dashed, however, when neuroscientists revealed that the brain is actually hard-wired by a child's experiences, especially during the first three years of life (U.S. Department of Education 1999; Carnegie Corporation 1994).

The brain is actually hard-wired by a child's experiences, especially during the first three years of life.

Other research established a direct connection between cognition and language. In the mid 1990s, Betty Hart and Todd Risley, for example, found that children reared by parents in professional careers developed more extensive vocabularies than their peers in working class and poor families. The difference was that professional parents talked more to their children and gave more encouragement (Early Education for All 2003).

Harlem Children's Zone

In 1997, Geoffrey Canada, who had operated social and educational programs for Harlem families for 25 years, created a network of programs for low-income children. The Zone offered a parenting education class for expectant parents and a charter middle school with extended hours that focused on raising students' test scores.

Before long, he developed a "conveyor belt" approach that would carry children from birth through the preschool years and into elementary and secondary school. Early results showed gains (Harlem Children's Zone n.d.). Though convinced that this approach works, Canada believes that older kids, who missed out on the conveyor belt, are worth the extraordinary measures needed to save them (Tough 2008).

Universal Pre-K
In the 2007–2008 school year, more than 80 percent of all 4-year-olds in the United States attended some kind of preschool. Roughly half of those were in a private program, and half were in a public program such as state pre-K, Head Start, or special education (National Institute for Early Education Research 2008).

The number and type of publicly funded programs varied widely from state to state. In one ranking, Oklahoma topped the list because it provides free public preschool to nearly 90 percent of its 4-year-olds (NIEER 2008).

National consensus for universal pre-K programs is growing (Pew Center on the States 2009). Most state governors recognize the educational and economic necessity of high-quality pre-kindergarten, but support is mixed. (For a state-by-state list of support, see www.preknow.org/documents/LeadershipReport_May2009.pdf.)

Where Do We Go from Here?
Four decades of research have led to a better understanding of the conditions in the home, school, and community that affect children's educational attainment.

We know what early childhood educators have long believed—that high-quality programs that teach parenting skills, enhance infant and toddler development, and expand preschool learning experiences can turn children's lives around. It's time to give these programs the added support they deserve.

References
Achievement Gap Initiative, Harvard University. n.d. "The Facts on the Gap." www.agi.harvard.edu/Topics/Gapstats.php.

Alliance for Excellent Education. August 2006. "Saving Futures, Saving Dollars: The Impact of Education on Crime Reduction and Earnings." www.all4ed.org/files/SavingFutures.pdf.

Bernstein, Jared. April 2007. "Is Education the Cure for Poverty?" *The American Prospect.* www.prospect.org/cs/articles?article=is_education_the_cure_for_poverty.

Carnegie Corporation of New York. 1994. *Starting Points: Meeting the Needs of Our Youngest Children.* www.carnegie.org/starting_points/index.html.

Clark, Jon, ed. 1996. *James S. Coleman.* Washington, D.C.: Falmer Press.

Day, Jennifer Cheeseman and Eric C. Newburger. July 2002. *The Big Payoff: Educational Attainment and Synthetic Estimates of Work-Life Earnings.* Washington, D.C.: U.S. Census Bureau. www.census.gov/prod/2002pubs/p23-210.pdf.

Early Education for All. June 2003. "Meaningful Differences in the Everyday Experience of Young American Children" (research summary). www.strategiesforchildren.org/eea/6research_summaries/05_MeaningfulDifferences.pdf.

Edmonds, Ronald R. December 1982. "Programs of School Improvement: An Overview," *Educational Leadership.* www.ascd.org/ASCD/pdf/journals/ed_lead/el_198212_edmonds.pdf.

Hanna, Julie. 2005. "The Elementary and Secondary Education Act: 40 Years Later," Harvard Graduate School of Education. www.gse.harvard.edu/news_events/features/2005/08/esea0819.html.

Harlem Children's Zone. n.d. "Promise Academy Charter Schools: Going beyond the walls of the classroom." www.hcz.org/programs/promise-academy-charter-schools.

HoltGWS.com. n.d. "John Holt and Growing Without Schooling." www.holtgws.com/johnholtpage.html.

Isaacs, Julia. September 2008. "Model Early Childhood Programs," The Brookings Institution. www.brookings.edu/papers/2008/~/media/Files/rc/papers/2008/09_early_programs_isaacs/09_early_programs_brief4.pdf.

Klein, Lisa G. and Jane Knitzer. January 2007. "Promoting Effective Early Learning: What Every Policymaker and Educator Should Know." National Center for Children in Poverty. www.nccp.org/publications/pub_695.html.

Luce, Tom. 1995. *Now or Never: How We Can Save Our Public Schools.* Dallas: Taylor Publishing.

McKinsey & Company. 2009. *The Economic Impact of the Achievement Gap in America's Schools.* www.mckinsey.com/clientservice/socialsector/achievementgap.asp.

National Assessment Governing Board. April 28, 2009. "News release: Long-term reading and math scores on the Nation's Report Card rise for 9- and 13-year-olds; 17-year-olds see fewer gains." http://nationsreportcard.gov/ltt_2008/media/pdf/ltt_news_release_2008.pdf.

National Center for Education Statistics. July 2009. "Achievement Gaps: How Black and White Students in Public Schools Perform in Mathematics and Reading on the National Assessment of Academic Progress." http://nces.ed.gov/nationsreportcard/pdf/studies/2009455.pdf.

National Center for Education Statistics. n.d. "Fast Facts: What are charter schools? How common are they, and who do they serve?" http://nces.ed.gov/fastfacts/display.asp?id=30.

National Commission on Adult Literacy. June 2008. *Reach Higher, America: Overcoming Crisis in the U.S. Workforce.* www.nationalcommissiononadultliteracy.org/ReachHigherAmerica/ReachHigher.pdf.

National Commission on Excellence in Education. April 1983. *A Nation at Risk.* www.ed.gov/pubs/NatAtRisk/risk.html.

National Head Start Association. June 19, 2008. "Head Start Leaders Have High Hopes for New President and Congress, But Budget 'Double Whammy' Expected to Force Cuts of Up to 14,000 Child Slots Nationwide." www.supportheadstart.org/News/releases2.cfm?releaseID=57.

National Institute for Early Education Research. 2008. *The State of Preschool 2008.* www.pewtrusts.org/uploadedFiles/wwwpewtrustsorg/Reports/Pre-k_education/yearbook(1).pdf.

Parents As Teachers. June 2002. "Evaluations." www.acf.hhs.gov/programs/ohs/about/fy2008.html.

Pew Center on the States. May 2009. *Leadership Matters: Governors Pre-K Proposals Fiscal Year 2010.* www.preknow.org/documents/LeadershipReport_May2009.pdf.

Rossell, Christine. Spring 2005. "Whatever Happened to Magnet Schools," *Education Next,* Hoover Institution, Stanford University. www.hoover.org/publications/ednext/3220691.html.

Rothstein, Richard. Dec. 22, 1999. "Lessons; 'Goals 2000' Score: Failure 8, U.S. 0," *The New York Times.* www.nytimes.com/1999/12/22/us/lessons-goals-2000-score-failure-8-us-0.html.

Sack, Joetta L. Jan. 6, 2005. "Kirst comments on effects of Prop 13 on education," in *Education Week,* Stanford University School of Education. http://ed.stanford.edu/suse/faculty/displayFacultyNews.php?tablename=notify1&id=264.

Texas Higher Education Coordinating Board. July 2009. *Closing the Gaps by 2015: A Progress Report.* www.thecb.state.tx.us/reports/PDF/1852.PDF?CFID=1789068&CFTOKEN=93029873.

Tough, Paul. 2008. *Whatever It Takes: Geoffrey Canada's Quest to Change Harlem and America.* Boston: Houghton Mifflin.

University of Arkansas for Medical Sciences. Dec. 6, 2001. "Bettye Caldwell Joins Galaxy of Early Childhood Leaders." www.uams.edu/today/120601/caldwell.htm.

U.S. Department of Education. n.d. "Innovations in Education: Creating Strong School District Choice Programs." www.ed.gov/admins/comm/choice/choiceprograms/programs_pg15.html.

U.S. Department of Education. July 1999. "Start Early and Finish Strong: How to Help Every Child Become a Reader." www.ed.gov/pubs/startearly/ch_1.html.

Weber, Bruce. July 30, 2008. "Dr. Julius B. Richmond, Who Led Head Start and Battled Tobacco, Dies at 91," *The New York Times.* www.nytimes.com/2008/07/30/us/30richmond.html.

Whitman, David. 2008. *Sweating the Small Stuff: Inner-City Schools and the New Paternalism.* Washington, D.C.: Thomas B. Fordham Institute.

The Workforce Alliance. 2009. *Toward Ensuring America's Workers and Industries the Skills to Compete.* www.workforcealliance.org/atf/cf/%7B93353952-1df1-473a-b105-7713f4529ebb%7D/SKILLSSTRATEGY_WEB VERSIONFINAL.PDF.

Yale University, Zigler Center. n.d. "Edward F. Zigler Festschrift (Tribute)." www.yale.edu/zigler/history.html.

Critical Thinking

1. Your state senator does not believe in using public money for the education of children prior to kindergarten. Write your senator a letter describing the financial and academic benefits for spending money on high quality preschool programs for at-risk children.

2. Go to the website listed in the article for the PewCenter on the States and find your state in the 28 page report. www.preknow.org/documents/leadershipreport_May2009.pdf. If you live in one of the 42 states that offer preschool programs for children, how does your state rank compared to others? What are the programs available for young children in your state?

Editor's note—Thanks to John Fessenden, director of accountability and research, Del Valle Independent School District, Del Valle, Texas, for reviewing this article.

The Messiness of Readiness

Instead of sorting children into those who are ready to learn and those who are not, schools should provide opportunities for all children to succeed.

PAMELA JANE POWELL

So many times I have heard, "Most of the children coming to kindergarten don't even know their ABCs!" This is usually followed by, "They aren't ready for school."

I've always found this attitude curious. Isn't that what school is about, to learn the ABCs? Does one have to get ready to learn? How do you get ready to learn? And what does a child who is ready to learn look like?

School readiness is an ubiquitous term. The definition varies depending on the context in which it's being discussed. Teachers have a different idea of school readiness than parents do, and politicians have a different notion than pediatricians. School readiness, seemingly easy to define, is just the opposite. The beliefs about and descriptions of school readiness are untidy.

> **Teachers have a different idea of school readiness than parents do, and politicians have a different notion than pediatricians.**

The problem with "readiness" is that its meaning is hard to pin down. It represents different things to different people and implies a sort-and-classify mentality. It is usually tied to the cognitive and social domains, and the gist of the term insinuates an ethereal threshold separating the haves from the have-nots.

Huey-Ling Lin, Frank R. Lawrence, and Jeffrey Gorrell write that, "Embedded in a sociocultural context, kindergarten teachers' readiness perceptions are shaped by many factors, including their own experiences as learners and teachers, school structure, school teaching conditions, the expectations of schools for children, social forces, community needs and values, children's backgrounds, and external societal attitudes toward early childhood education" (2003: 227). When discussing readiness, Elizabeth Graue states, "It is almost always conceptualized as a characteristic of an individual child that develops as the child grows. Different theories of readiness depict a variety of mechanisms for readiness development, but

all seem to agree that readiness is something within a child that is necessary for success in school" (1993: 4). It would be reasonable to suggest that it is adults, then, who harbor concepts about readiness, and these concepts are informed by the experiences and expectations of these adults.

Readiness differs from eligibility for school entrance. Eligibility is straightforward, a date on a calendar. Readiness, on the other hand, implies something that resides within the child. Readiness is also tied to the concept of age-graded schools.

> **Eligibility is straightforward, a date on a calendar. Readiness, on the other hand, implies something that resides within the child.**

The Quandary of Being Ready

The way our schools are organized contributes to the confusion about readiness. And now, with many children in day care and preschool, the age-graded structure is an issue as well. Age-gradeness organizes children into age cohorts with a birthday cutoff date, thus ensuring at least a one-year chronological span in most classrooms. However, children in even a one-year age span can be vastly different. When you total other factors, such as being overage for grade, being young for grade, being small for grade, being socially immature, and a myriad other variables, the pursuit of "readiness" becomes even more muddied.

A classroom of preschoolers or kindergartners varies widely because of students' cognitive abilities and their socioemotional functioning. Those who perform well across domains are the ideal incoming students. But those who have difficulty may not be welcomed in classrooms already overtaxed with the pressure of large class sizes, understaffed centers or classrooms, and the need to make Adequate Yearly Progress.

But even if schools had clearly defined "readiness" criteria, that static goal still could be dynamic because there still would be children who wouldn't be "quite as ready" as others. In other words, the range of abilities still would be there.

Through various assessments and observations, children may be deemed ready (or not) to enter a school. There are proponents with various assessments to determine if young children are ready, and there are also detractors. But it is troubling that some assessments could be used to prevent school entry at the normal age. We can't account for all the differences that might affect the score on such assessments, and it might not be just to permit or deny entry to school on the basis of such assessments.

However, the ideas behind these threshold assessments seem reasonable. That is, children "need" certain skills to succeed in school. Therefore, if they don't have them, school will be a struggle. The question that must be posed, though, is who will struggle: the child, the teacher, other students, all of them? Does the struggle ensue because of an erroneous notion that we can somehow package what "ready" looks like?

Perceptions about readiness, fueled by conventional wisdom, also add to this messiness. A self-fulfilling prophecy may begin as the young-for-grade, small-for-age, clinging child walks through the doors of a kindergarten. The not-so-uncommon phenomenon of a child being booted out of preschool may be a current example of those deemed "not ready." But teachers, caregivers, parents, and the public may be part of the problem because they are unaware of what is developmentally appropriate.

All children do not have the same experiences and opportunities, and comparing children to children is an unreasonable comparison when you consider the vast variations between them. Comparing the child with himself or herself, based on growth over time, seems more logical.

Looking for growth does not deny the excellence of academic achievement. In fact, it may spawn more academic achievement because children will be succeeding within their own learning frames. Excellence, then, can be based on individual achievement and can be rooted in the mastery of many skills and, if you like, standards. Instead of lamenting the supposedly low levels of some children, accolades may be given to children for their steps forward.

The National Association for the Education of Young Children (2009) calls for a definition of readiness to be "flexible and broadly defined." This includes all the domains that reside within the child. Furthermore, teachers of young children must be proficient in assessing the needs and being able to meet the needs of children where the children are, not where they're expected to be.

Ready Schools

Some states and organizations understand that ready children must be paired with ready schools. One example is North Carolina's Ready Schools Initiative, which states:

A ready elementary school provides an inviting atmosphere, values and respects all children and their families, and is a place where children succeed. It is committed to high quality in all domains of learning and teaching and has deep connections with parents and its community. It prepares children for success in work and life in the 21st century. (Smart Start and NC Ready School Initiative 2007)

Ready schools understand that children are at different places at different times. They expect them to be. Ready schools are schools that meet children where they are and help them grow. Ready schools understand the importance of teachers being steeped in child development and how that can affect teaching and learning. Ready schools open their arms to every child with the expectation that all children will learn. Ready schools understand that children may have different learning styles/preferences and thus provide multiple opportunities for growth. Ready schools have teachers who are professionals and know what to do for children's growth. They understand the importance of assessment and its ability to inform instruction. They are accountable and can meet the needs of children through various means. Ready schools are keenly aware that one size does not fit all. Ready schools are about the success of all children.

The Illusion of Readiness

The truth is that we will never be able to have uniform readiness in an age-graded system. Children are living organisms, and education is not what we do to them, but what we do with them. Defining readiness is akin to trying to catch the wind. Readiness exists in the minds of adults, not in the minds of children, who are ever curious and always ready to learn.

Education is the right of every child. Children are perpetually ready to learn, and we have the responsibility to provide rich opportunities for them to do so. Let's provide opportunities for them to succeed.

We can do this by engaging entire communities in the pursuit of helping children succeed. We need to exchange competitiveness for collaboration and educate cities and communities about the needs and the stages of children. Strategic and purposeful planning to engage parents, children, and other community members in enhancing the foundation for young children can ultimately strengthen the citizenry of communities, states, and the nation as a whole.

References

Graue, M. Elizabeth. *Ready for What? Constructing Meanings of Readiness for Kindergarten.* Albany, N.Y.: State University of New York Press, 1993.

Lin, Huey-Ling, Frank R. Lawrence, and Jeffrey Gorrell. "Kindergarten Teachers' Views of Children's Readiness for School." *Early Children Quarterly* 18, no. 2 (2003): 225–237.

Smart Start and NC Ready School Initiative. "Pathways and Definitions to a Ready School." Raleigh, N.C.: North Carolina Ready Schools Initiative, 2007. www.ncreadyschools.org/defandpath.html.

National Association for the Education of Young Children. "Where We Stand on School Readiness." NAEYC Position Statement. Washington, D.C.: National Association for the Education of Young Children, 2009. www.naeyc.org/files/naeyc/file/positions/Readiness.pdf.

Critical Thinking

1. What would one expect to find happening in a school setting ready to accept all children?
2. What makes readiness so challenging to assess? How would you define readiness for kindergarten?

PAMELA JANE POWELL is an assistant professor of literacy and early childhood at Northern Arizona University, Flagstaff, Ariz.

Invest in Early Childhood Education

We need expanded federal leadership in early education to develop an excellent, coherent, and equitable system. The authors recommend 13 ways for the government to develop a universal and sustained approach to early childhood education.

SHARON LYNN KAGAN AND JEANNE L. REID

The federal government's role in early education has a long and contentious history. While the nature and amount of federal engagement has shifted in response to changing social, political, and economic needs, the lack of long-term planning or coordination has yielded an array of programs, dispersed across federal agencies and legislative committees, which begs for greater excellence, coherence, and equity in early childhood education.

The history of American early education is one of changing roles and goals. From the privately funded Infant Schools for indigent families in the earliest days of the republic, to the federal government's foray into early childhood with Depression-era nursery schools, to more recent investments in Head Start, federal early education policies can best be understood as a series of responses to shifting social, economic, and political phenomena (Beatty 1981; Cahan 1989; Cohen 1996). Amid these changes, four durable polemics have shaped the federal response.

First, American society has long questioned whether young children should be served outside their homes at all. From the nation's birth, the primacy and the privacy of the home were ideological mantras, forcing early education programs to legitimate their existence; such programs have never been considered an entitlement akin to K-12 education.

Federal support for early education grew during times of national crises and declined as the crises ebbed.

Second, because public values haven't generally supported out-of-home, nonmaternal care, federal support for early education grew during times of national crises and declined

as the crises ebbed, leaving early education bereft of three essential mainstays: vision, permanence, and infrastructure.

Third, there has been an enduring ambivalence regarding which children should be served and how. Most public programs have targeted children from low-income families, while the private sector has served children from middle- and upper-income families. Leaving a legacy of services segregated by income, which often translates into quality differences, early education policy defies deeply held American values regarding the equal opportunity that all young children need in order to thrive and learn.

Fourth, there is no consistent agreement about the mission of early education. Should early education focus on care as the day nurseries did? Should it focus on socialization and education as nursery schools purported to do? Although increasingly regarded as a false dichotomy because good early education does both, federal and state policy makers still must tussle with the question as they debate early education's departmental jurisdictions and funding amounts.

5 Cornerstones

Recognizing this historical context and building on the past, we first recommend five cornerstones for American early education:

- Keep early education voluntary before kindergarten.
- Maintain a diverse delivery system with both public and private providers for both fiscal prudence and choice for parents.
- Foster developmentally oriented pedagogy that stresses cognitive, language, social, emotional, and physical development for all children.

- Honor linguistic, cultural, and programmatic diversity.
- Conceptualize early education as a partnership among families, programs, and communities.

Second, we see a need for expanded federal leadership and investments in early education. However, such investments must be guided by clearly defined roles for federal and state governments. These roles must frame and bound the public early childhood policy agenda. In addition to role clarity, the goals of federal intervention must be clear. Early education efforts should focus on advancing excellence, coherence, and equity.

Third, at the community and family level, we seek a combination of demand- and supply-side strategies for direct provision, noting that a focus on demandside policy alone seriously erodes excellence, coherence, and equity. A mixed delivery system will encourage myriad providers of early education and care and encourage higher quality, irrespective of funding mechanisms. In particular, we encourage the development of high-quality choices for low- and middle-income families—two aspects of early education that the current market fails to address effectively.

Early childhood services should be regarded as a fundamental right of all American children, from birth to age five, whose parents wish to enroll them.

Fourth, we would reposition the debate over universal versus targeted services. Early childhood services should be regarded as a fundamental right of all American children, from birth to age five, whose parents wish to enroll them. Even on a sliding-scale fee basis, this goal will not be achieved for years. But a universal goal would enable us to systematically expand high-quality early education services. This means abandoning the program-of-the-year approach to early education and substituting a clear and steady agenda for reform; it means converting the policy zeitgeist from one that permits multiple idiosyncratic department-by-department and state-by-state efforts and moving to thoughtful, evidence-based policy efforts that fit within a conceptually coherent scheme for universality.

Early education is valuable for all children, but parents should be able to choose whether their children will participate.

Our recommendations address the polemics of early care and education by asserting that early education is valuable for all children, but parents should be able to choose whether

The Role of the Federal Government

- Provide the coordinated long-term vision and leadership for the development of a comprehensive, integrated, early childhood system that makes high-quality early education available to all preschool-age children on a voluntary basis.
- Establish research-driven standards regarding the expectations for children, the skills and competencies their teachers require, the provision of programs that serve children, and the requirements for states regarding their duties in advancing the early childhood system.
- Foster building an infrastructure at the state and local levels as a prerequisite for quality and an integral component of all early education efforts by advancing:

  a. teacher quality and workforce enhancements and credentialing;
  b. governance;
  c. the development of assessment tools and the collection of usable data;
  d. preschool to K-12 school linkage/transition efforts;
  e. parental and public engagement; and
  f. research.

- Fund, in conjunction with the states, essential direct services for children at high risk of school failure and children of the working poor as a first step toward fulfilling the mission of universality.
- Promote a spirit of innovation and the development and use of new knowledge regarding early childhood development, pedagogy, curriculum, assessment, and program effectiveness. This includes the funding and effective dissemination of basic research, longitudinal studies, program evaluations, and a series of research and demonstration efforts to guide policy and practice.

their children will participate. Those who remain ideologically opposed to early education do not have to participate. The universal goal would encourage policies that would not, by design, segregate children by family income. We assume high-quality early education programs would offer both care and education, with the paramount goal of readiness for school and life. Finally, we recognize that federal, state, and local governments have specific roles in relation to early childhood education. (See the box "The Role of the Federal Government," "The Role of State Governments," "The Role of Local Communities".)

Recognizing the special role that the federal government plays in early childhood education, we offer 13 specific recommendations for federal action in the next three years. For some, these recommendations may seem too modest. Advancing a fiscally and operationally prudent policy agenda, we take a steady incremental approach that addresses significant and simultaneous increases in direct services and in the early childhood infrastructure.

Recommendation #1
Establish and Fund a Federal Early Learning Council

Composed of representatives from diverse federal agencies, states, and philanthropic organizations, the council will develop a 10-year plan for the federal government's role in advancing early childhood education. This plan would address government roles and responsibilities to young children and their families and determine how best to handle diverse federal funding streams and ensure that all early education efforts meet standards of excellence, coherence, and equity.

Recommendation #2
Establish Federal Guidelines for Children, Teachers, and Programs

To promote greater consistency across states, guidelines should be established that specify what children should know and be able to do, how teachers should be qualified to teach young children, and what foundational elements of quality should characterize early childhood programs. Developed by three national task forces over a two-year period, the guidelines would not be mandated, but would guide states as they develop and modify their own standards.

Recommendation #3
Modify the NCLB Successor

To promote a continuity of experience for children as they transition from early childhood settings into schools, modify the successor to NCLB to ensure that states align their standards, curricula, and assessments across these age groups and that elementary schools are ready for young children and their families.

Recommendation #4
Set Aside an Additional 10% of All New Federal Early Education Funds

Regardless of funding streams, all new federal direct service dollars for children should have a 10% earmark (on top of all new federal dollars invested in early education) for infrastructure and quality enhancement. States would use these funds to enhance personnel preparation, development, compensation, and credentialing services and systems; standards development and implementation; coordinated assessment, monitoring, and accountability systems; coordinated governance efforts; and program quality enhancement systems.

The Role of State Governments

- Ensure equitable access to early education for all children in ways that do not segregate children along socioeconomic lines.
- Create and monitor long-range state plans so that early education services, irrespective of departments, are coordinated and cohesive.
- Review federal standards; set and monitor state standards for children, programs, and personnel. Inherent in this function is the establishment of state accountability systems that capture young children's access to services and their progress over time.
- Fund and monitor direct services for young children.
- Fund and monitor infrastructure advancements.

Recommendation #5
Enhance Early Childhood Teacher Preparation and Credentialing

Given the importance of teacher quality to early childhood program quality and child outcomes, funding must be considered over and above what is currently provided by the Higher Education Act reauthorization and the infrastructure recommendation above. Increase the Higher Education Act budget by 1% and sustain that increase in each of the three years, with these funds targeted to preparing and credentialing early education personnel.

Recommendation #6
Support Parents with Young Children

Parents are their children's first and most important teachers, but many young low-income women become parents without the requisite supports and knowledge to advance their children's development. In the next fiscal year, the federal government should provide parenting education and support to 100,000 low-income mothers with infants or toddlers. For each of the two subsequent fiscal years, an additional 100,000 mothers should be added. Each mother should be served for two years.

Recommendation #7
Expand Services to Low-Income Infants and Toddlers through Early Head Start

Quadruple funding for Early Head Start in year one, and sustain this increase in subsequent years, so that its services can reach more children and families and its quality can be enhanced.

The Role of Local Communities

- Implement state mandates and reporting requirements.
- Provide funding for programs to reflect a local commitment to young children.
- Engage parents and community leaders in the design and distribution of services.

Recommendation #8
Expand Services to Low-Income Children through Head Start and the Child Care and Development Block Grant (CCDBG)

To enhance the availability of services to preschool-age children, expand Head Start funding by 5% annually. The CCDBG budget should also experience a 5% annual increase with the goal of expanding its direct services to low-income children from birth to age five.

Recommendation #9
Expand the Child and Dependent Care Tax Credit

Increase the value of the credit by 25% for families whose annual incomes are below $40,000.

Recommendation #10
Support States as they Develop Pre-kindergarten and Other Early Education Efforts

For the next three years, provide states 25 cents on each additional dollar the states invest to launch or expand their current enrollments in pre-K, with first priority accorded to children from low-income families, children for whom English is not the home language, or those at high risk of school failure. Eligibility for these funds is contingent on states having a long-term plan to provide universal preschool for three- and four-year-old children.

Recommendation #11
Expand and Coordinate Federal Research on Young Children and their Families

Dedicate $100 million in new funds for research on young children and sustain this increase in each of the three years. Such funds would be distributed between education and health and human services and would ensure the funding of two early childhood research centers and the continuation of the Early Childhood Longitudinal Studies.

Recommendation #12
Establish an Electronic National Clearinghouse on Early Education Innovations

Given that early educators are experimenting with innovative pedagogical and systems-infrastructure approaches, the federal government should oversee the review of such efforts and make the results widely available through a national clearinghouse. Such a clearinghouse should include results from and links to high-quality research efforts that could affect policy and practice.

Recommendation #13
Award Challenge Grants to States to Promote Innovation and Quality

The federal government should award competitive challenge grants, which require a state match, to 10 states in the amount of $10 million each in the first year; such grants should be sustained for three years. The challenge grants should select highly promising cross-funding stream (public and private sector) efforts that will significantly enhance early education excellence, coherence, and equity, and that offer strong promise of replicability.

Clear and pointed, these recommendations convey the urgent action required to enact an effective federal commitment to young children. In no other field is the evidence of efficacy so compelling, and in no other field is the potential for future investment so promising. Advancing a piecemeal approach would only perpetuate the fragmentation and lack of quality and equity that has characterized American early education to date. To that end, we recommend finally that the new President and new Congress avoid viewing these recommendations as a menu and instead regard them as an integrated package.

We urge federal policy makers to build an infrastructure, as outlined above, that will strengthen current efforts to expand access to early education and increase the return on a sustained early childhood investment. Only by providing the leadership for both direct services and a durable infrastructure will early childhood education finally square with the excellence, coherence, and equity that it—and this nation—have deserved for so long.

References

Beatty, Barbara R. "A Vocation from on High: Preschool Advocacy and Teaching as an Occupation for Women in 19th-Century Boston." Doctoral dissertation, Harvard Graduate School of Education, 1981.

Cahan, Emily D. *Past Caring: A History of U.S. Preschool Care and Education for the Poor, 1820–1965*. New York: National Center for Children in Poverty, 1989.

Cohen, Abby J. "A Brief History of Federal Financing for Child Care in the United States." *The Future of Children* 6, no. 2 (1996): 26–40.

Critical Thinking

1. Read the following quote found on the second page of the article to three people not in the field of education and ask them to agree or disagree with the statement and describe why. "Early childhood services should be regarded as a fundamental right of all American children, from birth to age five, whose parents wish to enroll them."

2. In the article, Kagan and Reid list recommendations for improvements in education. Find a program in your local community that you believe is meeting one of the recommendations listed in the article.

SHARON LYNN KAGAN is the Virginia and Leonard Marx Professor of Early Childhood and Family Policy, associate dean for policy, and co-director of the National Center for Children and Families at Teachers College, Columbia University, New York. **JEANNE L. REID** is a graduate research fellow at the National Center for Children and Families at Teachers College, Columbia University.

This article is based on a paper commissioned by the Center on Education Policy (CEP). The complete paper, with citations to individual studies and evaluations, is available at www.cep-dc.org.

Joy in School

Joyful learning can flourish in school—if you give joy a chance.

STEVEN WOLK

Two quotes about schooling particularly resonate with me. The first is from John Dewey's *Experience and Education* (1938): "What avail is it to win prescribed amounts of information about geography and history, to win the ability to read and write, if in the process the individual loses his own soul?" (p. 49). If the experience of "doing school" destroys children's spirit to learn, their sense of wonder, their curiosity about the world, and their willingness to care for the human condition, have we succeeded as educators, no matter how well our students do on standardized tests?

The second quote comes from John Goodlad's *A Place Called School* (1984). After finding an "extraordinary sameness" in our schools, Goodlad wrote, "Boredom is a disease of epidemic proportions. . . . Why are our schools not places of joy?" (p. 242). Now, a generation later, if you were to ask students for a list of adjectives that describe school, I doubt that *joyful* would make the list. The hearts and minds of children and young adults are wide open to the wonders of learning and the fascinating complexities of life. But school still manages to turn that into a joyless experience.

So what can schools and teachers do to bring some joy into children's formal education? Children typically spend from six to seven hours each day in school for nearly 10 months each year. During the school year, children generally spend more time interacting with their teachers than with their parents. What happens inside schools has a deep and lasting effect on the mind-sets that children develop toward lifelong learning.

Dewey's point about the destructive power of our schools should make us ask ourselves some fundamental questions: What is the purpose of school? What dispositions about learning, reading, school, the world, and the self do we want to cultivate? Ask young adults why they go to school. You will hear nothing about joy.

I am not using the word joy as a synonym for *fun*. For many children, having fun is hanging out at the mall, watching TV, text-messaging their friends, or zipping down a roller-coaster. Having fun certainly brings us joy, but students don't need to be having fun in school to experience joy. According to my Random House dictionary, *joy* means, "The emotion of great delight or happiness caused by something good or satisfying." Surely our schools can do some of that. Joy and learning—including school content—are not mutually exclusive. Many of our greatest joys in life are related to our learning. Unfortunately, most of that joyful learning takes place outside school.

As educators, we have the responsibility to educate and inspire the whole child—mind, heart, and soul.

As educators, we have the responsibility to educate and inspire the whole child—mind, heart, and soul. By focusing on the following essentials, we can put more joy into students' experience of going to school and get more joy out of working inside one.

JOY 1:
Find the Pleasure in Learning

Why do people learn? I don't mean inside school—I mean learning as a part of life. Surely a large part of our learning is necessary for survival and a basic quality of life.

But there is another, entirely different, reason to learn. Learning gives us pleasure. This kind of learning is often (but not always) motivated from within, and no outside forces or coercions are needed. We also don't mind the possible difficulties in this learning. We often expect the challenges we encounter; we tend to see them as a natural part of the learning process, so we are far more open to taking risks. Some love to learn about cars, others love to learn about history, and some find great joy in learning how to dance. According to Mihaly Csikszentmihalyi (1990), such learning is an example of *flow*, which he defines as

> the state in which people are so involved in an activity that nothing else seems to matter; the experience itself is so enjoyable that people will do it at even great cost, for the sheer sake of doing it. (p. 4)

By helping students find the pleasure in learning, we can make that learning infinitely more successful.

If we want students to experience more flow in school—if we want them to see school and learning as joyful—we need to rethink how and what we teach. No longer can schooling be primarily about creating workers and test takers, but rather about nurturing human beings (Wolk, 2007). By helping students find the pleasure in learning, we can make that learning infinitely more successful.

JOY 2:
Give Students Choice

Outside of school, children are free to pursue their interests, and they do so with gusto. They learn how to play baseball or the drums; they learn how to ice skate or play video games; they read comic books, graphic novels, skateboard magazines, and Harry Potter.

But during a typical six-hour school day, how much ownership do students have of their learning? Practically none. It's not surprising that their interest in learning dissipates and that teachers complain of unmotivated students.

Joy in learning usually requires some ownership on the part of the learner. Students can own some of their school learning in several ways. They can choose the books they want to read through independent reading. In writing workshop, we can inspire them to be real writers and choose for themselves what genres to write in. During units in math, science, art, and social studies, they can choose specific subtopics to study; then, as "experts," they can share their learning with the class. Students can also choose which products they want to create to demonstrate their learning. What brings more joy—studying the civil rights movement in the United States through a textbook and lectures or creating comic books, writing and performing plays, interviewing people to create podcasts, and proposing your own ideas? Which would *you* rather do?

I advocate giving students one hour each day to study topics of their choice in what I call "Exploratory" (Wolk, 2001). In Exploratory, teachers collaborate with students to help shape student-initiated ideas into purposeful, inquiry-based investigations. During this time, students are scattered around the room, absorbed in an endless variety of topics that matter to them. While one student is studying the life of ants, a second is researching the workings of the FBI, and a third is exploring the life of Frida Kahlo. While two students work together to investigate the history of soccer, another is engrossed in surveying adults on their opinions of video games. Exploratory can teach students that school can be a place that nurtures curiosity, inspires them to ask questions, and helps them find the joy in learning.

JOY 3:
Let Students Create Things

People like to make stuff. Having control of our work and using our minds and hands to create something original give us a tremendous sense of agency. There is a special pride in bringing an original idea to fruition. It empowers us and encourages us; it helps us appreciate the demanding process of creating something from nothing.

The list of what students can create across the curriculum is virtually limitless: newspapers and magazines, brochures, stories, picture books, posters, murals, websites, podcasts, PowerPoint presentations, interviews, oral histories, models, diagrams, blueprints and floor plans, plays and role-plays, mock trials, photographs, paintings, songs, surveys, graphs, documentary videos—the list goes on and on. At its best, school should help and inspire students to bring their own ideas and creations to life.

JOY 4:
Show Off Student Work

Our schools and classrooms should be brimming with wonderful, original student work. School spaces that are devoid of student work perpetuate a sterile and joyless environment. I tell my teacher education students that the walls of their classrooms should speak to people; they should say exactly what goes on in that space throughout the school day. I can tell what teachers value by simply walking into their classrooms and looking at the walls.

The same is true for a school building. My son, Max, is in 4th grade, and his school, Augustus H. Burley School in Chicago, is a joyous place to visit. The hallways and classrooms are filled with remarkable student work, and there is rarely a worksheet in sight. The teachers also show off the students themselves. There are photographs of students next to their favorite books, above their posted work from writing workshop, and next to the doors of some classrooms.

JOY 5:
Take Time to Tinker

Gever Tulley has started a unique summer school in California called the Tinkering School. His blog describes it this way:

The Tinkering School offers an exploratory curriculum designed to help kids—ages 7 to 17—learn how to build things. By providing a collaborative environment in which to explore basic and advanced building techniques and principles, we strive to create a school where we all learn by fooling around. All activities are hands-on, supervised, and at least partly improvisational. Grand schemes, wild ideas, crazy notions, and intuitive leaps of imagination are, of course, encouraged and fertilized (Tulley, 2005).

At Tinkering School, students are allowed to dream. They come up with their own ideas for an object, and the faculty and staff help them sketch, design, and build it. When have you seen a public school that encouraged students to come up with "grand schemes, wild ideas, crazy notions, and intuitive leaps of imagination"? In fact, schools actually work to prevent this from happening.

Our school days are too planned, leaving no room for spontaneity and happenstance. Kindergarten is the last refuge in school for letting kids tinker. Once they enter 1st grade, students must banish the joy of "fooling around" with objects and ideas and, instead, sit at their desks most of the day listening to lectures, reading textbooks, and filling out worksheets.

Sometimes the best ideas come from tinkering—and teachers, not just students, should be doing more of it. We must push beyond the teacher-proof curriculum the textbook industry has created, which tries to plan every subject for every hour of the day. Far from being think tanks or workshops, our schools continue to be assembly lines. We need to free teachers to take risks, experiment, play with the art of pedagogy, and feel the joy that comes from tinkering with their teaching.

JOY 6:
Make School Spaces Inviting

Why do classrooms need to look so much like, well, *classrooms,* with desks in rows or arranged in groups, with a chalkboard or whiteboard at the front? When I walk into a classroom in my son's school, I usually see a space that looks a lot like a family room. There's a large rug, a class library with the best in children's and young adult literature, bean bags, couches, comfortable chairs, pillows, colorful curtains, fabric hung over the ceiling lights, and lamps scattered about the classroom. In fact, sometimes the ceiling lights are off, and the lamps warmly light the room.

And what about the public spaces inside and outside the school—the hallways, foyers, meeting areas, and school grounds? Anyone who has spent time at a university knows how integral these spaces are to the learning and social dynamics of the campus. The same can be true for a school. Why not transform these often unused and sterile spots into places for small groups of students to work or cozy nooks for kids to read or write? How about filling a foyer with plants and flowers? Why not give a large wall to the students to create and paint a mural? One colorful mural can transform a barren hallway or entrance into a vibrant and joyful sight. And schools can turn outdoor spaces into gardens, sculpture parks, walking paths, and quiet reading areas.

JOY 7:
Get Outside

I am bewildered by how much time students spend inside schools. I don't mean that the school day should be shorter; I mean that more of the school day should be outside. We adults know all too well how much we like to get outside for a respite during the workday, and the same applies to students and teachers in school. They need a break from being confined inside a classroom all day. Fresh air, trees, and a sunny day can do miracles for the human spirit.

Interacting with nature brings a unique joy. Gavin Pretor-Pinney (2006) writes, "I have always loved looking at clouds. Nothing in nature rivals their variety and drama; nothing matches their sublime, ephemeral beauty" (p. 9). Naturalist and artist David Carroll (2004) describes his childhood enthrallment of seeking out turtles as he walked the ponds and marshes:

> The sheer joy of being there, of simply bearing witness, continued to be paramount. I went out neither to heal my heartbreaks nor to celebrate my happiness, but to be in nature and outside myself. Turtles, spotted turtles most significantly, were a living text moving upon an endless turning of the pages of the natural world. (p. 27)

The easiest way to get students outside is simply to have recess. There is a special joy in standing amidst the students as they burst from the school and spread out like a swarm of hungry ants. Kids say that recess is their favorite time in school. Recess was also one of my favorite times of the day as a teacher because I was outside and surrounded by children having fun. Tragically, recess has become a rare sight, which may say more about our schools today than anything else. Why do so many schools find it so difficult to allow children 20 minutes each day to play?

As a teacher, I would often take my students outside to read, write, or have a class meeting. It is delightful for a student to sit under a tree and read or for a class to sit in a circle on the grass and talk. Much of our science curriculums could directly include the outdoors. A school does not have to be near a forest or the ocean for students and teachers to explore nature. Ecosystems are all around us. Have students dig a hole in a patch of dirt, and they will witness the flourishing life in the soil beneath their feet. Don't underestimate the power of sheer joy that children—and adults—can experience from tipping over a large rock and seeing the ground teeming with life.

JOY 8:
Read Good Books

Everyone loves a good story. We all know that if you have a 5-year-old sitting on your lap and a good book in your hands, you will soon experience the magic of stories. And what amazing stories there are! We are living in an astonishing time of children's and young adult literature. Immerse students in a culture of good books, and you surround them with joy.

For the past few years, I've been working on a grant with a Chicago public school, in part to help teachers make literature an important feature of their classrooms. I have brought loads of good books into the school. As I did book talks in 4th and 8th grade classrooms about dozens of new titles we ordered, the room was abuzz with students who could not wait to get their hands on the books. When I walk into a classroom now, I am met with the excited voices of the students telling me what books they're reading.

Of course, if we want joy in schools, then sometimes students should read books that aren't so "serious." I believe that books with important themes can make a better world, but we must also sometimes allow—even encourage—students to experience books for sheer pleasure. Have 3rd graders read Dav Pilkey's *Captain Underpants and the Perilous Plot of Professor Poopypants* (Scholastic, 2000). Have 5th graders read Jeff Kinney's *Diary of a Wimpy Kid* (Amulet, 2007). Have young adults read Sherman Alexie's very funny (and serious) *The Absolutely True Diary of a Part-Time Indian* (Little Brown, 2007). Encourage students to read thrillers; romance novels; action-adventure books; stories about sports, animals, and pop culture; graphic novels and manga; and nonfiction on topics they love. You will see plenty of joy.

JOY 9:
Offer More Gym and Arts Classes

In recent years, with our zeal for increasing test scores, "specials" in school have become nearly as rare as recess. It is not uncommon, especially in more impoverished schools, for students to have no art, music, and drama at all, and gym only once or twice a week. In my son's previous school in Chicago, he did not have gym until January.

With his work on multiple intelligences, Howard Gardner has helped us better appreciate the uniqueness of children and has spoken to the need to give students opportunities to use their varied strengths and interests in school. For the legions of children who have a special affinity for the visual arts, theater, music, or sports, classes in these subjects are golden times for them to experience joy in school. But how much joy can they experience when it's limited to 45 minutes each week?

JOY 10:
Transform Assessment

When I was a kid, I dreaded report card time. When I was a teacher, many of my students were anxious about their grades. For far too many students, assessment in its dominant forms—tests, quizzes, letter grades, number grades, and standardized tests—is a dark cloud that never seems to leave. Must it be this way?

The idea of assessment in school is not inherently bad; children assess themselves all the time. When they're busy doing something they love outside school, such as tae kwon do, baking, or playing the saxophone—when they're experiencing *flow*—they don't mind assessment at all. In fact, they see it as an important part of the process. But for most students, assessment in school is the enemy.

We can, however, make it a more positive experience. We need to help students understand the value of assessment. We also need to rethink "failure." Our schools see failure as a bad thing. But adults know that failure is a vital part of learning. Portraying failure as a bad thing teaches a child to avoid risk taking and bold ideas. Imagine if we graded toddlers on their walking skills. We would be living in a nation of crawlers.

We should limit how we use quantitative assessments and make more use of narrative assessments and report cards, portfolios of authentic work, and student presentations and performances. In addition, parent conferences should not only include students, but also encourage the students to do much of the talking, using the conference as an opportunity to present their work and discuss their strengths and areas to focus on for growth.

As a teacher, I had my students regularly do self-assessments. This gave them some real power over the process. They assessed most of their schoolwork before I did my own assessment. And during report card time, I passed out photocopies of a blank report card and had my students complete it, for both grades and behavior, before I filled it out. I don't recall a student ever abusing this opportunity. At another school in which I taught, I redesigned our report card to include space for a photograph of the student inside; the cover was left blank so students could either draw a picture or write something meaningful there.

JOY 11:
Have Some Fun Together

Recently, when I was visiting a school, I was standing in the hallway talking to a teacher when a tall 8th grade boy from another classroom exuberantly walked up to that teacher. They began some good-natured ribbing. Back and forth it went for a few minutes with smiles and laughter. What was this about? The teacher-student basketball game held earlier that week. Here were two people—an 8th grader and his teacher—having a joyous good time.

Schools need to find ways for students, teachers, and administrators to take a break from the sometimes emotional, tense, and serious school day and have some fun together. Sporting events, outdoor field days, movie nights, school sleep-ins, potluck meals, visits to restaurants, schoolwide T-shirt days, and talent shows can help everyone get to know one another better, tear down the personal walls that often get built inside schools, form more caring relationships, and simply have a wonderful time together.

Teaching as a Joyful Experience

Recently, I visited a former graduate student in her classroom. It is her third year as a teacher, and I was excited to see her creative and thoughtful teaching. But she said to me, "I never imagined this job would be so hard. I'm tired all the time."

Yes, teaching is hard. John Dewey's quote—about school sapping our souls—can be as true for teachers as it is for students. Considering the staggering turnover of new teachers in urban schools, it is in everyone's interest to help teachers find joy in their work. So teachers must strive in whatever ways they can to *own their teaching* so that each morning they can enter their classrooms knowing there will be golden opportunities for them—as well as for their students—to experience the joy in school.

References

Carroll, D. (2004). *Self-portrait with turtles.* Boston: Houghton Mifflin.

Csikszentmihalyi, M. (1990). *Flow.* New York: Harper Perennial.

Dewey, J. (1938). *Experience and education.* New York: Collier.

Goodlad, J. (1984). *A place called school.* New York: McGraw-Hill.

Pretor-Pinney, G. (2006). *The cloudspotter's guide.* New York: Perigee.

Tulley, G. (2005, May 4). About. *Tinkering School.* Available: www.tinkeringschool.com/blog/?p=11

Wolk, S. (2001). The benefits of exploratory time. *Educational Leadership,* 59(2), 56–59.

Wolk, S. (2007). Why go to school? *Phi Delta Kappan,* 88(9), 648–658.

Critical Thinking

1. Reflect on a recent learning experience you had and describe it as a joyful or joyless experience. Why do you think you rated it as such?

2. Choose three of the joys Steven Wolk describes in his article and indicate why they are most important to you in your education.

STEVEN WOLK is Assistant Professor of Teacher Education at Northeastern Illinois University, 5500 N. St. Louis Ave., Chicago, IL 60625; s-wolk@neiu.edu.

Early Education, Later Success

How do you sustain the momentum generated by your prekindergarten and full-day kindergarten programs? Start by considering an aligned and unified PK-3 unit.

SUSAN BLACK

D oes your district offer high-quality prekindergarten and full-day kindergarten programs? If so, your youngest students are off to a good start.

Research confirms that children in good prekindergartens are eager and successful learners in kindergarten. And children who attend good full-day kindergartens stand a better chance of succeeding in first grade. That's the encouraging news.

But there's a worrisome downside. Prekindergarten children's gains in language, literacy, and math often fade out by the end of first grade. The gains children make in kindergarten, whether they attend half-day or full-day, often fade out by third grade.

Don't give up hope. There are steps you can take to ensure that prekindergarten and kindergarten pay off in the long run.

What's Needed?

PK-3 units are a "promising solution" to the fade-out problem, says Kristie Kaurez, director of early learning at the Education Commission of the States.

In an issue brief for the New America Foundation, a nonprofit public policy institute, Kaurez says success requires more than high-quality programs at each grade. The first five grades, she says, must provide similar instruction, curriculum alignment, well-managed transitions between grades, smaller class sizes, parent involvement, and top-quality teaching.

Kaurez envisions a five-step ladder—a "succession of sturdy rungs"—that children climb with confidence during their first five years of schooling. At each rung, children gain and maintain a "strong foothold" in language, literacy, and math.

Studies show it can be done, and children can profit immeasurably.

An evaluation of New Jersey's Union City School District's PK-3 "base camp," a program which links standards, curriculum, and assessments, showed significant gains: When the youngsters reached fourth grade, they nearly doubled their proficiency on state tests in language arts and math.

Multi-year studies of the Chicago Child-Parent Centers, a PK-3 program established by the Chicago Board of Education, show long-lasting effects. Students had higher achievement and, in later years, were less involved in juvenile crime.

Arthur Reynolds, with the University of Minnesota's Institute for Child Development, reports two "striking effects" for children

in high-quality PK-3 units: By third grade, they're far less likely to be retained or to be placed in special education. While it's unproven that PK-3 units alone cause higher achievement, Reynolds stands by the "wisdom of high quality PK-3 programs."

Taking a Long View

Well-planned PK-3 programs help children master reading and math, according to researchers with the University of Michigan's Inter-University Consortium for Political and Social Research (ICPSR). Equally important, five-grade units help children develop "social, self-regulating, and motivating traits," attributes considered essential to learning.

PK-3 programs take a long view of children's learning and development, and they give children more time to succeed, ICPSR points out. Compared to school readiness programs, PK-3 programs provide a "richer, more detailed understanding and a better prediction of children's development outcomes," ICPSR says.

Success depends on getting PK-3 units right, and that can take time and effort.

Success depends on getting PK-3 units right, and that can take time and effort. ICPSR says these components are essential:

- School organization that supports PK-3 units
- Strong principal leadership
- Qualified teacher
- Classrooms designed as learning centers
- Curriculum and instruction that is aligned and coordinated across five grades
- Assessment and accountability systems for teachers and administrators
- Family and community engagement and support

An even longer view, beginning with infants and toddlers, adds to the benefits of PK-3.

A 2006 study in *Pediatrics* describes a 36-month health and educational program of home visits and parent support groups provided to families with low birth weight and premature infants. A follow-up study shows that, as teens, the children had higher achievement in math and reading; less tobacco, marijuana, and alcohol use; and less antisocial behavior and suicidal tendencies or attempts.

Citing such effects, some states have expanded early childhood education to include the years preceeding prekindergarten.

New York State's Board of Regents' early childhood education policy covers birth through fourth grade. It begins with prenatal care and extends to health services and educational programs for infants and toddlers. School districts are expected to "ensure that families have access to needed services," particularly families at or below the poverty level and those with children who speak limited English and whose children have disabilities.

Georgia's Department of Early Care and Learning oversees a statewide system that coordinates services for children from birth through age 4. Washington State's Department of Early Learning coordinates Head Start, child care, early reading programs, and prekindergarten.

All in the Family

How important are families? Linda Espinosa, with the University of Missouri-Columbia, says social-emotional development during an infant's first year contributes to learning language. By age 5, a child should have a large vocabulary, narrative skills, and the ability to verbalize thoughts, ideas, emotions, and observations.

Espinosa says children are more likely to succeed in school if they have these experiences during their first five years:

- Close, supportive relationships at home, in day care, and in nursery school
- Opportunities to describe and express feelings
- Opportunities to make choices and to develop self-control and self-regulated learning
- Enrichment, such as field trips to zoos, parks, and museums
- Playtime that includes role play and opportunities to be expressive and imaginative

A child's first relationships are the "prism through which they learn about the world," says Ross Thompson with the University of Nebraska. Social interactions during a child's early years have a greater effect on learning than educational toys, brain-stimulating activities, and nursery school lessons, he claims.

Thompson says infants and toddlers are more likely to succeed if they develop three types of skills: intellectual, including using simple numbers and clearly expressing ideas; motivational, including curiosity and confidence in learning; and social-emotional, including participating in groups, cooperating with others, and exerting self-discipline.

Family engagement is essential to "develop and sustain effective PK-3 programs," says Richard Weissbourd, co-chair of Pre-K to 3 Education: Promoting Early Success, Harvard University's new institute for school leaders. Superintendents, principals, and teachers enrolled in the institute study early childhood literacy, and they learn the importance of helping parents provide reading, math, and rich conversations during daily home activities; involving parents in literacy activities at school; and strengthening teacher-parent partnerships through home visits.

Creating a Good Program

A suburban school district administrator told me it takes "perseverance and pushiness" to create a high-quality PK-3 unit. She's been at it for three years, but progress is slow-going.

So far she's secured board approval for PK-3, found space for new prekindergarten classrooms, and provided teachers with training and supplies. But problems persist. An elementary principal is halfhearted about the PK-3 concept, and some teachers refuse to try new strategies, plan as a team, or conduct home visits.

Still, I'm pinning my hopes on this dedicated administrator and the teachers who have stepped forward and are willing to do all they can to help their youngest students.

Here's why.

A *Washington Post* story describes Johnny, a 5-year-old child of immigrants who entered kindergarten in Maryland's Montgomery County Public Schools. Education writer Jay Mathews says Johnny is part of an "unnerving language gap" that contributes to a wide achievement gap. (Most children from affluent families enter school knowing 13,000 English words, a sharp contrast to many children from poor and immigrant families who know a meager 500 English words.)

Operation Johnny began soon after the school year started. Working as a team, the little boy's kindergarten teacher, his parents, an interpreter, a speech pathologist, a special education consultant, and a social worker designed a year-long plan to help Johnny learn. The teacher was pivotal to the plan, agreeing to sit close to the boy, teach him new vocabulary through games and activities, and videotape classroom lessons for Johnny's parents to reinforce at home.

The district is determined to rescue Johnny and others like him. MCPS's board of education authorized Superintendent Jerry Weast to spend more than $21 million for an Early Success Performance Plan that's reduced class sizes and created full-day kindergartens in all 123 primary schools. The plan is paying off: In three years, the percentage of low-income 5-year-olds attaining grade-level goals has risen from 44 percent to 70 percent. Their fourth-grade passing rate on state tests is 86 percent.

Johnny is off to a good start. He's eager to learn, due in part to the district's plan and in part to his kindergarten teacher's determination and extra effort. Operation Johnny illustrates what all school leaders and teachers can and should do to help struggling students succeed at every step on the five-step ladder.

Critical Thinking

1. In the article, Linda Espinosa says children need one of the five listed experiences during their first five years of life. Share these five with a parent of a preschool child and ask them to describe how they provide one of these for their children.

2. Write a letter to the editor of your local paper in support of a PK-3 unit being developed for your local school district.

SUSAN BLACK, an *ASBJ* contributing editor, is an education researcher and writer in Hammondsport, N.Y.

Don't Dismiss Early Education as Just Cute; It's Critical

Lisa Guernsey

Picture an arborist puzzled by an ailing tree. He has tried giving it more water. He has protected it from blight. Why won't it grow?

If the tree stands for public education, the arborist is today's education reformer. Ideas continue to pour forth on how to help students, fix schools and revamp No Child Left Behind. But none tackles the environments the tree experienced as a sapling, when its roots never got the chance to stretch out and dig in.

Few would dispute that public education is in trouble. Last month's reading scores from the National Assessment of Educational Progress showed that two-thirds of U.S. fourth-graders cannot read well enough to do grade-level work. Many schools are not measuring up to federal standards.

Now consider what dominates the debate on how to make amends: charter schools, public school choice, dropout prevention programs, linking teacher pay to student performance. President Obama has embraced many of these ideas, which might help some children in some districts.

Misplaced Focus

But have we forgotten to look underfoot? Experts talk too often about poorly performing middle or high schools and dismiss elementary and preschool time as the "cute" years. But these are the years we should focus on.

Science continues to provide insights—and warnings—about how much of a person's capacity for learning is shaped from birth to age 8. Young children need to experience rich interactions with teachers, parents and other adults who read to them, ask questions of them, and encourage their exploration of a myriad of subjects.

Unfortunately, the state of early education is not good. In a 2007 national study in *Science,* researchers found that only 7% of children in the elementary grades were getting consistently high-quality instruction and attention to their emotional needs.

Kindergarten, which faces unstable funding, is troubled, too. School teachers get little training on the best methods for reaching 5-year-olds.

Lag in Preschool

And many children are still not getting the benefit of preschool. While a few states, such as Georgia and Oklahoma, offer universal prekindergarten, in others only 10% of children are enrolled in a public preschool program, according to the National Institute for Early Education Research. Expensive private programs are not an option for many working families.

To earn the label of true education reform, the reauthorization of No Child Left Behind must recognize these earliest years. The law should include a fund that extends to third grade. It should encourage districts to use their Title I dollars (which go to districts with economically disadvantaged families) to build better programs and partner with existing preschools. It should require districts to integrate data from children's earliest years with K–12 data so that parents, schools and communities can track how their children are progressing relative to the kinds of programs they experienced before and during elementary school. It should ensure that funding for professional development extends to preschool teachers and principals.

Above all, the law should reward states, districts and schools that create high-quality programs and have the data to show that they work.

If No Child Left Behind cannot help foster better learning environments from the beginning, we will forever be that arborist, scratching his head at why, despite so many fixes, our students still aren't reaching for the sky.

Critical Thinking

1. You are visiting a school and meet some upper elementary teachers. When they find out you are interested in early childhood education they mock work with young children as just babysitting and not important. How are you going to respond to these claims?

2. Explore the websites of three local programs serving preschool age children. What is the take away message parents would get from exploring these three sites while looking for a program for their preschool child?

LISA GUERNSEY is the director of the Early Education Initiative at the New America Foundation. She is the co-author of a new report, "A Next Social Contract for the Primary Years of Education."

Are We Paving Paradise?

In our rush to promote achievement, we've forgotten how 5-year-olds really learn.

ELIZABETH GRAUE

Kindergarten teacher Celia Carlson passionately describes kindergarten in terms of transitions—it's the *only* first time that children will begin school, and it should be a place where both children and families adjust to a new, challenging context. She worries, though, that we've let go of what makes kindergarten a safe place for children to start. In our push to do more, sooner, faster, we fragment children into little pieces of assessment information and let go of the activities that enabled us to get to know them in more personal and integrated ways.

We've let go of the developmental piece that makes kindergarten a safe place for children to start school.

Across town, teacher Wendy Anderson feels like a rebel. Working in a high-poverty school, she struggles to maintain a semblance of a child-centered program. When she found a sensory table stacked with extra materials in another classroom, she asked whether she could have it. The kids flock to it, in need of kinesthetic experience and the joy of pouring, measuring, and comparing. "Where did you *get* that?" a colleague whispered, as though Wendy had brought in a unicorn or something illegal. Hers is also the only classroom that goes out for recess in the morning. Again, her colleagues ask, "How do you find the time?" Although she doesn't know why no one else goes out for recess, she wonders whether other classes lose precious time because of behavior issues associated with children who have not had a chance to play.

Teacher Pamela Gordon thinks that many people see her as old and eccentric. While everyone else uses worksheets, she continues to do projects with her students. They research together; and as they go, they integrate content required in the kindergarten curriculum. Currently, they're studying the lives of American Indians, figuring out how they obtained food and water and how the environment shaped their lives.

One reason so many of Pamela's colleagues favor worksheets is that they provide evidence for parents of what their children are doing. Instead of sending home worksheets, Pamela carefully writes a weekly letter to parents detailing activities and related learning, a great complement to children who answer the question, "What did you do at school today?" with a generic "We played."

These three teachers work hard to cultivate a children's garden within their classrooms. But just like in Joni Mitchell's well-known song, kindergarten seems threatened by developers who want to pave paradise and put up a parking lot. These teachers aren't mindlessly resisting new methods in favor of an outdated tradition; rather, they're fighting to keep children at the center of kindergarten.

The Evolution of Kindergarten
From a Focus on Children . . .
Kindergarten has always been a bit of an odd duck. It was a latecomer to the elementary school. Its teachers were educated in different programs, and its classrooms often looked like home, with gingham curtains and play kitchens. Teachers were left to craft a program that focused on the social and physical as well as on the academic. Guided by knowledge of human development, kindergarten teachers were interested in *children* rather than *curriculum content*.

To a Focus on Outcomes . . .
As kindergarten was incorporated into elementary school, programming slowly moved from half to full day in many areas and became governed by a desire for more academic content. Two movements prompted these shifts. First, as the number of women in the workforce increased, so did the number of children in child care. Kindergarten's traditional role of socializing children into group experiences seemed less relevant. Second, the notion of early intervention captured the interest of policymakers and the public. When Hart and Risley (1985) noted that middle-class children typically heard 8 million more words in a year than children living in poverty did, investing in preschool programs seemed just the right solution. Justified as a way to close the achievement gap; reduce special education referrals, teen pregnancy, and incarceration rates; and enhance earning

power in adulthood, these early intervention programs evolved over time to be more literacy and mathematics focused. Child outcomes, rather than children's experiences, became the major element of program evaluation.

To a Focus on Literacy and Math

At the same time that preschool was changing, the elementary school was changing, too. States and districts developed grade-level standards, measurable and organized by content area. A key element in this process was research that stated that if students did not read at grade level by grade 3, they would never catch up (Stanovich, 1986). Districts mapped trajectories for students to hit the 3rd grade mark as well as interventions to nudge along the stragglers. Expectations were made explicit at each grade level, with a greater focus on literacy and mathematics.

For the first time, kindergarten was included in this map, with curriculum often designed by content-area specialists with limited experiences with 4-, 5-, and 6-year-olds. Although early learning standards covered kindergarten programs, the standards that counted—the content standards—were used to define a new kindergarten program. With the advent of pacing guides and high-pressure progress monitoring in literacy and math, attention to other elements of the kindergarten curriculum underwent a dramatic shift.

The Report Card: Then and Now

An easy way to see this shift is in the kindergarten report card. The report card I received as a kindergartner in 1960 was one page long; it focused on my ability to listen and play with others. In 1998—the year my oldest son started kindergarten—the progress report had sections on reading, speaking and listening, writing, science, social studies, social skills and work habits, and math, plus a large section for teacher comments. Each area included affective and behavioral information as well as skills. The social skills section was particularly informative, addressing issues of independence, flexibility, work habits, and peer interaction.

In contrast, the 2009 report card from that same school—note the name change from *progress report* to *report card*—reports on performance relative to expectations in language arts, mathematics, science, and social studies. It includes a lean section called the Child as Learner and Community Member. There's a single line for comments for each content area.

Unseen by families are thick grading guides that direct teacher ratings for each content area, requiring days of pains-taking assessment—not to inform instructional practice but to make sure that students are meeting learning targets. For many kindergarten teachers, the report card obscures their ability to know students because as one teacher told me, "I don't have time to listen to children anymore." The report is more about tracking progress for administrative purposes than informing families about how their children are doing.

The Kindergarten Chimera

Thus, kindergarten has become a sort of *chimera,* a mash-up that has the genetic makeup of more than one species.

Kindergarten has the genetic code of early childhood, with its attention to multiple dimensions of development and its focus on nurturing social relationships, along with the DNA of the content-focused elementary school. The current political, educational, and social context supports the elementary school elements of kindergarten's existence. However, the early childhood parts are losing ground; they should be on the endangered species list.

As someone who taught kindergarten for many years, I agree with standards-based teaching and the need to align expectations and practices across the education system. However, I worry that in the rush to promote content achievement we've forgotten that children are multidimensional beings who learn in complicated ways. Because the curriculum increasingly reflects the expertise of content specialists in the district office, the parts of kindergarten not explicitly listed on the report card are withering away or, at least, are not cultivated in a way that supports a balanced program and a balanced child. We do not attend, for example, to the future architect who builds with blocks, designing structures, managing materials, and testing the laws of physics. We also ignore the aesthetic child who paints, draws, sings, and dances.

This lack of focus on the early childhood part of kindergarten is especially important in the context of transition. A child who moves from a developmentally appropriate preschool program to a content-focused kindergarten experiences a kind of whiplash. We need a more ecological approach to kindergarten (see "Elements of a Hybrid Kindergarten," p. 16).

Making the Case
For Play

The growing allocation of kindergarten time to academic content has firmly pushed play to the edges. What counts as play in many classrooms are highly controlled centers that focus on particular content labeled as "choice" but that are really directed at capturing a specific content-based learning experience, such as number bingo or retelling a story exactly as the teacher told it on a flannel board. It's like calling the choices of doing the laundry, grocery shopping, or cleaning out your closet "playful." It also means that in-depth project work that involves research into child-initiated questions just takes too much time. If students become fascinated with the birds at the feeder outside the classroom window, for example, this cannot become a focus of learning because it's not listed in the standards.

What's lost with this shift? Attention to anything but clearly defined cognitive aspects of development. Although vitally important, learning content is inherently intertwined with other elements like motor skills, aesthetic experiences, and social-emotional development. In an increasingly sedentary, structured context, students have few opportunities for rich experiences of moving, creating, or interacting.

The early childhood community, which has traditionally valued play as a learning tool, has not been very articulate about play's importance in our evidence-based school economy. It's no longer enough to argue that play is the work of children;

we're now required to prove what children *get* from play. What they get must translate to increased achievement or reduced risk. So let's nail the evidence base.

Wendy Anderson takes her kindergartners out for recess and schedules free play because she recognizes that play is a complex activity that has many benefits beyond the pure joy it gives children. Learning to negotiate, share, and empathize are all key to playing; we deny children the opportunity to learn these skills in a kindergarten without play. Yes, Robert Fulghum (2004) was right: Everything you need to know, you learn in kindergarten. But the kindergarten he's talking about is one that values the social, the emotional, and the aesthetic; it's one that teaches through modeling, practice, and nurturing.

Rich play environments enable children to develop what psychologists call *executive function*. When children play, they learn to shift attention, remember, and inhibit impulses; as a result, they are able to plan, solve problems, and work toward a goal. These skills relate to later achievement in social areas and in academic content, such as mathematics and literacy (Bodrova & Leong, 2007; Diamond, Barnett, Thomas, & Munro, 2007). Doing away with play does away with opportunities to develop these skills.

In recent years, some have called for a kindergarten curriculum that once again includes attention to social and emotional competence (Raver, 2002), an important reminder that for children to succeed in school, a complex set of capacities must be carefully balanced.

For Relationships and Trust

Celia Carlson describes how students can no longer take the scenic route in kindergarten—her students are fast-tracked so they can get to the reading level mandated by the district by the end of the year. Although important, such reading supports often involve pulling students out of the classroom. Celia worries that she's not getting a chance to build the foundation that students need to be resilient learners who can handle frustration, work through problems, and focus on the essentials.

Relationships and trust take time—and time is in short supply in today's kindergarten. Celia sees students crumble when they hit any tiny bump—in the classroom, in the cafeteria, and on the playground. Her students dissolve into tears or pick fights in situations that challenge them. In the past, she would have better known their triggers and could have built opportunities for them to be resilient. The students have no reserves to draw from because teachers simply haven't had enough time to do this important work.

Relationships and trust take time—and time is in short supply in today's kindergarten.

The Cutoff Conundrum

Policymakers have addressed perennial concerns about readiness by requiring children to be older before they can enter school. The kindergarten entrance date has slowly but surely moved back from January so that most states now require children to be 5 in September. Some states have moved it even earlier, to a summer cutoff.

Elements of a Hybrid Kindergarten

- It addresses all areas of child development: social-emotional, physical, aesthetic, cognitive, linguistic.
- It's balanced, with time for whole-group, small-group, and independent activities. It provides opportunities for teacher-directed lessons and student choice. Some activities require physical activity; others focus on the mind.
- It's intellectually engaging, addressing issues of interest to 5-year-olds, respecting their curiosity and encouraging them to develop inquiry and problem-solving skills. It provides support for skills related to literacy and mathematics.
- It devotes *real* time to play, both indoors and out, and provides extended periods for children to choose activities.
- Its physical environment includes a dramatic play area, art supplies, unit blocks, equipment for sensory experiences, musical instruments, books, manipulatives, soft and hard surfaces, and a place to cuddle. Yes, cuddling is a requirement even in this touch-phobic society.
- It recognizes that kindergartners are eager learners who do not march lockstep through the curriculum. It toes a fine line between supporting students' current developmental levels and stretching them to attain standards.
- Its teacher has a background in early childhood education and knows the value of both guided reading and project inquiry, of both solving mathematics problems and exploring social issues. He or she advocates a balanced program and has support from colleagues, the principal, and the community.

I lived through such a move when I taught kindergarten in Missouri in the mid-1980s. As the cutoff date moved from October 1 to July 1, my students got bigger and bigger—and the baseline for "typical" followed suit.

I have to wonder if this solution is, in fact, contributing to the problem it's meant to solve. With slightly older students, the expectations become a little more intense, which makes people worry about the kids who can't cope with the demands—which makes us once again try new strategies to ensure readiness. Is kindergarten caught in a recursive cycle where every fix induces more problems?

Kindergarten: A Hybrid Version

I recognize that today's children are different from those of even a decade ago and that kindergarten must evolve in the same way a garden does. But that evolution must support the very children that kindergarten should nurture. We need to step back and consider whether all the innovations and interventions, all the programs and progress monitoring, are actually getting us what we want. In our work to develop assessment-driven instruction, have we driven off without the child?

The assessment that kindergarten children deserve is broad-based, contextual, and inclusive of *all* dimensions of development—not just those few that feed the accountability machine. We need to reassess both the means and ends of kindergarten, remembering that under all the data we generate are real live children. Those children need us to create education experiences that are responsive, challenging, and nurturing of all the complexity that is a 5-year-old.

References

Bodrova, E., & Leong, D. J. (2007). *Tools of the mind: The Vygotskian approach to early childhood education.* Upper Saddle River, NJ: Prentice Hall.

Diamond, A., Barnett, W. S., Thomas, J., & Munro, S. (2007). Preschool program improves cognitive control. *Science, 318*(5855), 1387–1388.

Fulghum, R. (2004). *All I really need to know I learned in kindergarten.* New York: Ballantine Books.

Hart, B., & Risley, T. (1985). *Meaningful difference*s. Baltimore: Brookes Publishing.

Raver, C. (2002). Emotions matter: Making the case for the role of young children's emotional development for early school readiness. *Social Policy Report, 16*(3), 3–18.

Stanovich, K. E. (1986). Matthew effects in reading: Some consequences of individual differences in the acquisition of literacy. *Reading Research Quarterly, 21*(4), 360–407.

Critical Thinking

1. Describe some of the characteristics of a hybrid kindergarten.
2. Why is play, both inside and outside, so important for kindergarten children?

ELIZABETH GRAUE is a professor of early childhood education in the Department of Curriculum and Instruction at the University of Wisconsin, Madison. She is also associate director of Faculty, Staff, and Graduate Development at the Wisconsin Center for Education Research; graue@education.wisc.edu.

Author's note— All teacher names are pseudonyms.

UNIT 2

Young Children, Their Families and Communities

Unit Selections

Learning Outcomes

After reading this Unit, you will be able to:

- Provide teachers and parents with a list of some general characteristics most often found in children of a particular birth order.

- Develop strategies for making connections with all the families with whom you come in contact.

- List steps to helping children develop positive eating behaviors.

- Describe some of the factors affecting school achievement over which the educational setting has no control.

- Plan ways to collaborate with families for the success of their children.

- Identify ways school personnel can assist homeless children and families.

- Incorporate communication strategies for staying in touch with parents not living in the local community.

- Describe ways to connect with babies and assist them as they navigate their time in your care.

- Provide guidelines for families and teachers on appropriate use of technology for young children.

- Develop strategies for helping parents deal with the influence of media and commercialism.

Student Website

www.mhhe.com/cls

Internet References

Administration for Children and Families
www.dhhs.gov

The AARP Grandparent Information Center
www.aarp.org/relationships/grandparenting

All About Asthma
www.pbskids.org/arthur/parentsteachers/lesson/health/#asthma

Allergy Kids
http://allergykids.com

Changing the Scene–Improving the School Nutrition Environment
www.fns.usda.gov/tn/Resources/changing.html

Children, Youth and Families Education and Research Network
www.cyfernet.org

National Network for Child Care
www.nncc.org

National Safe Kids Campaign
www.babycenter.com

Zero to Three
www.zerotothree.org

Many different issues are addressed in this unit titled "Young Children, Their Families and Communities," and I invite you to reflect on your family, the types of experiences children today have as opposed to you, and the ways educators can help families as they navigate the ever-changing, fast-paced world while raising children.

One's position within a family setting, and the number of siblings, if any, has been a great area of research interest for years. This unit on young children and their families begin with an examination of the most fascinating topic of birth order in Linda DiProperzio's "The Power of Birth Order." Every reader can relate to the information in the article as they reflect on their own birth order and how parents or siblings may have treated you differently based on your birth order.

When examining the partnership between educational settings, young children, their families, and the communities in which they live, one word keeps coming up again and again: *relationships*. The importance of developing healthy relationships between the adults in the early childhood setting and the young children and their families is critical. You will see the word relationships in many of the articles in this unit, including "Teachers Connecting with Families—In the Best Interest of Children" by Katharine C. Kersey and Marie L. Masterson. They provide excellent specific suggestions for educators to not only initiate relationships but to also foster them throughout the year. The chance to interact with families diminishes as the learner gets older until it is almost nonexistent at the secondary level. Early childhood educators who recognize and fully embrace the rich contributions families can make as partners in the education process will benefit and so will the children. Sharing between the parents and teachers about the strengths and needs of the child become the path to student success.

Many of the articles read for possible inclusion in this edition focused on the effects of poverty on young children. There is increased attention on narrowing the achievement gap among minorities and children living in poverty. Some say the best way for children to achieve higher test scores is for teachers to teach better. Others say higher achievement among minorities and children living in poverty cannot be possible without attention to the living conditions and the support families receive. Jayne Boyd-Zaharias and Helen Pate-Bain discuss this most important issue in "Class Matters—In and Out of School." They focus on the needs of affordable housing, access to health care, and early childhood education, along with improved instruction from teachers in class sizes that have proved to support education, especially for children in poverty. There is substantial research indicating that high-quality prekindergarten programs can help narrow the achievement gap. The research is so solid that 39 states now provide publicly funded preschool education of some form that serve more than one million preschoolers. This unit also includes the article, "Creating a Welcoming Classroom for Homeless Students." With a 50 percent increase in the homeless population since 2008, school personnel must do all they can to meet the needs of homeless children and families.

As the United States continues to send soldiers on long deployments overseas, some for multiple tours of duty, there

© JGI/Jamie Grill/Getty Images

are ramifications for the over 700,000 children with a parent serving in the U.S. military. Educators are also finding that the challenging economic times means families are separated for long periods of time while one parent works in a distant city just to have a secure job. Recognizing the child may go through various stages of separation is important for teachers to understand. Suggestions for teachers working with children living in a stressful family situation are included. Support from the teacher and consistent communication with family members can help to ease the separation anxiety that children face. Educators living in areas with a high number of military families will especially benefit from reading "Making Long-Term Separations Easier for Children and Families" by Amy M. Kim and Julia Yeary.

Dr. Alice Honig shares her wisdom on making vital connections with infants in "Keys to Quality Infant Care: Nurturing Every Baby's Life Journey." She provides 11 strategies teachers and caregivers can incorporate into their repertoire of skills when interacting with babies. After reading Honig's article you will want to go out and spend some time getting to know an infant.

With technology being so readily accessible these days, 75 percent of mothers in a study at babycenter.com reported they have given their young children a phone to play with. It is time we examined any policies related to the use of technology by young children. In "Gaga for Gadgets," Margery D. Rosen shares strategies for families. The American Academy of Pediatrics recommends no screen time for children under the age of two; however, many parents will report that recommendation is most often not followed in their home. There are many strategies for introducing young children to technology in an age appropriate way since it will play a significant role in their lives. Already there are over 1,000 phone and computer applications for children three and under. An adult needs to supervise any use of technology by children so they don't become frustrated or worse, get connected to an inappropriate site. There is a balance to using technology with young children, and many experts recommend that when children can easily have access to the actual materials such as playing with blocks at home, that should be the preferred method in learning but when it is not convenient, for instance when riding in a car, a computer app may fill in nicely.

Families can provide a wealth of information about their child, and teachers who develop strong relationships with families are beneficiaries of this knowledge. Upon doing a check of websites at a local school district, I came across a principal's page at one school. There the principal posted pictures of herself as an elementary student and shared some of her likes and skills when she was younger. Children and families form connections with those who take the time to get to know them. Share a bit about yourself and your interests, and you may be rewarded with information from families about the children in your class. Build on this information to provide learning experiences that are relevant and meaningful to your children.

The Power of Birth Order

How on earth did your kids turn out to be so different from each other? It may have to do with where they sit in the family tree.

LINDA DIPROPERZIO

Each time Elizabeth Moore returns from the supermarket, she expects her sons to help her unload groceries from the car. Her oldest, 13-year-old Jake, is always the first to help, while her youngest, 8-year-old Sam, complains the whole time. Meanwhile, her middle son, 10-year-old Ben, rarely makes it out of the house. "He gets held up looking for his shoes. By the time they've turned up, we're done," says the West Caldwell, New Jersey, mom. "It amazes me how different my children are from one another."

How do three kids with the same parents, living in the same house, develop such distinct personalities? A key reason seems to be birth order. Many experts believe that a child's place in the family is intertwined with the hobbies he chooses, the grades he'll earn in school, and how much money he'll make as an adult. "For siblings, the differences in many aspects of personality are about as great as they would be between a brother and a sister," says Frank Sulloway, Ph.D., author of *Born to Rebel: Birth Order, Family Dynamics, and Creative Lives.* Birth order isn't the only factor that contributes to how a kid turns out, but giving it consideration can help you understand your kids' personalities—so you can help them succeed in their own unique ways.

The Firstborn
Innate Strengths
The firstborn is often used to being the center of attention; he has Mom and Dad to himself before siblings arrive (and oldest children enjoy about 3,000 more hours of quality time with their parents between ages 4 and 13 than the next sibling will get, found a study from Brigham Young University, in Provo, Utah). "Many parents spend more time reading and explaining things to firstborns. It's not as easy when other kids come into the picture," says Frank Farley, PhD, a psychologist at Temple University, in Philadelphia, who has studied personality and human development for decades. "That undivided attention may have a lot to do with why firstborns tend to be overachievers," he explains. In addition to usually scoring higher on IQ tests and

generally getting more education than their brothers and sisters, firstborns tend to outearn their siblings (firstborns were more likely to make at least $100,000 annually compared with their siblings, according to a recent CareerBuilder.com survey).

Common Challenges
Success comes with a price: Firstborns tend to be type A personalities who never cut themselves any slack. "They often have an intense fear of failure, so nothing they accomplish feels good enough," says Michelle P. Maidenberg, PhD., a child and family therapist in White Plains, New York. And because they dread making a misstep, oldest kids tend to stick to the straight and narrow: "They're typically inflexible—they don't like change and are hesitant to step out of their comfort zone," she explains.

Firstborns tend to be type A's who don't cut themselves slack.

In addition, because firstborns are often given a lot of responsibility at home—whether it's helping with chores or watching over younger siblings—they can be quick to take charge (and can be bossy when they do). That burden can lead to excess stress for a child who already feels pressure to be perfect. "I'm constantly reminding my oldest daughter, 9-year-old Posy, that I'm the mom; I should be the one worrying about everyone else," says Julie Cole, a mother of six from Burlington, Ontario. "I don't want her to be a little grown-up, but it's also easy to give her responsibilities; I really can trust her."

Necessary Nurturing
Firstborns are constantly receiving encouragement for their achievements, but they also need to know it's okay if they don't succeed at everything, says psychologist Kevin Leman, PhD, author of *The Birth Order Book.* So tell your eldest about that time you didn't make the cheerleading squad or got fired from your first job—any situation in which you tried something and

it didn't work out exactly as you planned. Be sure to emphasize why it was okay in the end and how you learned from your mistakes. You want her to see that making a few of her own is nothing to worry about and can actually be a good thing.

The Youngest
Innate Strengths

Lastborns generally aren't the strongest or the smartest in the room, so they develop their own ways of winning attention. They're natural charmers with an outgoing, social personality; no surprise then that many famous actors and comedians are the baby of the family (Stephen Colbert is the youngest of 11!), or that they score higher in "agreeableness" on personality tests than firstborns, according to Dr. Sulloway's research.

Youngests also make a play for the spotlight with their adventurousness. Free-spirited lastborns are more open to unconventional experiences and taking physical risks than their siblings (research has shown that they're more likely to play sports like football and soccer than their older siblings, who preferred activities like track and tennis).

Common Challenges

Youngests are known for feeling that "nothing I do is important," Dr. Leman notes. "None of their accomplishments seem original. Their siblings have already learned to talk, read, and ride a bike. So parents react with less spontaneous joy at their accomplishments and may even wonder, 'Why can't he catch on faster?'"

Lastborns also learn to use their role as the baby to manipulate others in order to get their way. "They're the least likely to be disciplined," Dr. Leman notes. Parents often coddle the littlest when it comes to chores and rules, failing to hold them to the same standards as their sibs. "My youngest is carefree and doesn't worry about details," says Freedom, Pennsylvania, mom of five, Christine Kiefer. "I expected more from my oldest when he was his age."

Necessary Nurturing

The long-term result of too much babying could be an adult who is dependent on others and unprepared for the world. So don't underestimate your child. Youngests are masters at getting out of chores and are often seen as "too little" to participate. But even a 2-year-old can manage tasks like putting away toys, so be sure she has responsibilities. "Keep a consistent set of rules that all of the kids must follow," says Dr. Maidenberg. "If you don't make them follow the rules, you really can't be angry when they get into trouble."

The Middle One
Innate Strengths

Middleborns are go-with-the-flow types; once a younger sibling arrives, they must learn how to constantly negotiate and compromise in order to "fit in" with everyone. Not surprisingly,

---

Special Order

Experts weigh in on what you should know if you've got a singleton or twins.

- **All in One** You've probably heard that "lonely onlies" grow up selfish and socially inept. Not true, says Dr. Frank Sulloway: "Only kids learn people skills from their parents and peers." In fact, most only children turn out to be movers and shakers with similar traits to firstborns: They're ambitious and articulate. And since they spend so much time with their parents, they're comfortable interacting with adults. The downside: Onlies may have difficulty relating to kids their own age. "So make sure your child spends time with his peers from early on," says Dr. Michelle Maidenberg. Sign him up for playgroups, sports teams, and other organized activities—so he's guaranteed lots of kid time.

- **Double Happiness** Even if they have other sibs, twins (and other multiples) generally grow up as an entity unto themselves—because that's how others see them, says Dr. Kevin Leman. The firstborn twin typically acts as the older child in the twosome, while the secondborn will have traits of a younger sib. Outside of their relationship, however, they often get lumped together as "the twins." This can be a source of frustration when twins get older and each seeks to carve out an individual identity. So encourage your duo to develop their own passions. While they might prefer to do things together, it's important for each kid to establish his or her own interests and personality.

Dr. Sulloway notes, mid kids score higher in agreeableness than both their older and younger sibs.

Because they receive less attention at home, middletons tend to forge stronger bonds with friends and be less tethered to their family than their brothers and sisters. "They're usually the first of their siblings to take a trip with another family or to want to sleep at a friend's house," says Linda Dunlap, PhD, professor of psychology at Marist College, in Poughkeepsie, New York. Tracie Chuisano, a mom of three from Wilmington, North Carolina, sees these traits in her middle son: "I let him stay over at a friend's house in the second grade, even though I'd thought his older brother had been too 'young' for it."

Common Challenges

Middle kids once lived as the baby of the family, until they were dethroned by a new sibling. Unfortunately, they're often acutely aware that they don't get as much parental attention as their "trail-blazing" older sibling or the beloved youngest, and they feel like their needs and wants are ignored. "Middle kids are in a difficult position in a family because they think they're not valued," says Dr. Maidenberg, "It's easy for them to be left out and get lost in the shuffle." And there is some validity to their complaint: A survey by TheBabyWebsite.com, a British parenting resource, found that a third of parents with three children admit to giving their middle child far less attention than they give the other two.

Necessary Nurturing

Find small ways to put your middleton in the spotlight. The biggest complaint among middle children is that they aren't "heard" within the family. But making simple gestures—like letting her choose the restaurant or the movie that everyone goes to—can mean the world to her. "A lot of the time, middle children end up deferring to the oldest's wants and the youngest's needs," Dr. Maidenberg says. So do what you can to make her feel empowered.

Critical Thinking

1. Describe some of the characteristics most often found in firstborn and youngest children. Using the birth order of you and your siblings, reflect on any similar traits you possess to those described in the article.

2. Why would it be useful for a teacher to know a student's birth order in their family?

From *Parents*, October 2010, pp. 180–184. Copyright © 2010 by Meredith Corporation. Reprinted by permission.

Teachers Connecting with Families—
In the Best Interest of Children

Katharine C. Kersey and Marie L. Masterson

When parents are involved in school, their children's achievement improves. Children make friends more easily and are more successful learners (NCPIE, 2006). Children whose families participate in school activities stay in school longer and take more advanced classes (Barnard 2004). But the greatest benefit to children of a successful home-school partnership is that children are more motivated to succeed (Hoover-Dempsey et al. 2005).

To connect parents with school, teachers need to learn the best ways to share information and thereby build bridges and strong ties with families. They need to find ways to establish positive relationships by shifting from a focus on children's problems to affirming children's strengths. Such approaches can improve classroom-home communications and encourage all families to become involved.

Knowing and Understanding Families

Most parents can remember what it felt like to take their child to school for the first time. Those hours seemed endless. Was she OK—smiling, crying, or hurt? Could you hardly wait to see her? What positive things did her teacher have to say when you picked up your child after her first day at kindergarten? If you waited to learn what she did on her first day and the teacher didn't say anything at all, were you crushed? Had you hoped that she would tell you what a nice little girl you had (in other words, that you'd done a good job)?

There are reasons a parent might feel intimidated by a teacher or hesitant to come to a conference. One parent expressed frustration that he left a meeting at work and drove 45 minutes during the worst traffic of the day, only to have 10 or 15 minutes with his child's teacher! Other parents say that they did not feel welcome at their children's school. Sometimes, parents can feel a teacher is questioning their competence, and so when they come for a meeting, they are defensive. Parents could be anticipating bad news. They may be surprised if the teacher has something nice to say. Teachers need to build parents' confidence that their school encounters will result in positive interactions and success for their child.

At times, when parents hesitate to become involved, it may be because they feel inadequate in terms of their education or perhaps are unable to read. Teachers may use language a parent doesn't understand or describe a child's progress in educational jargon, which the parent is reluctant to admit confuses him. Parents may cringe at the thought of being asked questions they can't answer. And most of all, parents don't want to feel judged for their child's problems, behaviors, or poor progress.

Distrust and uncertainty work both ways. Teachers themselves can feel intimated by parents. In some cases, a parent's strong personality comes across as demanding or accusatory, Teachers may worry about being caught off guard or asked a question not easily handled. They too could fear being judged or embarrassed. One teacher said that at the end of a parent teacher conference, she experienced an awkward moment when she tried to shake hands with the parent, a practice she didn't know was considered disrespectful in the family's culture. She now takes the time to learn about the cultures of the children in her class. Setting parents at ease and helping them know that as teachers we want the same things they want for their children is well worth the time and energy it takes.

Sharing Information with Families

The positive interactions teachers use to create connections with parents are in the best interest of the child (Hamre & Pianta 2005). Successful teachers make it their business to connect with families and plan ways to build strong relationships with children and parents. Setting up an open and positive system of teacher availability supports cooperative and productive teacher-parent relationships.

The following suggestions illustrate some specific ways to build bridges and strengthen the bond between teacher and parent. Using strategies such as these can ensure that when challenges come, a strong foundation is already in place.

Before School Starts

- **Send a personalized postcard** to every child saying "See you soon at school. You'll make friends and enjoy learning!"
- **Make a phone call** to each child: "I am calling to talk to Maria. I am your new teacher, and I look forward to seeing you."
- **Have an open house** for children and families as an orientation to school. Let the children explore the room so they will feel safe. Join the children at their level when you talk to set them at ease. Introduce children and families with common interests.
- **When the school year begins,** hold a Welcome Parents meeting [AQ3a Indicate when this takes place.] to show families that you care about their ideas and interests. Ask each family to complete a questionnaire to help you learn children's interests, strengths, pets, and hobbies. Ask for information about allergies and special concerns.

Begin the meeting with a **Family Introduction Circle:** "Whose mom or dad are you?" "Tell us something about _____ [child's name]." "What would you like everyone to know?" "Do you have something you would like to share with the children about your job, hobby, or a special interest?" Hand out copies of daily schedules, menus, and other items. Provide copies in the home languages of the families in the group. Plan time for a group of parents to get to know each other, and help them find ways to connect.

Make and share a **"Me Bag."** Bring special items that show and tell about you personally. Let families get to know you and about the things you love. You can share the same Me Bag with the children when school begins, and let the children bring in their Me Bags as well.

Throughout the Year

- **Call children at home.** Leave a message on the home answering machine during the school day. "Jamal, I am calling to say I noticed you help Brandon on the playground. He seemed grateful for your help." It takes 15 seconds, and Jamal may never want to erase it. Set aside a time each week to make these calls, and keep a list to make sure to include every child.

- **Send home a Great Moments! Certificate.** Attach a digital photo to the certificate and highlight a special contribution, a kind gesture, or clever words a child has used. Send three to five certificates each day to ensure each child receives one during the week.
- **Use the phone to share news.** Ask parents to let you know when they are available, and then set up a schedule so they can look forward to hearing from you. Be available for parents to call you at a set time if they have questions or want to talk. When a child is sick, it is appropriate to call her home to let her know she is missed.
- **Send e-mail communications.** "Today we had a picnic. We went outside under a tree. Ask Carmen to tell you what she did." Do this frequently so parents come to associate e-mails with memories of their children's experiences.
- **Say at least one positive thing each** time you see a parent. "Danny has such a wonderful sense of humor." "Teresa told me about your camping trip." Run after a parent to say, "I want to tell you . . . !" Parents will enjoy hearing about interesting things their child has done and learned.
- **Record the positive things children do.** Place them on 3 × 5 cards in a notebook you can share each time you see a parent—another opportunity to connect. Focus on conveying the message, "I notice your child!"
- **Encourage parent volunteers.** Any time you invite a parent to class, the child will feel excited and special. Encourage parents to read, share some expertise, or tell about a special interest. Let the parent's child help. Find creative ways for parents to make meaningful contributions to the classroom that can fit in their schedules (organizing child portfolios, photo copying, planning parties, or preparing for an art, music, or dramatics activity).
- **Send home weekend project packs** with activities parents and children can do together. An example could be a class mascot—a stuffed animal that takes turns going home with the children and have the families keep a diary of his activities. Children will take pride in bringing home the pet and then sharing their diary entry with classmates when the mascot returns to school.

During Parent Conferences

- **Focus on a child's natural strengths.** Affirm the child. Share special traits and unique capabilities. "Judy's block buildings are complex and inventive." "Joey shows compassion to his peers." "Jasmine enjoys exploring new art materials." A teacher can help parents see the potential in their child and encourage them to support and nurture the child's gifts at home.

- **Always get the parent to talk first.** Say, "Tell me about your child?" The parent may ask, "What do you want to know?" You can respond, "Anything you want to tell me." Such an approach lets parents take the lead and feel relaxed and open to a conversation.
- **Ask parents for their perspectives.** Parents are experts about their child and may describe a child's strength or need. When they mention a strength, ask, "How do you support her at home?" When they tell you about a problem, ask, "How do you deal with that?"
- **Ask for help!** If the child is experiencing difficulty at school and you think the parent needs to get involved, you might introduce your concern by saying, "There is something I'd like your help with."
- **Focus on one important issue.** When you have concerns, choose one that you think can be helped or fixed. First, identify it, and then brainstorm some solutions. Together with the family you can agree to a plan. "I will work on this at school, while you work on it at home. Let's set an appointment to get together again in two weeks." This tells parents that by working together you can help the child succeed.
- **Start and end on positive notes.** Tell something good first. It lets the parents relax and know you notice special things about their child. Make sure to end with a commitment. "I appreciate and value the time that I share with your child, and I want to help her develop and learn."
- **Send a reminder.** Call or send an e-mail the day before to confirm the next appointment. "If you can't come that day, when is it convenient for you to come?"

When Parents Are Not Able to Come to School

- **Share successes immediately.** With parental permission, allow a child to call a parent during the day to tell about something great he just did. You can call also: "I want you to know that Joshua counted to six in Spanish today!"
- **Videotape children's activities,** presentations, and special accomplishments. Send the tape home on loan for parents to appreciate what they see their child learning and doing. Or upload the video to the school or classroom website.
- **Send home daily sheets.** Use photos and descriptions to show parents the activities and learning in which the children are engaged.
- **Fill a class newsletter with highlights** of community activities, parenting and positive guidance tips, and information about the class curriculum. Children can help write the news for this newsletter!

Use Affirmations to Connect with Families

With parents, use every opportunity to connect positively: "I can't wait to see you and tell you all of the wonderful things your child is doing!" When a teacher adopts this attitude in her interactions with parents, they will eagerly join in to support school and classroom activities for their child. Tell parents what the child is learning about himself, new friends, the world, and the outdoors. Parents need to hear what children are learning socially and how they are becoming successful. It is our job as teachers to help each child navigate the world successfully. We can give parents hope and confidence that their child is well on his way to achieving that goal.

It is always in the best interest of the child to connect with parents. When teachers and parents build connections and work together, children are more successful—both academically and socially. The relationships teachers form early with parents help children become socially and emotionally competent and do better in school (Walker et al. 2005). As a result, children have fewer behavior problems both at school and at home (NCPIE 2006). Family connections built, when children are young pay off in a lifetime of rich dividends for the child.

Teachers can tell families, "I hear about you all the time. I heard what a great thing you all did together last night." These positive affirmations make a parent feel relaxed and stand up tall. You're the teacher, are building bridges. You have a lasting impact on parents when you share your values and your goals for their children. You empower parents to be more successful in their parenting role when you connect them positively to their child's teacher and to school.

Once families feel comfortable and understand how important they are to their child's success, a strong relationship begins. The partnership strengthens as school and teacher become a source for positive information. Through this approach to building connections, teachers create authentic, caring relationships with families, and parents become active participants in their child's success.

References

Barnard, W.M. 2004. Parent involvement in elementary school and educational attainment. *Children and Youth Services Review* 26: 39–62.

Gladwell, M. 2005. *Blink: The power of thinking without thinking.* New York: Little, Brown.

Hamre, B., & R. Pianta. 2005. Can instructional and emotional support in the first-grade classroom make a difference for children at risk of school failure? *Child Development* 76 (5): 949–67.

Hoover-Dempsey, K., M. Walker, H. Sandler, D. Whetsel, C. Green, A. Wilkins, & K. Closson. 2005. Why do parents become involved? Research findings and implications. *Elementary School Journal* 2 (106): 105–30.

NCPIE (National Coalition for Parent Involvement in Education). 2006. What's Happening. *A new wave of evidence: The impact of school, family and community connections on student achievement.* www.ncpie.ore/WhatsHappening/researchJanuary2006.html

Walker, J.M., A.S. Wilkins, J.R. Dallaire, H.M. Sandler, & K.V. Hoover-Dempsey. 2005. Parental involvement: Model revision through scale development. *The Elementary School Journal* 106 (2): 85–104.

Critical Thinking

1. Interview two families with children attending a preschool setting and ask them to name specific relationship building actions taken by the staff at their children's school.

2. If asked at a job interview to describe why it is important for you to develop a trusting relationship with the families of children in your class; how will you respond?

KATHARINE C. KERSEY, EdD, is professor of early childhood, an educator, and the director emeritus of the Child Study Center, Old Dominion University (ODU), in Norfolk, Virginia. She is the former chair of ODU's Department of Early Childhood, Speech Pathology, and Special Education and is a child behavior expert, TV consultant, teacher and parent educator, author, and speaker. kkersev@odu.edu

MARIE L. MASTERSON, PhD, is the early childhood specialist for the Virginia Department of Education and adjunct professor of early childhood education at Old Dominion University. She is coordinator of the ODU Director's Institute and an educational researcher, child behavior consultant, and speaker. mmasters@odu.edu.

The Impact of Teachers and Families on Young Children's Eating Behaviors

ERIN K. ELIASSEN

Young children depend on their families and teachers to support their well-being and promote positive development, including eating behaviors. Children's food preferences and willingness to try new foods are influenced by the people around them (Bellows & Anderson 2006).

The eating behaviors children practice early in life affect their health and nutrition—significant factors in childhood overweight and obesity (Clark et al. 2007)—and may continue to shape food attitudes and eating patterns through adulthood (Birch 1999; Campbell & Crawford 2001; Westenhoefer 2002). Eating environments—mealtime and snack—that make food fun, offer new foods and a variety, and encourage children to taste and choose the foods they want let children develop food attitudes and dietary practices that ultimately support good health (Campbell & Crawford 2001).

Developing Eating Behaviors

The development of eating behaviors is a dynamic process that begins in infancy and continues throughout life. In this article, *eating behaviors* refers to food preferences, patterns of food acceptance and rejection, and the types and amounts of food a person eats. Genetics and the contexts in which foods are presented are two key factors that underpin the development of eating behaviors. Although parents provide a child's biological predisposition, which may affect factors like taste perception, they are not the only adults influencing the development of a child's eating behaviors. Every family member and caregiver interacting with a child at meals or snacks has the potential to do so.

In center- and home-based child care settings, teachers and family child care providers influence children's eating behaviors by the foods they offer, the behaviors they model, and their social interactions with children at snack and mealtimes (Savage, Fisher, & Birch 2007). Here are a few examples of how these factors influence eating behaviors.

Repeated exposure to a new food reduces a child's fear of the food and helps increase acceptance. Observing families and teachers eating and enjoying a variety of foods makes these foods more appealing to children. In contrast, children who are

pressured to eat specific foods learn to dislike them. Restricted access to some foods, such as cookies or potato chips, often results in overconsumption of those foods when children are free to choose them (Savage, Fisher, & Birch 2007).

Educators and Families are Role Models

Based on research, the following six subsections discuss food fears, care environments, food behavior models, food restriction, pressures to eat, and food as a reward or celebration. Each area offers suggestions for educators and families to help children develop positive, early eating behaviors.

Food Fears

Most children naturally demonstrate fears of new foods. Neophobia, or fear of the new, is a protective behavior observed in omnivores, including humans, that helps prevent consumption of harmful substances (Birch 1999). Teachers help decrease children's fears by creating supportive environments with enjoyable, nutritious, and fun early food experiences.

For example, teachers could involve families by encouraging each family to bring every child a tasting sample of a unique food their child enjoys (or the teacher may offer suggestions of foods to taste). The teacher can arrange a tasting schedule, with a different family sharing a food tasting each week. Once every family has had an opportunity to share, host a classroom tasting party with all of the foods and invite parents to enjoy the event with their children. Although experiments vary, researchers tell us that offering a food 10 to 15 times appears necessary to increase a child's food acceptance (Savage, Fisher, & Birch 2007). Activities like tasting parties expose children to foods from different cultures and provide opportunities to learn more about their friends.

The acceptance of new foods is a slow process. Particularly through the ages 2 to 5, persistence is essential (Birch 1999; Satter 2008). A teacher/caregiver may think it is best to hold off on introducing food variety until children's fearful responses decrease. Instead, it is important to continue introducing a variety of foods throughout early childhood. Although children are skeptical of many foods during these early years, the variety of foods they accept is greater in this developmental phase than it is in later childhood (Skinner et al. 2002).

Enjoyable or satisfying experiences with a food highly influence a child's subsequent selection of the food on given occasions or its adoption into his or her regular diet. These experiences are as simple as frequent family meals during which the television is off and parents or caregivers are tuned in to the mealtime experience by talking and enjoying the foods themselves. Positive exposure to multiple foods helps children develop a taste for more foods, choose them as regular mealtime selections, and have needed dietary variety—whole grains, fruits, and vegetables. Many children lack opportunities to taste a variety of healthful foods, compared to the numerous chances our culture makes available for tasting high-fat, calorie-dense foods (Savage, Fisher, & Birch 2007).

Care Environments

Child care settings foster positive development of eating behaviors for 2- to 5-year-olds. Caregivers introduce variety in the foods served at meals and snacks and encourage families to do the same when they send lunches from home. Programs can guide parents by sharing comprehensive lists of foods that present a variety of grains, fruits, vegetables, nuts and seeds, and meats and beans, and an illustration of their nutritional value. For instance, using MyPyramid (www.mypyramid.gov) food groups helps families categorize foods and prepare lunches with variety and nutritional balance. Teachers can share examples of simple, creative lunches with variety in color, texture, and taste to appeal to young children.

Being persistent and providing repeated exposures to foods is important for both teachers and families. Avoid temptations to remove healthy foods from the program's meal or snack menus just because children reject them. Support families in continuing to offer lunch items even if their child does not consume the food on a given day. When serving a new item such as snap peas at snack time, include it two or three times a month and encourage children to look, smell, touch, and taste the new food. It is perfectly acceptable for a child to avoid a new vegetable the first several times it is offered. Inviting children to touch and smell the food helps them take small steps toward tasting. Encouraging rather than requiring children to eat a food is the key objective.

Food Behavior Models

Families are typically children's first significant models of eating behavior (Golan & Weizman 2001). Child care providers also are early role models. Positive role modeling correlates with an increased interest in food and less food fussiness among children (Gregory, Paxton, & Borzovic 2010). Poor role models influence children's perceptions of foods and mealtimes (Matheson, Spranger, & Saxe 2002). For example, negative comments about the taste or texture of a food will make a child less willing to try it. On the other hand, a child is more likely to try a food if he or she observes an adult enjoying it.

Teachers and caregivers become role models by engaging with children at mealtime and sitting down and eating with

Ten Steps to Positive Eating Behaviors

1. Provide a variety of foods at meals and snacks, especially whole grains, vegetables, and fruits.
2. Offer repeated opportunities to taste new foods.
3. Share with families nutrition resources, such as lists of foods (by category) to guide their food selections and offer new ideas for meals sent from home.
4. Apply the same guidelines to food selections in teachers' lunches brought from home.
5. Sit with children at meals, and enjoy conversation. Talk about the taste, texture, appearance, and healthful aspects of foods.
6. Plan adequate time for all children to finish eating.
7. Respect a child's expression of satiety or sense of being full.
8. Develop a routine for serving snacks, applying the same rules whether offering carrots, crackers, or cookies.
9. Wash hands before snack and mealtime; encourage touching and smelling a food as a step toward tasting.
10. Find alternatives to using food as a reward or serving foods high in fat, sugar, or salt as part of a celebration.

them. This practice is often called family-style dining. When early childhood programs provide meals, teachers and staff can model healthy eating behaviors by eating the same foods the children eat.

Staff who bring their lunches can model the same kinds of healthy eating as described in the guidelines the program suggests for families who send lunches with their children. For example, if parents send a fruit and a vegetable item, then teachers can include both of these items in their lunches. If children have milk, water, or 100 percent fruit juice as a beverage, teachers should drink these same beverages.

Interesting and engaging mealtime conversations create greater food enjoyment (Hughes et al. 2007). Adults can talk positively about the foods they are eating and also invite the children to describe colors, tastes (sweet, sour, salty), and textures (crunchy, smooth, stringy). However, the conversation should not be about the food alone. Also engage children in conversation about other appropriate topics, such as animals or family activities. Too much emphasis on the foods may decrease the children's interest.

Food Restriction

Many well-meaning adults try to control the way children eat. They may believe that restricting or forbidding unhealthy foods will decrease children's preference for them, but the opposite is true (Satter 2008). Pressuring a child to eat one type of food (such as fruit or vegetables) leads to resistance. When an adult restricts access to certain foods (such as sweets or french fries), a child may become preoccupied with the restricted food.

A study on the effect of restricted access to foods among a population of 3- to 6-year-olds (Fisher & Birch 1999) found that the children focused great attention on the visible but inaccessible food through spontaneous clapping and chanting. In a similar study (Fisher & Birch 1999), restricting a desired, palatable snack food substantially increased children's selection of that food compared to times when both it and similar foods were freely available.

Avoid making comments about children's frequency or quantity consumption of a given food. For example, when serving cookies for snack, offer them as all other snacks are served. Their quantity should not be restricted unless the quantity of all snack foods is restricted. Early childhood educators can develop routines for offering all snacks, both unfamiliar and favorite foods, in the same unbiased way.

Pressure to Eat

When families or teachers pressure children to eat at mealtimes, the practice negatively influences a child's food intake as well as attitude toward food (Galloway et al. 2006). Gregory, Paxton, and Brozovic (2010) report that children pressured to eat were less interested in food over time; whereas, when parents modeled healthy eating, the children expressed greater interest in food and less food fussiness. Coercion to eat specific quantities or types of foods may mean that children eat more at the given meal, but over time they will likely avoid the targeted food (Satter 2008).

In a study involving adults, Batsell and colleagues (2002) traced common food dislikes to the adults' childhood experiences in being pressured to consume certain foods. Galloway and colleagues (2006) learned that refraining from the use of pressure and simply eating with and talking to the children had a more positive impact on children's attitude toward the food offered.

While pressure to eat contributes to a dislike of certain foods, emphasis on having a "clean plate" may hinder children's recognition of the internal cues of hunger and satiety and contribute to overeating (Satter 2008). It is important for adults to respect the child's expression of food preference and fullness (particularly if the child tastes a food) and to follow a schedule that gives children enough time to eat.

Food as a Reward or Celebration

Food as reward or celebration is common in some early childhood settings. Such practices may be well intentioned but can have negative consequences and impact long-term eating behaviors (Birch 1999; Brown & Ogden 2004). Food rewards or party treats are often sweets or other "desired" snack items. Giving a desired food as a reward enhances a child's preference for the food (Puhl & Schwartz 2003).

By establishing guidelines for the use of food in the classroom, early childhood programs encourage families to provide alternatives to fast-food lunch parties or cupcake celebrations and to bring instead, for example, fruits or muffins. Class celebrations or everyday activities also give young children opportunities to prepare their own foods in the classroom. Children enjoy making edible art fruit or vegetable skewers, or snacks resembling animals.

Alternative practices for recognition and celebration are growing in variety in early childhood settings. Instead of food, teachers recognize children by giving them special opportunities, such as selecting a song for the group to listen or dance to, choosing a game to play with friends, or having first choice of equipment for gross motor play. Non-food-related activities, like bringing a favorite book or game to class to read or share with friends, are other ways to acknowledge individuals.

Conclusion

Early childhood educators who understand the importance of their role in the development of children's healthful eating behaviors can help improve the lifelong health of the children they serve. They can offer meaningful, positive experiences with food, including growing, preparing, and eating foods with children. Regardless of the foods offered at home, the early childhood educator has the opportunity to model selection and enjoyment of a variety of foods. Food in the program should be associated with opportunities and fun experiences rather than rules and restrictions. Tasting activities help children learn about foods, manners, and even other cultures.

Everyone caring for children needs to be aware that some food strategies have negative effects on the development of eating behaviors. Food practices involving pressure and restriction may not only affect childhood health but also have long-lasting implications, such as problematic behaviors of binge eating and dietary restraint among adults (Puhl & Schwartz 2003).

A supportive, caring early childhood environment offers guidance through adult modeling, serving a variety of nutritious foods at meals and snacks, and exposing children to new foods in the classroom. These practices encourage children's development of healthy eating attitudes and behaviors and promote positive long-term health outcomes.

References

Batsell, R., A. Brown, M. Ansfield, & G. Paschall. 2002. "You Will Eat All of That! A Retrospective Analysis of Forced Consumption Episodes." *Appetite* 38 (3): 211–19.

Bellows, L., & J. Anderson. 2006. "The Food Friends: Encouraging Preschoolers to Try New Foods." *Young Children* 61 (3): 37–39. www.naeyc.org/yc/pastissues/2006/may.

Birch, L. 1999. "Development of Food Preferences." *Annual Reviews of Nutrition* 19 (1): 41–62.

Brown, R., & J. Ogden. 2004. "Children's Eating Attitudes and Behaviour: A Study of the Modeling and Control Theories of Parental Influence." *Health Education Research* 19 (3): 261–71.

Campbell, K., & D. Crawford 2001. "Family Food Environments as Determinants of Preschool-Aged Children's Eating Behaviors: Implications for Obesity Prevention Policy. A Review." *Australian Journal of Nutrition and Dietetics* 58 (1): 19–25.

Clark, H., E. Goyder, P. Bissel, L. Blank, & J. Peters. 2007. "How Do Parents' Child-Feeding Behaviours Influence Child Weight?

Implications for Childhood Obesity Policy." *Journal of Public Health* 29 (2):132–41.

Fisher, J., & L. Birch. 1999. "Restricting Access to Palatable Foods Affects Children's Behavioral Response, Food Selection, and Intake." *American Journal of Clinical Nutrition* 69 (6): 1264–72.

Galloway, A., L. Fiorito, L. Francis, & L. Birch. 2006. "'Finish Your Soup': Counterproductive Effects of Pressuring Children to Eat on Intake and Affect." *Appetite* 46 (3): 318–23.

Golan, M., & A. Weizman. 2001. "Familial Approach to the Treatment of Childhood Obesity." *Journal of Nutrition Education* 33 (2): 102–07.

Gregory, J., S. Paxton, & A. Brozovic. 2010. "Maternal Feeding Practices, Child Eating Behavior and Body Mass Index in Preschool- Aged Children: A Prospective Analysis." *The International Journal of Behavioral Nutrition and Physical Activity* 7: 55–65.

Hughes, S., H. Patrick, T. Power, J. Fisher, C. Anderson, & T. Nicklas. 2007. "The Impact of Child Care Providers' Feeding on Children's Food Consumption." *Journal of Development & Behavioral Pediatrics* 28 (2): 100–07.

Matheson, D., K. Spranger, & A. Saxe. 2002. "Preschool Children's Perceptions of Food and Their Food Experiences." *Journal of Nutrition Education and Behavior* 34 (2): 85–92.

Puhl, R., & M. Schwartz. 2003. "If You Are Good You Can Have a Cookie: How Memories of Childhood Food Rules Link to Adult Eating Behaviors." *Eating Behaviors* 4 (3): 283–93. www.faeriefilms.com/images/Schwartz_-_If_You_Are_Good.pdf.

Satter, E. 2008. *Secrets of Feeding a Healthy Family.* Madison, WI: Kelcy Press.

Savage, J., J. O. Fisher, & L. Birch. 2007. "Parental Influence on Eating Behavior: Conception to Adolescence." *Journal of Law, Medicine & Ethics* 35 (1): 22–34.

Skinner, J., B. Carruth, W. Bounds, & P. Ziegler. 2002. "Children's Food Preferences: A Longitudinal Analysis." *Journal of the American Dietetic Association* 102 (11): 1638–47.

Westenhoefer, J. 2002. "Establishing Dietary Habits During Childhood for Long-Term Weight Control." *Annals of Nutrition & Metabolism* 46 (supplement): 18–23.

Critical Thinking

1. How many times does a young child need to be exposed to a food prior to accepting it into their diet? What early food experiences affected your eating habits today?

2. What steps can early childhood educators take to assist young children in developing healthy eating habits?

Class Matters—In and Out of School

Closing gaps requires attention to issues of race and poverty.

JAYNE BOYD-ZAHARIAS AND HELEN PATE-BAIN

Low achievement and high dropout rates among poor and minority students continue to plague U.S. society. And we say "plague" purposefully, because these children are all our children, and our nation will profit by or pay for whatever they become. While much attention over the past quarter century has focused on reforming the schools these students attend, little or no progress has been made in actually closing the achievement gaps or reducing the number of dropouts.

Why? Aren't Americans a "can-do" people? We eradicated the childhood scourge of polio, built the best road system since the Romans, put men on the moon, outlasted the Soviet Union, and created universities that are the envy of the world.

But the problem of underachievement by poor and minority students has confounded us. High-level commissions issue warnings, governors hold summits, think tanks produce reports, scholars write books, and Congress passes laws. But the U.S. has failed to deliver on its promise to provide a high-quality education to every child.

In the 1960s, Martin Luther King, Jr., forced our nation to face the inequities of race, poverty, and war. But today, these three inequities still exist in this country.

Rethinking the Problem

Surely schools need to be improved, especially the schools that serve poor and minority children. But school improvement alone will not suffice. We believe in the power of good teaching, but educators alone cannot do a job so large. We can inspire individual students to break through the boundaries of social class, but we cannot lift a whole social class of students to a higher level of achievement. Low achievement and dropping out are problems rooted in social and economic inequality—a force more powerful than curricula, teaching practices, standardized tests, or other school-related policies. Richard Rothstein summed it up best:

> For nearly half a century, the association of social and economic disadvantage with the student achievement gap has been well known to economists, sociologists, and educators. Most, however, have avoided the obvious implication of this understanding—raising the achievement of lower-class children requires amelioration of the social and economic conditions of their lives, not just school reform.[1]

Once acknowledged, this truth has profound implications for educators and policy makers alike.

If all efforts to close achievement gaps concentrate exclusively on schools and school reform, they will fail, leaving schools and teachers to shoulder the blame. In turn, good administrators and teachers, who are doing their best under difficult circumstances, will be driven *out* of the profession, a prospect that can only make matters worse. As Gary Orfield sums it up: "Doing educational reform while ignoring the fundamental cleavages in society is profoundly counterproductive."[2]

A useful way of visualizing the remedy for the chronic problem of low achievement of poor and minority students is to return to Abraham Maslow's 1954 hierarchy of needs for self-actualization. We have patterned a hierarchy of needs for a self-actualized society after Maslow's (see Figure 1).

Affordable Housing in Stable Neighborhoods

Nearly one-third of the nation's poorest children have attended three different schools by third grade. Such high mobility depresses achievement. One study found that reducing the mobility of low-income students to that of other students would eliminate 7% of the test-score gap by income and 14% of the

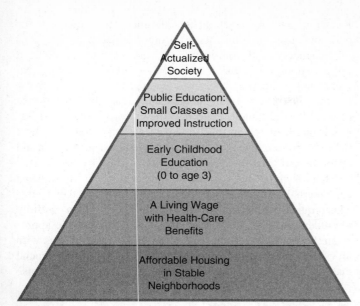

Figure 1 A hierarchy of needs for a self-actualized society.

black/white test score gap.[3] Other studies have shown that low-income families and children benefit when integrated into middle-class neighborhoods. This integration requires housing subsidies for poor families.[4]

After *Brown* v. *Board of Education,* "white flight" became common across the country. Middle-income white families moved to the suburbs, leaving only poor families in the inner cities. The challenge today is to integrate low- and middle-income families into stable neighborhoods. Margery Turner and Susan Popkin have identified several ways to afford this mix of income groups: 1) low-income housing tax credits, 2) housing choice vouchers, 3) HOPE VI (a public housing plan that has been successful in Seattle and Kansas City), 4) new communities, and 5) linking supportive services to affordable housing.[5] The most effective integrated communities will include:

- elected local committees to keep residents informed and active;
- public schools with small classes, teachers who make home visits, family resource centers with health-care services available to the community, active parent/teacher organizations, and after-school care and summer programs;
- support services: adult education, job training, and financial and budgeting classes.

A Living Wage with Health-Care Benefits

One in four American workers today earns poverty-level hourly wages. What's more, 33% of black and 39.3% of Hispanic workers earn poverty-level hourly wages.[6] These are appalling numbers, and they have a profound impact on poor and minority

children. Poverty, especially long-term, chronic poverty, takes a terrible toll on children's health and their readiness for school.

In 1968, 12.8% of America's children lived in poverty. In 2006, that proportion had risen to 17.4%—an increase of 1.2 million children.[7] Raising the minimum wage, protecting workers' rights to organize and join unions, and implementing living wage ordinances will certainly benefit poor children and families.

Early Childhood Education

There is no question that those poor and minority children who participate in prekindergarten programs are better prepared for school, especially in terms of letter/word recognition, pattern recognition, and ability to work with others. As Clive Belfield has noted, "Model pre-K programs show extremely powerful effects over the long term. There are significant reductions in special educational placement and grade retention. Pre-K participation reduces high school dropout rates dramatically."[8]

Arthur Rolnick and Rob Grunewald conclude that the case in favor of investing in early childhood education is closed. "Now," they continue, "it is time to design and implement a system that will help society realize on a large scale the extraordinary returns that high-quality early childhood programs have shown they can deliver."[9]

Today, we are indebted to researchers in education and to economists for providing us with proof that early childhood education saves money and children. By acting on their findings, we can improve the lives of the 13 million children living in poverty.

Public Education: Small Classes

Teachers have long known intuitively that small classes allow them to devote more attention to individual students. Hence, class size has been one of the most researched topics in education. But studies prior to Tennessee's Project STAR, with which we have both been intimately involved, were found to be inconclusive because of weak methodologies. STAR was independently reviewed by Frederick Mosteller of Harvard University, and he declared it to be "one of the most important educational investigations ever carried out and illustrates the kind and magnitude of research needed in the field of education to strengthen schools."[10]

Because of STAR's strong research design, there is widespread confidence in its major finding that small classes in K-3 provide extraordinary academic benefits to students, especially low-income and minority students. STAR is where intuition met empirical proof. And since STAR, other studies (SAGE, Success Starts Small, Burke County, etc.) have shown the positive impact of small classes in the primary grades.[11]

Small classes in the early grades also provide long-term positive outcomes. STAR students have been followed through high school and beyond. Research from follow-up studies indicates that students who entered small classes in kindergarten or first grade and had three or more consecutive years of small classes showed gains in academic achievement through at least eighth grade.[12]

Attending small classes in K-3 reduces the black/white gap in the rate at which students take college entrance exams by an estimated 60 percent.

In addition, Alan Krueger and Diane Whitmore found that attending small classes in K-3 reduces the black/white gap in the rate at which students take college entrance exams by an estimated 60 percent. Their research also showed that attending small classes raised the average score on the exams by 0.15–0.20 of a standard deviation for black students and by 0.04 of a standard deviation for white students.[13]

But cost is the bottom line when education budgets are developed. When the value of reducing class size was first introduced, the initial response of policy makers was that it would cost too much. However, recent research provides evidence that small classes produce long-term savings.

Follow-up data from STAR have shown that criminal conviction rates were 20% lower for black males assigned to small classes than for those assigned to regular size classes. Maximum sentence rates were also 25% lower for black males from small classes. Teen birth rates were shown to be one-third less for white females assigned to small classes than for their peers assigned to regular size classes, and the fatherhood rate for black teenage males from small classes was 40% lower than for those from regular size classes.[14]

Small K-3 classes have been identified as a cost-effective educational intervention that reduces high school dropout rates. They are a wise investment.

> From a societal perspective (incorporating earnings and health outcomes), class-size reduction would generate a net cost savings of approximately $168,000 and a net gain of 1.7 quality-adjusted life-years for each high school graduate produced by small classes. When targeted to low-income students, the estimated savings would increase to $196,000 per additional graduate.[15]

Although research related to small classes in later grades is somewhat scarce, new findings suggest that class size reduction at the middle-school level will also provide substantial benefits to students.[16] More studies need to be conducted to determine the impact of class size reduction beyond the primary grades.

Public Education: Improved Instruction

Most school improvement efforts don't focus sufficiently on instruction. It is time that policy makers recognize that teaching, which is at the very core of education, involves complex tasks that require specialized skills and knowledge. It is not enough, for example, for a teacher of mathematics to know mathematics.

Knowing math for teaching is different from knowing it for one's own use. The same holds for other subjects.

"Teachers can't learn for students," notes Deborah Ball, dean of the School of Education at the University of Michigan.[17] No matter the instructional format—lecture, small-group activity, or individualized assignment—students make their own sense of what they're taught. Ideas don't fly directly from teachers' minds into learners' minds. Effective teaching requires teachers to be able to assess what students are taking from instruction and adapt their instruction to meet the differing needs of students.

There is an old but wise saying in teaching, "If my students can't learn the way I teach, then I must teach the way they learn." This requires teachers to ask probing questions, listen carefully to student answers, and create assignments to provide appropriate help. Moreover, teachers today must do all of this with an ever-increasing variety of students, spanning gulfs of social class, language, and culture, to ensure that each student learns.

Confronting Three Inconvenient Truths

To achieve a high quality education for every child, policy makers in Washington, D.C., and in state capitals must confront three inconvenient truths.

Inconvenient truth #1. Our nation's social class inequalities are vast and growing. If we are serious about providing equal educational opportunity for every child, we must address these inequalities. They are not immutable. Barack Obama has addressed such inequalities directly and vowed:

> This time we want to talk about the crumbling schools that are stealing the future of black children and white children and Asian children and Hispanic children and Native American children. This time we want to reject the cynicism that tells us that these kids can't learn; that those kids who don't look like us are somebody else's problem. The children of Americans are not those kids, they are our kids, and we will not let them fall behind in a 21st century economy.[18]

Inconvenient truth #2. Schools alone cannot close the achievement gap or solve the dropout problem. The renowned sociologist James Coleman has written, "Inequalities imposed on children by their home, neighborhood, and peer environment are carried along to become the inequalities with which they confront adult life at the end of school."[19]

According to Thomas Bellamy and John Goodlad:

> Collaborative decision making and collective actions depend on leaders who can cross boundaries within and among various groups involved in setting school priorities. The ability to frame issues in ways that support broad participation, bridge communication gaps across groups, and facilitate local deliberation is critical, but often missing. Consequently one important way to support local renewal is by identifying individuals who are attempting such cross-sector leadership, connecting them with one another, and offering learning experiences related to local challenges.[20]

Inconvenient truth number #3. It is going to cost a lot of money to ameliorate the achievement-depressing social and economic conditions of lower-class children's lives and to improve the public schools they attend. But the costs of allowing another generation of children from lower-income groups to grow up undereducated, unhealthy, and unconnected with our economy or society will be even greater.

A black boy born in 2001 has one chance in three of going to prison in his lifetime. A Hispanic boy born in the same year has one chance in six of going to prison in his lifetime.[21] Faced with such stunning indicators of things gone wrong, one can only conclude that a serious course of correction is in order.

Advocating for Transformational Change

Educators have a special insight into the damage that deprivation does to children's learning. We and the organizations that represent us must speak up and keep the policy makers on task. It won't be easy. They are pushed and pulled in many different directions, so that even the more sympathetic ones are easily distracted. We will have to stop being so defensive and go on the offense. We will have to be bold without being belligerent. The stakes are high, but we must be heard.

In the words of David Labaree, "In a democratic society, everyone is affected by what schools accomplish as they educate the majority of each generation's voters, jurors, and taxpayers. So all have reasons to stay involved in the public conversation about school quality."[22]

As advocates for equal opportunity, we must insist on transformational change. Incremental change that merely nibbles around the edges of long-term problems will fall woefully short—again. When a swimmer is drowning 50 feet offshore, it does no good to throw a 10-foot rope. Yet that is precisely what we do, year after year, when it comes to poor and minority children.

The federal government can start by living up to its promises. It promised to cover 40% of the cost of educating disadvantaged students under Title I of the Elementary and Secondary Education Act (ESEA), and it has never done so. Since 2002, for example, when ESEA became No Child Left Behind, the federal government has shortchanged states and school districts by $54.7 billion.[23] School districts and states need fewer mandates and more monetary support.

We need a self-actualized society. We need massive public investments in our children, in their schools, and in our future. It has been more than half a century since *Brown v. Board of Education,* but if Linda Brown were a girl today, we still could not guarantee her a high-quality education. It's time we heed the words of Dr. Martin Luther King, Jr., "Save us from that patience that makes us patient with anything less than freedom and justice."[24]

Notes

1. Richard Rothstein, *Class and Schools: Using Social, Economic, and Educational Reform to Close the Black-White Achievement Gap,* Washington, D.C.: Economic Policy Institute, 2004, p. 11.

2. Gary Orfield, "Race and Schools: The Need for Action," *Visiting Scholars Series,* Spring 2008, National Education Association, Washington, D.C., www.nea.org/achievement/orfield08.html

3. Eric A. Hanushek, John Kain, and Steven G. Rivkin, "Disruptions Versus Tiebout Improvement: The Costs and Benefits of Switching Schools," *Journal of Public Economics,* vol. 88, 2004, pp. 1721–46.

4. Rothstein, pp. 135–38.

5. Margery Austin Turner and Susan J. Popkin, "Affordable Housing in Healthy Neighborhoods: Critical Policy Challenges Facing the Greater New Orleans Region," statement before the Committee on Financial Services, U.S. House of Representatives, 6 February 2007.

6. *The State of Working America 2005–07,* Economic Policy Institute, Washington, D.C., www.epi.org/content.cfm/datazoneindex

7. "CDF Examines Progress Made Since Dr. King's Death," Children's Defense Fund, 25 January 2008, www.childrensdefense.org

8. Clive R. Belfield, "The Promise of Early Childhood Education Interventions," in Clive R. Belfield and Henry M. Levin, eds., *The Price We Pay: Economic and Social Consequences of Inadequate Education* (Washington, D.C.: Brookings Institution Press, 2007), p. 209.

9. Arthur J. Rolnick and Rob Grunewald, "Early Intervention on a Large Scale," Federal Reserve Bank of Minneapolis, 2007, http://woodrow.mpls.frb.fed.us/Research/studies/earlychild/earlyintervention.cfm

10. Frederick Mosteller, "The Tennessee Study of Class Size in the Early School Grades," *The Future of Children: Critical Issues for Children and Youths,* Summer/Fall 1995, p. 113.

11. Student Achievement Guarantee in Education (SAGE), www.weac.org/sage; C. M. Achilles, "Financing Class-Size Reduction," SERVE, University of North Carolina, Greensboro, ERIC ED 419 288; and C. M. Achilles, Patrick Harman, and Paula Egelson, "Using Research Results on Class Size to Improve Pupil Achievement Outcomes," *Research in the Schools,* Fall 1995, pp. 23–31.

12. Jeremy D. Finn et al., "The Enduring Effects of Small Classes," *Teachers College Record,* April 2001, pp. 145–83.

13. Alan B. Krueger and Diane M. Whitmore, "The Effect of Attending a Small Class in the Early Grades on College-Test Taking and Middle School Test Results: Evidence from Project STAR," *Economic Journal,* January 2001, pp. 1–28.

14. Alan B. Krueger and Diane M. Whitmore, "Would Smaller Classes Help Close the Black-White Achievement Gap?" in John E. Chubb and Tom Loveless, *Bridging the Achievement Gap* (Washington, D.C.: Brookings Institution Press, 2002).

15. Peter Muennig and Steven H. Woolf, "Health and Economic Benefits of Reducing the Number of Students per Classroom in U.S. Primary Schools," *American Journal of Public Health,* November 2007, www.ajph.org/cgi/content/abstract/97/11/2020

16. Christopher H. Tienken and C. M. Achilles, "Making Class Size Work in the Middle Grades," paper presented at the annual meeting of the American Educational Research Association, New York City, March 2008.

17. Deborah Loewenberg Ball, "Improving Mathematics Learning by All: A Problem of Instruction?" *Visiting Scholars Series,* Spring 2008, National Education Association, Washington, D.C., p. 5.

18. Remarks of Senator Barack Obama: "A More Perfect Union," Philadelphia, 18 March 2008, www.barackobama .com/2008/03/18/remarks_of_senator_barack_obam_53.php

19. James S. Coleman et al., *Equal Educational Opportunity* (Washington, D.C.: United States Government Printing Office, 1966), p. 26.

20. G. Thomas Bellamy and John I. Goodlad, "Continuity and Change in the Pursuit of a Democratic Public Mission for Our Schools," *Phi Delta Kappan,* April 2008, p. 570.

21. "CDF Examines Progress Made Since Dr. King's Death."

22. David Labaree, quoted in Bellamy and Goodlad, p. 570.

23. "ESEA Title I-A Grants: Funding Promised in Law vs. Funding Actually Received, FY 2002–09, www.nea.org/lac/funding/ images/title1gap.pdf

24. Martin Luther King, quoted in Michael J. Freedman, "U.S. Marks 50th Anniversary of Montgomery Bus Boycott," International Information Programs, www .america.gov/st/diversity-english/2005/November/ 20080225140519liameruoy0.664715.html

Critical Thinking

1. In the article, David Labaree states, "In a democratic society, everyone is affected by what schools accomplish as they educate the majority of each generation's voters, jurors, and taxpayers. So all have reasons to stay involved in the public conversation about school quality." Using that statement as your base, how would you convince a retired couple, whose children have long graduated from their local public schools, to vote for an increase in property taxes to support the schools?

2. If you could wave a magic wand and make one change in a community to help improve academic achievement, what one change would you make and why?

JAYNE BOYD-ZAHARIAS began work on Project STAR in 1986 and was named director of Class Size Studies at Tennessee State University. She is currently executive director of Health & Education Research Operative Services, Inc. where she developed the National Class Size Database and continues her role as a co-principal investigator on STAR Follow-up Studies. HELEN PATE-BAIN was one of four original Project STAR principal investigators. She has been a classroom teacher, a professor of educational administration, and is a past president of the National Education Association. The authors wish to express their thanks to David Sheridan of the Human and Civil Rights Division of the National Education Association for his advice and input on this article.

From *Phi Delta Kappan,* by Jayne Boyd-Zaharias and Helen Pate-Bain, September 2008, pp. 40–44. Reprinted with permission of the authors and Phi Delta Kappa International, www.pdkintl.org, 2009. All rights reserved.

Creating a Welcoming Classroom for Homeless Students

One million homeless children and youth were enrolled in U.S. schools in 2009. Experts estimate that as many as half a million more went uncounted because they weren't enrolled in school. How can educators help students maintain their studies while living in an unstable environment?

JENNIFER J. SALOPEK

In the United States, the homeless child population has increased by 47 percent in the past two years. Increasing unemployment rates have combined with home foreclosures to render many more families homeless since 2007.

A homeless person is defined as someone who does not have a "fixed, regular, and adequate night-time residence," according to the PBS website article "Facts and Figures: The Homeless." By this definition, families living in campgrounds, motels, cars, and with other families are technically homeless. For families, the top three causes of homelessness are lack of affordable housing, poverty, and unemployment, according to the U.S. Conference of Mayors' 2008 Hunger and Homelessness Survey.

The odds are greater than ever that teachers will have highly mobile or homeless students in their classrooms. Educators can help by recognizing the indicators of such living situations and understanding students' legal rights and educational needs. Developing a plan to quickly and properly assess students, help them transition into a new school, and meet their basic needs will allow teachers to provide stability for students who may bounce from school to school as they move among temporary residences.

Understanding Students' Legal Rights

The homeless population is usually highly mobile. In such situations, school may be the only stabilizing influence in the life of a homeless child. Legislation is in place to help keep children in their schools of origin, if it is in their best interest, or to help them transition to another school.

Homeless children have certain legal rights under the McKinney-Vento Homelessness Assistance Act that was signed into law by President Ronald Reagan in 1987 and reauthorized as part of the No Child Left Behind Act in 2002. The act requires that state and local educational agencies provide homeless students with access to school, despite their housing situation.

The 2008 report *The Economic Crisis Hits Home: The Unfolding Increase in Child and Youth Homelessness,* from the National Association for the Education of Homeless Children and Youth (NAEHCY) and First Focus, identifies the key provisions of the act:

- Homeless students may remain in their school of origin, even if they are living temporarily in another district.
- Schools must provide transportation for these students to their school of origin.
- Children and youth who are homeless can enroll in school and begin attending immediately, even without normally required documents.

The act also requires every school district to designate a homeless liaison to ensure the act is implemented in the district. If an educator suspects that a student does not have a permanent home, he should contact the district liaison and check the National Center for Homeless Education (NCHE) at the SERVE Center's website for a list of state and local resources.

"Classroom teachers share the responsibility for ensuring that homeless children are identified," says Barbara Duffield, policy director for NAEHCY. "District liaisons can do sensitive, discreet inquiries into the family living situation and offer help."

Identifying and Helping Homeless Students

Some key characteristics indicate that a child in your classroom may be homeless or experiencing the effects of adverse economic circumstances, says Karen Fessler, director of Project Connect and liaison for homeless students for the Cincinnati (Ohio) Public Schools:

- **Physical:** fatigue, poor health and nutrition, poor personal hygiene, wears same clothes day after day, frequent respiratory ailments and asthma
- **Behavioral:** very possessive of belongings, secretive, unable to give home address, hoards food
- **Cognitive:** poor organizational skills, inability to conceptualize
- **Academic:** indications of lack of continuity in education; incomplete or missing records and transcripts; incomplete

or missing assignments; lack of materials and supplies; poor attendance; missed parental deadlines for permission forms, etc.; parents difficult to contact

These signs, especially multiple ones with one child, can indicate homelessness, Fessler says.

If you think a student is homeless, be sure to alert administrators and the district liaison, says Fessler. "We do not want teachers feeling pressured to confront children or families, and in fact we don't want to 'confront' anyone," explains Fessler. "When a teacher expresses concerns to me about a student, I contact the parents or family members, offering empathy and support. I offer to help them find solutions in a cooperative way."

The district's homeless liaison can ensure that the student is getting the services and support guaranteed by the law. The McKinney-Vento Act is an unfunded mandate, which means that available services will differ by district. The law is intentionally vague; the job of districts and liaisons is to "remove barriers to education" that homelessness causes.

Fessler describes Cincinnati's program for homeless students as "full-service." She can provide students with back-packs full of school supplies, uniform vouchers, adequate shoes, and winter coats if necessary.

As a teacher, you can ensure the child's needs are being met by helping enroll the child in free meal programs, provide classroom materials and supplies, plug him into extended-day programs, refer him for supplemental instructional support—whatever you can do to make sure the child feels safe and has adequate nutrition and ample time and space to complete classwork.

Creating a Welcoming Classroom

According to *The Economic Crisis Hits Home,* homeless children are 1.5 times more likely to perform below grade level in reading and spelling and 2.5 times more likely to perform below grade level in math.

And these adverse effects can snowball, according to Diana Bowman, director of the NCHE. "Every time a child changes schools, he or she can get several months behind. Only a few moves equal a whole grade."

If you learn in advance that you will be gaining a homeless or highly mobile student in your classroom, you can do many things to make his or her transition smoother, according to the NCHE. The organization's tip sheet for teachers lists these suggestions:

- Prepare a list of your class routines and procedures.
- Prepare a new student file with information for parents and guardians.
- Maintain a supply of materials for students to use at school.
- Prepare a "getting to know you" activity for the class to do on the first day.
- Post the class schedule in a visible place.

The next step is to assess the student for proper placement. It can be difficult to assess these students, particularly if the family has been highly mobile for some time and many or all transcripts and records are unavailable.

Develop an arsenal of quick, easy assessments and drills you can administer to discover where students are academically. On its website, NCHE provides a useful issue brief, *Prompt and Proper Placement: Enrolling Students Without Records,* for free download. The publication includes information-gathering techniques, questions to ask students and parents, affordable assessment instruments, and links to computer-based assessment tools.

Talk with new students about what they studied at their last school, and attempt to find out what texts they were using. If you discover learning gaps, use your creativity to close them. Assign special projects that will help the student catch up, or if the student is old enough, find out whether you can grant academic credit for a paying job or other activities. Many states have online courses that qualify for academic credit; find some that might help students close the gap. "Remember that many students do not have an environment conducive to doing homework," Bowman says. Allow homeless students to work in your classroom before or after class; help them gain access to a computer or study carrel in the library. "That student may only be in your classroom for a day, a week, or a month," says Bowman. "It's important to be very targeted about the most important things to accomplish, and to make every day productive."

Be sensitive in your curriculum and assignments as well, urges Fessler. Remember that not all families have the funds for optional field trips or supplies for large, home-based projects. You can also work with your district liaison to find out whether Title I funds might cover field trip fees and educational enrichment.

"It's important that teachers be aware of the needs of these students and that we support, understand, and encourage them," says John McLaughlin, federal coordinator for education of homeless children and youth programs for the U.S. Department of Education. McLaughlin was once a state coordinator, and he remembers a helpful job aid distributed by social workers in the Minneapolis Public Schools. The resource reminded educators that new students need "a warm welcome, the basics of life, a buddy, flexibility, and high expectations."

By greeting children in transitional living situations with affection and optimism and helping them get their basic needs met, educators can help set them on the path to stability and educational success.

Additional Resources

Campaign to End Child Homelessness:
www.homelesschildrenamerica.org

McKinney-Vento Act: www.hud.gov/offices/cpd/homeless/lawsandregs/mckv.cfm

National Association for the Education of Homeless Children and Youth: www.naehcy.org

National Center on Family Homelessness:
www.familyhomelessness.org

National Center for Homeless Education at the SERVE Center: www.serve.org/nche

Critical Thinking

1. Choose one of the additional resources websites listed at the end of the article and spend 15 minutes investigating the site. What services are available to assist teachers and families?

2. What are the key provisions of the McKinney-Vento Homelessness Assistance Act? Why are these so significant to require for each student?

Making Long-Term Separations Easier for Children and Families

Jenny, a teacher of young toddlers, notices that 18-month-old Kyle is very emotional this week. He cries and clings to his mother each morning, and Jenny has to hold him for quite a while after his mom leaves. Jenny sees that Kyle is eating less than normal, but he will let her spoon-feed him his lunch. Kyle's mom mentions that he is acting this way at home too. Since he has no fever or other symptom of illness, Jenny wonders if Kyle's mood change has to do with his dad leaving three weeks ago for a military deployment. Jenny decides she'll talk with Kyle's mom about this, and to see how she's coping as a "single parent."

AMY M. KIM AND JULIA YEARY

Jenny is very observant and tuned in to Kyle's emotional development. Often adult caregivers minimize or do not recognize the effects of long-term separation on young children. This may be due to a child's limited ability to express his discomfort or insecurity, coupled with the caregiver's assumption that the child is too young to be aware of his or her circumstances. Caregivers may attribute children's challenging behaviors or the return to previous developmental stages (such as wetting the bed after completing toilet training) to something other than a grief reaction to the separation from their parent.

The issues military families face when parents deploy, especially to combat zones, are quite complex; each family's circumstances, challenges, and stressors are unique.

In this article, we explore the importance of early attachments, the effects of separation on infants, toddlers, and 3-year-olds, and ways teachers can support children and families during separations. As difficult as a separation might be for an individual child and family, there are strategies to help them cope with this potentially challenging experience. The issues military families face when parents deploy, especially to combat zones, are quite complex; each family's circumstances, challenges, and stressors are unique. But all caregivers and teachers can learn from the methods used by military families who are very familiar with frequent extended parent-child separations.

Early childhood educators can explore the strategies that professionals supporting military families use to foster stronger parent-child relationships and, as appropriate, implement them in their own settings.

The Importance of Early Attachments

John Bowlby (1988) describes *attachment* as a lasting psychological connectedness between human beings. For young children, secure attachment develops when they know with certainty that a primary caregiver will respond to their emotional needs, such as by providing comfort or a calming presence if they are distressed or frightened, as well as their physical needs. Early relationships are critical, and the responsiveness of a parent is crucial to a child's healthy development. The benefits of a healthy attachment relationship may include the reduction of fear in challenging situations, an increase in self-efficacy, and the ability to build on skills to better manage stress (Shonkoff & Phillips 2000). These benefits extend into adulthood, supporting healthy adult relationships, the ability to maintain employment, and the capacity to care for one's own children (Edelstein et al. 2004; Onunaku 2005).

When a Caregiver Leaves

Bowlby, in referencing his work with researcher John Robertson, states that the effect of separation is considerable for the youngest children, who still rely on caregivers to help them regulate their emotions (Lieberman et al. 2003). Research shows that children who experience a prolonged separation may exhibit anxiety, withdrawal, hyper-vigilance, eating disorders, and possibly anger and aggression (Parke & Clarke-Stewart 2001). Young children may also have trouble sleeping, become clingy or withdrawn, and regress (for example, have a lapse in toilet learning).

It is important to remember that separation is not just a one-time event, but rather something experienced before, during, and after a departure.

It is important to remember that separation is not just a one-time event, but rather something experienced before, during, and after a departure. Often, the effects of separation continue after the reunion. One teacher offers an example from her classroom:

Three-year-old Bailey had previously experienced separation when her father was deployed to Iraq for six months. For the first couple of weeks after his return, she continually asked, "Who will pick me up today?" Bailey also had difficulty at nap times, often waking up, looking for a teacher, and then closing her eyes as soon as she spotted one. Later, teachers learned that Bailey was afraid that her father would leave again while she was at school, without her knowing.

Offering Parents Support Impacts Family Resiliency

By understanding what military families do to foster resiliency in their children, caregivers and teachers can provide better support and information to the families of young children experiencing a lengthy separation from a parent. There are numerous factors that predict the level of resiliency a family coping with long-term separations will show. However, military families who use active coping styles, receive social and community support, are optimistic and self-reliant, and give meaning to the separation are shown to function more effectively than those who don't (APA 2007).

An active coping style can be as simple as the family planning to have a neighbor watch the children one afternoon a week so the caregiver at home can run errands. A family that participates in a neighborhood play group or attends family activities at their church is receiving support from their community. A parent who believes that he or she can get through the separation and that there will be support if problems arise is self-reliant and optimistic. The military family who feels their service member is deployed to help others or to defend the country is giving meaning to the separation. Adopting these attitudes or following similar actions will foster resiliency in a family, a key to successfully meeting the challenge of separation.

Understanding the Emotional Cycle of Long-term Separation

Pincus and colleagues (2005) developed the Emotional Cycle of Deployment as a model to explain the emotional responses many military families experience during a deployment. While every family will not react to separation in exactly the same way, there are some predictable stages. This model can offer insights into the emotions nonmilitary families may experience when one parent leaves for an extended period of time.

The first stage begins when the family is notified of the deployment. During this stage, families enter a period of anticipatory grief. Though the separation hasn't yet taken place, the thought of the separation can begin the grieving process. Anticipatory grief has been defined as a feeling of loss before a dreaded event occurs (Hodgson 2005). Symptoms can include denial, mood swings, forgetfulness, disorganized and confused behavior, anger, depression, and feeling disconnected and alone. Physical symptoms such as weight loss or gain, sleep problems, nervous behavior, and general fatigue may also be present. At this stage, families are working to strengthen their bonds while letting go at the same time.

The second stage occurs when the individual leaves. During this phase, family members left at home may go through a period of grief or mourning. They may have periods of tearfulness and experience a change in their appetite and sleep patterns. These depression-like symptoms are typical, and they usually lessen after two to four weeks. In some cases, the remaining family members may experience relief at the departure of the military member. This also is a typical reaction, as families have dealt with many of their emotions prior to the departure and are ready to move to the next stage.

About a month after departure, the family typically settles into the third stage: a new family routine that usually lasts until just before the absent parent returns home. Adults and children typically do best if the newly established family routine is similar to what they did prior to separation. Families who take advantage of neighborhood and community support systems report fewer difficulties during a separation.

The fourth stage occurs about four to six weeks prior to reunion, when the family begins anticipating the return of the absent family member. For many families, this reunion stage is more stressful than the other stages (National Military Family Association 2005). Not knowing how each partner in the relationship has changed, how those changes will be accepted, and how children will accept the returning family member can raise many questions and anxieties.

Upon the return of the member who has been away, the family enters the fifth stage, when they must renegotiate the family roles and reestablish their relationships. This stage may begin with a happy, almost honeymoon-like period but can turn stressful quickly if family members do not recognize the need to communicate and work together. Professionals working with military families identify this stage as one of great concern. This time of disequilibrium may contribute to heightened risks for child or spouse abuse due to the increased stress.

Ongoing Communication

Communication is one of the primary concerns of military families coping with family separation (National Military Family Association 2005), and it is the most important aid in minimizing negative effects during every stage experienced during the separation. Communication is important not only between the adults, but also with children (in developmentally appropriate ways). Parents and teachers can help by offering children words for the emotions they might be experiencing. Providing the child with needed vocabulary and simple, factual information will help them begin to make sense of the situation and will make them feel like what they are experiencing is validated (Parke & Clarke-Stewart 2001).

Working to Stay Connected: Co-parenting Alliance

Families who cope successfully with frequent separations are likely to work together as partners in raising their children. Such parents are likely to communicate regularly, using letters, e-mail, or phone calls to discuss *all* aspects of raising their child. One mother shared as much information as possible, so the father, who was in Iraq, was able to ask their 3-year-old son specific questions about his child care friends and activities. Another father, who had been away for 17 months, found resuming his role as father in the home was a great deal easier because he knew about his children's daily routine and accomplishments while he was away.

Military parents demonstrate this co-parenting alliance by working hard to keep the child and absent parent connected. Rather than simply letting an absence take its course, they work to keep the absent parent in the child's mind through a variety of interactive means, and include that parent in all major decisions regarding the child. A teacher can support families experiencing separation. For example, after sharing that a couple's 19-month-old daughter was biting other children in the class and displaying aggressive behaviors, her teacher arranged for her father, in Korea on military assignment, to participate in the parent-teacher conference via Webcam so everyone could strategize together about how to help the toddler learn more appropriate ways to express her frustration and cope with her strong feelings.

For the Classroom

Teachers of young children play an important role in supporting the strong connections between families and children. The strength of these connections begins with the teacher being aware of the circumstances of the children in the classroom and their families.

Support the at-home parent. Simply taking a moment to ask a parent how he or she is doing will help strengthen connections between the parent, caregiver, and child. It is difficult to parent without the support of a second adult in the home.

Simply taking a moment to ask a parent how he or she is doing will help strengthen connections between the parent, caregiver, and child.

It is important that program directors and teachers know of community resources that can provide needed services. Mental health and financial concerns are two issues that may surface when a parent is faced with the long-term absence of his or her partner. It is helpful to have information or resources to discreetly give to parents should the need arise. These positive interactions may encourage parents to reach out to other agencies for assistance.

Maintain a consistent program environment. Although some change is inevitable, try to keep the classroom setting as consistent as possible, including maintaining a predictable daily routine. You may want to reconsider the timing of moving a child to a new class. Provide opportunities for a child to feel more in control of daily activities to help her feel more secure. Be aware of children's need to make choices whenever possible. For example, ask a child if he would like juice or water with his meal, or ask which center he would like to play in first.

Be aware of stages of child development. Separation anxiety is a normal part of development for infants and toddlers. Having a parent leave for an extended period of time adds another layer to the challenge of learning to separate from a parent. Children experiencing long separations from their parent are best supported in an environment that honors their need to stay connected to their parent.

Include parent-child photos. Place pictures of family members at children's eye level to help them feel closer to their parents, no matter the length of a separation. Teachers can have parents help create special memory books with laminated pictures for toddlers and young preschoolers to carry with them in the classroom.

Use video or audio tapes. Invite children's parents to create tape recordings of themselves singing or reading to their children. These tapes can bring the absent parent into the classroom while he or she is away. Such recordings help a child stay in touch with the parent and soothe the child when he or she is missing that parent. If video equipment is available, parents can record themselves playing with or reading to their children. Parents can take the videos home to watch with their child. Teachers can set up special viewing centers in the classroom. These ideas are extremely helpful to the child with an absent parent, but also are helpful for all young children as they learn to separate from their primary caregivers.

Use transitional objects. Transitional objects may help a child cope with strong feelings about a parent's absence. Programs can encourage parents to send their child's favorite cuddly toy to help the child feel more secure. These transitional objects, along with the voice recordings from parents, can be especially soothing for the older infant or young toddler.

To create a special transitional object for a young child, take a T-shirt the parent has worn and make it into a pillow. One mother made a pillow out of her nightgown because her young twins liked to feel the soft fabric while they rested. The scent of the parent adds an additional layer of comfort. Some military parents spray the pillow with the cologne or aftershave the absent parent uses to invoke memories of the parent for the child. Older infants and toddlers may hold onto the pillow and snuggle into it when they are missing their parent. (Note: Infants should not sleep with pillows.)

Teachers can establish a special place in the classroom for quiet reflection. Children can keep their transitional objects in that area and use them as needed.

Reinforce parent-child connections. Books can be a wonderful resource to connect a child with a caring adult. Some titles frequently used to emphasize the parent-child connection are *The Kissing Hand,* by Audrey Penn, *Owl Babies,* by Martine Waddell, and *Are You My Mother?* by P.D. Eastman. After reading books such as these, children can do follow-up activities. For example, after reading *The Kissing Hand* teachers can have young children trace their hands and place a kiss in the center to give to a parent. To extend this activity to home, ask parents to trace their hands and place a kiss in the palm. They can send the hands in with their children. This activity may also be done by a parent who is away.

If possible, mail items directly to the absent parent; this helps the parent know you are remembering to include him or her in the collaborative team caring for the child.

Review communication strategies. Ask yourself, "How can I share information with parents who are away?" Consider incorporating technology such as e-mail or Webcams to allow for conferences. Have the child make two different creations during a project; one to take home and one for the parent who is away. Teachers can make two copies of classroom reports or communications, so one can be mailed to the absent parent. If possible, mail items directly to the absent parent; this helps the

---

For More Resources on Separation

Many parents want to learn more ways to support their child through a period of separation and how to keep parent-child connections strong. The ZERO TO THREE website (www.zerotothree.org) has information to support families of young children and the professionals who work with them. Information specific to helping families cope with parental separation can be found in the Military Families section, under Key Topics. Links to organizations that support military families, including counseling and resource information, can also be found there.

---

parent know you are remembering to include him or her in the collaborative team caring for the child.

Conclusion

As a teacher or caregiver, you play a very important role in a young child's life while a parent is away. You serve as a valuable resource by supporting the parent at home and helping to foster the relationship between the away parent and the child. Incorporating a few strategies may help families to develop coping skills, build resiliency, and maintain important relationships crucial to the well-being of children and families.

References

APA (American Psychological Association). 2007. *The psychological needs of U.S. military service members and their families: A preliminary report.* www.apa.org/releases/MilitaryDeploymentTaskForceReport.pdf

Bowlby, J. 1988. *A secure base: Parent-child attachment and healthy human development.* New York: Basic Books.

Edelstein, R.S., K.W. Alexander, P.R. Shaver, J.M. Schaaf, J.A. Quas, G.S. Lovas, & G.S. Goodman. 2004. Adult attachment style and parental responsiveness during a stressful event. *Attachment and Human Development* 6(1): 31–52.

Hodgson, H. 2005. Anticipatory grief symptoms: What's the big deal? www.americanhospice.org/index.php?option=com_content&task=view&id=80&Itemid=13

Lieberman, A.F., N.C. Compton, P. Van Horn, & C.G. Ippen. 2003. *Losing a parent to death in the early years: Guidelines for the treatment of traumatic bereavement in infancy and early childhood.* Washington, DC: ZERO TO THREE Press.

National Military Family Association. 2005. *Report on the Cycles of Deployment Survey: An analysis of survey responses from April through September, 2005.* www.nmfa.org/site/DocServer/NMFACyclesofDeployment9.pdf?docID=5401

Onunaku, N. 2005. *Improving maternal and infant mental health: Focus on maternal depression.* Los Angeles, CA: National Center for Infant and Early Childhood Health Policy at UCLA. www.healthychild.ucla.edu/Publications/Maternal%20Depression%20Report%20Final.pdf

Parke, R., & K.A. Clarke-Stewart. 2001. Effects of parental incarceration on young children. Presented at the National Policy Conference: From Prison to Home: The Effect of Incarceration and Reentry on Children, Families, and Communities, Washington, DC, January 2002. http://aspe.hhs.gov/HSP/prison2home02/parke&stewart.pdf

Pincus, S.H., R. House, J. Christenson, & L.E. Adler. 2005. *The emotional cycle of deployment: A military family perspective.* www.hooah4health.com/deployment/Familymatters/emotionalcycle.htm

Shonkoff, J., & D. Phillips, eds. 2000. *From neurons to neighborhoods: The science of early childhood development.* Washington, DC: National Academy Press.

Critical Thinking

1. Describe three ways you can keep parents up to date with what their children are doing in your class while the parents are living away from their children.

2. Describe the four stages of the emotional cycle during long-term separation.

AMY M. KIM, MEd, is a training and consultation specialist for military projects at ZERO TO THREE, the National Center for Infants, Toddlers, and Families. Amy works on material development and trainings for military professionals and families. akim@zerotothree.org. **JULIA YEARY,** LCSW, is a senior training and consultation specialist with military projects at ZERO TO THREE, the National Center for Infants, Toddlers, and Families. Julia has worked extensively with military families; she is also a military spouse and mother. jyeary@zerotothree.org.

Keys to Quality Infant Care
Nurturing Every Baby's Life Journey

Teachers of infants need a large bunch of key ideas and activities of all kinds to unlock in each child the treasures of loving kindness, thoughtful and eloquent use of language, intense active curiosity to learn, willingness to cooperate, and the deep desire to work hard to master new tasks. Here are some ideas that teachers can use during interactions with infants to optimize each child's development.

Get to Know Each Baby's Unique Personality

At 4 months, Luci holds her hands in front of her face and turns them back and forth so she can see the curious visual difference between the palms and backs. Jackson, an 8-month-old, bounces happily in accurate rhythm as his teacher bangs on a drum and chants, "Mary had a little lamb whose fleece was white as snow!" Outdoors, 1-year-old Jamie sits in an infant swing peering down at his feet sticking out of the leg holes. How interesting! Those are the same feet he has watched waving in the air while being diapered and has triumphantly brought to his mouth to chew on.

Teachers can tune in to each child's special personality—especially the child's temperament. There are three primary, mostly inborn, styles of temperament (Honig 1997). Some babies are more low-key; they tend to be slow to warm up to new caregivers, new foods, and new surroundings. They need reassuring hand-holding and more physical supports to try a new activity. Others are more feisty and sometimes irritable. They tend to be impetuous, intense in their emotional reactions, whether of anger or of joy. Easygoing babies are typically friendly, happy, accept new foods and caregivers without much fuss, and adapt fairly quickly and more flexibly after experiencing distress or sudden change. Try to find out whether each baby in your care tends to be shy and slow to warm up *or* mostly feisty and intense *or* easygoing. A caring adult's perceptive responses in tune with individual temperament will ease a child's ability to adapt and flourish in the group setting.

Physical Loving

Your body is a safe haven for an infant. Indeed, some babies will stay happy as a clam when draped over a shoulder, across your belly as you rock in a rocking chair, or, especially for a very young baby, snuggled in a sling or carrier for hours. As Montagu (1971) taught decades ago, babies need *body loving:* "To be tender, loving, and caring, human beings must be tenderly loved and cared for in their earliest years. . . . caressed, cuddled, and comforted" (p. 138).

As you carry them, some babies might pinch your neck, lick your salty arm, pull at your hair, tug at eyeglasses, or show you in other ways how powerfully important your body is as a sacred and special playground. Teach gentleness by calmly telling a baby you need your glasses on to read a story. Use the word *gently* over and over and over. Dance cheek-to-cheek with a young child in arms to slow waltz music—good for dreary days! Also carry the baby while you do a routine task such as walking to another room to get something.

Provide lap and touch times generously to nourish a child's sense of well-being. Slowly caress a baby's hair. Rub a tense shoulder soothingly. Kiss one finger and watch as a baby offers every other finger to kiss. Rock a child with your arms wrapped around him for secure comfort. Babies learn to become independent as we confirm and meet their dependency needs in infancy. A sense of well-being and somatic certainty flows from cherishing adults who generously hold, caress, and drape babies on shoulders and tummies.

Create Intimate Emotional Connections

Scan the environment so you can be close to every baby. Notice the quiet baby sitting alone, mouthing a toy piece and rocking back and forth with vacant eyes. Notice shy bids for attention, such as a brief smile with lowered lids. The child with an easy or cautious temperament needs your loving attention as much as the one who impulsively climbs all over you for attention.

A caring adult's perceptive responses in tune with individual temperament will ease a child's ability to adapt and flourish in the group setting.

Shine admiring eyes at the children, whether a baby is cooing as she lies in her crib, creeping purposefully toward a toy she desires, or feeding herself happily with messy fingers. Speak each child's name lovingly and frequently. Even if they are fussing, most babies will quiet when you chant and croon their names.

Although babies do not understand the meanings of the words, they do understand *tonal* nuances and love when your voice sounds admiring, enchanted with them, and happy to be talking with them. While diapering, tell the baby he is so delicious and you love his plump tummy and the few wispy hairs on that little head. Watch him thrust out his legs in delight on the diapering table. Your tone of voice entrances him into a deep sense of pleasure with his own body (Honig 2002).

Harmonizing Tempos

Tempo is important in human activities and is reflected in how abruptly or smoothly adults carry out daily routines. Because adults have so many tasks to do, sometimes we use impatient, too-quick motions, for example, while dressing a baby to play outdoors. When dressing or feeding, more leisurely actions are calming. They signal to children that we have time for them. Rub backs slowly and croon babies into soothing sleep.

A baby busily crawling across the rug sees a toy, grasps it, then plops himself into a sitting position to examine and try to pull it apart. He slowly looks back and forth at the toy as he leisurely passes it from hand to hand. He has no awareness that a teacher is about to interrupt because she is in a hurry to get him dressed because his daddy is coming to pick him up. Young children need time and cheerful supports to finish up an activity in which they are absorbed. If they are hurried, they may get frustrated and even have a tantrum.

Enhance Courage and Cooperation

Your presence can reassure a worried baby. Stay near and talk gently to help a child overcome his fear of the small infant slide. Pascal sits at the top, looking uncertain. Then he checks your face for a go-ahead signal, for reassurance that he can bravely try to slide down this slide that looks so long to him. Kneeling at the bottom of the slide, smile and tell him that you will be there to catch him when he is ready to slide down.

Be available as a "refueling station"—Margaret Mahler's felicitous term (Kaplan 1978). Sometimes a baby's independent learning adventure comes crashing down—literally. Your body and your lap provide the emotional support from which a baby regains courage to tackle the learning adventure again.

Create loving rituals during daily routines of dressing, bath times, nap times, feeding times. Babies like to know what will happen and when and where and how. Babies have been known to refuse lunch when their familiar, comfortable routines were changed. At cleanup times, older babies can be more flexible and helpful if you change some chores into games. Through the use of sing-song chants, putting toys away becomes an adventure in finding the big fat blocks that need to be placed together on a shelf and then the skinny blocks that go together in a different place.

Young children need time and cheerful supports to finish up an activity in which they are absorbed. If they are hurried, they may get frustrated and even have a tantrum.

Address Stress

Attachment research shows that babies who develop secure emotional relationships with a teacher have had their distress signals noticed, interpreted correctly, and responded to promptly and appropriately (Honig 2002). At morning arrival times, watch for separation anxiety. Sometimes holding and wordlessly commiserating with a baby's sad feelings can help more than a frenzied attempt to distract her (Klein, Kraft, & Shohet 2010). As you become more expert at interpreting a baby's body signals of distress and discomfort, you will become more sensitively attuned in your responses (Honig 2010).

Learn Developmental Milestones

Learning developmental norms helps teachers figure out when to wonder, when to worry, and when to relish and feel overjoyed about a child's milestone accomplishments. Day and night toilet learning can be completed anywhere from 18 months to 5 years. This is a *wide* time window for development. In contrast, learning to pick up a piece of cereal from a high chair tray with just thumb and forefinger in a fine pincer grasp is usually completed during a *narrow* time window well before 13 months. By 11 months, most babies become expert at using just the first two fingers.

Hone Your Detective Skills

If a baby is screaming and jerking knees up to his belly, you might suspect a painful gas bubble. Pick up the baby and jiggle and thump his back until you get that burp up. What a relief, for you as well as baby. Maybe an irritable, yowling baby just needs to be tucked in quietly and smoothly for a nap after an expert diaper change. Suppose baby is crying and thrashing about, and yet he has been burped and diapered. Use all your detective skills to determine the cause. Is it a hot day? He might be thirsty. A drink of water can help him calm down.

Notice Stress Signs

Scan a child's body for stress signs. Dull eyes can signal the need for more intimate loving interactions. Tense shoulders and a grave look often mean that a child is afraid or worried (Honig 2010). Compulsive rocking can mean a baby feels forlorn. Watch for lonesomeness and wilting.

Some babies melt down toward day's end. They need to be held and snuggled. Murmur sweet reassurances and provide a small snack of strained applesauce to soothe baby's taste buds and worries. Check his body from top to bottom for signs of stresses or tensions, such as eyes avoiding contact, teeth grinding, fingernail chewing, frequently clenched fists, so that you can develop an effective plan for soothing. Be alert, and tend to children's worrisome bodily signs; these will tell you what you need to know long before children have enough language to share what was stressful (Honig 2009).

Play Learning Games

Parents and teachers are a baby's preferred playmates. While playing learning games with infants, pay attention to their actions. Ask yourself if the game has become so familiar and easy that it is time to "dance up the developmental ladder" (Honig 1982) and increase the game's challenge. Or perhaps the game is still too baffling and you need to "dance down" and simplify the activity so that the child can succeed.

Provide safe mirrors at floor level and behind the diapering table so children can watch and learn about their own bodies. Hold babies in arms up to a mirror to reach out and pat the face in the mirror. Lying on the floor in front of a securely attached safety mirror, a young child twists and squirms to get an idea of where his body begins and ends.

Your body can serve as a comforting support for some early learning activities. Sit an infant on your lap and watch as he coordinates vision and grasp to reach and hold a toy you are dangling. Babies love "Peek-a-boo! I see you!" These games nurture the development of object permanence—the understanding that objects still exist even when they are out of sight. Peek-a-boo games also symbolically teach that even when a special adult is not seen, that dear person will reappear.

Provide Physical Play Experiences

Play pat-a-cake with babies starting even before 6 months. As you gently hold a baby's hands and bring them out and then back together, chant slowly and joyously, "Pat-a-cake, pat-a-cake, baker's man; bake me a cake just as fast as you can. Pat it, and roll it, and mark it with a *B,* and put it in the oven for [baby's name] and me." Smile with joy as you guide the baby's hands rhythmically and slowly through the game, and use a high-pitched voice as you emphasize her name in the sing-song chant. Over the next months, as soon as you begin chanting the words, the baby will begin to bring hands to the midline and do the hand motions that belong with this game. Babies who are 9 to 11 months old will even start copying the hand-rolling motions that belong with this game.

To encourage learning, try to arrange games with more physical actions. Sit on the floor with your toes touching the baby's toes, then model how to roll a ball back and forth.

Introduce Sensory Experiences

Safe sensory and tactile experiences are ideal for this age group. As he shifts a toy from hand to hand, turns it over, pokes, tastes, bangs, and even chews on it, a baby uses his senses to learn about the toy's physical properties. Teachers can blow bubbles so babies can reach for and crawl after them. Provide play-dough made with plenty of salt to discourage children from putting it in their mouths. Older babies enjoy exploring finger paints or nontoxic tempera paint and fat brushes.

Play Sociable Games

Give something appealing to a seated baby. Put out your hand, smile, and say "Give it to me, please." The baby may chew on the "gift," such as a safe wooden block or chunky plastic cylinder peg. After the baby passes it to you, say thank you, then give the object back with a smile. Give-and-take games with you are a sociable pleasure for babies and teach them turn-taking skills that are crucial for friendly social interchanges years later.

Seated on a chair, play a bouncing game, with the baby's back resting snuggly against your tummy. After you stop bouncing and chanting "Giddyup, horsie," a baby often bounces on his or her tush as if to remind you to start this game over and over. An older baby vigorously demands "More horsie!" to get you to restart this game. Babies enjoy kinesthetic stimulation too, such as when you swing them gently in a baby swing. A baby will grin with glee as you pull or push him in a wagon around the room or playground.

Observe Babies' Ways of Exploring and Learning

Observe a baby to learn what and how she is learning, then adapt the activity to offer greater challenge. Observation provides information that lets teachers determine when and how to arrange for the next step in a child's learning experience. Watch quietly as a baby tries with determination to put the round wood top piece for a ring stack set on the pole. His eyes widen in startled amazement as he gradually realizes that when the hole does not go through the middle, then that piece will not go down over the pole—a frustrating but important lesson. Calmly, a teacher can demonstrate how to place the piece on top of the pole while using simple words to describe how this piece is different. She can also gently guide the baby's hands so he feels successful at placing the piece on top.

Enhance Language and Literacy in Everyday Routines

Talk back and forth with babies; respond to their coos and babbles with positive talk. When the baby vocalizes, tell her, "What a terrific talker you are. Tell me some more."

The diapering table is a fine site for language games. With young babies, practice "parentese"—a high-pitched voice, drawn-out vowels, and slow and simple talk. This kind of talk fires up the brain neurons that carry messages to help a baby learn (Doidge 2007). Cascades of chemicals and electrical signals course down the baby's neural pathways. A baby responds when you are an attentive and delighted talking partner. Pause so the baby gets a turn to talk too, and bring the game to a graceful close when baby fatigue sets in.

Talk about body parts on dolls, stuffed animals, yourself, and the babies in the room. Talk about what the baby sees as you lift her onto your lap and then onto your shoulders. Talk at mealtimes. Use every daily routine as an opportunity to enhance oral language (Honig 2007).

Daily reading is an intimate one-on-one activity that young babies deeply enjoy in varied spaces and at varied times of the day (Honig 2004). Hook your babies on books as early as possible. Frequent shared picture-book experiences are priceless gifts. Early pleasurable reading experiences empower success in learning to read years later in grade school (Jalongo 2007).

Cuddle with one or several children as you read and share books together every day. Use dramatic tones along with loving and polite words. You are the master of the story as you read aloud. Feel free to add to or to shorten picture-book text according to a particular child's needs. Group reading times can be pleasurable when infants lean against you as you sit on the rug and share a picture book. Teachers often prefer the intimacy of individual reading times with babies (Honig & Shin 2001). Individual reading can help a tense or fussy baby relax in your lap as he becomes deeply absorbed in sharing the picture-book experience.

Encourage Mastery Experiences

Children master many linguistic, physical, and social skills in the first years of life. Watch the joy of mastery and self-appreciation as a baby succeeds at a task, such as successfully placing Montessori cylinders into their respective sockets. Babies enjoy clapping for their own efforts. Mastery experiences arranged in thoughtful doses bring much pleasure, such an eagerness to keep on exploring, trying, and learning. Watch the baby's joy as he proudly takes a long link chain out of a coffee can and then stuffs it slowly back in the can. He straightens his shoulders with such pride as he succeeds at this game of finding a way to put a long skinny chain into a round container with a small diameter opening.

Mastery experiences arranged in thoughtful doses bring much pleasure, such an eagerness to keep on exploring, trying, and learning.

Vygotsky taught that the *zone of proximal development* is crucial for adult-child coordination in learning activities. You the teacher are so important in helping a child to succeed when a task may be slightly too difficult for the child to solve alone. Hold the baby's elbow steady when she feels frustrated while trying to stack one block on top of another. For a difficult puppy puzzle, a teacher taped down a few of the pieces so a baby could succeed in getting the puppy's tail and head pieces in the right spaces. If a baby has been struggling with a slippery nesting cup for a while, just steady the stack of cups so he can successfully insert a smaller cup into the next largest one.

Promote Socioemotional Skills

Babies learn empathy and friendliness from those who nurture them. Empathy involves recognizing and feeling the distress of another and trying to help in some way. A young baby who sees another baby crying may look worried and suck his thumb to comfort himself. Fifteen-month-old Michael tussles over a toy with Paul, who starts to cry. Michael looks worried and lets go of the toy so Paul has it. As Paul keeps crying, Michael gives him his own teddy bear. But Paul continues crying. Michael pauses, then runs to the next room and gets Paul's security blanket for him. And Paul stops crying (Blum 1987).

When teachers showed deeply respectful caregiving, then they observed that babies did develop early empathy and internalize the friendly interactions they had experienced.

Friendliness includes making accommodations so children can play together. For example, move a child over to make room for a peer, or make overtures to invite other babies to engage in peer play. Perhaps they could take turns toddling in and out of a cardboard house. Babies act friendly when they sit near each other and companionably play with toys, happy to be close together. McMullen and colleagues (2009) observed that positive social-emotional interactions were rare in some infant rooms. But when teachers showed deeply respectful caregiving, then they observed that babies did develop early empathy and internalize the friendly interactions they had experienced. One teacher is described below:

> Her wonderful gentle manner, the way she speaks to the babies, how they are all her friends . . . only someone who utterly respects and values babies could put that kind of effort into this the way she does, almost like she is setting a beautiful table for honored guests each and every morning. (McMullen et al. 2009, p. 27)

Conclusion

Later in life, a baby will not remember your specific innumerable kindly caring actions in the earliest years. However, a child's *feelings* of being lovable and cherished will remain a body-memory for life. These feelings of having been loved will permeate positive emotional and social relationships decades later.

Keep your own joy pipes open. How brief are the years of babyhood. All too soon young children grow into the mysterious world of teenagers who prefer hanging out with peers to snuggling on an adult lap. Reflect with deep personal satisfaction on your confidence and delight in caring for tiny ones—hearing the first words, seeing the joy at a new accomplishment, watching the entranced look of an upturned face as you tell a story, feeling the trust as a baby sleepily settles onto your lap for refreshment of spirit, for a breath of the loving comfort that emanates from your body.

Life has grown more complicated in our technological, economically difficult, and more and more urbanized world. But you, the teacher, remain each baby's priceless tour guide into the world of "growing up!" You gently take each little person by the hand—literally and figuratively—and lure each and every baby into feeling the wonder and the somatic certainty of being loved, lovable, and cherished so that each baby can fully participate in the adventure of growing, loving, and learning.

Your nurturing strengthens a baby's determination to keep on learning, keep on cooperating, keep on being friendly, and keep on growing into a loving person—first in the world of the nursery and later in the wider world. You can give no greater gift to a child than to be the best guide possible as each child begins his or her unique life journey.

References

Blum, L. 1987. Particularity and responsiveness. In *The emergence of morality in young children,* eds. J. Kagan & S. Lamb, 306–37. Chicago: University of Chicago Press.

Doidge, N. 2007. *The brain that changes itself.* New York: Penguin.

Honig, A.S. 1982. *Playtime learning games for young children.* Syracuse, NY: Syracuse University Press.

Honig, A.S. 1997. Infant temperament and personality: What do we need to know? *Montessori Life* 9 (3): 18–21.

Honig, A.S. 2002. *Secure environments: Nurturing infant/toddler attachment in child care settings.* Washington, DC: NAEYC.

Honig, A.S. 2004. Twenty ways to boost your baby's brain power. *Scholastic Parent and Child* 11 (4): 55–56.

Honig, A.S. 2007. Oral language development. *Early Child Development and Care* 177 (6): 581–613.

Honig, A.S. 2009. Stress and young children. In *Informing our practice: Useful research on young children's development,* eds. E. Essa & M.M. Burnham, 71–88. Washington, DC: NAEYC.

Honig, A.S. 2010. *Little kids, big worries: Stress-busting tips for early childhood classrooms.* Baltimore: Brookes.

Honig, A.S., & M. Shin. 2001. Reading aloud to infants and toddlers in childcare settings: An observational study. *Early Childhood Education Journal* 28 (3): 193–97.

Jalongo, M.R. 2007. *Early childhood language arts.* 4th ed. New York: Pearson.

Kaplan, L. 1978. *Oneness and separateness: From infant to individual.* New York: Simon & Schuster.

Klein, P.S., R.R. Kraft, & C. Shohet. 2010. Behavior patterns in daily mother-child separations: Possible opportunites for stress reduction. *Early Child Development and Care* 180: 387–96.

McMullen, M.B., J.M. Addleman, A.M. Fulford, S. Moore, S.J. Mooney, S.S. Sisk, & J. Zachariah. 2009. Learning to be *me* while coming to understand *we.* Encouraging prosocial babies in group settings. *Young Children* 64 (4): 20–28. www.naeyc.org/files/yc/file/200907/McMullenWeb709.pdf

Montagu, A. 1971. *Touching: The human significance of the skin.* New York: Harper & Row.

Critical Thinking

1. Observe a parent or caregiver as they interact with an infant. Watch for one of the keys Dr. Honig discusses in her article. What did the adult do that made an impact on you and why?

2. Some of the key ideas are geared more to teachers than parents. Choose the ones that can be easily adapted to the home environment and develop a one page handout that could be given to families to assist them in the home as they nurture their baby on his or her life journey.

ALICE STERLING HONIG, PhD, is professor emerita of child development in the College of Human Ecology at Syracuse University, where she has taught the QIC (Quality Infant/Toddler Caregiving) Workshop for 34 years. She is the author or editor of more than two dozen books and more than 500 articles and chapters on early childhood. As a licensed New York State clinician, she works with children and families coping with a variety of troubles, such as divorce or learning difficulties. ahonig@syr.edu

---

From *Young Children,* Vol. 65, No. 5, September, 2010, pp. 40–47. Copyright © 2010 by National Association for the Education of Young Children. Reprinted by permission.

Gaga for Gadgets

Your little kid is clamoring to get her hands on your cell phone or iPad so she can play games—or learn her letters. Whether you want to embrace or escape our high-tech world, you can help your child find the right balance.

MARGERY D. ROSEN

Four-year-old Ian Rich and his 6-year-old brother, Jason, didn't watch TV (or use any screen media) until they were 2½. After all, their father is Michael Rich, MD, MPH, director of the Center on Media and Child Health at Children's Hospital Boston. He knows that scientific evidence has shown that very young children don't benefit from screen time. However, now that the boys are older, Dr. Rich, a *Parents* advisor, is letting them test-drive his high-tech devices, and he's impressed by how quickly they master them. Recently, Ian figured out how to take pictures on his dad's iPhone—including some of his mom getting out of the shower.

"At least he hasn't figured out how to upload them to the Internet," says Dr. Rich. "Yet."

Yup, it's 2011, when most preschoolers don't know how to tie their shoelaces but they can understand—as if by osmosis—how to use the latest electronic gadget. Although we know that it's essential for our kids to be able to navigate the byways of our wired world in order to excel at school and beyond, it's hard not to be stunned by how technology seems to have taken over our lives.

A study conducted by the Kaiser Family Foundation last year found that school-age kids spend an average of 7½ hours a day in front of a television, a computer, a smartphone, or another digital device. That's one hour and 17 minutes more than they did when the last study was done five years ago. The fact that most devices are mobile gives kids access in places they never had it before: on the school bus, in the doctor's waiting room, or on a drive to Grandma's. Although the Kaiser study involved 8- to 18-year-olds, anyone who has more than one child knows that little brothers and sisters not only follow in their older siblings' footsteps, they're barely a baby step behind.

"My girls are 12 and 4, and I'm astonished at how much more technology Elena, the younger one, has been exposed to," says Stephanie Deininger, of Redlands, California. "She's learning to read from websites like PBSkids.org and knows how to use a laptop, a DS, and an MP3 player nearly as well as her sister does. We set time limits, but there's no question that technology is the big draw and sometimes getting Elena to turn it off can be a battle."

Even babies may log an average of two hours of screen time per day, despite the fact that the American Academy of Pediatrics (AAP) recommends that children under the age of 2 have no screen time at all. Last fall, in fact, the AAP urged all pediatricians to start asking parents about their child's technology usage at every well visit. "Digital media are as much a part of kids' lives as the air they breathe," says Dr. Rich. Whether this is good or bad is a moot point now—the real challenge is figuring out how to help our children benefit from high-tech tools while still making sure that they are playing and learning in the tried-and-true ways.

Brave New World

We've seen an explosion of media targeted at those very same infants and toddlers who aren't supposed to be watching—including TV shows, DVDs, digital books, and a huge array of software and portable gaming platforms. But given the choice, kids prefer to use Mommy's or Daddy's devices. "When my 20-month-old son, Isaac, gets antsy in a restaurant, my phone is a lifesaver," says Tricia Callahan, of Dayton, Ohio. In fact, 60 percent of the top-selling apps on iTunes target young children, according to a 2009 analysis by the Joan Ganz Cooney Center at Sesame Workshop, which studies the role of digital technologies in childhood literacy. (*Parents* offers its own line of apps, including Flash Cards, which teach colors, shapes, letters, and math.)

Two-year-old Madeline Horwitz, of East Amherst, New York, is another early adopter. Having mastered the iPhone apps her parents downloaded for her by the time she was 1, she was ready to tap and swipe the day her dad, Jeremy, brought home an iPad. "We're a high-tech family; we see it as an investment in our kids' future," says Horwitz, a technology journalist. Madeline's favorite apps include Duck Duck Moose's Baa Baa Black Sheep, Fisher Price's Little People, Shape Builder, and Montessorium Intro to Math. Says Horwitz, "The iPad is unusual—it's fun, educational, and portable. And there's no mess to clean up afterward!"

Experts who are worried about how immersed kids have become in interactive media point to studies linking heavy screen time to obesity, difficulty paying attention, an inability to make real-world friends, dulled imagination, low academic performance, and increased aggression. More important, they argue, digital technology robs kids of the hands-on creative play that's so essential for development. However, other experts and parents applaud the fact that technology makes learning fun and engages kids in exploring and problem-solving. In one study, researchers in Massachusetts, Texas, and Pennsylvania followed children from preschool through adolescence and found that those who'd watched small amounts of educational TV as preschoolers placed more value on achievement, read more books, and had higher grades as teens than those who watched entertainment TV at the same age.

"For kids under 2, however, the jury's still out," says Ellen Wartella, PhD, professor of communication and psychology at Northwestern University, in Evanston, Illinois. Most research has focused on the effects of TV and computer programs on kids preschool-age and up—and apps are just starting to be studied. A child may learn a letter that he sees on a phone app, much like he traces a letter on paper, says Dr. Wartella. "But we don't know yet if young kids learn anything from electronic media that they wouldn't learn otherwise, or what the long-term consequences are."

Content Counts

"Technology itself doesn't create problems," says Dr. Rich. "What matters is what we do with it." Just as you monitor the foods your kids eat, you should introduce quality media when they're ready, help them think about what they see and hear, and make sure they're not sacrificing time for homework, physical activity, family, or friends.

Especially when your kids are young, it's best to play or watch with them and discuss what they see. Sarah Kimmel, of Lehi, Utah, is a fan of "lapware," software designed for babies sitting in your lap. "Giggles Computer Funtime for Babies is simple and fun," she says. "We practice shapes, colors, letters, numbers." Giggles also gets a thumbs-up from educational psychologist Warren Buckleitner, editor of *Children's Technology Review,* which helps teachers, librarians, and parents find quality technology products for children. "It's something joyful that parents can do with their kids."

Research underscores the importance of one-on-one time for learning. A 2010 study, for example, found that when kids were read to by a parent—as opposed to watching a video in which a person read to them—the part of their brain that involves emotions and problem-solving lit up. "However, if you use technology with your child, he'll learn that it can be a collaborative tool," says Dr. Wartella. "You can nudge him along by stopping a video or a game and asking, 'What do you think will happen next?' or pointing out and labeling objects on the screen."

What makes a computer program, an app, or a TV show educational can be summed up in one word: content. "A well-designed program can improve literacy or math skills and boost

Take-Charge Rules

Only three out of ten kids ages 8 to 18 say that their parents set limits on their media use and stick to them, according to the Kaiser Family Foundation study. It's easier to establish boundaries when your child is 2 than 12, so take these steps now.

1. **Unplug Yourself**. Is the TV always on, even when no one is watching? Do you take your smartphone to the dinner table? You don't have to go cold turkey; just set a good example by limiting your tech time and using those free moments to be with your family.

2. **Fire The Electronic Babysitter.** Don't flip a switch whenever the kids are bored or you need a break. "When the TV is off, I'm 'on'—and that can be hard when I have a lot to do," admits Stephanie Deininger. "But my 4-year-old has a tough time entertaining herself." So Deininger keeps the computers in one location—the den, which she's converted into a media room. "If Elena doesn't see the computer, it's less tempting."

3. **Develop Healthy Media Habits Early.** Just because your kid can play with your iPad for hours doesn't mean he should. Watching a video on a two-hour car ride won't do any harm, but if you hand him a digital device every time you get in the car, he'll have a meltdown if he doesn't get that electronic fix. For toddlers and preschoolers, 20 to 30 minutes of screen time twice a day (*all* screens, not just TV) is plenty, says Dr. Michael Rich.

4. **Teach How Technology Can Aid Learning.** "What the World Book was to earlier generations, Google is today," says Dr. Ellen Wartella. Still, some experts are concerned that it provides instant information without any creative problem-solving. "We need to show our kids how to take advantage of Google but teach the importance of critical-thinking skills."

5. **Be Skeptical.** If a program is billed as educational, that doesn't necessarily mean it is. Check for recommendations from trusted sources such as Common Sense Media (commonsensemedia.org) and The Center on Media and Child Health (cmch.tv).

school readiness no matter what format it's delivered on," says Deborah Linebarger, PhD, director of the Children's Media Lab at the University of Pennsylvania. Software should be tailored to their developmental stage and have a simple story line (no flashbacks or cutaways). It also needs characters with whom kids can connect, as well as lots of repetition, and it should let a child move at her own pace.

Of course, it's also wise to shield young children from scary or violent media and overly commercial products. "Children under 7 can't always differentiate between fantasy and reality," says Liz Perle, editor-in-chief and cofounder of Common Sense Media, a nonprofit organization that helps parents better understand technology and its effect on kids. "Little kids learn from what they see and imitate it. So if a character on screen bops someone on the head, you may well see that same behavior in your living room."

Connected Kids

Even experts who are skeptical about younger children's growing media use recognize its value. Simply knowing how to use a computer translates into academic confidence. Simulation software and multimedia encyclopedias open windows (no pun intended) for students that weren't available even five years ago. Want to watch butterflies emerge from their chrysalis? Find out why Pluto is no longer a planet? A few clicks takes you inside the American Museum of Natural History to ask why.

Learning how to live in a high-tech world effectively, safely, and responsibly is a task we need to start teaching children earlier than ever. "As kids explore social networking sites such as Club Penguin or KidSwirl, parents must visit these sites with their child and

monitor all chats," says Perle. "Make sure you choose from age-appropriate games, since many have sexual or violent content as well as commercial characters embedded in them." By age 7, children begin to understand that commercials try to get them to want to buy things—so talk about how to be a smart media consumer.

Like all parents, Dr. Rich is doing his best to stay on top of his sons' digital exploits. Recently, he reports, Ian took a picture of his mom sleeping and installed it as the wallpaper on his dad's iPhone. "Now this one's a keeper," he says.

Critical Thinking

1. What are some of the problems researchers are seeing in children who have had a heavy dose of screen time during their early childhood years?
2. What advice would you give to parents who want to introduce their young children to technology?

UNIT 3
Diverse Learners

Unit Selections

Learning Outcomes

After reading this Unit, you will be able to:

- Explain the vicious cycle of poverty that can occur for children living in constant poverty.

- Describe strategies teachers can use to assist English language learners and their families.

- Explain why differentiating the learning environment is so important when working with children with disabilities.

- Develop a list of different learning needs for girls and boys.

- List what teachers can do to individualize instruction in a preschool classroom.

- Summarize successful strategies for working with children with autism spectrum disorder.

Student Website

www.mhhe.com/cls

Internet References

American Academy of Pediatrics
    www.aap.org
Child Welfare League of America (CWLA)
    www.cwla.org
The Council for Exceptional Children
    www.cec.sped.org/index.html
First Signs
    http://firstsigns.org
Make Your Own Web page
    www.teacherweb.com
National Resource Center for Health and Safety in Child Care
    www.nrc.uchsc.edu
Online Innovation Institute
    www.oii.org

This unit focuses on the many diverse learners who are in our early childhood programs and schools. This unit starts with an article aimed at school board members about the importance of reaching those most important young children even prior to their entrance into kindergarten. Annie Papero's "The Wonder Years" is geared for elected school board trustees, but it has implications for all citizens. An educated population is better for us all and ensuring from the very beginning that all children have the necessary tools to be successful learners benefits all society. It is less expensive to provide children early with the skills they will need and the resources to be successful learners than to provide remedial help for 13 years of education.

Also included in this unit on diversity is "Class Division" by Peg Tyre. This article is from a widely circulated magazine available in any grocery store, *Family Circle,* and sends a powerful message to parents and educators about the different educational needs for boys and girls. Tyre reminds us all that young boys generally require active learning experiences, need male role models in their lives, and need opportunities to read books and magazines geared to the interests of boys. Strategies are included for supporting the learning of girls including playing math games, planning activities centered on science and natural themes, and fostering a sense of independence and persistence.

Another issue with deep implications for the early childhood profession is how we care for and educate children in inclusive environments. Nationwide, college and university programs are adapting to new standards from the National Association for the Education of Young Children (NAEYC) and Council for Exceptional Children (CEC), which require programs educating teachers at two- and four-year institutions to include much more content and field experiences on working with children, especially children with disabilities in inclusive environments. As teacher preparation institutions adapt to meet the new standards, there will be more teachers out in the field better equipped to meet the needs of special-needs children and their families. The new standards are all encompassing in their focus on the diversity and richness in the children and families we serve. Secretary of Education Arne Duncan and Assistant Secretary, Office of Special Education and Rehabilitative Services, Alexa Posny have stated that inclusive education is the responsibility of all educators, and collaboration among the adults who work with children are significant contributors to their learning and education. Recruiting and retaining qualified teachers who are well prepared to work with all children in environments that are established to be inclusive and differentiated is the new normal in schools. In Mara Sapon-Shevin's "Learning in an Inclusive Community," the reader will find 10 strategies for creating positive, inclusive classrooms to meet the needs of all children. Preservice teachers need many experiences in settings serving diverse learners. This can be challenging for teacher-preparation institutions located in communities lacking diversity. Education students with limited experience traveling to other cultures or interacting with children and families who are different from themselves must supplement their own experiences to be

© Kablonk/Purestock/SuperStock

successful teachers able to meet the needs of all children and families. Assess your prior experiences with children and families and see if you need to volunteer or work in settings different from your past work to better equip yourself with skills needed to work with all families and children. We tend to gravitate to familiar and comfortable experiences, but good teachers stretch themselves to become familiar with the life experiences children in their classes bring to the learning environment. Spend some time with a family who has a child with a disability. Get to know the stresses that child as well as the parents and other siblings may deal with on a day-to-day basis. If you own a car and many of your families depend on public transportation, take the bus one day to more fully understand the frustrations that can come from depending on a fixed schedule. Shop for groceries in the local markets used by the families in your classroom. In short; really get to know the many different life experiences the families you work with face in their daily lives.

In "Young Children with Autism Spectrum Disorder: Strategies That Work" Clarissa Willis helps teachers recognize some of the characteristics of autism spectrum disorder. As more and more children are receiving this diagnosis, approximately one in every 150 children, teachers are feeling unprepared to best meet the learning needs of children with Autism. The author provides suggestions for teachers to implement in their classroom.

In "Individualizing Instruction in Preschool Classrooms" by Mary B. Boat, Laurie A. Dinnebeil and Youlmi Bae, the reader will explore the ongoing need for learning experiences to be differentiated. It is a reminder to all teachers that individualizing learning can be accomplished through a thoughtful and intentional approach. The authors provide strategies for involving children in their learning. This unit ends with "The Why Behind RTI." All educators, but especially those who work with young children, need familiarity with Response to Intervention (RTI) and the steps educators can take to, as my great Aunt Nene used to say, "do a stitch in time to, save nine." Early prevention is one of the cornerstones of our profession. The strong foundation we build early in a child's life will serve him or her well into the future. We know that if we can intervene early and work with the child and family we can help that child get on track and compete with peers.

There are more and more examples of teachers adjusting their image of diverse learners and families. Only when all educators are accepting of the wide diversity that exists in family structures and among individual children will all children feel welcomed and comfortable to learn at school. The collaboration of families, the community, and school personnel will enable children to benefit from the partnership these three groups bring to the educational, setting. The articles in this unit represent many diverse families and children and the issues surrounding young children today.

The Wonder Years

Children's success in public schools begins at birth, and it's time our attitudes and funding reflect the importance of education in the early years

ANNIE PAPERO

What if every child entered kindergarten ready to learn? What a difference it would make to school leaders, families, and our society if all children received high-quality care during their first three years of life. Evidence continues to grow that school success begins at birth. Our children will never achieve at their highest levels until we change our attitudes—and commit money and resources—to reflect the importance of the first three years of life.

As education leaders, we need to be aware of the established links between very early childhood experiences and later achievement. School leaders—who shoulder the responsibility of raising achievement—are in an extraordinary position to advocate for high-quality care for infants and toddlers. They can make a strong argument that early childhood education is a crucial part of any plan for student achievement and success.

The Risks of Growing Up Poor

Research overwhelmingly confirms the role of early childhood education in later school success. In spite of this, many in public education pay little attention to it, perhaps because teacher and school leaders believe it's out of their sphere of influence.

Although we typically view kindergarten as the beginning of formal schooling, it actually is a continuation of all the learning that has come before. For some children, the early years provide a wealth of developmental riches. In stark contrast, some children face a paucity of opportunity and start out far behind.

One well-recognized risk factor for young children is growing up poor. Children make up a quarter of the U.S. population. However, they are disproportionately represented in poverty, accounting for 35 percent of the nation's poor. Children under age 6 are the poorest demographic group in our country—important to note because, not surprisingly, poverty is more detrimental to the development of young children than to that of older children.

Poverty is associated with lower levels of school achievement and higher levels of behavioral problems. Early poverty shapes later school achievement in many ways. One factor is how language is used in each child's environment. Both parents and children from more affluent, professional backgrounds possess vocabularies that are twice the size of those used by parents and children on welfare. Research shows that these differences in language noted in children when they were 3 were found to be predictors of vocabulary and language development when they were 9 and 10.

Another risk factor faced by infants and toddlers is having a depressed or severely stressed primary caregiver. When a caregiver is unable, for any reason, to establish a warm, responsive relationship with a very young child, development can be affected. The risks include poorer regulation of negative emotion, higher levels of insecure attachment, lower rates of compliance, cognitive and language delays, and lower levels of social competence.

Many of these risks have the potential to alter children's future development paths. For example, the quality of an infant's attachment to a caregiver predicts later social competence, empathy, self-esteem, flexibility, and problem-solving abilities.

Interestingly, the ages of 6 months to 18 months appear to be particularly sensitive to the effects of the quality of caregiving. Many researchers have found that impairments in caregiving during this window of development lead to persistent developmental problems including cognitive impairment, difficulty with peers, hyperactivity, and difficulty regulating attention and emotion—even if conditions subsequently improve for these children.

Children learn to successfully express and regulate emotion through caring, ongoing interactions with significant others in their lives. This self-regulation is a skill that any educator recognizes as important for academic and social success in school.

That Ship Has Sailed

Public schools face significant challenges when children arrive for kindergarten with vastly different levels of development. Metaphorically, a majority of children are on a ship that departs at birth, sailing at a strong clip towards higher developmental levels, fueled by rich environments and quality interactions. Unfortunately, some children are left on shore, lacking the responsive interactions and enriched environments that would carry them along.

We expect those left on shore to catch up and perform at the same levels academically as those who have been on the ship for five years already. It would be quite the feat for a young child with few resources to swim fast enough to climb aboard that ship.

Both sets of children may sit in the same classroom with the same teacher at age 5. But some children have an easier time surrounded by familiar knowledge and skills, while others must simultaneously learn academics and stay afloat in a world where they have no prior experience and far fewer applicable skills. Some very capable and resilient children manage to excel under these difficult circumstances, while many more do not.

It is our responsibility to make sure all children have a chance at academic success. With such unequal starting points, we face a very difficult task. One child may be ready for advanced math, while another child is struggling to focus and learn in the classroom.

It is time for all of us, especially education leaders who are in the position to advocate nationwide, to declare that all children should be on that ship before it sails.

The Role of a High-Quality Program

Early high-quality programs for infants, toddlers, and preschoolers that are accessible and affordable to all families have the greatest potential to help with this goal. Early high-quality care has been found to improve the cognitive, language, and social development of children, particularly those who are low-income, with effects that stretch into the early school years.

Group size, caregiver/child ratio, adult responsiveness, and continuity are some of the factors that determine the quality of care. Infants need to form trusting relationships with a primary care provider. Frequent changes in caregiving have been found to be related to insecure attachment and more problematic behaviors. Many low-income parents are more likely to seek out informal arrangements with relatives or other community members. This type of care has the potential to be less stable than center-based care. Frequent daycare changes are associated with insecure attachment and lower levels of social competence.

In fact, children's relationships with trusted teachers appear to provide children with some of the same benefits as a secure attachment to a parent. In addition, research has found that stability of early care also appears to enhance school adjustment in first grade.

A low child-to-adult ratio is also an important factor in high-quality care. Higher child-to-adult ratios have been found to result in elevated stress levels in children. Sustained, elevated levels of cortisol production in children have been linked to chronic illness and to difficulties concentrating and controlling anger.

Economic Benefits

High-quality early childhood programs can produce significant economic benefits to our society. Research studies that have followed children for more than 40 years are now showing savings of $13 or more for every dollar spent 40 years ago on intervention for 3- and 4-year-old children at risk.

The children who received half-day preschool paired with weekly home visits by their teachers when they were 3 and 4 have been found longitudinally to have higher levels of school achievement, reduced pregnancy and delinquency rates in adolescence, higher high school graduation rates, higher levels of college attendance, increased employment, and lower rates of single parenthood.

Would even earlier intervention, before the age of 3, lead to even greater economic savings and a higher level of student achievement? A 1995 review of model intervention programs showed that IQ effects produced persisted for the longest amount of time among the children who were participants in the two experimental studies that enrolled them as infants in full-day programs.

The Carolina Abecedarian Project, which provided full-day care for low-income children beginning during the first three months of life, has produced evidence that the children who received intervention sustained an IQ advantage over their peers through adulthood, achieved higher levels in reading and math, completed more years of schooling, had lower rates of drug use and early parenthood, and had higher rates of college enrollment and employment.

In a subsequent experiment, researchers provided intervention beginning in kindergarten instead of infancy. Although the school-age intervention aided children's academic achievement, it did not impact their IQs and its effects were significantly weaker than they were for the children who received services as infants.

Often, people object to early childhood programs because they believe that society should not pay for the failure of individuals to provide for themselves and their children. To reframe that argument, consider that it may be preferable to invest in early, high-quality programs that improve student achievement than to pay a much greater sum for remedial education, juvenile detention, adult incarceration, and welfare payments. Research suggests that financial investment in the first few years of life would simultaneously save money and improve the conditions of poverty.

Advocate for Early Childhood

As school leaders, we serve all children, from the poorest of the poor to those who come from the wealthiest families. We exist in every community, and we have a voice that needs to be heard. The issue of early care affects us directly.

We can bring all individuals involved in the care and education of children from birth through adulthood to the same table to talk about what is working or not working for our children. We can each learn more about the resources and gaps in our communities for the families with young children, and we can advocate for improvements that include better care for infants and toddlers.

We can advocate in our own communities and at the national level, drawing attention to the early years, giving voice to a community of educators and children who receive very little of society's attention or resources. We are in the position to spread the word that K–12 public schools alone can not make up for the deficiencies experienced by so many children during the first five years of life. We can demand a more equal starting line for all children when they reach our schools.

From Diapers to Decimals

Any serious discussion of closing the achievement gap, almost by definition, must include a discussion of the provisions being made for infants and toddlers. For those children who arrive without adequate experiences, we are in the position to advocate for interventions that make sense from a developmental perspective, providing our most challenged children with the opportunities to form strong relationships with reliable adults, and not just provide for the practice of rote facts and measurable academic skills.

Understanding the research is the first step for us as leaders in education and for those who advocate for the children in this country. Research strongly suggests that we would experience higher levels of achievement in our public schools if we as a society ensure that all of our infants and toddlers are provided with the opportunity to relate to adults who provide responsive, sensitive care.

Prekindergarten is not the starting line. The journey began at birth, leaving many children behind. From diapers to decimals, development is a continuum, and we cannot as a society continue to view the first five years of life as a "private domain." Children's success in our public schools begins at birth, and both our attitudes and our funding structures should reflect that knowledge.

Critical Thinking

1. What are some risk factors children bring with them when they enter K–12 schools?

2. How can school administrators help combat how these risks affect young children entering their schools?

ANNIE PAPERO (alpapero@ship.edu) is an assistant professor of early childhood teacher education at Pennsylvania's Shippensburg University.

Class Division

They sit side by side and learn the same lessons, yet boys struggle with reading and writing, while girls avoid advanced math and physical science. The good news? By working together to teach more creatively, educators and parents can help raise grades and close the gender gap.

PEG TYRE

Amy Kramschuster and her husband, John, never thought much about the differences between boys and girls when they became parents to Sam and, two years later, daughter Molly. "We didn't paint the nursery blue or pink, or buy G.I. Joe and Barbie dolls," says Amy. But as the kids grew, it often seemed as if they really were from separate planets. "Sam, like a lot of his friends, was always moving around and roughhousing," says Amy. "Molly was active, but she enjoyed periods of quiet play much more." By the time the two were attending James W. Russell Elementary School in Gray, Maine, Amy, 41, who works at the cafeteria there, and John, 46, a manager at Prudential, discovered that Venus can be surprisingly far from Mars.

Although Molly did well in kindergarten, in first grade she began struggling with addition and subtraction, despite her best efforts. Sam was simply less engaged, and by third grade he'd fallen far behind in reading. Even worse, his teacher said he was disruptive and didn't follow directions. "Not, every boy and girl responds to school exactly the same, of course," says Amy. "But John and I didn't expect to see our son and daughter have such opposite attitudes toward learning."

Molly and Sam are textbook cases of the gender gap between boys and girls in schools across America, where female students shy away from math and science, while males consistently lag behind in reading and writing. What accounts for the differences? Some experts have suggested that minute variations in brain structure might be to blame; researchers; for example, have found that boys tend to be better in spatial relations while girls learn language faster. "Many people jumped on this research to explain the achievement gap," says Janet Hyde, professor of psychology at the University of Wisconsin–Madison. "But there's really not much hard scientific evidence that supports the notion of a 'boy' versus 'girl' brain." These days most education experts agree that the expectations of parents, the role models kids see around them, an unconscious bias in how classes are taught and whether teachers can adapt to the needs of individual students affect performance far more than mental hardwiring.

The good news is that schools are thinking more creatively and offering opportunities to help boys and girls succeed in subjects that don't come easily. Parents, too, have to step up at home. When Molly began second grade last year, Amy started sitting down at the kitchen table with her daughter to review her weekly math homework packet. She also looked over Molly's textbooks and worksheets every weeknight, reinforcing what she'd just learned in class. "The more we worked together, the more her confidence blossomed," she says. Amy was especially proud when the shy 8-year-old participated in the spring science presentation with a report on bugs.

As for Sam, after a series of probing questions, Amy and John discovered his reading was so poor he couldn't decode the instructions his teacher wrote on the board every morning. They borrowed phonics tapes and workbooks from the library to help him get up to speed. Around Christmas, Sam got hooked on graphic books and their irresistible blend of comic-strip pictures and complex story lines. First he tackled the *Calvin and Hobbes* series, about a hyperimaginative 6-year-old and his sardonic—albeit stuffed—tiger, then *Diary of a Wimpy Kid,* which chronicles the oh-so-lame life of an unathletic middle schooler. With his eyes and mind engaged, something clicked. Sam's reading got stronger, his behavior issues vanished and the 10-year-old is actually looking forward to fourth grade. "John and I finally figured out that boys and girls sometimes need different kinds of support to help them thrive," says Amy. And that, she says, was a lesson worth learning.

It's a Girl Thing

For years the conventional wisdom was that only girls get math block—and that their weakness with numbers makes them avoid science. But girls don't naturally start out that way. In an extensive survey by the U.S. Department of Education (DOE) 66% of female fourth-graders and 68% of males said they liked science. But by seventh grade half as many girls as boys felt the same. In high school females account for only 17% of students in advanced placement computer science and 15% in physics. The results of that disengagement are profound. According to the most recent data available, from 2006, women make up one-third of scientists in business and industry, and one-fifth of tenured science professors.

Educators are now realizing that beginning in elementary school they have to focus less on multiplication tables and more on instilling confidence. Young girls tend to be more critical of their mathematical ability than boys, even when they get the same grades. How to correct this? Drive home the point early and often that they're as smart as anybody else. That's the goal of Girlstart, an Austin, Texas–based educational enrichment program that offers hands-on exploration of math, science and technology. Through workshops and classes in schools throughout central Texas, first- to twelfth-graders tackle topics like cryptology and environmental engineering. One group of teens is creating a computer search engine to help Austin residents find parking spaces and cut down on auto emissions. "They're using math problems and binary numbers and making Web pages with HTML," says Deputy Director Julie Shannan. "And they're psyched about helping change the world."

Another stumbling block is the lack of role models. "The white-coated man working in isolation on an abstract problem in a laboratory just doesn't appeal to many young females," says National Science Foundation (NSF) spokesperson Maria Zacharias. To encourage girls to pursue science and physics, teachers need to emphasize the contribution of women and search out female experts for class presentations. Citing an NSF poll that found that girls get more excited about a field if they can see how it improves their lives and those of others, Zacharias says it's especially important for schools to recast science "not as an isolated pursuit of loners but something that helps communities, whether it's by curing diseases, improving communication or creating new technologies."

A lack of role models is just one reason girls avoid science. "The white-coated man working alone in a laboratory doesn't appeal to many females," says Zacharias.

One program that's opening middle schoolers' minds to a world of possibility is GROW (Girls Researching Our World), according to Jackie Spears, director of the Center for Science Education at Kansas State University. At the main campus, in Manhattan, Kansas, girls log hours in laboratories, taking apart small appliances like fans and mixers, and figuring out what makes motors run. On visits to organic farms, they run soil tests, learn about sustainable agricultural practices and then lend a hand harvesting crops. Where GROW leaves off, an initiative called EXCITE picks up, offering high schoolers a chance to program computers, test cars in a wind tunnel or build a robot. "It's about girl-bonding, mentorship and exposure to exciting aspects in science," says Spears. "We want them to see careers they can succeed in that they may not have considered."

Where the Boys Are

From elementary through high school, they're floundering. Boys are held back in kindergarten and first grade at twice the rate of girls, and have more learning disabilities and behavior problems. In middle school they do less homework and get more C's and D's. At every age, they struggle to stay at grade level in reading and writing. Among high school seniors who have at least one parent who graduated from college, 23% of males were reading at "below basic" levels—which means they couldn't understand written directions or a newspaper. They write far less well than girls, and worse than their male peers did 15 years ago. Most alarming, more than one-third drop out. "With boys we need to look at the early warning indicators and make sure we intervene," says Bob Wise, the former governor of West Virginia who heads the Alliance for Excellent Education, which seeks to increase federal funding and improve schools to help every child graduate.

Schools are trying out a wide range of solutions to give boys a foothold in class. In elementary school part of the problem is physical. In the last 15 years recess and other opportunities for play and movement have been whittled away; according to the DOE, some 40% of first-graders get 20 minutes or fewer a day, and 7% get none at all. While being sedentary is bad for all kids, "on average girls handle it better," says Kenneth Ginsburg, associate professor of pediatrics at the University of Pennsylvania School of Medicine, and author of *A Parent's Guide to Building Resilience in Children and Teens* (American Pediatric Association). "Boys need movement to thrive." In Marine-on-St. Croix, Minnesota, sixth grade teacher Abby Brown designed a stand-up desk for her students and had a furniture manufacturer produce them. The kids in her class can stand while they work, shift from foot to foot or swing their legs. "Boys who used to have problems paying attention are now finding school a whole lot easier," she says. Other schools, like those in Wilmette, Illinois, are letting restless kids—especially ants-in-the-pants boys—balance on exercise balls and foam wedges.

A Leg up for Boys

- Check your son's elementary school schedule. Not enough gym? Sign him up for a sports club or exercise class to curb restlessness and help him focus on learning.
- Make sure dad takes equal turns reading aloud. Boys in particular need such role models.
- Ask your school librarian what kind of books your son gravitates toward, then visit the library or bookstore. Keep it up through high school. All kinds of materials count—comic books, manga, sports bios, books based on movies or computer games. It's the quantity that matters.
- Instead of getting your tween another video or computer game, buy him a magazine subscription for, say, *Sports Illustrated* or *Car & Driver*.
- Give your teen a cool-looking notebook—unlined for doodling—and encourage him to express himself. And don't call it a diary. Just suggest that he "collect" stuff like sports ticket stubs, rock lyrics, funny jokes. The words will follow.

Giving Girls a Hand

- Play math games—counting, multiplying, fractions—while shopping, eating, traveling with your elementary school–age girls.
- Provide plenty of informal exposure to science by taking trips to natural history museums or participating in community projects like gardening or recycling.
- Banish the notion of being "good" or "bad" at math, and repeat the message often. Explain that persistence, not talent, is key.
- For middle schoolers, whose confidence and performance often take a nosedive, keep a close eye on math homework. Highlight her competency. If she's stumped or seems insecure, alert her teachers and devise a plan.
- Encourage your high school teen to take AP classes in science and physics. Since girls tend to be underrepresented, ask instructors to make sure she feels welcome.

To get boys reading, teachers are allowing them to call the shots. William Brozo, professor of literacy at George Mason University in Fairfax, Virginia, and author of *To Be a Boy, To Be a Reader* (International Reading Association), says they're pickier than girls about subject matter and favor books "with male protagonists and plenty of action." Alexis Bleich learned that lesson from one fourth-grader in her class in New York City. "He hated reading," she recalls. "Would not do it. Every book I gave him, he'd say, 'This is the dumbest thing I ever read.' So I let him choose his book, a graphic novel from the *Bone* comic/fantasy series. He devoured every volume, and soon moved on to a word-only fantasy series." Bleich has since stocked her room with books that have boy appeal. "Reading

is a process of discovery," says Brozo. "With boys you have to capture their imagination first, then worry about building their skills and widening their tastes."

> **With boys you have to capture their imagination first, then worry about building skills and widening tastes, says Brozo.**

Educators are also rethinking their goals when it comes to teaching writing. "Most teachers tend to value serious, heartfelt and personal stories over humorous or violent subjects, which boys gravitate toward," says Ralph Fletcher, author of *Boy Writers: Reclaiming Their Voices* (Stenhouse). "We need to welcome how boys express themselves, what they choose to write about and how they choose to write it," he says, even if that means a little more conflict, blood and weapons. Literacy coach Jennifer Allen, who works at an elementary school in Waterville, Maine, started a boys-only writing club. Once a week a small group spends recess in her classroom, notebooks open, refining their stories. Many begin by working out the plot. Others cover the same topic over and over but write longer each time, with more detailed descriptions or a deeper understanding. They don't always finish their stories, but that's okay. "Unlike many other boys at school, they're writing, and writing a lot," says Allen. Fletcher approves. Practice, he says, can make perfect.

Critical Thinking

1. Compile a list of five specific strategies that would address the active learning needs of boys.
2. Write a paragraph for a school newsletter using the data reported in the article on the decrease in interest in science and math for boys and girls as they age. Include some suggestions for changing the statistics.

Learning in an Inclusive Community

Inclusive classrooms create students who are comfortable with differences, skilled at confronting challenging issues, and aware of their interconnectedness.

MARA SAPON-SHEVIN

Schools are increasingly acknowledging the heterogeneity of their student populations and the need to respond thoughtfully and responsibly to differences in the classroom. It's understandable that educators often feel overwhelmed by growing demands for inclusion, multi-cultural education, multiple intelligences, and differentiated instruction to deal with the growing diversity.

But what if including all students and attending thoughtfully to diversity were part of the solution rather than part of the task overload? What if we put community building and the emotional climate of the classroom back at the center of our organizing values? What if we realized that only inclusive classrooms can fully support the goal of creating thoughtful, engaged citizens for our democratic society?

Redefining the Inclusive Classroom

After years of struggle about the politics and practice of inclusion and multicultural education, it's time we understand that inclusive, diverse classrooms are here to stay. But inclusion is not about disability, and it's not only about schools. Inclusion is about creating a society in which all children and their families feel welcomed and valued.

Inclusion is about creating a society in which all children and their families feel welcomed and valued.

In truly inclusive classrooms, teachers acknowledge the myriad ways in which students differ from one another (class, gender, ethnicity, family background, sexual orientation, language, abilities, size, religion, and so on); value this diversity; and design and implement productive, sensitive responses. Defining inclusion in this way requires us to redefine other classroom practices. For example, *access* can mean, Is there a ramp? But it can also mean, Will letters home to parents be written in a language they can understand?

Differentiated instruction can mean allowing a non-reader to listen to a book on tape. But it can also mean organizing the language arts curriculum using principles of universal design, assuming and planning for diversity from the beginning rather than retrofitting accommodations after the initial design.

Positive behavior management can be a system of providing support to students with diagnosed emotional problems. But it can also mean ongoing community building, classroom meetings, cooperative games, and a culture of appreciation and celebration for all students.

What does it mean to think inclusively, and how can this framework enhance the learning of all children? There are many lessons that inclusive education settings can teach us. Here are just a few.

Comfort with Diversity

In our increasingly diverse world, all people need to be comfortable with diversity. Inclusion benefits all students by helping them understand and appreciate that the world is big, that people are different, and that we can work together to find solutions that work for everyone.

Inclusion teaches us to think about *we* rather than *I*—not to ask, Will there be anything for me to eat? but rather to wonder, How can we make sure there's a snack for everyone? Not, Will I have friends? but rather, How can I be aware of the children here who don't have anyone to play with? When we are surrounded by people who are different from us, we are forced to ask questions that go beyond the individual and address the community. When we have friends who use wheel-chairs, we notice that there are steep stairs and no ramps. When we have friends who wear hearing aids, we listen differently to comments like "What are you, deaf or something?" When we have friends with different skin colors, we become more alert to racist and exclusionary comments. When we have friends from different religious backgrounds, we are more aware that the decorations in the mall are about only one religion.

Inclusion teaches us to think about *we* rather than *I*.

In the absence of diversity, it's hard to learn to be comfortable with difference. The white college-age students I teach are often confounded about how to talk about people of color: "Is the right term *African American* or *black?* What if the person is from Jamaica or Haiti? How do I describe people?" Similarly, many adults are nervous about interacting with people with disabilities, unsure whether they should offer help or refrain, mention the person's disability or not.

The only way to gain fluency, comfort, and ease is through genuine relationships in which we learn how to talk to and about people whom we perceive as different, often learning that many of our initial assumptions or judgments were, in fact, erroneous. The goal is not to make differences invisible ("I don't see color"; "It's such a good inclusive classroom, you can't tell who the kids with disabilities are") but to develop the language and skill to negotiate diversity. Classrooms cannot feel safe to anyone if discussions of difference are avoided, discouraged, or considered inappropriate.

I am always delighted, and a bit stunned, when I see young people easily negotiating conversations about difference that would have been impossible a decade ago and that are still out of reach for many of us. I recently witnessed a discussion of different kinds of families during which children from ages 5 to 8 spoke of adoption, same-sex parents, known and unknown donors, and the many ways they had come to be members of their family.

These students, growing up in an inclusive, diverse community, will not need a book that says, "There are many kinds of families." That understanding is already part of their lived experience.

As a teacher, you can successfully facilitate discussions like this by doing the following:

- Familiarize yourself with the current terminology and debates about what people are called: Do Puerto Ricans call themselves *Latino?* Why is the term *hearing impaired* preferred by some but not all "deaf" people? If there are disagreements about terms—for example, some people prefer the term *Native American* and *some Indian*—find out what that conversation is about. Model appropriate language when discussing differences in the classroom.

- Provide multiple opportunities for talking about diversity. When a news story is about a hurricane in Haiti, pull down the map: Where is that country? What languages do the people there speak? Do we have anyone at our school from Haiti?

- If you hear teasing or inappropriate language being used to discuss differences, don't respond punitively ("I don't ever want to hear that word again!"), but don't let it go. As soon as possible, engage students in a discussion of the power of their language and their assumptions. Teach students the words *stereotype, prejudice,* and *discrimination* and encourage them to identify examples when they see them: "On the commercial on TV last night, I noticed that all the people they identified as 'beautiful' were white."

Inclusion is not a favor we do for students with disabilities, any more than a commitment to multicultural education benefits only students of color. Inclusion is a gift we give ourselves: the gift of understanding, the gift of knowing that we are all members of the human race and that joy comes in building genuine relationships with a wide range of other people.

Honesty about Hard Topics

Inclusion not only makes students better educated about individual differences, but also provides a place to learn about challenging topics. In inclusive classrooms, teachers and students learn to talk about the uncomfortable and the painful.

Often, as adults, we don't know what to do when we are confronted by people and situations that frighten, surprise, or confound us. Children, through their eagerness to engage with the world and seek answers to their questions, can learn important repertoires of communication and interaction in inclusive settings: How can I find out why Michelle wears that scarf on her head without hurting her feelings? How can I play with Jasper if he doesn't talk? Learning how to ask questions respectfully and how to listen well to the answers are skills that will provide a smoother entry into the complexities of adulthood.

In one school, a young boy who required tube feeding provided the opportunity for all the students to learn not only about the digestive system but also about ways to help people while preserving their dignity and autonomy. In another school, a child whose religion kept him from celebrating birthdays and holidays gave other students the opportunity to not only learn about different religions but also brainstorm ways of keeping Jonah a valued and supported member of the classroom. And when a young Muslim child was harassed on the way home from school in the months after the attack on the World Trade Center, the whole class was able to engage in an important discussion of racism and being allies to those experiencing prejudice and oppression.

A student in one classroom was dying of cancer. The teachers, rather than excluding the student and avoiding the subsequent questions, helped all the other students stay informed and involved in his life (and eventually, in his death). With close communication with parents, the teachers talked to students about what was happening to Trevor and how they could support him: "Of course we would miss you if you died." "Yes, it's very, very sad." "No, it's not fair for a 6-year-old to die; it doesn't happen very often." On days when Trevor was in school and feeling weak, the students took turns reading to him. On days when he was not able to come to school, they wrote him notes and made cards. When he died, many of them went to the funeral. Tears were welcomed and tissues were widely used; the teachers were able to show their sadness as well. Teachers had to be thoughtful about discussions of religious beliefs in order to be inclusive: "Yes, some people believe in heaven, and they think that's where Trevor is going."

Although no parents would want their children to have to deal with the death of a classmate, the sensitivity and tenderness of the experience helped bond the class and enabled students to connect to both the fragility and the sacredness of life. When they experience death again later in their lives, they will have some understanding of what it means to offer and receive support and will be able to seek the information and caring they need for their own journeys.

Ten Strategies for Creating a Positive, Inclusive Classroom

1. Make time for community building throughout the year. Time spent building community is never wasted.
2. Proactively teach positive social skills: how to make friends, how to give compliments, what to do if someone teases you or hurts your feelings. Don't wait for negative things to happen.
3. Be explicit in explaining to your students why treating one another well and building a community is important. Use key terms: *community, inclusion, friends, support, caring, kindness.* Don't let those words become empty slogans; give lots of examples of positive behaviors.
4. Adopt a zero-indifference policy. Don't ignore bullying in the hope that it will go away. Don't punish the participants, but be clear about what is acceptable. Say, "I don't want that word used in my classroom. It hurts people's feelings and it's not kind."
5. Share your own learning around issues of diversity and inclusion. When students see that you are also learning (and struggling), they can share their own journeys more easily. Tell them, "You know, when I was growing up, there were some words I heard and used that I don't use anymore, and here's why." "You know, sometimes I'm still a little uncomfortable when I see people with significant physical differences, but here's what I've been learning."
6. Think about what messages you're communicating about community and differences in everything you do, including the books you read to your students, the songs you sing, what you put on the walls, and how you talk about different families and world events.
7. Seize teachable moments for social justice. When students say, "That's so gay," talk about the power of words to hurt people and where such oppressive language can lead. When a student makes fun of another student, talk about different cultures, norms, and experiences.
8. Provide lots of opportunities for students to work together, and teach them how to help one another. End activities with appreciation circles: "What's something you did well today?" "How did Carlos help you today?"
9. Don't set students up to compete with one another. Create an atmosphere in which each student knows that he or she is valued for something.
10. Keep in mind that your students will remember only some of what you taught them but everything about how they felt in your classroom.

In inclusive classrooms, I have seen students learn to support a classmate with cerebral palsy, become allies in the face of homophobic bullying, and help a peer struggling with academic work. All of these were possible because the teachers were willing and able to talk to the students honestly about what was going on, creating a caring, supportive community for all students rather than marginalizing those who were experiencing difficulty.

Mutual Support

Sadly, teasing and exclusion are a typical part of many students' school experience. Bullying is so common that it can become virtually invisible. But inclusive classrooms foster a climate in which individual students know they will not be abandoned when they experience injustice. Inclusion means that we pay careful attention to issues of social justice and inequity, whether they appear at the individual, classroom, or school level or extend into the larger community.

I have used Peggy Moss's wonderful children's book *Say Something* (Tilbury House, 2004) to engage students and teachers in discussions about what we do when we see someone being picked on. In the book, a young girl goes from witnessing and lamenting the mistreatment of her classmates to taking action to change the patterns she observes.

This book and similar materials encourage students to talk about the concept of courage, about opportunities to be brave in both small and large ways, and about how they can make a difference.

Inclusive classrooms give us many opportunities to be our best selves, reaching across our personal borders to ask, Do you want to play? or Can I help you with that? Our lessons about how we treat one another extend beyond the specificity of rules (Don't tease children with disabilities) to broader, more inclusive discussions: How would you like to be treated? What do you think others feel when they're left out? How could we change this activity so more kids could play? How do you want others to deal with your challenges and triumphs, and what would that look like in our classroom?

Teachers in inclusive classrooms consider helping essential. The classroom becomes a more positive place for everyone when multiple forms of peer support—such as peer mentoring and collaborative learning—are ongoing, consistent, and valued. Rather than saying, "I want to know what you can do, not what your neighbor can do," inclusive teachers say, "Molly, why don't you ask Luis to show you how to do that," or "Make sure everyone at your table understands how to color the map code."

Inclusive settings provide multiple opportunities to explore what it means to help one another. By challenging the notion that there are two kinds of people in the world—those who need help and those who give help—we teach all students to see themselves as both givers and receivers. We recognize and honor multiple forms of intelligence and many gifts.

Courage to Change the World

When students develop fluency in addressing differences, are exposed to challenging issues, and view themselves as interconnected, teachers can more easily engage them in discussions about how to improve things.

Having a personal connection profoundly shifts one's perception about who has the problem and who should do something about it. When students have a classmate who comes from Mexico and is undocumented, discussions of immigration rights, border patrols, and fair employment practices become much more real. When students have learned to communicate with a classmate with autism, they understand at a deep level that being unable to talk is not the same as having nothing to say. When a classmate comes from a family with two mothers, reports of gay bashing or debates about marriage rights become more tangible.

A powerful way to combat political apathy is by helping young people make connections between their lives and those of others and giving them opportunities to make a difference in whatever ways they can. Although it's certainly possible to teach a social-justice curriculum in a fairly homogeneous school, inclusive classrooms give us the opportunity to put social-justice principles into action. In inclusive classrooms, students can *live* a social-justice curriculum rather than just study it.

A powerful way to combat political apathy is by helping young people make connections between their lives and those of others.

Inclusive classrooms that pay careful attention to issues of fairness and justice bring to the surface questions that have the potential to shift students' consciousness now and in the future: Who gets into the gifted program, and how are they chosen? How can we find a part in the school play for a classmate who doesn't talk? Why do people make fun of Brian because he likes art and doesn't like sports? How can we make sure everyone gets to go on the field trip that costs $20?

Inclusive classrooms put a premium on how people treat one another. Learning to live together in a democratic society is one of the most important goals and outcomes of inclusive classrooms. How could we want anything less for our children?

Critical Thinking

1. Think back to some of your favorite classes, either in K-12 or college, and describe what the teacher did to develop a caring, inclusive community in the classroom. Which of those teaching techniques will you incorporate in your own classroom?

2. Obtain a copy of the book, *Say Something* mentioned in the article. After reading the book write action steps you could take with a group of young children to get them to share feelings of mistreatment.

MARA SAPON-SHEVIN is Professor of Inclusive Education, Syracuse University, New York; msaponsh@syr.edu. She is the author of *Widening the Circle: The Power of Inclusive Classrooms* (Beacon Press, 2007).

Young Children with Autism Spectrum Disorder

Strategies That Work

Alexis is new to Ms. Roxanne's preschool classroom and spends a lot of time wringing her hands and staring out the window. She has been diagnosed with Asperger's syndrome, one of five conditions classified as an autism spectrum disorder. Roxanne wonders about Asperger's and what she can do to help Alexis adjust to being in the classroom.

Autism spectrum disorder (ASD) affects about one and a half million people in the United States. One in every 150 babies is diagnosed with autism spectrum disorder, and boys are four times more likely than girls to have a form of the neurological disorder (Autism Society of America 2006). Many children with ASD, especially those with Asperger's syndrome, are fully included in regular early childhood classrooms with their typically developing peers (Willis 2009).

> **The term *spectrum* is used because the characteristics of the disorder occur along a continuum, with severe symptoms at one end and very mild behaviors at the other.**

ASD is a broad-based term under which there are five recognized types of autism. The term *spectrum* is used because the characteristics of the disorder occur along a continuum, with severe symptoms at one end and very mild behaviors at the other. Where a child falls on the continuum helps determine how to plan for his education. For example, a child may be at the mild end in his ability to communicate with others, but at the severe end regarding his behavior around others.

ASD is a medical condition usually diagnosed by a developmental pediatrician and/or a team of specialists that may include a speech-language pathologist, occupational therapist, or child psychologist. Early intervention offering behavorial, social, and skill-building training is vital. Most children with ASD have an Individual Family Service Plan (IFSP) or an Individual Education Program (IEP) in place by the time they enter the classroom. These plans are designed with input from the child's family and can serve as a guide for planning activities and making modifications to the curriculum. They outline the broad goals and objectives written with a child's individual strengths and weaknesses in mind.

This article discusses the major characteristics associated with autism and offers some simple strategies for helping children with autism function in preschool settings (see "Characteristics of Autism Spectrum Disorder"). While each child with autism is unique and exhibits characteristic/symptomatic behaviors in varying degrees, most children diagnosed with an autism spectrum disorder have difficulty with communication and social relationships, including interactive play; display behaviors not typical of their peers; and respond to sensory stimuli by screaming or reacting strongly to light, sound, or motion (Sicile-Kira 2004).

> **Families and educators should focus on what the child can learn, rather than what cannot be learned.**

It is important to view a child with autism as a person with talents, strengths, and potential. In other words, families and educators should focus on what the child can learn, rather than what cannot be learned. Remember,

- Always put the child first. He is a "child with autism" not an "autistic child." Use the child's name as often as possible.
- Each child is unique, and no two children with autism have the same strengths and weaknesses.

Characteristics of Autism Spectrum Disorder

Autism	To be diagnosed with autism, a child must exhibit a significant number of the following characteristics: a significant delay in social interaction, such as eye contact or expression; a communication delay; behaviors including stereotypical behavior, such as intense, almost obsessive, preoccupation with objects; the need for nonfunctional and ritualistic routines, such as lining up books or food in a certain manner; and repeated movements, such as finger popping or hand flapping.
Pervasive development disorder not otherwise specified (PDD-NOS)	This classification is used when it is determined that a child has autism, but the characteristics displayed by the child are not like the characteristics of other children with autism. This diagnosis is also used when the onset of the disorder happens after age 3. Of all the autism classifications, this is the most vague and confusing for both families and teachers. However, this classification allows a child with a few, but not all, of the characteristics of autism to be classified as having autism, so that he can receive needed services.
Asperger's syndrome	Children with Asperger's typically behave much like children with other types of autism when they are young. However, as they grow into middle school age or in adolescence, they often learn how to socialize, communicate, and behave in a more socially acceptable manner. Most children with Asperger's have normal or above normal intelligence, so they learn new skills as quickly or in many cases more quickly than their typical peers.
Rett's syndrome	This is a degenerative disorder, meaning it gets worse with time. It begins in the first two years of life and is found almost exclusively in girls. Unlike other types of autism, children with Rett's develop normally prior to the onset of the disorder. Characteristics include loss of motor skills, hand-wringing or repetitive hand washing, and a decrease in head growth. Seizures and sleeping disorders may also develop.
Childhood disintegrative disorder	Sometimes called Heller's syndrome, this is a degenerative condition in which a child may begin to develop normally but start to lose skills or seem to forget how to do things over a few months. Loss of skills usually happens in the area of toilet training, play, language, or problem solving, typically between ages 3 and 4.

Adapted with permission from C. Willis, *Teaching Young Children with Autism Spectrum Disorder* (Beltsville, MD: Gryphon House, 2006).

- Not all information about autism (including what is shown on television and found on the Internet) is accurate.
- While there are several approaches to teaching a child with autism, there is no single method, specific program, or magic cure that can *fix* autism. Many programs and methods are successful with some children, yet may not be successful with others (Willis 2006).

How Might a Child with Autism Behave in My Classroom?

Children with an autism spectrum disorder may display in varying degrees some or all of the following behaviors: obsession with specific objects, such as collecting forks or having an attachment to a piece of cloth; prolonged interest in common occurrences like watching water as it swirls down the drain; adherence to rituals, such as arranging food in a certain order; and repetitive (stereotypic) behaviors like hand flapping or repeating the same phrase over and over.

What Is Stereotypic Behavior?

Stereotypic behavior is usually defined as a behavior carried out repeatedly and involving either movement of the child's body or movement of an object (Edelson 1995). Some of the most common stereotypic behaviors seen in young children with autism include flapping one or both hands, pulling or tapping the ears, rocking back and forth or from side to side, sniffing the air, or sucking on the upper lip.

Stereotypic actions allow the children to move further into their own world and away from reality. While stereotypic behavior is not usually physically harmful, it often interferes with a child's ability to focus on what is going on around her (Lee, Odom, & Loftin 2007). Of course, all children, from time to time, tune out activities they want to avoid. Unlike typically developing children, however, many children with autism learn that by doing a specific thing, such as rocking, they can consistently tune out everything around them.

Knowing the reason for a behavior can often help teachers determine what a child is trying to communicate through his or her actions.

Attempting to understand the function behind the behavior is important. Knowing the reason for a behavior can often help teachers determine what a child is trying to communicate through his or her actions. Behavior specialists and teachers can work together to conduct a functional behavior assessment, which involves observing the child's particular behavior across time to help determine its function.

How Do We Know What a Child with Autism Is Trying to Communicate with a Behavior?

It is very difficult for a teacher to be responsive when she does not know what a child is trying to say. To try to understand the child's communication, ask yourself the following questions:

1. **What was the child doing immediately before the behavior started?** For example, if Aaron is sitting down for small group time and suddenly stands up and screams, his teacher can try to recall what occurred just before his outburst. Perhaps she had stopped interacting with him and is now talking to the group. If Aaron typically has a tantrum during group activities, it may indicate that he is using the tantrum to regain the teacher's attention.

2. **What in the environment might have triggered the behavior, outburst, or tantrum?** Did something make a loud noise? Did the classroom suddenly get brighter? Is there a smell unfamiliar to the child?

3. **What is the child trying to say by his behavior?** Sometimes a child will act a certain way as a protest, while other times she may cry out to express "There's too much going on here; I can't think!" One key to identifying the function of a child's behavior is to look at what happens after the behavior. If the child's tantrums are often followed by some kind of interaction with an adult (even if the interaction seems negative), the child may be communicating (in a maladaptive way) that he wants attention.

4. **Can I predict when the child will behave in a certain way?** The behaviors of children with autism are not always predictable. However, sometimes knowing what will happen next can allow a teacher to step in to prevent an outburst. If Candice starts biting herself every day after coming in from the playground, it is probably safe to assume that she enjoys being outside and does not want to come indoors. In this case, the teacher can try cuing Candice with a special signal right before it is time to come inside. This gives the child time to end the activity she is enjoying and transition to the next one.

Other Ways a Child with Autism Might Communicate

Approximately 40 percent of all children with ASD are nonverbal (Charlop & Haymes 1994). However, just because a child is nonverbal, it does not mean she cannot learn to communicate. Several alternative or augmentative forms of communication are used with children with autism. These include

Sign language. Some children with autism can use the same signs used by people who are deaf.

Communication devices. Computer-like tools can speak for the child when activated by the push of a button or selection of a picture.

Communication pictures. A child can point to specific pictures to tell what is happening, what he needs, or what he wants. Many children with autism respond better to real pictures than to line drawings (Willis 2009).

Among the many tools commercially developed for children with communication deficits is the Picture Exchange Communication System (PECS) (Frost & Bondy 1994). PECS is simple to use, relatively inexpensive, and helps children with autism develop a way to communicate with others (Charlop-Christy et al. 2002). Because of communication and behavior issues, many children with ASD do not initiate interactions with others. What makes the PECS system unique is that, unlike other systems of communication, it requires that the child initiate interaction by using a representative picture (Bondy 2001). In general, when used consistently, the PECS helps children with autism have more meaningful communication interactions. Communication with others is an important social skill that helps any child make friends.

What Do We Do When a Child Won't Interact with Others?

Because children with autism generally do not initiate interactions, social skills training, including how to respond in social situations, should begin as early as possible and continue throughout the child's education (Stichter & Conroy 2006). Some strategies can help a child learn how to greet people and introduce himself (for an example, see "Strategy 1: Making New Friends").

It is important to work with the child's family and other teachers and specialists to prioritize which social skills should be taught. Learning too many new skills without enough time for practice can be overwhelming, and the child may react with maladaptive behavior. To encourage positive social interactions, it is vital to structure the environment to help the child succeed.

How Do We Arrange a Preschool Environment for Success?

Children with autism function best when they have

- structure and a predictable routine,
- environments that do not distract,
- verbal reminders of what will happen next, and
- picture schedules.

Teachers should define the environment as much as possible for a child with autism. To reduce the child's anxiety, create and post in each center or learning area a picture schedule using photographs or other images to display the day's events. The child can look at the picture to get an idea of what is supposed to occur in that area. Children with autism like to know what they are supposed to do, so a picture schedule is reassuring.

In learning centers, teachers also can set up activities that encourage interaction, such as group art projects or activities

Strategy 1: Making New Friends

Objective: To help develop social interaction by showing the child how to introduce himself.

1. Make an introduction cue card with two cues, one for the child's name and one to remind him to wait for the other person to respond. If possible, laminate the card.
2. Explain to the child that the cue card will help him know what to do when he meets someone new.
3. Ask several children to help you and the child practice meeting people.
4. Sit in a circle and practice what to say and how to wait for the other person to respond.
5. Remind the children that when you are meeting someone for the first time, it is a good idea to look at him or her.
6. Look for opportunities for the child to practice using the cue card to introduce himself.

Helpful Hints

- When the child becomes familiar with this routine, add additional cues, such as one showing something that he likes to do or asking a new friend to play a game.
- Make a set of cue cards for the child to take home.
- Alert the family that the child is working on introducing himself and other social skills, so they can help him practice.

Adapted with permission from C. Willis, *Teaching Young Children with Autism Spectrum Disorder* (Beltsville, MD: Gryphon House, 2006).

---

that require two people to complete them. Remember, children with autism may not be particularly interested in an activity or specific center. Allowing use of a child's preferred object can greatly increase the probability that the child will take part in an activity (Schwartz, Billingsley, & McBride 1998).

Transitions are times when a child with autism is likely to have an outburst. Plan smooth transitions. Music makes an excellent transition tool. Use the same song for each transition so the child learns that the song is a cue that something new is about to happen.

Here are some other ideas to facilitate smooth transitions:

- Go with the child to the picture schedule and point to the next activity.
- Set a timer to indicate that in a few minutes it will be time to change activities. Hourglass timers are less distracting than timers with loud continuous bells.
- Tap the child gently on the shoulder as a cue that it is almost time to stop.
- Ring a service bell (with one quick ring) or soft chime, such as wind chimes, as a reminder that it is time to change activities.

Note that making loud noises or flashing lights on and off are not good ways to signal transitions for a child with autism. The sensory stimulation can be overwhelming.

It is critical to remember that most children with autism will, in some fashion, have difficulty with sensory stimuli. They require an environment that is sensitive to their unique needs.

Why Do Children with Autism Have Difficulty with Sensory Stimuli?

Most children with autism have some form of sensory integration disorder whereby they cannot filter or screen out sensory-related input (Kranowitz 2005). The common "feely box" that many preschool teachers use to introduce new textures can be very distressing for many children with autism. For them, the information they receive from their environment—such as through a feely box—becomes distorted and unreliable.

The quiet center is also a space where a child can go to complete especially stressful activities, such as counting, working a puzzle, or writing her name.

Children with autism need a special place in the classroom where they can go without distraction and without all the sensory input they receive elsewhere. Locate this place in the quietest part of the room and provide soft, indirect lighting, a comfortable chair or cushion, and some activities that the child likes. Teachers should always be able to observe the child in the special place. This quiet center is also a space where a child can go to complete especially stressful activities, such as counting, working a puzzle, or writing her name (Willis 2006).

After the child spends time in the quiet center, allow her to return and finish any activity she started before visiting the quiet center. Quiet centers should be used routinely to allow the child to be in a place where she feels safe and secure. They should *never* be used as a form of punishment.

How Can We Prepare for a Child with Autism?

The best way teachers can prepare themselves and the other children in the class for a child with autism is to get to know as much as possible about the child before enrollment. Encourage the family to come with their child to visit your classroom before the first day of school. This initial visit is an opportunity to meet the family and the child and let him become familiar with the classroom. This introductory visit should happen when other children are not present, and more than one visit may be necessary. One way to help a child learn more about his new classroom is to take the child on a classroom hunt (see "Strategy 2: Classroom Hunt—I Spy!").

Strategy 2: Classroom Hunt— I Spy!

Objective: To encourage the child with autism to explore areas of the classroom, interact with toys, or try new activities.

Materials: A basket with a handle and one item from each learning center.

1. Gather one representative item from each of the centers in the room—a block from the block area, a magnetic letter from the literacy center, a paint-brush from the art area, a book from the reading center, and so on.
2. Place the items in a basket or box. A basket works best because you can carry it on your arm. The child may even want to carry it for you.
3. Tell the child you need help putting the things in your basket back in the centers where they belong.
4. Start each hunt with the same phrase, "Here is a ____. I wonder where it goes."
5. Refocus a child who looks away or appears disinterested by holding the item in front of her.
6. Hold up an object and ask, "____ [the child's name], where do you think this goes?"
7. Prompt a child who does not reply or does not take the object by walking to a center and asking, "Do you think it goes here?"
8. When the child figures out where the object belongs, ask her to place the item in/on the correct bin or shelf. Continue with the other objects in the basket.

Helpful Hints

- Say the name of the object aloud.
- Vary the activity. For example, if you use picture cards, match the object to the correct picture card before returning it to its proper location.
- Put the object in the wrong location if the child appears uninterested or bored. Wait to see if she corrects you. Sometimes, even nonverbal children have an extraordinary sense of place and know in fine detail where items belong.

(Later, after the child has gotten used to being at school, it might be fun to do the activity with a second child so that the three of you look for the correct center.)

Adapted with permission from C. Willis, *Teaching Young Children with Autism Spectrum Disorder* (Beltsville, MD: Gryphon House, 2006).

Many preschools have a family information form, but you will need to find out much more about the child than is typically included on such forms. Here are some questions to ask the family before a child with ASD arrives at the program:

1. What does she like to eat? Are there foods that she will not eat or that cause her to react in a certain way?
2. What are her particular interests? Does she have an object that she is attached to?
3. Does she have a favorite activity or song?
4. How does she communicate with others?
5. What might cause her to become upset or frustrated?
6. What do you see as her strengths?
7. What do you consider her challenges?
8. What other services has she been receiving? Speech therapy? Occupational therapy? Who provides the services? How often and in what setting?
9. What do you do when/if she has an outburst at home?
10. How much experience has she had interacting with other children?
11. What is her daily routine?

How Do We Set up the Daily Routine for a Child with Autism?

Children with autism are less frustrated when they can follow predictable and organized routines. When setting up a daily routine for a child with autism, it is important for the child to understand what you are asking him to do. How the day begins often determines how the child will behave during the rest of the day. If there is any variation in the schedule, even a minor change, let the child know in advance.

When the child arrives, greet him and discuss the daily schedule. Use familiar picture cards to show each activity for the day. Make sure the schedule is on a level the child can understand. For some children, this may be an object schedule, and for others, a simple first–then card. A first–then card is a series of picture pairs in which the first shows what happens first and the second shows what happens next (Small & Kontente 2003; Willis 2006). When possible, use the identical daily routines, such as saying the same morning greeting each day (see "Strategy 3: Morning Greeting").

Concluding Thoughts

Jim Sinclair puts it best: "Autism isn't something a person has, or a 'shell' that a person is trapped inside. There's no normal child hidden behind the autism. Autism is a way of being. It is pervasive; it colors every experience, every sensation, perception, thought, emotion, and encounter, every aspect of existence. It is not possible to separate the autism from the person—and if it were possible, the person you'd have left would not be the same person you started with" (1993, n.p.).

All children can learn, and children with autism spectrum disorder are no exception. To help them be as successful as possible in your classroom, remember that they function best when they have the following:

- structure and a predictable routine,
- environments that do not distract,
- verbal reminders of what will happen next,
- picture schedules to give them clues about what to do,
- a quiet place to go where they can be alone for a few minutes, and
- nothing to overwhelm their senses with too much light or noise.

Strategy 3: Morning Greeting

Objective: To establish a morning routine that starts the day on a positive note.

1. Use the same words and phrases each day, perhaps something as simple as "Good morning, *[child's name]*." Wait to see if the child responds, then say, "Let's check and see what we do first."
2. Bend down to eye level and use a picture schedule to show the child what you want him to do.
3. Try singing to a child who does not respond to a spoken welcome. You might sing the following to the tune of "Three Blind Mice" (first verse):

   [Child's name], welcome.
   [Child's name], welcome.
   I'm glad you're here.
   I'm glad you're here.

4. Direct the child to his cubby. If he hesitates, walk with him. A picture of the child above the cubby will help him identify it more easily. Show him the picture cards that relate to putting up his backpack, coat, and so on.
5. Tell him what to do next: "After you put up your backpack, go to the ____ center." Even if you start the day with independent center time, direct the child to a specific place each morning.
6. Say or sign thank you.
7. Guide the child to the center if he does not go on his own; walk with him.
8. Vary the welcome only after he is accustomed to the morning routine. For example, suggest two or more center choices. Expect that when you first tell him to choose where he wants to go, he will likely stand still or hide in his cubby.

Helpful Hints

- Stay focused on your primary objective, which is to start each day with a calm and predictable sequence.
- Keep in mind, regardless of your morning routine, that consistency will make the child with autism feel more secure.
- Accept that some children, even children without autism, are just not morning people and need a little more time to wake up. If the child is prone to rugged mornings, begin each day by allowing him to go to the quiet center until he has adjusted to the routine.
- Make sure that when you are absent, the substitute or teacher's assistant follows your morning welcome routine.

Adapted with permission from C. Willis, *Teaching Young Children with Autism Spectrum Disorder* (Beltsville, MD: Gryphon House, 2006).

References

Autism Society of America. 2006. *Autism facts.* www.autism-society.org/site/PageServer?pagename=about_whatis_factsstats.

Bondy, A. 2001. PECS: Potential benefits and risks. *The Behavior Analyst Today 2* (2): 127–32.

Charlop, M.H., & L.K. Haymes. 1994. Speech and language acquisition and intervention: Behavioral approaches. In *Autism in children and adults: Etiology, assessment, and intervention,* ed. J.L. Matson. Pacific Grove, CA: Brooks/Cole.

Charlop-Christy, M.H., M. Carpenter, L. Loc, L. LeBlanc, & K. Kellet. 2002. Using the Picture Exchange Communication System (PECS) with children with autism: Assessment of the PECS acquisition, speech, social-communicative behavior, and problem behavior. *Journal of Applied Behavior Analysis 35* (3): 213–31.

Edelson, S. 1995. Stereotypic (self-stimulatory) behavior. www.autism.org/stim.html

Frost, L.A., & A.S. Bondy. 1994. *The Picture Exchange Communication System training manual.* Cherry Hill, NJ: Pyramid Educational Consultants.

Kranowitz, C. 2005. *The out-of-sync child: Recognizing and coping with sensory processing disorder.* New York: Perigee.

Lee, S., S.L. Odom, & R. Loftin. 2007. Social engagement with peers and stereotypic behavior of children with autism. *Journal of Positive Behavior Interventions 9* (2): 67–79.

Schwartz, I.S., F. Billingsley, & B. McBride. 1998. Including children with autism in inclusive preschools: Strategies that work. *Young Exceptional Children 2* (1): 19–26.

Sicile-Kira, C. 2004. *Autism spectrum disorders.* New York: Penguin.

Sinclair, J. 1993. Don't mourn for us. *Our Voice: The Newsletter of the Autism Network International* 1 (3). http://ani.autistics.org/dont_mourn.html

Small, M., & L. Kontente. 2003. *Everyday solutions: A practical guide for families of children with autism spectrum disorder.* Shawnee Mission, KS: Autism Asperger Publishing.

Stichter, J.P., & M.A. Conroy. 2006. *How to teach social skills and plan for peer social interactions.* Series on autism spectrum disorders. Austin, TX: Pro-Ed.

Willis, C. 2006. *Teaching young children with autism spectrum disorder.* Beltsville, MD: Gryphon House.

Willis, C. 2009. *Creating inclusive learning environments for young children: What to do on Monday morning.* Thousand Oaks, CA: Corwin.

Critical Thinking

1. Neighbors of yours just inform you that they were told their six-year-old son has autism. They have no prior knowledge of Autism Spectrum Disorders and ask you to provide them with a summary they can read and share with other family members. Write a two page summary you would share with the family,
2. Following up on the first task, the family then asks you for strategies they can give their son's teacher. What are some specific strategies you would provide for the teacher?

CLARISSA WILLIS, PhD, is a speaker and consultant based in Winston-Salem, North Carolina; author of *Teaching Young Children with Autism Spectrum Disorder* and *Creating Inclusive Learning Environments for Young Children;* and coauthor of *Inclusive Literacy Lessons for Early Childhood.* In addition to earning a doctorate in early childhood special education, Clarissa worked more than 20 years in schools and child development centers and as a speech pathologist. Clarissa@clarissawillis.com

Individualizing Instruction in Preschool Classrooms

Increasing numbers of young children with diagnosed disabilities and unique learning needs are enrolled in early childhood programs. Individualizing learning opportunities is one widely accepted practice for successful inclusion.

MARY B. BOAT PhD, LAURIE A. DINNEBEIL PhD, AND YOULMI BAE MEd

In 2003, 34 percent of young children with disabilities received special education services in community-based early childhood programs such as child care centers, Head Start classrooms, and nursery schools (U.S. Department of Education, 2005). These services are provided by early childhood special educators.

However, these special education professionals usually spend just a few hours each week with the children. If early childhood inclusion is to be a successful educational approach, it is imperative that ALL early childhood teachers understand and are able to provide individualized instruction to young children with special needs. This article describes teaching techniques that preschool teachers can use to support the learning needs of all children with whom they work, including young children with disabilities and special needs.

The term *instruction* refers to the methods used to teach a curriculum (Bredekamp & Rosegrant, 1992). In early childhood education, instruction encompasses many different types of learning experiences ranging from non-directive to directive (Wolery, 2005; Wolery & Wilbers, 1994).

Just as children's learning falls along a continuum from passive to active, so does the process of instruction. Instruction may be as basic as modeling how to put on a coat, or it can be as complex as helping children learn to read. The degree to which teacher direction or guidance is used depends on the objective of the experience and the children's individual needs. Thus, for teaching to be *instruction*, it must be intentional. The result of appropriately individualized instruction is meaningful learning for all young children.

How to Individualize Instruction

The process of individualizing instruction consists of four primary steps (Pretti-Frontczak & Bricker, 2004):

- **Get to know each child's** interests, needs, and abilities
- **Create opportunities for learning** that build on children's interests

---

What Is Instruction?

Instruction refers to intentional teaching methods.

When is something teachers do or say considered to be *instruction*? When a teacher draws a young child in to a conversation about a picture or experience, is that teacher providing instruction? Perhaps it is, if the teacher is creating an opportunity for the child to express herself verbally or practice turn-taking skills. Teaching is instructive if it is done *intentionally* to provide support or opportunities for children's learning.

Teachers who are aware of children's learning needs continuously look for ways to support their learning.

- **Scaffold children's learning** through supportive interactions
- **Monitor children's progress** toward achieving important goals

These components are interrelated and form the framework for decision making around individualization.

To successfully create engaging learning opportunities for children, teachers must know

- what children enjoy and value,
- what children are capable of doing, and
- what adults can and should expect from each child (skills as well as appropriate content standards)

Teachers who know about the children can then create learning opportunities based on that information and support their learning through instructional strategies that promote growth.

Skilled teachers determine whether children are making appropriate progress toward achieving goals by monitoring progress (assessment) *and* using that information to change instructional strategies and intensity as appropriate.

Get to Know Each Child

Most children are naturally curious about their surroundings and eagerly participate in learning activities. For some children, however, it is difficult to identify what motivates them to be more fully engaged. Teachers who pay attention to what children do and say can usually find out what motivates them. This is true for all children, but even more so for children with disabilities because they may not exhibit the same kinds of behaviors as their typically developing peers.

Teachers who successfully work with children who have special needs are diligent in identifying child interests by collaborating with families and other service providers who know the child. This knowledge, coupled with teaching skills, is essential to determine how to use individual information about children to work toward desired outcomes for them.

For example, identifying familiar, common objects is a skill mastered by most preschool children and is a goal on many individualized education plans (IEPs). Some young children, however, have little interest in typical objects in early childhood classrooms. This does not mean that these children are not interested in objects, but rather that their interests fall outside the spectrum of items that appeal to most young children.

Teachers certainly want to encourage young children to be able to identify and name common objects. This skill is necessary for language and literacy development, and provides a common frame of reference for interactions with peers. Teachers who know children well can identify what is likely to motivate them to develop an interest in everyday early childhood learning materials.

Create Opportunities for Learning

The ability to generate and sustain children's interest in learning is a critical skill for effective early childhood teachers. Teachers who can pique children's curiosity and then use appropriate instructional strategies to convey information and skills provide children with rich learning environments (Sandall & Schwartz, 2008).

Maya, a 4-year-old, was diagnosed with a language delay. Maya's teacher, Mr. Flores, is working with her on using words for common objects and activities in the classroom rather than gestures such as pointing or grabbing objects. Mr. Flores seeks a way to motivate Maya's use of vocabulary. He carefully observes what interests Maya and uses this information to set up learning opportunities.

Mr. Flores notes that Maya enjoys working in the art center and especially painting and cutting paper. To provide her with an opportunity to practice using words for common objects, he places crayons and scissors just out her reach, creating a situation in which Maya must ask for the items. He does not hand the objects to her until she names or attempts to name them.

Mr. Flores may further support Maya's learning by modeling the correct words and asking Maya to repeat them. She is then rewarded by receiving the objects she desires.

This scenario may be repeated, but should be utilized only to help Maya use her vocabulary to obtain what she desires or get her needs met. Mr. Flores actively reinforces Maya's independent attempts to use her vocabulary, because independence is the ultimate goal.

The strategy described here works well for Maya, but effective teachers know that it will not work for every child. Thus, it is imperative that teachers know individual children's interests, cultures, and values before determining the best way to create learning opportunities (Copple & Bredekamp, 2009). For example, a Native American child whose family culture teaches that it is not polite to ask for objects may not respond to the strategy that worked for Maya.

Early childhood teachers use a variety of strategies to facilitate learning opportunities for children. The seven techniques in Table 1 vary in level of teacher direction as well as in the degree to which a child must respond (Ostrosky & Kaiser, 1991). The first several strategies do not require a child's response for an activity to continue. The later strategies are much more directive.

When creating opportunities for learning, make sure that children are ultimately in control of the situation. Even though the intent is to entice a child into the interaction, the child may or may not respond. Teachers try to create opportunities that interest and engage children in learning, but there is no way to make them be interested.

All of the strategies mentioned here are effective ways to engage all children, not just those who have disabilities. Instructional strategies are intended to provide the minimal assistance necessary for the child to successfully attempt the skill (Wolery, 2005; Wolery, Ault, & Doyle, 1992). When using these strategies, do not single out children or foster their dependence. Drawing attention to differences in how children are supported may decrease the likelihood the target children will participate in the opportunity. When planning an intervention, always ask if the strategy is appropriate for the individual child, necessary, and sufficient to promote success.

Scaffold to Support Learning

When teachers support learning, the key is to determine what type and intensity of support will be most helpful to individual children. A teacher's simple glance may draw one child's attention to an inappropriate behavior. Another child may need a verbal reminder. Yet another may benefit from specific guidelines or examples of positive behavior. One child may follow when the teacher demonstrates how to properly hold scissors to cut paper, while another may need hand-over-hand support for the same activity.

In all likelihood, children only need support temporarily, so savvy teachers know that fading their support is critical to children's independence. Effective teachers know how to individualize support to be just the right amount of help. What criteria facilitate this decision-making? Beyond knowing children's individual interests and preferences, there are indicators that may help teachers think about individual situations. Table 2 provides examples of how support from teachers or families may be matched to children's needs.

Table 1   Teaching Strategies That Pique Children's Interest

1. **Comment** about an event that appears to interest the child. This technique prompts the child to repeat, respond to, or expand on the comment. A teacher looking at a child's painting might say, "Look at all of the bright colors you used! I see pink, green, and purple."

2. **Expand** on a child's statement. Elaborate with one or two key words that are likely to build the child's expressive vocabulary. A child may say, "I have truck," and the teacher may elaborate by saying, "Yes, you have a red fire truck."

3. Introduce an **unexpected event**. Set up situations that capture a child's attention through novelty and create cognitive dissonance. A teacher might do something that is inconsistent with the daily routine or the way children typically perceive their environment. For example, hold a child's name card upside down or start to dress a doll by putting a shoe on its hand.

4. Initially provide **inadequate portions or insufficient materials**. Without sufficient quantity to complete a task, the child is likely to ask for more. If only a small ball of modeling compound is available, the child may ask for more to roll out and use a cookie cutter to make shapes.

5. **Block access**. When a teacher subtly denies a child access to a preferred object or event, the child is likely to request the object or ask for assistance. The teacher might set out bright balls in a plastic container with a tight lid. A child who is interested in playing with the balls will request help to open the container.

6. Create **opportunities to choose**. When children are given choices among objects, events, or activities, they are more likely to actively participate. Choices provide children with opportunities to develop expressive language and cognitive skills. Some choices may be routine, such as offering either crackers or cereal at snack time. Other choices capitalize on children's interests by building on their activities: "Would you like the letter you wrote to go in the mailbox? Or do you want to take it home with you?"

7. Make a **direct request** to say or do something that requires more than a yes or no answer. For example, insist that a child state the name of an object before it is available for play: "Please say 'ball' if you want the orange ball."

Table 2   Match Support to Children's Needs

Support	Child Needs	Examples of Teaching Strategies
Time	Time to process information and to act on a request.	Ask a child to begin cleaning up. Provide plenty of wait time after the request to see if the child complies before making a further intervention.
		Ask a child to share something he enjoyed about a field trip. Provide enough wait time for the child to reflect and respond.
Gesture	A reminder to perform a skill.	Point to the trash can as child gets up from snack and leaves her milk carton.
		Make a "shh" sign to remind children to be quiet during a story.
Verbal Prompt	More explicit information to successfully perform a skill.	Verbally remind a child to put away the toys she used in one center before moving to another.
		Verbally remind a child to put on a smock before waterplay.
Model or Demonstration	How to do a challenging skill or help remembering how to perform a skill.	Demonstrate how to put on a glove. Show how to spread fingers and pull on the glove one finger at a time.
		Suggest that a child watch how a peer holds a pitcher to pour a beverage.
Physical Prompt	When acquiring a skill, child needs physical guidance to be successful.	Use a hand-over-hand techniques to help a child figure out how to balance table blocks.
		Physically help a child grasp and hold a coat zipper.

Scaffolding Strategies

Response-prompting strategies (Wolery, 2005; Wolery, et al., 1992) is a phrase used to describe the process of providing help (or prompts) in order for the learner to make a desired response. Levels of prompting can be ordered from most-to-least or least-to-most.

- **A most-to-least strategy** can be implemented if the child is learning a complex motor skill such as dressing. At first, adults provide children with a great deal of help and gradually reduce the amount of assistance as the child acquires the skill.

- **Least-to-most prompting** can be used when the child knows how to do something, but must be supported to use the skill. For example, children often need help to generalize the skill of turn taking to new situations. While they might be proficient at taking turns when playing Peek-a-Boo with an adult, they might not be comfortable taking turns when they play with a stacking toy. The teacher provides the least amount of help necessary for the child to successfully take turns, providing more help as needed in order for the child to be successful.

The amount of help provided is planned and structured to match the child's skill level and desired outcome.

Peer-mediated strategies are another type of technique that can be used to support individual child learning (DiSalvo & Oswald, 2002; Kohler & Strain, 1999; Robertson, Green, Alpers, Schloss, & Kohler, 2003). These strategies are implemented when a more accomplished peer is paired with one who needs to develop or hone skills.

Peer mediation often occurs naturally in preschool settings. Children typically observe and interact with others in ways that scaffold development. An important aspect of designing curriculum and the learning environment is to make sure that young children have ample opportunities to interact with and learn from one another.

Formal peer-mediated strategies go a step further, when a teacher intentionally pairs children. A teacher typically identifies a peer who possesses a desired (target) skill and works with that child to show him or her how to support a child who has yet to develop the skill.

- First, the teacher coaches the more accomplished peer on how to interact with the target child in a supportive manner, typically through role playing.
- The teacher then structures situations in which the peer "mentor" and the child developing the skill can play or work together utilizing the target skill.

For example, Matthew may have difficulty entering peer group play situations. He often resorts to disrupting the group or aggressive behavior when his attempts to join are rebuffed. The teacher may coach Tarin, a socially-skilled child who is frequently a part of the group Matthew tries to join, to prompt Matthew to use appropriate words to request participation or materials. The teacher role-plays (practices) with Tarin the specific prompts he might use. In turn, Matthew is prompted to use more appropriate interaction strategies. The teacher provides Tarin with statements he can use with Matthew to positively reinforce his use of the target skill(s).

Pay attention to what children do and say.

Just as learners have choices about whether or not to engage in an instructional interaction, more accomplished peers must also be given choices about their involvement as mentors with other children.

Monitor Children's Progress

Effectively individualizing instruction is a cycle that involves knowing individual children, knowing effective instructional strategies, and determining whether or not the choices made resulted in child learning. The final step in this cycle of individualized instruction—monitoring and documenting children's progress—is just as important as knowing the best strategy to use (Pretti-Frontczak & Bricker, 2004).

Without this step, the capacity of teachers to meaningfully affect children's learning is minimized and time is wasted. Determining whether or not instruction is effective must be an evidence-based process in which children's learning is documented. To accomplish this:

- First give a strategy time to work—most meaningful learning does not occur overnight.
- Then, determine the best way to collect and use evidence of children's learning.

Identify the target skill or behavior in order to keep track of children's developmental or academic progress. Choose a method of recording observations that can be incorporated into daily routines and activities.

Focused observation helps teachers plan and implement meaningful curriculum and teaching strategies. Table 3 outlines some ways to document observations that can fit into a busy classroom schedule.

Table 3   Observation Techniques to Document Children's Learning

1. **Observe and record children's behavior at specific times of the day or week.** Choose a time during which the target child is likely to use a skill or behavior AND when enough adults are present.

2. **Make quick checks throughout the day.** If the skill or behavior is something that occurs fairly often, a relatively easy way to monitor progress is to pick a standard time (perhaps every hour) and record whether or not the behavior occurred at that time. While this does not yield detailed information, it indicates how often the behavior occurred.

3. **Use found objects to help keep track.** Use objects (in multiple pockets of an apron, for example) to help keep track of children's behavior. Claire is trying to keep track of how often Shoshanna initiates an interaction with a peer during 90-minute center time. Every time she sees Shoshanna initiate an interaction, she moves a small block (or other object) from one pocket to another. At the end of the day, she counts the number of blocks and records the number of initiations observed.

4. **Record the level of help a child requires.** For some children who have disabilities or special needs, it takes a long time to achieve a goal. Break down a task into smaller steps and document those steps to check for progress. Or track the amount of help a child needs to be successful. With Shoshanna, at first she might need very direct verbal prompts to approach another child (Claire asks Shoshanna to say, "Ashley will you play with me?"). After a while though, the teacher might just have to say "Shoshanna, what do you want Ashley to do?" in order to help Shoshanna approach Ashley. Finally, Claire might just need to gesture (point a finger at Ashley) in order to help Shoshanna know what to do. While Shoshanna still is not initiating interactions independently, she is certainly learning and making important progress toward that goal.

Make Sound Decisions Based on Data

The information that teachers collect as they observe and document children's learning is critically important to inform curricular decisions. Understanding when to introduce new content or increase support for a difficult skill depends on using the information collected as part of the observation process. Teachers must analyze and use the data they gather to determine if their teaching strategies are effective and make changes when the data suggests that they are not (Luze & Peterson, 2004).

The Role of IEPs

Individualization is the foundation of IEP development. IEP annual goals and objectives or benchmarks are target skills for the child to reach. While the annual goals provide a framework for a minimum level of accountability for individual children, they do not reflect the total of what children with disabilities learn in a given year, nor are they the curriculum.

IEP annual goals provide outcomes and direction that help young children access the general curriculum and developmentally typical environments. Although IEPs may include information that supports identifying appropriate instructional strategies, often it is up to the classroom teacher to determine the best way to help a child achieve his or her goals.

Appropriately individualized instruction leads to meaningful learning.

Fortunately, all of the strategies discussed here can help teachers implement instructional strategies that support the diverse learning needs of all children in a classroom. Effective teachers understand that, although IEPs may specify annual goals, these goals will be achieved when the skills to be learned are embedded in the classroom routine with strategies that facilitate children's development.

Individualizing instruction enables skilled teachers to provide meaningful learning experiences to all young children, including those with special needs (McWilliam, Wolery, & Odom, 2001). In order to provide effective instruction, teachers must

- be knowledgeable about the learners, including their abilities, interests, and needs
- create learning opportunities that are embedded in daily routines, activities, or experiences that capture children's interest and draw them into an instructional interaction
- implement a planned and structured approach for curriculum content
- make thoughtful decisions about the right kind and amount of support for children to be successful

- monitor the success of instruction to make sound decisions to support children's learning and development

Teaching is a reflective and intentional process. When scaffolding children's learning, teachers can choose from a variety of tools in their instructional toolbox!

References

Bredekamp, S., & Rosegrant, T. (1992). Reaching potentials through appropriate curriculum: Conceptual framework for applying the guidelines. In S. Bredekamp & T. Rosegrant (Eds.), *Reaching potentials: Appropriate curriculum and assessment for young children,* (Vol. 1.), (pp. 9–25). Washington, DC: National Association for the Education of Young Children.

Copple, C., & Bredekamp, S., (2009). *Developmentally appropriate practice in early childhood programs* (3rd ed.). Washington, DC: National Association for the Education of Young Children.

DiSalvo, C.A., & Oswald, D.P. (2002). Peer-mediated interventions to increase social interaction of children with autism. *Focus on Autism and Other Developmental Disabilities, 17*(4), 198–207.

Kohler, F.W., & Strain, P.S. (1999). Maximizing peer-mediated resources in integrated preschool classrooms. *Topics in Early Childhood Special Education, 19,* 92–102.

Luze, G.J., & Peterson, C.A. (2004). Improving outcomes for young children by assessing intervention integrity and monitoring progress: "Am I doing it right and is it working?" *Young Exceptional Children, 7*(2), 20–29.

McWilliam, R.A., Wolery, M., & Odom, S.L. (2001). Instructional perspectives in inclusive preschool classrooms. In M.J. Guralnick (Ed.), *Early childhood inclusion: Focus on change* (pp. 503–527). Baltimore, MD: Brookes.

Ostrosky, M.M., & Kaiser, A.P. (1991). Preschool classroom environments that promote communication. *Teaching Exceptional Children, 23,* 6–10.

Pretti-Frontczak, K., & Bricker, D. (2004). *An activity-based approach to early intervention* (3rd ed.). Baltimore, MD: Brookes.

Robertson, J., Green, K., Alpers, S., Schloss, P.J., & Kohler, F. (2003). Using a peer-mediated intervention to facilitate children's participation in inclusive childcare activities. *Education and Treatment of Children, 26,* 182–197.

Sandall, S.R., & Schwartz, I.S. (2008). *Building blocks for teaching preschoolers with special needs* (2nd ed.). Baltimore, MD: Brookes.

U.S. Department of Education, Office of Special Education Programs. (2005). *Twenty-fifth annual report to Congress on the implementation of the Individuals With Disabilities Education Act.* Washington, DC: Author.

Wolery, M. (2005). DEC recommended practices: Child-focused practices. In S. Sandall, M.L. Hemmeter, B.J. Smith, & M.E. McLean (Eds.), *DEC recommended practices: A comprehensive guide for practical application* (pp. 71–106). Longmont, CO: Sopris West.

Wolery, M., Ault, M.J., & Doyle, P.M. (1992). *Teaching students with moderate and severe disabilities: Use of response prompting strategies.* White Plains, NY: Longman.

Wolery, M., & Wilbers, J. (1994). *Including children with special needs in early childhood programs.* Washington, DC: National Association for the Education of Young Children.

Critical Thinking

1. Reflect back to a previous experience with young children when you observed another adult or implemented yourself one of the teaching supports listed in Table 2 in the article. Describe the behavior and what happened after you implemented the specific support.

2. Ask a teacher of young children to describe strategies they implement to get children's interest in a learning experience.

MARY B. BOAT, PhD, is Associate Professor and Program Coordinator, Early Childhood Education, University of Cincinnati, Ohio. She has worked directly and conducted research with young children with, or at risk for, disabilities. **LAURIE A. DINNEBEIL,** PhD, is the Judith Daso Herb Chair in Inclusive Early Childhood Education at the University of Cincinnati. She is a former preschool special education teacher and has worked extensively in the fields of early intervention and early childhood special education. **YOULMI BAE,** MEd, is a doctoral student and research assistant in Early Childhood Special Education at the University of Toledo, Ohio. She was an early childhood teacher in Korea and has worked with preschool Korean American children in a Korean Academy in Toledo.

From *Dimensions of Early Childhood,* vol. 38, no. 1, Winter 2010, pp. 3–10. Copyright © 2010 by Southern Early Childhood Association (SECA). Reprinted by permission.

The Why behind RTI

Response to Intervention flourishes when educators implement the right practices for the right reasons.

AUSTIN BUFFUM, MIKE MATTOS, AND CHRIS WEBER

We educators are directly responsible for crucial, life-saving work. Today, a student who graduates from school with a mastery of essential skills and knowledge has a good chance of successfully competing in the global market place, with numerous opportunities to lead a rewarding adult life. In stark contrast, students who fail in school are at greater risk of poverty, welfare dependency, incarceration, and early death. With such high stakes, educators today are like tightrope walkers without a safety net, responsible for meeting the needs of every student, with little room for error. Fortunately, compelling evidence shows that Response to Intervention (RTI) is our best hope for giving every student the additional time and support needed to learn at high levels (Burns, Appleton, & Stehouwer, 2005).

RTI's underlying premise is that schools should not wait until students fall far enough behind to qualify for special education to provide them with the help they need. Instead, schools should provide targeted and systematic interventions to *all* students as soon as they demonstrate the need. From one-room schoolhouses on the frozen tundra of Alaska to large urban secondary schools, hundreds of schools across the United States are validating the potential of these proven practices.

In light of this fact, why are so many schools and districts struggling to reap the benefits of RTI? Some schools mistakenly view RTI as merely a new way to qualify students for special education, focusing their efforts on trying a few token regular education interventions before referring struggling students for traditional special education testing and placement. Others are implementing RTI from a compliance perspective, doing just enough to meet mandates and stay legal. For still others, their RTI efforts are driven by a desire to raise test scores, which too often leads to practices that are counter productive to the guiding principles of RTI. Far too many schools find the cultural beliefs and essential practices of RTI such a radical departure from how schools have functioned for the past century that they are uncomfortable and unwilling to commit to the level of change necessary to succeed. Finally, some schools refuse to take responsibility for student learning, instead opting to blame kids, parents, lack of funding, or society in general for students' failures.

Although the specific obstacles vary, the underlying cause of the problem is the same: Too many schools have failed to develop the correct thinking about Response to Intervention. This has led them to implement some of the right practices for the wrong reasons.

The Wrong Questions

The questions an organization tries to answer guide and shape that organization's thinking. Unfortunately, far too many schools and districts are asking the wrong questions, like these.

How do we Raise our Test Scores?

Although high-stakes testing is an undeniable reality in public education, this is a fatally flawed initial question that can lead to incorrect thinking. For example, many districts that focus first on raising test scores have concluded that they need strictly enforced pacing guides for each course to ensure that teachers are teaching all required state standards before the high-stakes state tests. Usually, these guides determine exactly how many days each teacher has to teach a specific standard. Such thinking makes total sense if the goal is to *teach* all the material before the state assessments, but it makes no sense if the goal is to have all students *learn* essential standards. This in itself is problematic because, as Marzano (2001) notes, "The sheer number of standards is the biggest impediment to implementing standards" (p. 15). Assigning arbitrary, pre-determined amounts of time to specific learning outcomes guarantees that students who need additional time to learn will be left in the wake as the teacher races to cover the material.

This faulty thinking also leads to misguided intervention decisions, such as focusing school resources primarily on the "bubble kids" who are slightly below proficient. Administrators who adopt this policy conclude that if these students can improve, the school's test scores will likely make a substantial short-term jump. Consequently, the students far below basic often receive less help. This is deemed acceptable, as the primary goal of the school is to make adequate yearly progress, and the lowest learners are so far behind that providing them intensive resources will likely not bring about immediate gains in the school's state assessment rankings.

How Do We "Implement" RTI?

Frequently, we have worked with schools that view RTI as a mandated program that they must "implement." Consequently, they create an abundance of implementation checklists and time lines. Like obedient soldiers, site educators take their RTI marching orders and begin to complete the items on their RTI to-do list, such as administering a universal screening assessment, regrouping students in tiered groups, or creating a tutorial period.

Such an approach is fraught with pitfalls. First, it tends to reduce RTI to single actions to accomplish, instead of ongoing *processes* to improve teaching and learning. In addition, this approach fails to understand that what we ask educators to "do" in RTI are not ends in themselves, but means to an end. In other words, a school's goal should not be to administer a universal screening assessment in reading but to ensure that all students are able to read proficiently. To achieve this goal, it would be essential to start by measuring each student's current reading level, thus providing vital information to identify at-risk students and differentiate initial instruction.

How Do We Stay Legal?

Because RTI was part of the reauthorization of the Individuals with Disabilities Education Improvement Act (IDEIA) in 2004, many schools view its implementation from the perspective of legal compliance. This concern is understandable, as special education is by far the most litigated element of public education, and the potential costs of being out of compliance or losing a fair hearing can cripple a district.

Unfortunately, a large number of schools and districts are making RTI unreasonably burdensome. We find many districts creating unnecessarily complicated, laborious documentation processes for every level of student intervention, in fear that the data may be needed someday if a specific student requires special education services.

Teachers tell us that they often decide against recommending students for interventions "because it's not worth the paperwork." Other teachers complain that they "hate" RTI because they spend more time filling out forms than working with at-risk students. We have also worked with districts that refuse to begin implementing RTI until there is a greater depth of legal interpretation and case precedent; all the while, their traditional special education services are achieving woefully insufficient results in student learning.

If there is one thing that traditional special education has taught us, it's that staying compliant does not necessarily lead to improved student learning—in fact, the opposite is more often the case. Since the creation of special education in 1975, we have spent billions of dollars and millions of hours on special education—making sure we meet time lines, fill out the correct forms, check the correct boxes, and secure the proper signatures. A vast majority of schools are compliant, but are students learning?

Consider these facts:

- In the United States, the special education redesignation rate (the rate at which students have exited special education and returned to general education) is only 4 percent (U.S. Department of Education, 1996).
- According to the U.S. Department of Education, the graduation rate of students with special needs is 57 percent (National Center on Secondary Education and Transition [NCSET], 2006).
- It is estimated that up to 50 percent of the U.S. prison population were identified as students with special needs in school (NCSET, 2006).

There is little evidence to suggest that greater levels of legal compliance lead to greater levels of learning. If schools or districts would like to stay legal, they should start by focusing on student learning; parents rarely file for a fair hearing because their child is learning too much.

What's Wrong With This Kid?

At most schools, when a student struggles in the regular education program, the school's first systematic response is to refer the student for special education testing. Traditionally, schools have believed that "failure to succeed in a general education program meant the student must, therefore, have a disability" (Prasse, 2009). Rarely does special education testing assess the effectiveness and quality of the *teaching* that the student has received.

RTI is built on a polar opposite approach: When a student struggles, we assume that we are not teaching him or her correctly; as a result, we turn our attention to finding better ways to meet the student's specific learning needs. Unless schools are able to move beyond this flawed question, it is unlikely that they will ever see RTI as anything more than a new way to identify students for special education.

The Right Questions

Schools cannot succeed by doing the right things for the wrong reasons. So what are the right questions that should lead our work?

What is the Fundamental Purpose of Our School?

Our schools were not built so educators would have a place to work each day, nor do they exist so that our government officials have locations to administer high-stakes standardized tests each spring. If we peel away the various layers of local, state, and federal mandates, the core mission of every school should be to provide every student with the skills and knowledge needed to be a self-sufficient, successful adult.

Ask parents what they want school to provide their child, and it is doubtful the answer would be, "I just want my child to score proficient on state assessments," or "I want my child to master standard 2.2.3 this year." Learning specific academic standards and passing state tests are meaningless if the student does not become an intelligent, responsible adult who possesses the knowledge and quality of character to live a happy, rewarding adult life.

What Knowledge and Skills will our Children Need to be Successful Adults?

Gone are the days when the only skills a child needed to become a successful adult were a desire to work and some "elbow grease." Today's economy is driven by technology, innovation, and service. Because technology and human knowledge are changing at faster and faster rates, the top 10 in-demand jobs today probably didn't exist five or six years ago (Gunderson, Jones, & Scanland, 2004). Our high school graduates will most likely change careers at least four times by the age of 40—not jobs or employers, but *careers*. Alvin Toffler has been said to have suggested that, because of this acceleration of human knowledge, the definition of *illiterate* in the 21st century will not be "Can a person read and write?" but rather "Can a person learn, unlearn, and relearn?"

How do we prepare students for jobs that don't exist? How do we teach our students knowledge that we've not yet discovered? Teaching them comprehension and computation skills will not be enough—they need to be able to analyze, synthesize, evaluate, compare and contrast, and manipulate and apply information. We will erode our children's and world's future by limiting our vision to teaching only the skills and knowledge presented in our state assessments.

What Must We do to Make Learning a Reality for Every Student?

If we took the research on effective teaching and learning and condensed it into a simple formula for learning, it would look like this:

$$\text{Targeted Instruction} + \text{Time} = \text{Learning}$$

Because learning styles and instructional needs vary from student to student, we must provide each student with *targeted instruction*—that is, teaching practices designed to meet his or her individual learning needs. We also know that students don't all learn at the same speed. Some will need more time to learn. That is the purpose of RTI—to systematically provide every student with the additional time and support needed to learn at high levels.

Transforming the Tiers

If a school has asked the right questions, then how would this new way of thinking affect a school's RTI efforts? Quite honestly, it would transform every tier.

Tier 1

In Tier 1, the school would start by ensuring that every student has access to rigorous, grade-level curriculum and highly effective initial teaching. The process of determining essential student learning outcomes would shift from trying to cover all required standards to a more narrow focus on standards that all students must master to be able to succeed in the future.

A collective response will be required to ensure that all students learn, so teacher teams would work collaboratively to define each essential standard; deconstruct the standard into discrete learning targets (determine what each student must be able to know and do to demonstrate proficiency); identify the prior skills needed to master the standard; consider how to assess students on each target; and create a scope and sequence for the learning targets that would govern their pacing. Schools may continue to use such resources as textbooks as primary Tier 1 resources, but only by selecting those sections that align to what the team of teachers has determined to be essential for all students to master.

The school would understand that differentiation for individual student needs cannot be optional at Tier 1. Whether in an elementary math lesson or a secondary social studies lesson, teachers must scaffold content, process, and product on the basis of student needs, setting aside time to meet with small groups of students to address gaps in learning.

The direct, explicit instruction model contains the structures through which differentiation can take place. This thinking contradicts the approach taken by many schools that have purchased a research-based core instructional program and dictated that this program constitutes the *only* instructional material that teachers can use. This quest for fidelity sometimes becomes so rigid that each teacher is required to teach the same lesson, on the same day, following the same script.

Although we agree that schools should implement scientifically research-based resources, we also know that not all students learn the same way. In addition, because not all students learn at the same speed, we would plan flexible time into our master schedule to allow for reteaching essential standards for students who require it as well as providing enrichment learning for students who have already demonstrated mastery. To achieve these collective Tier 1 outcomes, we firmly believe that the only way for an organization to successfully implement RTI practices is within the professional learning community (PLC) model (Buffum, Mattos, & Weber, 2009).

Tier 2

At Tier 2, the school would use ongoing formative assessment to identify students in need of additional support, as well as to target each student's specific learning needs. In addition, teachers would create common assessments to compare results and determine which instructional practices were most and least effective in Tier 1. Giving students more of what *didn't* work in Tier 1 is rarely the right intervention!

Most Tier 2 interventions would be delivered through small-group instruction using strategies that directly target a skill deficit. Research has shown that small-group instruction can be highly effective in helping students master essential learnings (D'Agostino & Murphy, 2004; Vaughn, Gersten, & Chard, 2000).

Intervention is most effective when the interventions are timely, structured, and mandatory; focused on the *cause* of a student's struggles rather than on a symptom (for example, a letter grade); administered by a trained professional; and part of a system that guarantees that these practices apply no matter which teacher a student is assigned to (Buffum, Mattos, & Weber, 2009). Finally, because the best intervention is prevention, the effective RTI school would use universal screening data to identify students lacking the prerequisite skills for an essential standard and then provide targeted Tier 2 or Tier 3 support before delivering core instruction on that standard.

Tier 3

At Tier 3, we would start by guaranteeing that all students in need of intensive support would receive this help in *addition* to core instruction—not in place of it. If our goal is to ensure that all students learn at high levels, then replacing core instruction with remedial assistance not only fails to achieve this outcome, but also tracks at-risk students into below-grade-level curriculum.

Because Tier 3 students often have multiple needs, intensive help must be individualized, based on a problem-solving approach. It is unlikely that a single program will meet the needs of a student in Tier 3, as many of these students are like knots, with multiple difficulties that tangle together to form a lump of failure. Because of this, a school focused on meeting the needs of every student would develop a problem-solving team, composed of a diverse group of education experts who can address the students' social, emotional, and learning needs. The purpose of this team would not be to determine what is wrong with the student but to identify the specific needs the student still experiences after Tier 2 intervention, quantify them, and determine how to meet them.

Schools need to deliver Tier 3 interventions with greater intensity than Tier 2 interventions. They can do this by increasing both the duration and frequency of the intervention and lowering the student–teacher ratio (Mellard, 2004). At Tier 3, it is also important to quantify the student's specific learning needs. It would not be enough to say that a student's problem is "reading." Instead, a school team might find that a 2nd grade student is reading grade-level passages at a rate of 20 words read correctly (WRC) per minute compared with the expectation of 45 WRC for 2nd grade students at that point in the school year.

If a school diligently applies these practices, a vast majority of students will never need to be referred for special education testing. When all students have guaranteed access to rigorous curriculum and effective initial teaching, targeted and timely supplemental support, and personalized intensive support from highly trained educators, few will experience failure (Sornson, Frost, & Burns, 2005). In the rare case that this level of support does not meet a specific students' needs, the student may indeed have a learning disability. In this case, special education identification would be fair and appropriate.

Although the purpose of RTI is not special education identification, a school will identify far fewer students for these services if they ask the right questions and take preventative steps. Schools that fail to do so will continue to blame students for failing, which will perpetuate the over-identification of minority, English language learning, and economically disadvantaged students into special education.

Doing the Right Work for the Right Reasons

The secret to capturing the right way of thinking about RTI comes down to answering this question: Why are we implementing Response to Intervention?

The answer lies in why we joined this profession in the first place—to help children. Our work must be driven by the knowledge that our collaborative efforts will help determine the success or failure of our students. RTI should not be a program to raise student test scores, but rather a process to realize students' hopes and dreams. It should not be a way to meet state mandates, but a means to serve humanity. Once we understand the urgency of our work and embrace this noble cause as our fundamental purpose, how could we possibly allow any student to fail?

References

Buffum, A., Mattos, M., & Weber, C. (2009). *Pyramid response to intervention: RTI, professional learning communities, and how to respond when students don't learn.* Bloomington, IN: Solution Tree.

Burns, M. K., Appleton, J. J., & Stehouwer, J. D. (2005). Meta-analytic review of response-to-intervention research: Examining field-based and research-implemented models. *Journal of Psychoeducational Assessment, 23,* 381–394.

D'Agostino, J. V., & Murphy, J. A. (2004). A meta-analysis of reading recovery in United States schools. *Educational Evaluation and Policy Analysis, 26*(1), 23–38.

Gunderson, S., Jones, R., & Scanland, K. (2004). *The jobs revolution: Changing how America works.* n.p.: Copywriters Inc.

Marzano, R. J. (2001). How and why standards can improve student achievement: A conversation with Robert J. Marzano. *Educational Leadership, 59*(1), 14–18.

Mellard, D. (2004). *Understanding responsiveness to intervention in learning disabilities determination.* Retrieved from the National Research Center on Learning Disabilities at www.nrcld.org/about/publications/papers/mellard.pdf

National Center on Secondary Education and Transition (NCSET). (2006, March). Promoting effective parent involvement in secondary education and transition. *Parent Brief.* Retrieved from www.ncset.org/publications/viewdesc.asp?id=2844

Prasse, D. P. (2009). *Why adopt an RTI model?* Retrieved from the RTI Action Network at www.rtinetwork.org/Learn/Why/ar/WhyRTI

Sornson, R., Frost, F., & Burns, M. (2005). Instructional support teams in Michigan: Data from Northville Public Schools. *Communique, 33*(5), 28–29.

U.S. Department of Education. (1996). Eighteenth Annual Report to Congress on the Implementation of the Individuals with Disabilities Education Act. Retrieved from www2.ed.gov/pubs/OSEP96AnlRpt/chap1c.html

Vaughn, S., Gersten, R., & Chard, D. J. (2000). The underlying message in LD intervention research: Findings from research syntheses. *Exceptional Children, 67,* 99–114.

Critical Thinking

1. These authors are also critical of how schools implement RTI; however, they believe that school personnel misunderstand the true purpose for RTI. What are those misunderstandings? Do you agree?

2. The authors suggest that placing students into special education may not be the right intervention for many failing students. What are their reasons? Do you agree?

3. Return to the first RTI article for reading teachers; compare the implementation of RTI tiers with the suggestions for transforming the tiers in this article. Are there differences in the implementation process? What are they?

4. Now what do you think? Write a brief reflection summarizing what you believe are the most important points for you to understand, why these points are important, and how you might implement them for a student struggling in your content area.

AUSTIN BUFFUM is former senior deputy superintendent of the Capistrano Unified School District, California, and is currently a PLC associate with Solution Tree; austinbuffum@cox.net. **MIKE MATTOS** is a former elementary and middle school principal; mikemattos@me.com; and **CHRIS WEBER** is director of K–6 instructional services in Garden Grove Unified School District in Orange County, California; chrisaweber@me.com.

From *Educational Leadership*, Vol. 68, No. 2, October 2010, pp. 1–7. Copyright © 2010 by Austin Buffum, Mike Mattos, and Chris Weber. Reprinted by permissions of the authors. The material is from their book, "Simplifying Response to Intervention: Four Essential Guiding Principles". Bloomington, IN Solution Tree Press 2011.

UNIT 4

Supporting Young Children's Development

Unit Selections

Learner Outcomes

After reading this Unit, you will be able to:

- Develop a plan for ongoing professional development.

- Plan appropriate play experiences that allow children to develop peer relationships.

- Plan for large motor physical play experiences for young children on a daily basis.

- Describe why it is important for children to play throughout childhood.

- Explain why children tattle and the importance of developing appropriate social skills during the early childhood years.

- Identify why childhood obesity has become such an epidemic in our country today.

Student Website
www.mhhe.com/cls

Internet References

Action for Healthy Kids
www.actionforhealthykids.org
American Academy of Pediatrics
www.aap.org
You Can Handle Them All
www.disciplinehelp.com

This unit begins with a topic I haven't included in the past; one focused on the professional instead of the young children we serve. Care and education of young children is a profession as defined by the need for initial preparation and ongoing professional development. In "Take Charge of your Personal and Professional Development," Carla B. Goble and Diane M. Horm help educators see the importance of ongoing professional development and the need to be an active lifelong learner in the field. Just as we would not want to go to a physician who attended medical school over 25 years ago and has never attended a conference or read a professional journal, we would not advocate that same lack of professional development for our field. The added benefit of developing a professional development plan is that you are able to interact with others who share your passion for the care and education of young children and interaction with their families. It is a wonderful way to build your network of contacts and friends, whether you are new to an area or a long -time resident. Get out and get involved in our wonderful profession. Become an active member of a student ECE organization on your campus or start one if none exists. Look to attend professional development opportunities in your community. If funds are available, consider joining a professional organization. Often student membership rates are available for full-time students.

Recently I conducted a professional development in-service session for all the kindergarten and first-grade teachers in a school district located in the suburbs of a large Midwest city. The one issue about which the teachers were most concerned was the lack of time for play in their class, especially in light of the research on the importance of play-based learning experiences. "Helping Children Play and Learn Together" by Michaelene M. Ostrosky and Hedda Meadan is a resource for any staff looking for research that supports the need for play in programs serving children in the early childhood years. The development of important social and emotional skills during the early childhood years will serve the children well as they move through childhood and into adulthood.

Educators receive many questions from parents about what is called rough-and-tumble play among young children. The need for children to engage in appropriate rough play is strong, and the development of large muscles and the ability to control those muscles is a valuable skill to learn. In "Rough Play: One of the Most Challenging Behaviors" Frances M. Carlson provides teachers with many suggestions for big body play and strategies for supporting that play in educational settings. As educators we constantly straddle that line between what is developmentally appropriate for children's development and legal restrictions placed on educators from school administrators and insurance companies. A balance can be found, and there is no need to eliminate playgrounds or recess for legal issues if there is proper supervision and appropriate and well-maintained equipment. Many insurance companies serving educational institutions have developed outstanding resource materials that provide appropriate guidelines.

Normally as editor I wouldn't consider an article for *Annual Editions: Early Childhood Education* with the word *middle* in the title. There is an *Annual Editions: Education* that may be better suited for an article aimed at middle childhood, those years from

© Design Pics/Hammond HSN

age 8 through age 12. But on a second and then third reading of the article "Play and Social Interaction in Middle Childhood" by two very well known early childhood educators, Doris Bergen and Doris Pronin Fromberg, I realized the message is vitally important for all early childhood educators to read as well. The middle years follow early childhood and build on children's initial encounters with their family, environment and formal learning experience. Children in the middle years are now undergoing tremendous pressure to often, act, dress, and perform like teenagers. Recognition of the importance and value of play and other experiences unique to the middle years are important for early childhood educators. The middle childhood years continue to build on the strong foundation established during the early childhood years and when supported by family members and educators can serve to strengthen the experiences children will take into their teen and adult years. I do find it disheartening to read the first sentence in Bergen and Fromberg's summary, "Play has always been important in middle childhood, but its forms have changed with society and, in some cases, its very existence has been threatened." Unfortunately that statement could also be applied to play during the early childhood years. Schools are eliminating recess and reducing the opportunities for free choice play materials in preschool, kindergarten and primary classrooms all across the country. Both early and middle childhood educators must advocate for hands-on experiential -based experiences for the children in our schools. I am saddened by the lack of opportunities for play available for many children and remember with fondness the times my sister and I spent making a tree fort and inventing games during our middle childhood years.

When I was a primary teacher, tattling was an everyday occurrence in the classroom or on the playground. I tried many strategies aimed at dealing with this practice. "Is Tattling a Bad Word?" by Katharine C. Kersey and Marie L. Masterson provides excellent suggestions for adults helping children as they acquire appropriate social skills. Skilled teachers are constantly monitoring and adjusting their teaching skills to best meet the needs of their students.

Issues related to the health of young children continued to emerge this year. "Keeping Children Active: What You Can Do to Fight Childhood Obesity" addresses the importance of a healthy body for optimal educational performance. Childhood obesity is noticeable every time one enters a fast-food restaurant and hears a child order a meal by its number on the menu because they are so familiar with the selection at that particular restaurant. It is also evident on a playground where children just sit on the sideline not wanting to participate with their peers due to negative body image. Teachers can apply the suggestions provided in "Keeping Children Active: What You Can Do to Fight Childhood Obesity," which will help children develop appropriate eating habits and an active lifestyle. Parents and educators must work together to promote healthy living, with one-third of children classified as overweight and one-fifth of children as obese. Teachers should also participate in healthy-living activities. Only then will our society begin to realize that a lifestyle that includes good nutrition and exercise is one of the best ways to lead a long and healthy life. Teachers can model an active healthy lifestyle for the children in their classroom. Teachers can walk around the playground when the children are outside instead of standing in a group and talking to the other teachers. They can also talk about the foods eaten for breakfast, lunch, and dinner and share healthy eating tips with the children.

The title of this unit, once again, must be stressed: Supporting Young Children's Development. Teachers who see their job of working with young children as finding the approach that best supports each child's individual development will be most successful. We are not to change children to meet some idealistic model, but become an investigator whose job it is to ferret out the individual strengths and learning styles of each child in our care. Enjoy each day and the many different experiences awaiting you when you work with young children and their families.

Take Charge of Your Personal and Professional Development

CARLA B. GOBLE AND DIANE M. HORM

As the instructor gathered up books and materials one evening after a community college teacher-inservice class, one student lingered and then came up to the front of the room. She said, "My director made me take this class, and I really didn't want to have to go to school, especially at night. I work all day, and it is difficult for me to find time to study." Then she brightened, saying, "But I have learned new things in this class, and I like being here where I can talk to other teachers like myself. In my classroom I've started using the positive guidance strategies we're learning, and I already see such a difference in the children's behavior and learning. I only wish I had known all this before—earlier in my teaching. I could have been a better teacher and avoided some mistakes."

Comments like these are not uncommon. Although a reluctant student at first, the teacher in the scenario recognizes the benefits of professional development as she learns new, effective teaching approaches. Her program's director, like many a counterpart, responded to the increased call for higher levels of professional development for early care and education teachers by "making" the teacher take college classes. Many state licensing agencies and prekindergarten, Head Start, and Early Head Start employers are becoming more aware of the growing body of research (Bowman, Donovan, & Burns 2001; Barnett 2004) that supports the benefits of professional development for early childhood educators, early childhood education programs, and, most important, young children.

The need for professional development is universal, whatever a person's profession. Professionals must continually enrich their knowledge and increase their sense of professionalism over the course of their careers so as to implement current research based practice. Relative to early care and education, NAEYC emphasizes that "it is through caring, committed, and competent early childhood professionals that young children and their families experience the excellent curriculum, the appropriate teaching strategies, the thoughtful assessment practices, the supportive services, and the effective public policies" evident in high-quality early care and education settings (Hyson 2003, 1). To deliver this range and type of high-quality services, early care and education staff must complete ongoing professional development.

Professionals must continually enrich their knowledge and increase their sense of professionalism over the course of their careers so as to implement current research-based practice.

Early childhood professional development brings to the forefront the significance of the early years for children's learning and development and highlights the central role early childhood educators play in children's successful outcomes. The purpose of this article is to help early childhood teachers recognize the importance of their professional development and to encourage them to be proactive about their own personal and professional growth and development.

The Early Childhood Education Profession

Like the field of nursing, early childhood education has changed and evolved from a job or occupation into a professional field and career. Similarities between the two fields include increased education requirements, differentiated levels of staffing with corresponding levels of education, and expectations of lifelong learning

The Importance of Professional Development for Early Childhood Teachers

Teaching young children is serious work that requires high-quality, dedicated, professional teachers who see the importance of what they do and are eager to increase their effectiveness, knowledge, and skills.

- **Research findings** indicate that "quality encompasses a broad array of knowledge, skills, and behaviors" (Early et al. 2007, 575). The researchers say further that "by definition, teachers who provide instruction that leads to positive child outcomes are high-quality teachers."
- **A report by NCEDL** (National Center for Early Development and Learning) on connecting professional development to child outcomes "revealed that it is high-quality interactions between children and teachers that are the active ingredients through which pre-K programs foster the academic, language, and social competencies of children" (2008, 4). The report further says, "Improving teacher–child interactions requires continuing and consistent professional development opportunities . . ."
- **A study** on the relationship between teaching behaviors, college education, and child-related professional preparation (Berk 1985) found that early childhood education teachers with two- or four-year college degrees offered more direction and suggestions to children and were more responsive and encouraging than teachers who did not have college degrees. Teachers who had child-related, college-level professional development emphasized oral language development almost three times as much as did teachers with a high school education.

and professional development (NAEYC 1993; Parkin 1995; Gerrish, McManus, & Ashworth 2003; Cameron, Armstrong-Stassen, & Out 2004). More than 20 years ago, Lilian Katz (1987) identified attributes in the early childhood education field that are inherent in any profession: a code of ethics, a specialized body of knowledge, standards of practice, a professional organization, district associations, and at least one professional credential.

The work of Feeney and Freeman (Feeney 1995; Feeney & Freeman 2002; Freeman & Feeney 2006) explores early childhood education as a profession and documents the changes and challenges as new dimensions of professionalism have been added. Freeman and Feeney (2006, 16) ask early childhood educators to consider "what opportunities today's leaders may pursue to increase this professionalism." Mitchell (2007) points out improved public perceptions of early childhood education as evidence that progress has been made in professionalizing the field (see "The Importance of Professional Development for Early Childhood Teachers").

Growing Professionally

Professional development is more than taking a college class or attending a workshop. Just as children's development encompasses more than the old "nature versus nurture" debate, the growth of teaching competence involves more than just believing that *we* can make decisions that impact our own professional development and teaching quality. Wittmer and Petersen tell us that becoming a professional "requires courage, commitment, and caring" (2006, 358). They add that to be "a reflective, theory-based professional is to reflect on your vision for children and families, professional philosophy, ethical values, and professional plan (your vision for yourself)."

Knowledge Development

Because professional development is connected to developmentally appropriate early childhood teaching and children's development and learning, early childhood teachers should take charge and actively seek and complete ongoing professional development. Essential first steps are identifying your personal characteristics and then assessing your professional knowledge, skills, and behaviors. Upon entry and throughout a career in early childhood education, give thoughtful attention and planning to your personal development and the demands of the field—the necessary knowledge, skills, and behaviors.

To maximize your professional development opportunities, it is important to set goals, plan for and seek professional development opportunities, map a career path, and acquire ongoing knowledge and skills. Be sure your professional development path is designed to advance both personal and professional competencies and, most important, to prepare you to be the best early childhood teacher you can possibly be.

Be sure your professional development path is designed to advance both personal and professional competencies.

Personal Development

Laura Colker (2008) asks what it takes to be an effective early childhood teacher and identifies a dozen personal characteristics: passion, perseverance, willingness to take risks, pragmatism, patience, flexibility, respect, creativity, authenticity, love of learning, high energy, and sense of humor. Analysis reveals that the characteristics are clustered in the social-emotional domain. These dispositions or temperament variables were self-identified by 43 early childhood practitioners in interviews by Colker. Her survey focused on a discussion about how the teachers chose early childhood education as a field and why early childhood care and teaching was a good career match for them as individuals.

To further their personal development, early childhood educators can use the attributes listed by Colker (2008) to help pinpoint personal strengths as well as characteristics that may require modification. Teachers can modify their own style and develop new ways of relating to and interacting with children and others. Talking with other teachers about patience or having a sense of humor, keeping a personal reflection journal, and developing healthy outlets for stress are some strategies to consider. Enlisting the help of a mentor, coach, or role model who exhibits the desirable personal characteristics is a potentially helpful method for making changes in one's own personal practices and habits.

Professional Development

Freeman and Feeney (2006) recommend that to progress in the early childhood education profession, teachers need to recognize the distinctive features inherent in the educator role. As early childhood education practitioners, we can consider how these distinctions can guide "the creation of a unique professionalism that honors our field's particular ways of working effectively with young children and their families" (Freeman & Feeney 2006, 16). The field of early childhood education has particular ways of approaching and addressing programming for young children, including partnering with families (Briggs, Jalongo, & Brown 2006).

The core values and specific features of early childhood education include, and go beyond, the personal qualities noted by Colker (2008). They are specialized knowledge, philosophical foundations, research-to-practice applications, and ethical guidelines (NAEYC 2005; Feeney 2010).

Taking Charge

An important step in taking charge of your own professional growth is to develop a statement defining your early childhood education professional philosophy and to know what's expected of an early childhood education professional. This is essential not only for your own understanding of how and why you teach young children but also to be able to communicate to families and others how children develop and why you use certain teaching practices.

1. **Write out your philosophy.** Wittmer and Petersen (2010) explain the purpose and use of a professional philosophy: "A professional's philosophy statement includes what you believe about the rights of children, goals for children, what

children need, how they learn best, the definition of *quality* in programs, and why it matters for children and families" (p. 380). Early childhood educators should review their philosophy statement often and, as they learn and grow professionally, make changes that reflect new knowledge and understandings. The philosophy statement should be kept in a professional portfolio (Priest 2010) that documents not only your professional development activities but also your advances in knowledge and skill. Learning and professional development are lifelong, and Wittmer and Peterson remind us, "Developing a philosophy is a process rather than a product. It is ongoing and professionals should rewrite it often in their careers as they grow in knowledge and experience. Professionals can use their philosophy statement to reflect on their values and stay true to their principles as they progress in the profession" (2010, 380).

2. **Know what's expected of a professional.** The field of early childhood education has identified specific knowledge, skills, and dispositions that are inherent in the preparation of high-quality early childhood teachers. These professional attributes include six broad standards that "promote the unifying themes that define the early childhood profession" (NAEYC 2009, 2). The standards and key elements (pp. 11–17, www.naeyc.org/files/naeyc/file/positions/ProfPrepStandards09.pdf) can be used as a guide to plan and track your professional development.

These core standards are used in NAEYC accreditation of associate degree programs and NAEYC recognition of baccalaureate, master, and doctoral programs in National Council for Accreditation of Teacher Education (NCATE) accredited schools of education. The standards describe what well-prepared students (at associate, BA/BS, and graduate levels of professional preparation) should know and be able to do, and thus outline the scope of our field's professional knowledge and skills. Progression through the various levels of formal education deepens one's knowledge base and expertise in these core areas.

Types of Professional Development

As you develop an NAEYC standards-based plan for professional development, it is important to recognize the various forms of professional development available. Purposefully select those tailored to your short- and long-term career goals.

Formal professional development opportunities bearing academic credit are available through colleges and universities in the forms of certificate programs and degrees, such as associate, bachelor, and advanced graduate degrees. Some two- and four-year colleges work together to ensure career pathways beginning with CDA preparation, going on to the associate degree, and then a bachelor's degree.

These pathways are created through partnerships called *articulation agreements.* In some communities, articulation agreements do not exist. Where they are in place, it is important to recognize that they may vary in the number of credit hours that can be transferred from the two-year to the four-year college. Thus, it is valuable to meet with academic counselors from both institutions to make certain that credits are recognized and will transfer.

College credits from specialized early childhood and child development courses are applicable in meeting CDA renewal and state licensing requirements as well as degree requirements. Continuing education units, known as CEUs, are also available for some workshops and other professional development seminars. These can be applied to CDA renewal and child care licensing and requirements, and as documentation of training required by programs.

Teachers may use a variety of methods for self-study and informal professional development, depending on their individual learning style, needs, and circumstances. Examples include reading professional journals and books; viewing professional multimedia presentations, taking online courses, and participating in staff meetings and in-house workshops; receiving reflective supervision and mentoring by more experienced practitioners; discussing issues with peers and supervisors; visiting and observing in other classrooms; and using professional development websites as well as attending professional development institutes and conferences.

Teachers may use a variety of methods for self-study and informal professional development, depending on their individual learning style, needs, and circumstances.

Several online resources can help you develop and plan your own professional development (see "Online Resources for Professional Development"). Head Start's Early Childhood Learning and Knowledge Center website provides descriptions of various types of professional development opportunities as well as tips and strategies. The Child Care and Early Education Research Connections website links early childhood curriculum to research. Membership in NAEYC

Online Resources for Professional Development

Child Care and Early Education Research Connections. This site provides comprehensive, up-to-date, easy-to-use resources from the many disciplines related to the field of early childhood education. www.researchconnections.org

Council for Professional Recognition. Here are resources for the Child Development Associate (CDA) Credential as well as other professional development opportunities and materials. www.cdacouncil.org

Early Childhood Educator Professional Development Program. This U.S. Department of Education website provides professional development programs for improving the knowledge and skills of early childhood educators who work in communities with high levels of poverty and who teach children of families with low incomes. www.ed.gov/programs/eceducator/index.html

Early Childhood Learning and Knowledge Center. The Office of Head Start offers lists of professional development opportunities, tools and resources, information on professional organizations, and links to other websites for early childhood educators. http://eclkc.ohs.acf.hhs.gov/hslc/Professional percent 20Development

National Association for the Education of Young Children. NAEYC's online Early Childhood Professionals pages provide resources for improving professional practice and links to resources for self-study, courses, training sessions, and professional development specialists. www.naeyc.org/ecp (see also www.naeyc.org/yc/pastissues and www.naeyc.org/tyc for online articles)

National Child Care Information and Technical Assistance Center. The Child Care Bureau offers this national clearinghouse and technical assistance center to provide child care information resources and services, state and territory information, federal information, research, and other tools and resources. http://nccic.acf.hhs.gov

National Professional Development Center on Inclusion. The NPDCI works with states to offer professional development to support inclusion. Resources available include information for families, early intervention providers, schools and administrators, and early

intervention agencies. http://community.fpg
.unc.edu/npdci

The National Registry Alliance. This private,
nonprofit, voluntary organization maintains
state early childhood and school-age workforce registries and professional development leaders; also provides information,
briefs, and conference information. www
.registryalliance.org

provides professional publications and opportunities for professional development and for linking with
other early childhood professionals at national, state,
and local levels. NAEYC publications *Young Children*
and *Teaching Young Children* make many articles and
resources available online.

Conclusion

The quality of an early childhood program is directly
related to an individual teacher's professional development. By designing and completing a professional development plan, early childhood educators ready themselves
for each step on the professional development ladder.
The process enhances their own personal and professional development and assists them in effectively meeting a broad scope of demands in today's evolving early
childhood education profession. Most important is the
empowerment that comes from taking charge of your own
personal and professional development. You will become
the best qualified educator you can be for each child whose
life you touch and change during the course of your career
as an early childhood educator.

References

Barnett, W.S. 2004. Better teachers, better preschools:
Students' achievement linked to teacher qualifications.
Preschool Policy Matters Issue 2. New Brunswick, NJ:
National Institute for Early Education Research.

Berk, L.E. 1985. Relationship of caregiver education to child-
oriented attitudes, job satisfaction, and behaviors toward
children. *Child Care Quarterly* 14 (2): 103–29.

Bowman, B.T., M.S. Donovan, & M.S. Burns. 2001. *Eager to learn:
Educating our preschoolers.* Report of the National Research
Council. Washington, DC: National Academies Press.

Briggs, N.R., M.R. Jalongo, & L. Brown. 2006. Working with
families of young children: Our history and our future
goals. In *Major trends and issues in early childhood
education,* eds. J.P. Isenberg & M.R. Jalongo, 56–69. New
York: Teachers College Press.

Cameron, S., M.S. Armstrong-Stassen, & J. Out. 2004.
Recruitment and retention of nurses: Challenges facing
hospital and community employers. *Canadian Journal of
Nursing Leadership* 17 (3): 79–92.

Colker, L.J. 2008. Twelve characteristics of effective early
childhood teachers. *Young Children* 63 (2): 68–73. www
.naeyc.org/yc/pastissues/2005/march

Early, D.M., K.L. Maxwell, M. Burchinal, R.H. Bender, C.
Ebanks, G.T. Henry, J. Iriondo-Perez, A.J. Masburn, R.C.
Pianta, S. Alva, D. Bryant, K. Cai, R.C. Clifford, J.W.
Griffin, C. Howes, J. Hyun-Joo, E. Peisner-Feinberg,
N. Vandergrift, & N. Zill. 2007. Teachers' education,
classroom quality, and young children's academic skills:
Results from seven studies of preschool programs. *Child
Development* 78 (2): 558–80.

Feeney, S. 1995. Professionalism in early childhood teacher
education: Focus on ethics. *Journal of Early Childhood
Teacher Education* 16 (3): 13–15.

Feeney, S. 2010. Celebrating the 20th anniversary of
NAEYC's Code of Ethical Conduct—Ethics today in
early care and education: Review, reflection, and the
future. *Young Children* 65 (2): 72–77.

Feeney, S., & N.K. Freeman. 2002. Early childhood education
as an emerging profession: Ongoing conversations. *Child
Care Information Exchange* (Jan/Feb): 38–41.

Freeman, N.K., & S. Feeney. 2006. Viewpoint. The new face
of early care and education: Who are we? Where are we
going? *Young Children* 61 (5): 10–16.

Gerrish, K., M. McManus, & P. Ashworth. 2003. Creating
what sort of professional? Master's level nurse education
as a professionalizing strategy. *Nursing Inquiry* 10 (2):
103–12.

Hyson, M., ed. 2003. *Preparing early childhood professionals:
NAEYC's standards for initial licensure, advanced, and
associate degree programs.* Washington, DC: NAEYC.

Katz, L.G. 1987. The nature of professions: Where is early
childhood education? In *Current topics in early childhood
education, Vol. 7,* ed. L.G. Katz. Norwood, NJ: Ablex.

Mitchell, A. 2007. Developing our profession. *Young Children*
62 (4): 6–7.

NAEYC. 1993. A conceptual framework for early childhood
professional development: A position statement of
the National Association for the Education of Young
Children. Washington, DC: Author. (Under revision
2010–11.) www.naeyc.org/files/naeyc/file/positions/
PSCONF98.pdf

NAEYC. 2005. Position Statement. Code of ethical conduct &
statement of commitment. Revised. www.naeyc.org/files/
naeyc/file/positions/PSETH05.pdf

NAEYC. 2009. Position Statement. NAEYC standards for early
childhood professional preparation programs. www.naeyc
.org/files/naeyc/file/positions/ProfPrepStandards09.pdf

NCEDL (National Center for Early Development and
Learning). 2008. Connecting professional development
to child outcomes. *Professional Development & Teacher-
Child Interactions* 12 (1): 4.

Parkin, P.A.C. 1995. Nursing the future: A reexamination of the professionalization thesis in the light of some recent developments. *Journal of Advanced Nursing* 2l (3): 561–67.

Priest, C. 2010. The benefits of developing a professional portfolio. *Young Children* 65(1): 92–96. www.naeyc.org/yc/pastissues/2010/january

Wittmer, D.S., & S.H. Petersen. 2010. *Infant and toddler development and responsive program planning: A relationship-based approach.* 2nd ed. Upper Saddle River, NJ: Merrill/Pearson.

Critical Thinking

1. If you haven't already, write a professional philosophy. Start by keeping a list of terms that you feel describe how you believe children best learn and the types of learning experiences you will provide for young children.

2. If you are currently in a professional preparation program, think of all the ways you receive information about the profession. If you are no longer in a formal preparation program, develop a plan for keeping up to date with the ECE profession and how you will continue to learn and improve your teaching practices.

CARLA B. GOBLE, PhD, is the George Kaiser Family Foundation Endowed Professor of Child Development at Tulsa Community College in Oklahoma. She teaches child development and early childhood education courses, coordinates the child development program, and facilitates the professional development of early childhood teachers. cgoble@tulsacc.edu. **DIANE M. HORM,** PhD, is the George Kaiser Family Foundation Endowed Chair of Early Childhood Education and director of the Early Childhood Education Institute at the University of Oklahoma at Tulsa. Along with colleagues, she implements a bachelor's degree completion program in early childhood education in partnership with Tulsa Community College as the primary collaborator. dhorm@ou.edu

Helping Children Play and Learn Together

The preschoolers in Ms. Mimi's classroom are very busy throughout the day, working on emerging pretend-play skills, turn taking, conflict management, phonological awareness, math knowledge, and other academic, behavioral, and social skills. Ms. Mimi knows that young children's readiness for school comes with increased expectations for academic skills, but she worries that her preschoolers are not getting enough experience with social skill building. When her supervisor comes for a visit, Ms. Mimi shares her concern that she may not be meeting her preschoolers' social needs. She says, "Some days I find myself worrying so much about teaching literacy, numeracy, and all the other academic skills that I wonder if the children have enough opportunities to learn how to get along with each other."

MICHAELENE M. OSTROSKY, PHD AND HEDDA MEADAN, PHD

Ms. Mimi's concern is an important one. Young children's "readiness for school" has taken center stage for educators and policy makers, while their social development, a powerful predictor of school adjustment, success in school, and later success in life, is often ignored (Bowman, Donovan, & Burns 2000; Shonkoff & Phillips 2001).

During the early childhood years, children learn to interact with one another in ways that are positive and successful (Bovey & Strain 2003a). For example, young children use social skills to get a friend's attention, offer or ask to share something, and say something nice to a friend.

Researchers stress the importance of positive peer relationships in childhood and later life (Ladd 1999). Several national reports—for example, *A Good Beginning* (Peth-Pierce 2000), *Eager to Learn* (Bowman, Donovan, & Burns 2000), *From Neurons to Neighborhoods* (Shonkoff & Phillips 2001), the Ewing Marion Kauffman Foundation (2002) report on social emotional development—discuss the significant role of social emotional development in children's readiness for success in school. These studies identify a number of social emotional skills and abilities that help new kindergartners be successful:

- confidence,
- the ability to develop good relationships with peers,
- concentrating on and persisting with challenging tasks,
- attending and listening to instructions,
- being able to solve social problems, and
- effectively communicating emotions.

The absence of positive social interactions in childhood is linked to negative consequences later in life, such as withdrawal, loneliness, depression, and feelings of anxiety. In addition, low acceptance by peers in the early years is a predictor of grade retention, school dropout, and mental health and behavior problems (Ladd 1999).

The Pyramid for Teaching Social Skills

Educators can do many things to promote and support positive social interactions and prevent challenging behavior. They can develop a positive relationship with each child, structure the physical and social classroom environments to support positive interactions, and teach individual children specific social skills that they lack.

Fox and colleagues (2003) describe a pyramid framework for supporting social competence and preventing young children's challenging behavior (see www.vanderbilt.edu/csefel and www.challengingbehavior.org). The pyramid includes four levels of practice to address the needs of all children: (1) building nurturing and responsive relationships with children, families, and colleagues; (2) implementing high-quality supportive environments; (3) using social and emotional supports and teaching strategies; and (4) planning intensive individualized interventions. The focus of the pyramid model is on promotion and prevention, with the top level, individualized interventions, used only when necessary; the premise is that when the bottom three levels are in place, only a small number of children will require more intensive support.

This article highlights environmental and teaching strategies that support and facilitate the development of preschoolers' peer interaction skills—the skills children use to successfully interact with one another, such as sharing, taking turns, asking for assistance, and helping one another. We use a question-and-answer format to describe strategies that support the teaching pyramid's second and third levels (creating supportive environments and fostering positive social interactions), with the questions coming from many early childhood educators across the United States.

Structuring the Physical Environment

The 18 children in my classroom have a variety of strengths and come from diverse cultural and linguistic backgrounds. The class does not have the community feeling I had hoped to achieve by this point in the school year. While I realize that most of the children did not know one another prior to entering the group, I try to encourage relationships between them. What can I do to my classroom setting to support peer interactions (such as talking, playing, and enjoying being together), especially during center time?

When considering the design of the classroom's physical environment, two factors related to social emotional development warrant careful attention: strategies to promote engagement and ideas for preventing challenging behavior. Effective physical and social emotional aspects of early childhood classroom environments can enhance children's learning (Curtis & Carter 2005). Teachers need to ensure that the classroom is a place where children want to be. In addition, it is important to teach children the skills they need to be successful with their peers.

Well-planned and well-stocked learning centers increase the likelihood that children will engage in play and learning with each other. They decrease the likelihood of challenging behaviors. Consider the following when designing and maintaining learning centers:

> **Well-planned and well-stocked learning centers increase the likelihood that children will engage in play and learning with each other.**

1. **Placement.** Set clear boundaries to let children know where a center begins/ends, prevent overcrowding, and to separate noisy centers from quieter ones so children can concentrate on their play and learning.
2. **Number.** Make sure there are enough centers to accommodate all the children, but not so many that children play by themselves most of the time. The ratio of centers to the number of children is affected by the overall personality of the group, group and individual needs and interests, and the physical setting (such as the size and shape of the room and permanent fixtures that influence where centers are located).
3. **Materials.** Offer items that promote social play, such as dramatic play props and dress-up clothes, art materials for collaborative projects, and toy farm/zoo animals and

diverse family figures. Provide enough items so children can carry out their plans and do not get frustrated waiting for what they want to use.
4. **Images.** Display posters and photographs of children and adults shaking hands, hugging, and otherwise enjoying each other's company. Include books that reflect the diversity of the community and highlight important social emotional skills (see the book list at www.vanderbilt.edu/csefel/resources/strategies .html) (Lawry, Danko, & Strain 1999; Bovey & Strain 2003b).

NAEYC (Copple & Bredekamp 2009) and the Division for Early Childhood (Sandall et al. 2005) offer recommendations and guidelines for creating developmentally appropriate early childhood settings. The ideas offered by these professional organizations can assist teachers in creating early childhood environments that foster peer interaction.

Some of my centers seem to promote peer interaction, while in others children tend to play alone. What types of toys, activities, and materials are most likely to support peer interaction?

Most children are drawn to centers that are highly engaging and reflect their interests. Teachers who offer materials and activities that follow and build on children's interests are more likely to have classrooms in which children are busily making and carrying out plans. Center materials need to be meaningful, responsive, and relevant to children's needs, interests, and lives (including culturally appropriate materials such as books, puzzle images, and restaurant menus that reflect the ethnic and linguistic diversity of the community).

Changing or rotating center materials on a regular basis also can increase engagement, since children sometimes approach familiar materials in a different center as if they are new. Naturalistic props within the housekeeping center or miniature people or vehicles in the block area are more likely to spur peer interaction than items such as art easels or clay, which children are likely to enjoy alone (Ivory & McCollum 1999; Bovey & Strain 2003b). In addition, teachers can structure the way children work with materials or activities to encourage social play. For example, limiting the number of glue sticks or scissors can encourage children to share while doing a small group activity (initially, teachers may need to support and model sharing). Also, structuring activities, such as a puzzle activity whereby each partner has some of the pieces and the children work collaboratively to put the puzzle together, can support peer interaction. Finally, make sure the classroom has some quiet, solitary-play centers. Most children need time alone or downtime occasionally; some need it quite often.

Enhancing the Social Environment

My teaching assistant and I notice that all of the table groups are sometimes very talkative at mealtimes, while at other times one or two of the tables are so quiet you could hear a pin drop.

Given that the children can choose where to sit, how does group composition influence peer interaction?

Individual child characteristics such as temperament and confidence, along with the size of a group, can influence the ways children talk and interact with each other (Bovey & Strain 2003b). Observing natural interactions among children who seek out each other as play partners is an excellent way to collect information to use later to foster peer interaction. Grouping children who are outgoing with peers who tend to be shy can facilitate interactions and the development of relationships during activities such as snack or large group time. Creating an atmosphere in which conversation is encouraged is an excellent way to build communication and social skills. During snack and mealtimes, for example, carefully observe children and occasionally assign seats (perhaps through the use of creatively designed placemats) based on what you know about each child's language skills and approach to engaging with others. Teachers also can pair children to pass out materials (such as napkins, cups, snacks), play guessing games (like I Spy or 20 Questions), and use conversation starters (Tell me one fun thing you did over the weekend. If you were an animal, what would you be and why? What is your favorite sports team?).

Two children in my class have never been in group care before. Both are extremely quiet. What can I do to help children who appear to be withdrawn or really shy play and make friends with others?

Placing children with less developed social skills alongside or near more socially skilled children during large and small group activities is a minimally intrusive way to encourage interaction (Lawry, Danko, & Strain 1999; Bovey & Strain 2003b). Try partnering a child who is shy with a classmate who is more outgoing—perhaps for a dance activity, to share a bingo card, or to distribute props for a finger play. Activities such as Special Friend of the Week, in which the designated child tells the group about his or her favorite foods, activities, and toys, allow classmates to learn about common interests.

Strategies to Support Peer Interaction

A child in my class rarely makes eye contact, only occasionally approaches other children, and rarely responds to other children's invitations to play.

What can I do to help her build social skills so she can enjoy playing and learning with others in the class?

Role-playing, modeling playful activities, providing descriptive feedback, and prompting peer interactions are excellent ways to support peer interaction (Vaughn et al. 2003). For children who lack specific social skills, such as sharing or inviting a friend to play, teachers can provide frequent skill-building opportunities and take advantage of teachable moments. For example, it is better to teach sharing before a struggle over a favorite toy occurs or after children calm down from an argument. A teacher, for example, might suggest to a small group of children in the housekeeping area that each child take a turn with the popular cash register for two or three minutes, then let a classmate have a turn. By helping children learn to share, the teacher also helps ensure, through prompting and facilitation, that one child does not dominate use of the desired material.

For children who lack specific social skills, such as sharing or inviting a friend to play, teachers can provide frequent skill-building opportunities and take advantage of teachable moments.

If some children in my class are struggling with peer interactions, should I "teach" social skills to them individually or to all of the children during large or small group time? Or would I be better off teaching each child in a one-to-one situation?

The format for teaching social skills depends on the child and the skill being taught (Sugai & Lewis 1996). If numerous children share the same needs in terms of social skill instruction—for example, several children might be struggling with taking turns or entering into an existing play situation—using large group time to discuss and practice a skill might be most beneficial. However, if one child is struggling in isolation with a skill (such as how to enter into a play situation), it might be better to walk through the steps with this child alone and then support him as he attempts to use the new skill.

I know it is important to give children feedback when they learn and use new skills, such as hanging up their coat, using scissors, and picking up their toys. What strategies should I use to reinforce positive peer interaction?

Pay attention to children when they are engaged in positive social interactions by using verbal ("You are playing so nicely together") and nonverbal (high fives and smiles) reinforcers. Be careful not to interrupt children's activities to provide feedback. The key is finding the right time. For example, if two children are working together on an art project, wait for them to complete their work and then provide positive, descriptive feedback ("Skye and Lizzy, I noticed that the two of you shared the molds, rollers, and pipe cleaners when making your clay creations. You seemed to enjoy yourselves and you both made interesting creations.").

Several parents have asked me how they can help their children make friends. It breaks their hearts when they repeatedly see their children playing alone or struggling to enter into a play situation. What can families do at home to help children make friends?

We must remember that, while we want children to develop peer social skills, some children need more alone time than others, a personal characteristic that should be respected. The number of friends a child has is not as important as whether the child uses appropriate social skills when interacting with peers. When suggesting ways a family could foster a child's social skills with peers, teachers also should consider the family's culture, beliefs, and values.

While we want children to develop peer social skills, some children need more alone time than others, a personal characteristic that should be respected.

Taking into consideration individual child and family differences, families can arrange play dates, model how to interact with others, and spend time with their children in places where other children and families participate in enjoyable activities, such as parks, museums, or sports events (Ladd 1999; Ostrosky, McCollum, & Yu 2007). At home, adults can support children in learning and practicing new skills—turn taking, sharing, initiating, and responding—with siblings or other family members. Parents can play board games that involve turn taking, and they can structure pretend play focusing on relationship building (playing school or animal hospital with stuffed animals is a fun way for children to connect with other family members). Parents can also support their children in learning the give-and-take of conversation at mealtime and other social skills that can be fostered during household routines like cooking, folding laundry, and gardening (by taking turns, responding to questions). Adults model social skills by the way they treat each other within the family and beyond—when they invite other neighbors over for activities and celebrations, when they get together with extended family members, and when they involve their children in family rituals (such as game nights and special person of the day).

Conclusion

Carefully arranging the environment, focusing on children's skills and strengths, and regularly celebrating these strengths within early childhood settings can help promote peer interaction among all children. The pyramid model (Fox et al. 2003) provides a framework for critical thinking about how to support young children's social emotional development and prevent challenging behavior. By using the model, teachers can reflect on their own practice (see "Tips for Enhancing Positive Peer Interactions," p. 109) and how to best facilitate children's peer-related social interaction skills. It is only by reflecting on our own behavior and evaluating the physical and social environments that we can best support the development of all young children in our care.

References

Bovey, T., & P. Strain. 2003a. *Promoting positive peer social interactions.* Center on the Social and Emotional Foundations for Early Learning. www.vanderbilt.edu/csefel

Bovey, T., & P. Strain. 2003b. *Using environmental strategies to promote positive social interactions.* Center on the Social and Emotional Foundations for Early Learning. www.vanderbilt.edu/csefel

Bowman, B.T., M.S. Donovan, & M.S. Burns, eds. 2000. *Eager to learn: Educating our preschoolers.* Report of the National Research Council. Washington, DC: National Academies Press. www.nap.edu/openbook.php?isbn=0309068363

Copple, C., & S. Bredekamp, eds. 2009. *Developmentally appropriate practice in early childhood programs serving children from birth through age 8.* 3rd ed. Washington, DC: NAEYC.

Curtis, D., & M. Carter. 2005. Rethinking early childhood environments to enhance learning. *Young Children* 60 (3): 34–38.

Ewing Marion Kauffman Foundation. 2002. *Set for Success: Building a strong foundation for school readiness based on the social-emotional development of young children.* The Kauffman Early Education Exchange, vol. 1, no. 1. Kansas City, MO: Author. http://sites.kauffman.org/pdf/eex_brochure.pdf

Fox, L., G. Dunlap, M.L. Hemmeter, G.E. Joseph, & P.S. Strain. 2003. The teaching pyramid: A model for supporting social competence and preventing challenging behavior in young children. *Young Children* 58 (4): 48–52. www.challengingbehavior.org/dc/pyramid_model.htm

Ivory, J.J., & J.A. McCollum. 1999. Effects of social and isolate toys on social play in an inclusive setting. *Journal of Special Education* 32 (4): 238–43.

Ladd, G.W. 1999. Peer relationships and social competence during early and middle childhood. *Annual Review of Psychology* 50: 333–59.

Lawry, J., C. Danko, & P. Strain. 1999. Examining the role of the classroom environment in the prevention of problem behavior. In *Young exceptional children: Practical ideas for addressing challenging behaviors,* eds. S. Sandall & M. Ostrosky, 49–62. Longmont, CO: Sopris West.

Ostrosky, M.M., J.A. McCollum, & S.Y. Yu. 2007. Linking curriculum to children's social out-comes: Helping families support children's peer relationships. In *Young exceptional children: Linking curriculum to child and family outcomes,* eds. E. Horn, C. Peterson, & L. Fox, 46–54. Missoula, MT: Division for Early Childhood of the Council for Exceptional Children.

Peth-Pierce, R., ed. 2000. *A good beginning: Sending America's children to school with the social and emotional competence they need to succeed.* Monograph of The Child Mental Health Foundations and Agencies Network (FAN). www.casel.org/downloads/goodbeginning.pdf.

Sandall, S., M.L. Hemmeter, B.J. Smith, & M. McLean. 2005 *DEC Recommended practices: A comprehensive guide.* Longmont, CO: Sopris West.

Shonkoff, J.P., & D.A. Phillips, eds., Committee on Integrating the Science of Early Childhood Development; National Research Council and Institute of Medicine. 2001. *From neurons to neighborhoods: The science of early childhood development.* Washington, DC: National Academies Press. http://books.nap.edu/catalog.php?record_id=9824#toc

Sugai, G., & T.J. Lewis. 1996. Preferred and promising practices for social skills instruction. *Focus on Exceptional Children* 29 (4): 1–16.

Vaughn, S., A. Kim, C.V. Morris Sloan, M.T. Hughes, B. Elbaum, & D. Sridhar. 2003. Social skills interventions for young children with disabilities. *Remedial and Special Education* 24 (1): 2–15.

Critical Thinking

1. Describe some of the strategies, both in terms of establishing the environment and specific teaching skills that foster the development of children's social interactions with peers.

2. Observe young children engaged in free play either inside or in an outside setting for at least 30 minutes. Describe the ways you observe them interacting with each other and how the adults may have encouraged the interactions. What would you have done differently in the situation?

MICHAELENE M. OSTROSKY, PhD, is professor of special education at the University of Illinois at Urbana-Champaign. She is a faculty collaborator with the Center on the Social and Emotional Foundations for Early Learning and has been involved in research on promoting social emotional competence and preventing challenging behavior. ostrosky@illinois.edu. **HEDDA MEADAN,** PhD, is an assistant professor of special education at Illinois State University. Her areas of research include social and communication behavior of young children with disabilities. hmeadan@ilstu.edu.

From *Young Children,* Vol. 65, No. 1, January 2010, pp. 104–109. Copyright © 2010 by National Association for the Education of Young Children. Reprinted by permission.

Rough Play

One of the Most Challenging Behaviors

Frances M. Carlson

Young children enjoy very physical play; all animal young do. This play is often vigorous, intense, and rough. You may know this "big body play" as *rough-and-tumble play, roughhousing, horseplay,* or *play fighting.* In its organized play forms with older children, we call it many names: King of the Mountain, Red Rover, Freeze Tag, Steal the Bacon, Duck-Duck-Goose, and so on.

From infancy, children use their bodies to learn. They roll back and forth, kick their legs, and wave their arms, sometimes alone and sometimes alongside another infant. They crawl on top of each other. They use adults' bodies to stand up, push off, and launch themselves forward and backward.

As toddlers, they pull each other, hug each other tightly, and push each other down. As children approach the preschool years, these very physical ways of interacting and learning begin to follow a predictable pattern of unique characteristics: running, chasing, fleeing, wrestling, open-palm tagging, swinging around, and falling to the ground—often on top of each other.

Sometimes young children's big body play is solitary. Preschoolers run around, dancing and swirling, rolling on the floor or on the ground, or hopping and skipping along. Children's rough play can include the use of objects. For example, early primary children might climb up structures and then leap off, roll their bodies on large yoga balls, and sometimes tag objects as "base" for an organized game. More often, this play includes children playing with other children, especially with school-age children who often make rules to accompany their rough play.

Children's big body play may resemble, but does not usually involve, real fighting (Schafer & Smith 1996). Because it may at times closely resemble actual fighting, some adults find it to be one of the most challenging of children's behaviors. In spite of its bad reputation, rough play is a valuable and viable play style from infancy through the early primary years—one teachers and families need to understand and support.

Misconceptions About Rough Play

Teachers and parents often mistake this play style for real fighting that can lead to injury, so they prohibit it (Gartrell & Sonsteng 2008). This play style has also been neglected and sometimes criticized at both state and national levels.

The Child Development Associate (CDA) *Assessment Observation Instrument,* which is used to observe and evaluate a CDA candidate's classroom practices, states, "Rough play is minimized. Example: defuses rough play before it becomes a problem; makes superhero play more manageable by limiting time and place" (Council for Professional Recognition 2007, 31). In Georgia, a 2010 statewide licensing standards revision includes a rule change that states, "Staff shall not engage in, or allow children or other adults to engage in, activities that could be detrimental to a child's health or well-being, such as, but not limited to, horse play, rough play, wrestling" (Bright from the Start 2010, 25). Standards or expectations like these are based on the assumption that play fighting typically escalates or that children are often injured while playing this way. Neither assumption is true (Smith, Smees, & Pellegrini 2004).

Play fighting escalates to real fighting less than one percent of the time (Schafer & Smith 1996). And when it does, escalation typically occurs when participants include children who have been rejected (Schafer & Smith 1996; Smith, Smees, & Pellegrini 2004). (Children who are rejected are those "actively avoided by peers, who are named often as undesirable playmates" [Trawick-Smith 2010, 301].)

Attempts to ban or control children's big body play are intended to protect children, but such attempts are ill placed because children's rough play has different components and consequences from real fighting (Smith, Smees, & Pellegrini 2004). Rather than forbidding rough-and-tumble play, which can aid in increasing a child's social skills, teachers' and parents' efforts are better directed toward supporting and supervising this type of play, so that young children's social skills and friendship-making skills can develop (Schafer & Smith 1996).

What it is and What it is Not

Big body play is distinctly different from fighting (Humphreys & Smith 1987). Fighting includes physical acts used to coerce or control another person, either through inflicting pain or through the threat of pain. Real fighting involves tears instead of laughter and closed fists instead of open palms (Fry 2005). When open palms are used in real fighting, it is for a slap instead of a tag. When two children are fighting, one usually runs away as soon as possible and does not voluntarily return for more. With some practice, teachers and parents can learn to discern children's appropriate big body play from inappropriate real fighting.

In appropriate rough play, children's faces are free and easy, their muscle tone is relaxed, and they are usually smiling and laughing. In real fighting, the facial movements are rigid, controlled, stressed, and the jaw is usually clenched (Fry 2005). In rough play, children initiate the play and sustain it by taking turns. In real fighting, one child usually dominates another child (or children) and the other child may be in the situation against his or her will. In rough play, the children return for more even if it seems too rough to adult onlookers. In real fighting, children run away, sometimes in tears, and often ask the teacher or another adult for help.

Why it Matters

Rough-and-tumble play is just that: play. According to Garvey, all types of play

- are enjoyable to the players;
- have no extrinsic goals, the goal being intrinsic (i.e., pursuit of enjoyment);
- are spontaneous and voluntary; and
- involve active engagement by the players (1977, 10).

Rough play shares these characteristics; as in all appropriate play, when children involve their bodies in this vigorous, interactive, very physical kind of play, they build a range of skills representing every developmental domain. Children learn physical skills—how their bodies move and how to control their movements. They also develop language skills through signals and nonverbal communication, including the ability to perceive, infer, and decode. Children develop social skills through turn taking, playing dominant and subordinate roles, negotiating, and developing and maintaining friendships (Smith, Smees, & Pelligrini 2004; Tannock 2008). With boys especially, rough play provides a venue for showing care and concern for each other as they often hug and pat each other on the back during and after the play (Reed 2005). Rough play also allows young children to have their physical touch needs met in age- and individually appropriate ways (Reed 2005: Carlson 2006), and provides an opportunity for children to take healthy risks.

From an evolutionary developmental perspective, play-fighting allows children to practice adult roles (Bjorklund & Pellegrini 2001). That is, big body play helps prepare children for the complex social aspects of adult life (Bjorklund & Pellegrini 2001). Other researchers speculate that it is practice for future self-defense, providing vital practice and the development of critical pathways in the brain for adaptive responses to aggression and dominance (Pellis & Pellis 2007). There is a known connection between the development of movement and the development of cognition (Diamond 2000), and researchers believe there is a connection between this

very physical, rowdy play style and critical periods of brain development (Byers 1998). Rough play between peers appears to be critical for learning how to calibrate movements and orient oneself physically in appropriate and adaptive ways (Pellis, Field, & Whishaw 1999). There is evidence that rough-and-tumble play leads to the release of chemicals affecting the mid-brain, lower forebrain, and the cortex, including areas responsible for decision making and social discrimination; growth chemicals positively affect development of these brain areas (Pellis & Pellis 2007). In other words, rough-and-tumble play, this universal children's activity, is adaptive, evolutionarily useful, and linked to normal brain development.

Supporting Rough Play

One of the best ways teachers can support rough play is by modeling it for children. When adults model high levels of vigorous activity, the children in their care are more likely to play this way. Children also play more vigorously and more productively when their teachers have formal education or training in the importance of this type of play (Bower et al. 2008; Cardon et al. 2008).

Besides modeling, teachers can do three specific things to provide for and support rough play while minimizing the potential for injury: prepare both the indoor and outdoor environment, develop and implement policies and rules for rough play, and supervise rough play so they can intervene when appropriate.

Environments That Support Big Body Play

The learning environment should provide rich opportunities for children to use their bodies both indoors and outdoors (Curtis & Carter 2005). When planning for big, rough, vigorous body play, give keen, thoughtful attention to potential safety hazards. Children need to play vigorously with their bodies, but they should do so in a safe setting.

To support rough play with infants during floor time, provide safe, mouthable objects in a variety of shapes, colors, and textures. Place the items near to and away from the baby to encourage reaching and stretching. Also provide a variety of large items—inclined hollow blocks, large rubber balls, sturdy tubes, exercise mats—so infants can roll on, around, over, and on top of these items. Get on the floor, too so infants can crawl around and lie on you. Allow babies to be near each other so that they can play with each other's bodies. Supervise their play to allow for safe exploration.

Indoor environments encourage big body play when there is ample space for children to move around freely. Cramped or restricted areas hamper children's vigorous play. When usable space is less than 25 square feet per child, children tend to be more aggressive (Pellegrini 1987). Boys, especially play more actively when more space is available (Fry 2005; Cardon et al. 2008).

Some teachers find it helpful to draw or mark off a particular section of the room and dedicate it to big body play. One teacher shares the way she established a "wrestling zone" in her preschool classroom:

> First, I cleared the area of any furniture or equipment. Next, I defined the area with a thick, heavy comforter and pillows. After setting up the area, I posted guidelines for the children's rough play on the wall near the wrestling zone.

Designate an area for rough play where there is no nearby furniture or equipment with sharp points and corners. Firmly anchor furniture so that it doesn't upturn if a child pushes against it. All flooring should be skid-free, with safety surfaces like thick mats to absorb the shock of any potential impact.

Policies and Rules for Rough Play

Programs need policies about rough play. Policies should define this type of play, explain rules that accompany it, specify the level of supervision it requires, and include specific types of staff development or training early childhood teachers need to support it. In addition, policies can address how to include it in the schedule and how to make sure all children—especially children with developmental disabilities and children who are socially rejected—have access to it. Clear policies about supervision are vital, as this play style requires constant adult supervision—meaning the children are both seen and heard at all times by supervising adults (Peterson, Ewigman, & Kivlahan 1993).

Even with its friendly nature and ability to build and increase children's social skills, this play style is more productive and manageable when guidelines and rules are in place (Flanders et al. 2009). Children can help create the rules. By preschool age, children are learning about and are able to begin participating in games with rules. Involving the children in creating rules for their play supports this emerging ability.

The rules should apply to children's roughhousing as well as to big body play with equipment and play materials. Wrestling, for example, may have rules such as wrestling only while kneeling, and arms around shoulders to waists but not around necks or heads. For big body play with equipment, the rules may state that the slide can be used for climbing on alternate days with sliding, or that a child can climb up only after checking to make sure no one is sliding down, and that jumping can be from stationary structures only and never from swings. Other rules may say that tumbling indoors always requires a mat and cannot be done on a bare floor, and that children may only roll down hills that are fenced or away from streets and traffic.

Some general rules for big body play might be

- No hitting
- No pinching
- Hands below the neck and above the waist
- Stop as soon as the other person says or signals stop
- No rough play while standing—kneeling only
- Rough play is optional—stop and leave when you want (A Place of Our Own, n.d.)

Write the rules on white poster board, and mount them near the designated rough play area.

Supervise and Intervene

Teachers should enforce the rules and step in to ensure all children are safe, physically and emotionally. It's important to pay attention to children's language during rough play and help them use words to express some of the nonverbal communication. For example, if two boys are playing and one is on top of the other, say, "He is pushing against your chest! He wants you to get up!" Help the larger boy get up if he needs assistance. Instead of scolding, simply point out, "Because you are larger than he is, I think he felt uncomfortable with you on top of him." Allow the smaller boy to say these words, too. Help children problem solve about ways to accommodate their size differences if they are unable to do so unassisted. Say, "How else can you wrestle so that one of you isn't pinned under the other one?"

Children who are rejected

When supervising children with less developed social skills, remember that for these children, big body play can more easily turn into real fighting. Many children who are socially rejected lack the language skills needed to correctly interpret body signals and body language, which makes rough play difficult for them. The children often lack the social skill of turn taking or reciprocity. A child may feel challenged or threatened by another child's movement or action instead of understanding that rough play involves give-and-take and that he or she will also get a turn.

Although more difficult for them, engaging in big body play can help such children build social skills. When supervising these children, remain closer to them than you would to other children. If you see or sense that a child may be misunderstanding cues or turn taking, intervene. Help clarify the child's understanding of the play so it can continue. Strategies like coaching, helping the child reflect on cues and responses, and explaining and modeling sharing and reciprocity help a child remain in the play and ultimately support his or her language and social competence.

Communicating with Families

Some children already feel that their rough body play is watched too closely by their early childhood teachers (Tannock 2008). Not all parents, though, find children's rough play unacceptable. Several mothers, when interviewed, stated that rough play is empowering for their daughters and that they appreciate how this play style makes their girls feel strong ("Rough and Tumble Play" 2008). In industrialized countries, rough play is probably the most commonly used play style between parents and their children after the children are at least 2 years old (Paquette et al. 2003).

If children learn that rough play is acceptable at home but not at school, it may be difficult for them to understand and comply with school rules. Children are better positioned to reap the benefits of rough play when both home and school have consistent

Sample Handbook Policies for Big Body Play

Big Body Play for Preschool and School-Age Children

Here at [name of school or program], we believe in the value of exuberant, boisterous, rough-and-tumble play to a child's overall development. This vigorous body play allows children opportunities to use language—both verbal and nonverbal—and learn how to negotiate, take turns, wait, compromise, sometimes dominate and sometimes hold back, and make and follow rules. They are learning about cause and effect and developing empathy. Big body play also supports optimum physical development because it is so vigorous and because children—since they enjoy it so much—tend to engage in it for an extended amount of time.

To support the use of big body play, we do the following:

- Provide training to all staff on the importance of big body play and how to supervise it
- Prepare both indoor and outdoor environments for this play style
- Establish classroom and playground rules with the children to keep them safe and help them know what to expect

- Encourage staff to use big body games with the children
- Supervise the play constantly, which means ensuring an adult is watching and listening at all times
- Model appropriate play; coach children as they play so that they are able to interact comfortably with each other in this way

The following indoor and outdoor environmental features of our program support big body play:

- At least 50 square feet of usable indoor play space per child, free from furniture and equipment so that children can tumble and wrestle (for example, a wrestling area for two children would consist of at least 100 square feet with no furnishings in the area)
- At least 100 square feet of usable outdoor play space per child, free from fixed equipment so that children can run, jump, tag, roll, wrestle, twirl, fall down, and chase each other (for example, a group of six children playing tag would have at least 600 square feet in which to play)
- Safety surfaces indoors under and around climbers, and furniture that children might use as climbers (a loveseat, for example)
- Safety surfaces outdoors under and around climbers, slides, balance beams, and other elevated surfaces from which children might jump

From F.M. Carlson, *Big Body Play: Why Boisterous, Vigorous, and Very Physical Play Is Essential to Children's Development and Learning* (Washington, DC: NAEYC 2011). 87–88. © 2011 by NAEYC.

---

rules and messages. Children thrive in early childhood programs where administrators, teachers, and family members work together in partnerships (Keyser 2006). Partnership is crucial for children to feel supported in their big body play.

Teachers who decide to offer big body play must make sure that families are aware of and understand why rough play is included. Communicate program components to families when they first express interest in the program or at events such as an open house before the first day of school. Explain the use of and support for big body play in a variety of ways:

- Include in your family handbook a policy on big body play—and how it is supported and supervised in the program or school (see "Sample Handbook Policies for Big Body Play").
- Send a letter to families that explains big body play and its many benefits.
- Show photographs of children engaged in big body play
  — in newsletters
  — in documentation panels
  — in promotional literature, like brochures and flyers
  — on bulletin boards at entryways

Going Forward

Most children engage in rough play, and research demonstrates its physical, social, emotional, and cognitive value. Early childhood education settings have the responsibility to provide children with what best serves their developmental needs. When children successfully participate in big body play, it is "a measure of the children's social well-being and is marked by the ability of children to . . . cooperate, to lead, and to follow" (Burdette & Whitaker 2005, 48). These abilities don't just support big body play; these skills are necessary for lifelong success in relationships.

References

A Place of Our Own, n.d. "Rough Play Area." http://aplaceofourown.org/activity.php?id=492.

Bjorklund, D., & A. Pellegrini. 2001. *The Origins of Human Nature.* Washington, DC: American Psychological Association.

Bower, J.K., D.P. Hales, D.F. Tate, D.A. Rubin, S.E. Benjamin, & D.S. Ward, 2008. "The Childcare Environment and Children's Physical Activity." *American Journal of Preventive Medicine* 34 (1): 23–29.

Bright from the Start. Georgia Department of Early Care and Learning. 2010. Order Adopting Amendments to Rule Chapter 591-1-1. Rule Chapter 290-2-1 and Rule Chapter 290-2-3." 25. http://decal.ga.gov/documents/attachments/OrderAdoptingAmendments080510.pdf.

Burdette, H.L., & R.C. Whitaker. 2005. "Resurrecting Free Play in Young Children: Looking Beyond Fitness and Fatness to Attention, Affiliation, and Affect." *Archives of Pediatrics & Adolescent Medicine* 159 (1): 46–50.

Byers, J.A. 1998. "The Biology of Human Play." *Child Development* 69 (3): 599–600.

Cardon, G., E. Van Cauwenberghe, V. Labarque, L. Haerens, & I. De Bourdeaudhuij. 2008. "The Contributions of Preschool Playground Factors in Explaining Children's Physical Activity During Recess." *International Journal of Behavioral Nutrition and Physical Activity* 5 (11): 1186–192.

Carlson, F.M. 2006. *Essential Touch: Meeting the Needs of Young Children.* Washington, DC: NAEYC.

Council for Professional Recognition. 2007. "Methods for Avoiding Problems Are Implemented." *CDA Assessment Observation Instrument.* Washington. DC: Author.

Curtis, D., & M. Carter. 2005. "Rethinking Early Childhood Environments to Enhance Learning." *Young Children* 60 (3): 34–38.

Diamond, A. 2000. "Close Interrelation of Motor Development and Cognitive Development and of the Cerebellum and Prefontal Cortex." *Child Development* 71 (1): 44–56.

Flanders, J.L., V. Leo, D. Paquette, R.O. Pihl, & J.R. Seguin. 2009. "Rough-and-Tumble Play and Regulation of Aggression: An Observational Study of Father-Child Play Dyads." *Aggressive Behavior* 35: 285–95.

Fry, D. 2005. "Rough-and-Tumble Social Play in Humans." In *The Nature of Play: Great Apes and Humans,* eds A.D. Pellegrini & P.K. Smith, 54–85. New York: Guilford Press.

Gartrell, D., & K. Sonsteng. 2008. "Promote Physical Activity—It's Proactive Guidance." Guidance Matters. *Young Children* 63 (2): 51–53.

Garvey, C. 1977. *Play.* Cambridge, MA: Harvard University Press.

Humphreys, A.P., & P.K. Smith. 1987. "Rough and Tumble, Friendships, and Dominance in School Children: Evidence for Continuity and Change with Age." *Child Development* 58: 201–12.

Keyser, J. 2006. *From Parents to Partners: Building a Family-Centered Early Childhood Program.* Washington, DC: NAEYC: St. Paul, MN: Redleaf.

Paquette, D., R. Carbonneau, D. Dubeau, M. Bigras, & R.E. Tremblay, 2003. "Prevalence of Father-Child Rough-and-Tumble Play and Physical Aggression in Preschool Children." *European Journal of Psychology of Education* 18(2): 171–89.

Pellegrini, A.D. 1987. "Rough-and-Tumble Play: Developmental and Educational Significance." *Educational Psychology* 22 (11): 23–43.

Pellis, S.M., & V.C. Pellis. 2007. "Rough-and-Tumble Play and the Development of the Social Brain." *Association of Psychological Science* 16 (2): 95–8.

Pellis, S.M., E.F. Field, & I.Q. Whishaw, 1999. "The Development of a Sex-Differentiated Defensive Motor Pattern in Rats: A Possible Role for Juvenile Experience." *Developmental Psychobiology* 35 (2): 156–64.

Peterson, L., B. Ewigman, & C. Kivlahan. 1993. "Judgments Regarding Appropriate Child Supervision to Prevent Injury: The Role of Environmental Risk and Child Age." *Child Development* 64: 934–50.

Reed, T.L. 2005. "A Qualitative Approach to Boys' Rough and Tumble Play: There Is More Than Meets the Eye." In *Play; An Interdisciplinary Synthesis,* eds F.F. McMahon, D.E. Lytle, & B. Sutton-Smith, 53–71. Lanham, MD: University Press of America.

"Rough-and-Tumble Play." Ontario: TVO, 2008. Video, 10 min. www.tvo.org/TVO/WebObjects/TVO .woa?videoid?24569407001.

Schafer, M., & P.K. Smith. 1996. "Teachers' Perceptions of Play Fighting and Real Fighting in Primary School." *Educational Research* 38 (2): 173–81.

Smith, P.K., R. Smees, & A.D. Pellegrini. 2004. "Play Fighting and Real Fighting: Using Video Playback Methodology with Young Children." *Aggressive Behavior* 30: 164–73.

Tannock, M. 2008. "Rough and Tumble Play: An Investigation of the Perceptions of Educators and Young Children." *Early Childhood Education Journal* 35 (4): 357–61.

Trawick-Smith, J. 2010. *Early Childhood Development: A Multicultural Perspective.* Upper Saddle River, NJ: Pearson Merrill Prentice Hall.

Critical Thinking

1. Observe young children in an organized program playing outside on a playground. What opportunities are available for large muscle play and how is it encouraged?

2. Write a paragraph that could be included in a newsletter to families about the importance of rough play and how you will supervise that play with the children in your care.

FRANCES M. CARLSON, MEd, is the lead instructor for the Early Childhood Care & Education department at Chattahoochee Technical College in Marietta, Georgia. She is the author of a book from NAEYC, *Big Body Play: Why Boisterous, Vigorous, and Very Physical Play Is Essential to Children's Development and Learning* (2011). francescarlson@bellsouth.net

Play and Social Interaction in Middle Childhood

Play is vital for a child's emotional and cognitive development. But social and technological forces threaten the kinds of play kids need most.

DORIS BERGEN AND DORIS PRONIN FROMBERG

Play is important to the optimum development of children during their middle childhood years. Unfortunately, though there is abundant research evidence showing that play supports young children's social, emotional, physical, and cognitive development, it has often been ignored or addressed only minimally (Fromberg and Bergen 2006). However, when young adults are asked to recall their most salient play experiences, they typically give elaborate and joyous accounts of their play during the ages of eight to 12 (Bergen and Williams 2008). Much of the play they report involves elaborate, pretense scripts conducted for a long duration at home, in their neighborhood, or in the school yard. The respondents report that they either personally played the roles or used small objects (action figures, cars, dolls) as the protagonists. They also report games with child-generated rules that they adapted during play. For example, they might have had bike-riding contests or played a baseball-like game that uses fence posts for bases and gives five-out turns to the youngest players. These young adults believed that their middle childhood play helped them learn "social skills," "hobbies," and often "career decisions" that influenced their later, adult experiences.

Many schools, especially those considered to be poor performers, have reduced or eliminated recess.

For many children, the opportunities for such freely chosen play are narrowing. Much of their play time at home has been lost to music, dance, or other lessons; participation on sport teams (using adult-defined rules); and after-school homework or test preparation sessions. At the same time, many schools, especially those considered to be poor performers, have reduced or eliminated recess (Pellegrini 2005). Often, the only outdoor time in the school day is the 10 to 15 minutes left from a lunch period, with rules such as "no running allowed." Thus, the importance of play during middle childhood must be reemphasized by educators who understand why it facilitates skilled social interaction, emotional regulation, higher cognitive processing, and creativity.

Defining Middle Childhood Play

At any age, for an activity to count as play, it must be voluntary and self-organized. Children identify an activity as play when they choose it, but they define the same activity as work when an adult chooses it for them (King 1992). Play differs from exploring an object because such exploration answers the question: "What can it do?" In contrast, play answers the question: "What can I do with it?" (Hutt 1976).

Play in middle childhood continues to include practice play (repeating and elaborating on the same activities, often in the service of increasing skill levels), pretense (using symbolic means to envision characters and scenarios, using literary and other media experiences, as well as real-life experience sources), games with rules (revising existing games or making up elaborate games that have negotiated rules), and construction play (building and designing structures or artistic works). All of these types of play show increasing abilities to deal with cognitive, social, and emotional issues, as well as increases in physical skills.

The rules of play become apparent as children oscillate between negotiating the play scenarios and seamlessly entering into the activities, whether in selecting teams and rules for game play or borrowing media characters to "become" the pretend characters. Script theory, a kind of grammar of play (Fromberg 2002), outlines this oscillating collaborative process. The play process develops throughout the middle childhood years with 1) props becoming more miniaturized, 2) play episodes more extended, 3) language more complex, 4) themes more coherent, and 5) physical prowess more refined.

The Value of Middle Childhood Play

As the memories of young adults testify, play continues to be very valuable during the middle childhood years. Social and emotional competence, imagination, and cognitive development are fostered by many types of play.

Social and emotional competence. Although adults may provide the space and objects with which their children play, during play children practice their power to self-direct, self-organize, exert self-control, and negotiate with others. Even when engaged in rough-and-tumble play, if it was a mutual decision, the children involved demonstrate self-control (Reed and Brown 2000). Such experiences build confidence in deferring immediate gratification, persevering, and collaborating. Even when the play deals with hurtful themes, the children's intrinsic motivation ensures that the play serves a pleasurable, meaningful purpose for the players. For example, role playing threat, aggression, or death can help children deal with the reality of such issues.

Affiliation. Children who negotiate their play together fulfill their need for affiliation. How to enter into play successfully is a negotiation skill, and it requires practice and the opportunity to be with peers. The loner child who stands on the outside of a group and observes may not have these skills; these children may meet their needs for affiliation by joining a gang or by resorting to bullying and violence.

Cognitive development. Middle childhood play fosters cognitive development. Children exercise their executive skills when planning pretense scripts, using symbols in games, designing constructions, and organizing games with rules. For example, in construction play with blocks, exploratory manipulation precedes the capacity to create new forms. These three-dimensional constructions help older children develop the visual-spatial imagery that supports learning in mathematics, chemistry, and physics. Outdoor seasonal games that require eye-hand coordination and aiming—such as hopscotch, jump rope, tag, and baseball—also build the imagery that supports such concepts. Fantasy play can involve scripts that go on for days and become extremely elaborate. Sociodramatic play is a form of collaborative oral playwriting and editing, which contributes to the writer's sense of audience (Fromberg 2002). Thus, scripts often are written to guide the play.

Most humor involves cognitive incongruity, which demonstrates what children know.

Humor is very evident in middle childhood play, and although some is "nonsense" humor, most involves cognitive incongruity, which demonstrates what children know. That is, by using puns, jokes, exaggerations, and other word play, they show their knowledge of the world and gain power and delight in transforming that knowledge in incongruous ways. Much of this joking is designed to shock adults, but it also demonstrates children's increasing knowledge of the world. Playful use of language also shows up in "Pig Latin" and other code languages, which both include the play group and exclude others. Learning and performing "magic" tricks is also a delight and requires understanding the laws of objects and thus how to appear to bypass those laws.

Imagination and creativity. Children dramatize roles and scenarios with miniature animals, toy soldiers, and media action figures, using themes from their experiences, including "playing school." Some urban children might dramatize cops and gangs. Children in both urban and rural areas engage in such pretense, trying on a sense of power and independence, by imagining "what if" there were no adult society. As they try roles and pretend possible careers, they seek privacy from adults during much of this play, preferring tree houses, vacant lots, basements, or other "private" spaces. Symbolic games, such as Monopoly (using a board or online forms), as well as other computer or board games, add to the development of social learning and competence as children increasingly become precise about following the rules of the game.

When children have had opportunities to practice pretense and use their imaginations, researchers have found that they're more able to be patient and perseverant, as well as to imagine the future (Singer and Singer 2006). Being able to imagine and role play a particular career, rent and furnish an apartment, and negotiate other aspects of daily living makes those actions seem less daunting later on.

Contemporary Middle Childhood Play

Play for children in this age group has changed. Today, there are virtual, technology-enhanced play materials, a constriction of play space from the neighborhood to one's own home and yard, and the actual loss of free time and school time to devote to active play.

Technology. For children in the middle childhood years, virtual reality technology now provides three-dimensional interactive games, such as Nintendo's Wii, which uses hand-held devices that can detect motion. These interactive games may be so engaging that children, mainly boys, abandon other activities that build negotiation skills and social competence with other children. Children also increasingly "instant message," creating abbreviation codes—a form of power—and demonstrate their deepening digital literacy. In addition, they listen to music on iPods, play virtual musical instruments, and make virtual friends with whom they interact. This period of childhood affords different opportunities for children in less affluent families, however, resulting in a widening gap in types of technology-enhanced play materials and experiences among children from different socioeconomic levels. For example, though children can initially access some websites without cost, devices and software require purchases that are seductive, with consoles and accessories rising in cost.

Gender roles also are affected by technology. Virtual reality computer games for girls, such as Mattel's Barbie Girls, reinforce stereotypes. Boys are especially interested in virtual action games.

Suburban parents may believe that homes are too far apart to allow children to walk to friends' houses.

Spaces for play. Many parents are reluctant to allow their children to range far in their neighborhoods for the kinds of social experiences that were common for earlier generations. This could be caused by frequent media reports of potential dangers (Louv 2008). Parents may see city environments as too dangerous, and suburban parents may believe that homes are too far apart to allow children to walk to friends' houses or gather in neighborhood outdoor areas.

Time for freely chosen play. Administrators and teachers pressured to increase academic performance often reduce recess to a short period or omit it altogether because they believe this time is "wasted" or that it just will be a time for children to engage in bullying or other unacceptable behaviors. They also may fear lawsuits because of perceived dangers in freely chosen play, as indicated by prohibitions against running. In spite of research indicating that attention to school tasks may be greater if periods of recess are interspersed (Opie and Opie 1976), some adults don't seem to realize the potential of play as a means of supporting academic learning. Thus, time for play has been reduced both in the home and school environments.

Adult Facilitation of Play

Because middle childhood play is so valuable for social, emotional, cognitive, and physical development and because some trends seem to prevent play's full elaboration and development during these years, adults must become advocates for play and facilitators of play in middle childhood. There are a number of ways they can do this.

Providing play resources. When adults provide indoor and outdoor space and materials, children can adapt and use them creatively. The best kinds of materials have more than a single use but can be modified by interaction with others and elaborated with imagination.

Engaging in play interaction. When adults provide real choices, children can build the trust they need to cope with solving physical problems and negotiating emerging interpersonal play. Adults should appreciate process and effort without judging outcomes. They might assist less play-competent children's interactions by offering relevant materials to help

their children be invited into pretense games that other children have started.

Assessing play competence. Educators, in particular, often find that most children comply with their suggestions about play activities, but there may be one or two who do not appear to be participating or, on closer observation, appear to comply, but in their own ways. Teachers, in particular, need to appreciate the multiple ways in which children may represent experiences and display a sense of playfulness. In addition, teachers' assessments should also include observations of children's play competence, especially as it relates to development of imaginative and creative idea generation.

Supporting gender equity. Gender equity and children's aspirations are affected by sanctions and warrants. For example, boys have traditionally dominated play involving 3-D constructions, though some girls are now participating in Lego Robotics teams. To make girls more likely to participate, teachers should place themselves near 3-D construction areas or planned "borderwork" (Thorne 1993). Teachers should be sure to provide materials and equipment that do not have gender-suggestive advertising (Goldstein 1994). In this way, all children can be encouraged to have greater expectations for themselves.

Summary

Play has always been important in middle childhood, but its forms have changed with society and, in some cases, its very existence has been threatened. Parents and educators can facilitate aspects of play that support emotional, social, cognitive, and creative growth. To understand the importance of play for these children, they only have to recall the salience of their own play during this age period.

References

Bergen, Doris, and Elizabeth Williams. "Differing Childhood Play Experiences of Young Adults Compared to Earlier Young Adult Cohorts Have Implications for Physical, Social, and Academic Development." Poster presentation at the annual meeting of the Association for Psychological Science, Chicago, 2008.

Fromberg, Doris P. *Play and Meaning in Early Childhood Education.* Boston: Allyn & Bacon, 2002.

Fromberg, Doris P., and Doris Bergen. *Play from Birth to 12.* New York: Routledge, 2006.

Goldstein, Jeffrey H., ed. *Toys, Play, and Child Development.* New York: Cambridge University Press, 1994.

Hutt, Corinne. "Exploration and Play in Children." In *Play: Its Role in Development and Evolution,* ed. Jerome S. Bruner, Alison Jolly, and Kathy Sylva, 202–215. New York: Basic Books, 1976.

King, Nancy. "The Impact of Context on the Play of Young Children." In *Reconceptualizing the Early Childhood Curriculum,* ed. Shirley A. Kessler and Beth Blue Swadener, 42–81. New York: Teachers College Press, 1992.

Louv, Richard. *Last Child in the Woods: Saving Our Children from Nature-Deficit Disorder.* Chapel Hill, N.C.: Algonquin Books, 2008.

Opie, Iona A., and Peter M. Opie. "Street Games: Counting-Out and Chasing." In *Play: Its Role in Development and Evolution,* ed. Jerome S. Bruner, Alison Jolly, and Kathy Sylva, 394–412. New York: Basic Books, 1976.

Pellegrini, Anthony D. *Recess: Its Role in Education and Development.* Mahwah, N.J.: Lawrence Erlbaum Associates, 2005.

Reed, Tom, and Mac Brown. "The Expression of Care in Rough and Tumble Play of Boys." *Journal of Research in Childhood Education* 15 (Fall-Winter 2000): 104–116.

Singer, Dorothy G., and Jerome L. Singer. "Fantasy and Imagination." In *Play from Birth to 12: Contexts, Perspectives, and Meanings,* ed. Doris P. Fromberg and Doris Bergen, 371–378. New York: Routledge, 2006.

Thorne, Barrie. *Gender Play: Girls and Boys in School.* New Brunswick, N.J.: Rutgers University Press, 1993.

Critical Thinking

1. Describe the characteristics most prominent in the play of children between the ages of eight to twelve.

2. How has play for children during the middle childhood years changed from when you were that age? What are the most popular forms of entertainment and play during the middle childhood years?

DORIS BERGEN is distinguished professor of educational psychology at Miami University, Oxford, Ohio, and co-director of the Center for Human Development, Learning, and Technology. With Doris Pronin Fromberg, she co-edited the book, *Play from Birth to Twelve,* 2nd ed. (Routledge, 2006). **DORIS PRONIN FROMBERG** is a professor of education and past chairperson of the Department of Curriculum and Teaching at Hofstra University, Hempstead, New York.

From *Phi Delta Kappan*, by Doris Bergen and Doris Pronin Fromberg, February 2009, pp. 426–430. Reprinted with permission of Phi Delta Kappa International, www.pdkintl.org, 2009. All rights reserved.

Is Tattling a Bad Word?
How To Help Children Navigate the Playground

Katharine C. Kersey and Marie L. Masterson

The most often suggested strategy given to children if they are bothered by bullies is to tell their teacher or to get help from an adult (American School Health Association, 2005). Yet when teachers are asked to list their biggest frustration, one of the most frequent responses is—**tattling!** A major disconnect ensues if children are told to go to teachers for help, yet teachers feel annoyed and irritated when they come to them for support (Gartrell, 2007; National Education Association, 2009). Why is it that teachers are not more receptive and helpful when children come to them with complaints (Charach, Pepler, & Ziegler, 1995)? Why are children often sent away or shamed for tattling (Brewster & Railsback, 2001; Cohn & Canter, 2006; Skiba & Fontanini, 2000)?

Teachers may have to hear tattling many times a day, and thus it can become a time-consuming nuisance. Consequently, teachers tend to minimize the concern and sometimes excuse the person who teases by saying, "Oh, Sammy is just having a rough day. Find someone else to play with." Other teachers feel that it is important for children to "toughen up" in order to deal with life, and that enduring "sticks and stones" is just a part of growing up.

Why Children Come to You to Tattle

We would like to propose another way of looking at "tattling." Instead of seeing it as a nuisance, consider seeing it as an "honor." The child is at her teacher's elbow because she feels in need of something. When she is dismissed or turned away, a unique opportunity to make a connection is lost. How the teacher responds to tattling will determine what the child will do in the future when she needs help. If she does not find her teacher to be a resource for help, she will have to look elsewhere for answers.

In the middle of a busy playground, then, what is a teacher to do? If we view tattling from the child's perspective, we are less likely to brush it off as "snitching" or "gossiping." If we go to our principal with a problem we have experienced with another teacher, how would we feel if the principal were to tell us: "It's not a big deal." "You'll be OK." "Toughen up."

Children honestly don't know how to solve their problems and they need our help. When children approach us, they have a reason for coming and they feel safe doing so. We want to encourage them to seek help from a trusted adult, as opposed to modeling the inappropriate responses of their peers. More positive ways of responding to tattling will empower children and give them some healthy options for solving their own problems in the future. We need to reassure them so they will know we want to maintain our connection with them.

How to Respond to Tattling When It Occurs

The first and easiest way to validate the child is to simply say, "I'm sorry," followed by such statements as "I would never do that to you" and "Thank you for telling me." Other quick responses include, "I'm sorry your ears had to hear that." "I am sorry your eyes had to see that." "I am sorry you feel sad." "That must have hurt your feelings." Validating the child gives him words to describe what he feels, so he will be more likely to say, "I feel sad when I get left out" when he encounters a similar experience in the future, rather than to act out or retaliate (Denham et al., 2002).

When children come to us complaining about another child, one of these short responses usually is enough to satisfy their need for validation. If, however, it is obvious that the child is still troubled, we can offer some simple solutions, such as, "Did you tell him how that made you feel?" "Can you take care of it?" "Is there something I can do to help you take care of it?" "Do you want me to go with you while you tell him how you feel—or what you would like him to do?" A child may need your help negotiating a safe solution.

If the child is still not satisfied, and it is obvious that his intent is to get someone else in trouble, you need to make sure that his goal is not realized. It is important never to blame or punish a child for something that you did not see. *Make sure that his actions do not get the other child in trouble.* You can tell him that you will take care of it. Later, you can check on the situation by yourself. You might go to the other child or children and ask them what happened. Sometimes, they will tell on themselves. "I didn't hit Johnny!" Other times, they will improve their behavior just because you are near. At least, you are now aware that you need to be more vigilant in the future, so that you can see for yourself if children are mistreating each other.

Never blame a child for something you didn't see. Never ask a child a question you already know the answer to. Never ask, "Why?"

On the other hand, if you do witness the behavior, it is best not to challenge the child's honesty by asking, "Did you do it?" Once you actually see the behavior for yourself, you can confront the issue. "Mary, I saw you push Suzanne off the swing. Friends are not for pushing. If you want to push something, you can push the wagon or the doll carriage." You should be careful not to ask the child a question when you already know the answer.

It is also critical *not* to ask a child, "Why did you do that?" It is difficult to know what really happened in a teasing situation, since each person's perspective is different. A child may be responding to something that happened a minute ago or may be retaliating for something that happened earlier in the day. When we ask children for explanations, we put them in the unfortunate position of needing to defend themselves.

To support the goal of authentic connections, it is also important not to force a child to apologize. If we do so, we set him up to lie about what he feels. He may not feel sorry at all, but only regret that he got caught. Instead, we want to apologize for him to the child who has been hurt. "I am sorry that

---

What We Can Say to Children:

I'm sorry.
Thank you for telling me.
I would never do that to you.
I am sorry your ears had to hear that.
I am sorry your eyes had to see that.
I am glad you told me.
You must have felt so sad.
I am sorry your feelings were hurt.

What do you think you could do to work it out?
Can you tell him/her how that made you feel?
Could the two of you choose a third person to help you solve this problem?
What is your brain telling you about that?
Kiss your brain for doing the right thing—coming to tell an adult and not hitting or hurting someone else!
Would you like my help?
Do you want me to go with you so you can tell him how that made you feel?

---

hurt you. I would never do that to you." Modeling respect will make a lasting impression on both children. Soon, children will begin to apologize for themselves. Our goal is to help children have authentic empathy toward one another.

Suppose a child comes to you and says, "Sara threw paper down the hall." What will you do? The child who has told is watching you. You can respond, "Thank you for telling me. I'll take care of it." Later, on the way to recess, you can point to the paper in the hall and say, "Sara, will you please pick up the paper?" She says, "That's not mine." You respond, "I didn't say it was, but will you pick it up for me, please?" Sara knows that you know. There are many respectful ways to help children to become responsible for their actions.

How to Use Tattling to Build Connections

A proactive approach to making connections through tattling is to set aside time to address it later. We can use class meetings to make up a story about children who struggled with the same problem and encourage them to brainstorm solutions. A "third party" story will let children consider the situation objectively, and learn lessons about empathy, kindness, and respect, without putting anyone on the spot. Role-play and brainstorming will help children find solutions that make sense and validate what will work best. The goal is to create a classroom where children feel safe, and where they sincerely care about the feelings and thoughts of others.

If you find that a particular child is often the target of other children's complaints, the best thing you can do is spend some extra time with him. You can sit beside him at lunch or ask him to go with you to the library. Inquire about his favorite dog or sports team. The next day, you can ask him about those things and he will be amazed that you remembered. He will be surprised there is an adult who cares. Every child has something special and meaningful that he would like to share. Teachers need to spend time getting to know each child well. A child's behavior usually improves when he feels the sincere interest of a caring adult. Other children will be more likely to connect with him when they see your example, and less likely to find reasons to tattle.

Sometimes, teachers report that "the child being picked on doesn't seem to be upset." Therefore, they tend to minimize the concern. Bauman and Del Rio (2006) caution that children may not show when they are upset. The authors suggest that children learn very quickly to hide their "upset" feelings, knowing that their negative emotions may not attract help from an adult and may quickly provoke more teasing from peers.

How to Model So Children Will Learn from Our Example

Children are watching our responses to tattling, and they are learning from our actions. When we praise a child, he learns to praise others. When we say what children are doing right, they learn to say what is right with others. When we support and

What Children Can Do or Say:

Walk away.

"No thank you."

"I don't like that."

"Please stop."

"Cut it out."

"That hurts my feelings."

respect others, children learn to support and respect each other. We want to talk about them positively to others and affirm our confidence in them as often as possible. Children will want to "live up" to our expectations. When they see us respond to them calmly and responsively, they develop the skills to handle these challenges calmly in the future.

The more we stay respectful of and connected to children, the more they want to please us and become like us. They learn what is *important* to us. We want to model kindness, courage, empathy, and responsibility. When children see us truly caring and giving, they will internalize those values (Deci & Ryan, 1985).

How Responding Positively to Tattling Changes a Child's Future

Having positive relationships with teachers helps children see school as a safe place where they can be successful—and where they want to be (Baker, 1999). Warm, sensitive responses help children achieve more and become more successful in school (Pianta, Hamre, & Stuhlman, 2003). The ability to connect meaningfully when they are young will make all the difference when children face the social pressures and challenges of the upcoming middle school years (Birch & Ladd, 1997; Hamre & Pianta, 2001, 2005).

Children have a difficult time outgrowing the label of not being liked, and this reputation can stay with them through adolescence (Buhs, Ladd, & Herald, 2006). These children are at greater risk of school failure in subsequent grades, and so teachers must take every opportunity to connect and intervene early. Reacting calmly, modeling empathy, and teaching about emotions (Denham, 2005) when tattling occurs will give teachers the opportunity to positively affect the outcome of a child's life.

Wouldn't it be nice if all teachers (and parents) could see themselves as agents of change when children approach them with a complaint or worry? Wouldn't it be wonderful if, instead of trying to get rid of tattling, we could see it as an opportunity to strengthen our connection by validating and giving children the necessary tools to better navigate their world?

References

American School Health Association. (2005). Bullying in the school community: Everyone has a role to play in preventing bullying. *Health in Action, 3*(4), 1–23.

Baker, J. (1999). Teacher-student interaction in urban at-risk classrooms: Differential behavior, relationship quality, and student satisfaction with school. *The Elementary School Journal, 100,* 57–78.

Bauman, S., & Del Rio, A. (2006). Preservice teachers' responses to bullying scenarios: Comparing physical, verbal, and relational bullying. *Journal of Educational Psychology, 98*(1), 219–231.

Birch, S., & Ladd, G. (1997). The teacher-child relationship and children's early school adjustment. *Journal of School Psychology, 35,* 61–79.

Brewster, C., & Railsback, J. (2001). *Schoolwide prevention of bullying.* Northwest Regional Educational Laboratory. Retrieved January 15, 2009, from www.nwrel.org/request/dec01/bullying.pdf

Buhs, E. S., Ladd, G. W., & Herald, S. L. (2006). Peer exclusion and victimization: Processes that mediate the relation between peer group rejection and children's classroom engagement and achievement? *Journal of Educational Psychology, 98*(1), 1–13.

Charach, A., Pepler, D., & Ziegler, S. (1995). Bullying at school—a Canadian perspective: A survey of problems and suggestions for intervention. *Education Canada, 35*(1), 12–18.

Cohn, A., & Canter, A. (2006). *Bullying: Facts for teachers and parents.* Retrieved January 15, 2009, from www.nasponline.org/resources/factsheets/bullying_fs.aspx.

Deci, E. L., & Ryan, R. M. (1985). *Intrinsic motivation and self-determination in human behavior.* New York: Plenum.

Denham, S. A. (2005). The emotional basis of learning and development in early childhood education. In B. Spodek (Ed.), *Handbook of research in early childhood education* (pp. 85–103). Mahwah, NJ: Lawrence Erlbaum.

Denham, S., Caverly, S., Schmidt, M., Blair, K., DeMulder, E., Caal, S., Hamada, H., & Mason, T. (2002). Preschool understanding of emotions: Contributions to classroom anger and aggression. *Journal of Child Psychology and Psychiatry, 43,* 901–916.

Hamre, B., & Pianta, R. (2001). Early teacher-child relationships and the trajectory of children's school outcomes through eighth grade. *Child Development, 72,* 625–638.

Hamre, B., & Pianta, R. (2005). Can instructional and emotional support in the first grade classroom make a difference for children at risk of school failure? *Child Development, 76*(5), 949–967.

National Education Association. (2009). *Tools and ideas: Tattling.* Retrieved January 15, 2009, from www.nea.org/home/20570.htm

Pianta, R., Hamre, B., & Stuhlman, M. (2003). Relationships between teachers and children. In W. M. Reynolds & G. E. Miller (Eds.), *Handbook of psychology: Educational psychology* (Vol. 7, pp. 199–234). Hoboken, NJ: Wiley.

Skiba, R., & Fontanini, A. (2000). *Fast facts: Bullying prevention.* Bloomington, IN: Phi Delta Kappa International.

Resources to Build Caring and Connection When Tattling Occurs

The goal is to respond to tattling by building connections, empathy, cooperation, and respect. The following books focus on children's gifts and talents, responsibility and generosity, friendships, and caring.

American Girl. (2008). *Go for it! Start smart, have fun, and stay inspired in any activity.* Middleton, WI: American Girl Publishing.

Brandenberg, A. (1990). *Manners/Aliki.* New York: Greenwillow Books.

Brown, L. K., & Brown, M. (1998). *How to be a friend: A guide to making friends and keeping them.* New York: Little, Brown and Co.

Curtis, J. L. (2007). *Today I feel silly & other MOODS that make my day.* New York: Joanna Cotler Books. (Also see: *Letting off a little self-esteem.*)

Dyer, W. W. (2007). *Incredible you! 10 ways to let your GREATNESS shine through.* Carlsbad, CA: Hay House.

Dyer, W. W. (2008). *Unstoppable me: 10 ways to soar through life.* Carlsbad, CA: Hay House.

Kersey K. (2004). *The 101s: A guide to positive discipline.* Available at www.odu.edu/~kkersey/101s/101principles.shtml

Henkes, K. (1991). *Chrysanthemum.* New York: Greenwillow Books.

McCloud, C. (2006). *Have you filled a bucket today? A guide to daily happiness for kids.* Northville, MI: Ferne Press.

O'Keefe, S. H. (2005). *Be the star that you are! A book for kids who feel different.* St. Meinrad, IN: Abbey Press.

Critical Thinking

1. What are some ways teachers can use tattling as a way of building connections among children?

2. Develop a list of three strategies you can implement with a group of children when tattling occurs in your classroom.

KATHARINE C. KERSEY is Professor, Early Childhood Education, and Director Emeritus, Child Study Center, Old Dominion University, Norfolk, Virginia. **MARIE L. MASTERSON** is Early Child Specialist, Virginia Department of Education and Adjunct Professor, Old Dominion University.

From *Childhood Education*, vol. 86 no. 4, Summer 2010, pp. 260–263. Copyright © 2010 by the Association for Childhood Education International. Reprinted by permission of Katharine C. Kersey and Marie L. Masterson and the Association for Childhood Education International, 17904 Georgia Avenue, Suite 215, Olney, MD 20832.

Keeping Children Active
What You Can Do to Fight Childhood Obesity

RAE PICA

Just when you think that no more can be said about the childhood obesity crisis, along comes another frightening piece of information. We already know that today's children are fatter than they should be; approximately one-third of American children are overweight and one-fifth are obese. We know that overweight and obesity contribute to all manner of diseases, including heart disease, stroke, diabetes, and even several types of cancer. We've been told that overweight and obesity track from childhood to adulthood (the "baby fat" does not simply go away), meaning that children who start life overweight and obese already have a major strike against their health.

Now new studies, reported this past fall at an American Heart Association conference, have determined that obese children as young as 10 years old have the arteries of 45-year-olds, as well as other heart abnormalities that increase their risk for heart disease (Marcione, 2008).

Clearly, this trend must be reversed. And early childhood is the place to start.

Energy In/Energy Out

The formula for a balanced weight is pretty straightforward: energy in/energy out. This is the term nutritionists use to describe the intended balance between calories consumed and calories burned. If the level of physical activity is not great enough to burn the amount of calories taken in, weight increases. If this imbalance continues, overweight and possibly obesity result.

Given our fondness for fast food (an ever-growing fondness, due to ever-busier lives) and our tendency to "super-size," it's easy to imagine that caloric intake is the crux of the obesity problem. And certainly it is part of the problem, especially considering the quality of the calories consumed. (Evidence indicates that children get a full quarter of their vegetable servings in the form of potato chips and French fries! [Schlosser, 2005].) But studies both here and abroad have indicated that the greater problem may lie with the second half of the equation: energy out. Children are simply not moving enough!

The Need for Physical Activity

The trend toward greater accountability has not helped. Even at the preschool level children are expected to do more and more seatwork. And at the elementary-school level, physical education and recess are being eliminated in favor of more "academic" time. Since school is where children spend the majority of their waking hours, it's clear that under such conditions children are not meeting even the minimum requirements for physical activity.

The National Association for Sport and Physical Education (NASPE, 2002) recommends that:

- Young children should not be sedentary for more than 60 minutes at a time, except when sleeping.
- Toddlers should accumulate at least 30 minutes a day of structured physical activity and at least 60 minutes a day of unstructured physical activity.
- Preschoolers are encouraged to accumulate at least 60 minutes a day of both structured and unstructured physical activity.

While 60 minutes a day is the suggested minimum, it is further recommended that children accumulate "up to several hours" of physical activity daily.

For the early childhood professional, the concept of "accumulation" is comforting. It means you don't have to worry about setting aside huge blocks of time exclusively devoted to physical activity. Although it's developmentally appropriate for children to be engaged in active play most of the time (and that would certainly make the children happy), today's educational culture does not allow for that possibility. It's good to know, therefore, that you can fit in "bouts" of physical activity throughout the day and still meet the national guidelines and contribute to the fight against obesity.

Encouraging Unstructured Physical Activity

Unstructured physical activity, which involves free choice on the part of the children, is typically best experienced outdoors, where the children can run and jump and expend energy. While time spent outdoors has traditionally been considered "break" time—an opportunity for children to play without interference from adults and for teachers and caregivers to relax a bit—more and more early childhood professionals are realizing the potential of the outdoors as an extension of the indoor setting, with that time viewed as yet another opportunity to enhance children's development. Certainly, the outdoor setting provides the perfect opportunity to enhance the children's physical development and physical fitness.

If this is to happen, teachers and caregivers must become involved in children's outdoor play. This is not to say that they must go to the extreme of preparing structured lesson plans for every outdoor session, but many activities begun indoors can be continued and extended outdoors, including movement activities. (Batteries in the CD player mean even music can be a part of outdoor movement experiences.) Also, during playtime, adults can and should interact naturally and informally with the children, offering guidance and suggestions to extend the children's play.

Frost (1996) tells us the role of the teacher supporting outdoor play is that of a play leader, whom he defines as someone who interacts with the child by asking leading questions and providing guidance for certain skills. A play leader also "helps children plan where they will go to play, helps them deal with problems that come up, and talks with them about their play" (p. 27). Of course, teachers can also play with children in order to encourage more moderate to vigorous physical activity. For example, blowing bubbles for the children to catch encourages them to run and jump, contributing to both cardiovascular endurance and muscular strength and endurance.

Fitting Structured Physical Activity into the Day

Structured physical activity is organized and planned. It involves children in specific activities in which they're expected to achieve certain results. Naturally, that makes structured physical activity more challenging to incorporate into the curriculum than unstructured movement.

Early childhood professionals are charged with caring for the development of the whole child; therefore it is not unreasonable to expect that they will set aside a minimum of 30 minutes a day to focus on the acquisition and refinement of motor skills. Motor skills do not develop automatically from an immature to a mature level, so they must be taught and practiced just like any other skill in early childhood. While the prevailing belief may be that instruction in motor skills is less important than instruction in literacy and numeracy skills, children who are comfortable and confident with their motor skills are more likely to be physically active throughout their lives, helping to ensure a lifetime of physical fitness!

Of course, finding time for such instruction is a critical factor. Here are some simple solutions:

- Utilize substantial chunks of what is set aside for circle time.
- Take movement breaks throughout the day. These can incorporate moderate- to vigorous-intensity physical

activity (like walking briskly or running in place, pretending to be in a track meet), thereby contributing to cardiovascular endurance.
- Include gentle stretching that promotes both relaxation and flexibility, an important component of health-related fitness.

Transitions and Movement

Perhaps the simplest way to incorporate structured physical activity into your program is to utilize transition times. Because transitions usually require moving from one place to another, movement is the perfect tool for transition times. Children naturally enjoy movement, so transitions can become pleasurable experiences—even something to be looked forward to. And although you may be reluctant to make them more "active," the truth is that the more active they are, the more engaged children will be. As long as transitions are planned, as are other daily components of your program, the fewer discipline problems you'll have. Here are some activities to use for transitions.

Stand up/sit down. Upon arrival, once the children have removed outerwear and gathered in the center of the room, an activity called Stand Up/Sit Down can get both the brain and the body warmed up, while also working on the concepts of up and down. Doing this quickly will get the heart pumping, and because the children think it's funny, it's a great way to start the day.

Sit with the children, who are either in a circle or scattered throughout the space. Invite the children to alternately stand up or sit down if:

- they're glad to be there
- they're feeling good that day
- they're happy to see their friends
- they're happy to see their teacher
- they're looking forward to learning something new
- they're wearing something blue (green, yellow, etc.)
- if they're a boy (girl)
- if they have a cat (dog) at home

If the children are going to transition to another area of the room, end with a standing challenge. If you are going to do another activity with them for which they need to be seated, end with a sitting challenge.

Quick clean-up. Put on a piece of music with a fast tempo and challenge the children to clean up before the song ends!

Get ready, spaghetti. When it's time for lunch or snack, using a food-related transition makes the most sense. This activity encourages the children to consider the "before" and "after" of pasta. It also serves as a relaxation exercise (contracting and releasing the muscles) as the children wait for snack or lunch.

Talk to the children about the differences between uncooked and cooked spaghetti, letting them come up with ideas on their own. If they need prompting, you can ask them to tell you which is straighter and harder, and which is limp and squiggly. Then invite them to demonstrate uncooked and cooked spaghetti with their bodies. Alternate between the two, ending with the cooked version so the children's muscles are relaxed.

Here we go. Use this activity when it is time to move from where the children have gathered to another part of the classroom. This activity offers an opportunity for the children to experience a variety of locomotor (traveling) skills.

Challenge the children to move to their next destination in one of the following ways, making sure to ask them only to perform skills within their capabilities:

- jumping (two feet)
- hopping (one foot)
- marching
- walking (lightly; stomping)
- jogging
- galloping
- skipping

An alternate activity is to play Follow the Leader, using brisk and/or forceful movements (e.g., stomping) to transition.

Moving like animals. Moving like an animal stimulates the imagination, allows an opportunity to practice a variety of movements, and helps create empathy for the world's creatures. You can either designate the animal the children are to portray or allow them to choose the animal they would each like to be.

Conclusion

Use these examples as a starting point, creating and collecting other ideas as you work with children. If you plan for transitions, using movement to add personality, learning opportunities, physical activity, and fun to parts of the day that might otherwise be routine and dull, you will know that you and the children are making the most of every day. If you additionally encourage unstructured physical activity, set aside time for instruction in motor skills, and make movement breaks part of your curriculum, you will know that you are making the most of every day and contributing to the fight against childhood obesity.

Because the children spend so much of their time with you, and because teachers of preschoolers can be more realistic than parents in assessing children's physical activity levels (Noland et al., 1990), your role as an early childhood professional is essential in combating obesity and promoting healthy lifestyles from an early age.

What are your thoughts? What activities do you use to get children moving to positively impact childhood obesity? *Exchange* invites you to share them in their online survey. Visit www.ChildCareExchange.com/ comments to submit your ideas!

References

Frost, J. L. (1996). Joe Frost on playing outdoors. *Scholastic Early Childhood Today, 10*, 26–28.

Marcione, M. (2008). Fat kids found to have arteries of 45-year-olds. http://news.yahoo.com/s/ap/20081112/ap_on_he_me/med_ obese_kids_arteries

NASPE. (2002). *Active start: physical activity for children birth to 5 years.* Reston, VA: National Association for Sport and Physical Education.

Noland, M., Danner, F., & Dewalt, K. (1990). The measurement of physical activity in young children. *Research Quarterly for Exercise and Sport, 61*(2): 146–53.

Schlosser, E. (2005). *Fast food nation.* New York: Harper Perennial.

Critical Thinking

1. Why is it important to plan for active learning experiences throughout the day? How much activity do young children need each day?

2. Plan three active transition activities you can incorporate into your daily routine with children.

RAE PICA is a children's physical activity specialist and the author of 17 books, including the award-winning *Great Games for Young Children* and *Jump into Literacy*. Rae is known for her lively and informative workshop and keynote presentations and as host of the radio program "Body, Mind and Child" (www.bodymindandchild.com), in which she interviews experts in education, child development, the neurosciences, and more.

UNIT 5

Educational Practices That Help Children Thrive in School

Unit Selections

Learning Outcomes

After reading this Unit, you will be able to:

- Describe strategies teachers could use to develop positive working relationships with children.
- Describe how teachers can build positive relationships with children.
- What can teachers do to encourage young boys to be successful learners?
- Explain the concept of academic redshirting and why some parents choose to not send their children to kindergarten when they are age eligible to attend.
- Share some strategies that will allow young boys have a positive and successful time in early childhood programs.
- Develop a brief list of the components of developmentally appropriate practice.
- Justify the inclusion of play-based learning experiences in a primary grade classroom.
- List the causes for the pressure to push the curriculum down from the primary grades into preschool. How can teachers of young children resist that pressure?
- Describe the research teachers can use when making decision about grade retention.
- What are some examples of items that could be collected to provide evidence of the learning occurring in your classroom?
- List the components of an appropriate school lunch.
- Describe what teachers can do to advocate for daily recess.
- Develop the components of successful homework experiences.

Student Website
www.mhhe.com/cls

Internet References

Association for Childhood International (ACEI)
www.acei.org

Busy Teacher's Cafe
www.busyteacherscafe.com

Donors Choose
www.donorschoose.org

Future of Children
www.futureofchildren.org

Reggio Emilia
http://reggioalliance.org

Teacher Planet
www.teacherplanet.com

The title of this unit sums up what I see to be a key role for an educator; Helping Young Children Thrive in School. After all, we want all children to be successful learners who feel good about themselves and are challenged to grow in their educational setting. When talking to a group of educators about what constitutes good teaching practices in early childhood education many thoughts were shared, but the conversation always returned to one word; action. Good early childhood teaching is distinguished by action, good practice is children in action: children busy constructing, creating with materials, enjoying books, exploring, working in small groups, experimenting, inventing, finding out, building and composing throughout the day. Good practice is teachers in action: teachers busy holding conversations, guiding activities, questioning children, fostering the environment, challenging children's thinking, observing, drawing conclusions, planning and monitoring activities, and documenting the learning occurring throughout the day.

Make sure there is action in your classrooms; both children in action as they ask questions and work to find the answers to their questions as well as teachers in action supporting the ongoing investigations in their classrooms. One of the benefits of action-oriented learning is the opportunity for children to develop relationships with adults who are close by to support them in their learning. The importance of strong relationships is vital for learning. Recent research cites key components of effective teaching to be: intentional teaching, appropriate learning activities based on content standards and assessment, organized classroom practices, adults responsive to children and strong relationships developed with each child in the classroom. Kathleen Cranley Gallagher and Kelley Mayer expand on the important topic of relationships in "Enhancing Development and Learning through Teacher–Child Relationships."

Early childhood teaching is all about being proactive and establishing policies that support young children's development and learning. Good teachers are problem solvers just as children work to solve problems. Every day, teachers make decisions about how to guide children socially and emotionally. In attempting to determine what could be causing a child's emotional distress, teachers must take into account myriad factors. They should consider the physical, social, environmental, and emotional factors, in addition to the surface behavior of a child. Whether it is an individual child's behavior or interpersonal relationships, the pressing problem involves complex issues that require careful reflection and analysis. Even the most mature and seasoned teachers spend many hours thinking and talking about the best ways to guide and support young children's behavior: What should I do about the child who is out of bounds? What do I do to best prepare the learning environment to meet the needs of all children? How can I develop effective relationships with children and their families? These are some of the questions teachers ask as they interact with young children on a day-to-day basis. "Promoting Emotional Competence in the Preschool Classroom" by Hannah Nissen and Carol J. Hawkins includes critical information on the many roles of the teacher in helping the children build emotional competence. The teacher is a relationship builder, a coach and role model, and a creator

of healthy environments, all essential components in a quality early childhood setting. In fact, they are essential components for all teachers, no matter what age group the learner.

As the mother of two very active boys I often worried about their need for physical movement while they were confined in a classroom with a teacher who may not have always recognized the need for boys to be in motion while learning. Gropper et al., provide strategies in "Helping Young Boys Be Successful Learners in Today's Early Childhood Classrooms" for educators to better adjust their classrooms and teaching to meet the needs of all students, but particularly boys. A noted Yale educator, James Comer, states in the article, "The focus on child development that is largely missing from the preparation of educators probably contributes more to creating dysfunctional and underperforming schools than anything else." Teachers need to be knowledgeable of child development and put that knowledge to work in establishing their classrooms.

The articles in this unit will help teachers establish positive relationships with children. "Developmentally Appropriate Child Guidance: Helping Children Gain Self-Control" supports the need for positive relationships as the cornerstone for building rapport. The other theme that is woven throughout the articles in this unit is the importance of social and emotional development on all areas of development. Teachers who rush to teach academic skills at the expense of fostering the children's social and emotion development will find there are many unexpected hurdles to jump. Children who are not secure or confident in their surroundings or comfortable with the adults in their life will not be strong learners. Determining strategies for guidance and discipline is important work for an early childhood teacher. Because the teacher–child relationship is the foundation for emotional well-being and social competence, guidance is more than applying a single set of guidance techniques. Instead of one solitary model of classroom discipline strictly enforced, a broad range of techniques is more appropriate. It is only through careful analysis and reflection that teachers can look at children individually, assessing not only the child but the impact of family cultures as well, and determine appropriate and effective guidance. Recently one of my graduate students shared that the teachers at her school decided to stop using the traffic light system of management they had used for the past few years. The traffic light system is a light that resembles a traffic light and allows children to talk quietly when the light, located in the classroom or cafeteria, is green, whisper when the light is moved to yellow, and not talk at all when it is red. Some lights are noise sensitive so the noise level of the children determines the color of the light displayed, not the adult in the room. My student said the teachers recognized the program was not working and had many negative consequences. I am always pleased to hear when teachers and administrators alter programs based on observation and the gathering of data. Some educators stay with one practice that does not prove to be effective, yet they don't know what else to do so they stick with a poor plan. I applaud teachers who are constantly searching for ways to reach their children and will modify practice when needed.

Children crave fair and consistent guidelines from caring adults in their world. They want to know the consequences of their behavior and how to meet the expectations of others. When the expectations are clear and the students see a direct relationship between their behavior and the consequences, they begin to develop the self-control that will be so important as they move through life.

Parents not enrolling children in kindergarten when they are age eligible to attend is often called "academic redshirting," named after the practice of a college athlete sitting out a year to develop and grow stronger. Parents often want their child to be the most academically ready and oldest child in the class, but educators warn of potential long-term costs to this practice. Stephanie Pappas explores some of these issues in "Kindergarten Dilemma: Hold Kids Back to Get Ahead?" Economists and educational experts warn parents to consider all angles, not simply the child's birth-date, when making this most important decision about when to send their child to kindergarten. Parents and teachers should also keep in mind all professional early childhood organizations recommend sending children to kindergarten when they are age eligible in the state they reside. It is not the job of the children to get ready for school; educational personnel must be ready to meet the needs of all children.

An article that will lead to some rich discussion is Erika Christakis and Nicholas Christakis's "Want to Get Your Kids into College? Let Them Play." This article reminds me of one I included years ago in the 93/94 edition of Annual Editions: ECE titled, "Serious Play in the Classroom: How Messing Around Can Win You the Nobel Prize" by Selma Wassermann. Both Christakis and Wassermann stress the importance of allowing children ample time to play and mess around, or what Orville and Wilbur Wright called tinkering. They, along with Thomas Edison and Henry Ford, grew up in homes that encouraged playing around and figuring things out. Their play led to great discoveries. Children need time to let their minds wander as they manipulate and interact with a variety of materials.

I am distressed with the increasing push to have young children do things at an earlier and earlier age as the life expectancy keeps increasing. Children born today have an excellent chance of living into their 90s and beyond. There is no great need to rush and acquire skills that can easily be learned when the child is a little older at the expense of valuable lifelong lessons that are best learned when they are young. How to get along with others, make wise choices, negotiate, develop a sense of

compassion, and communicate needs are all skills that require introduction and practice during the preschool years. The basics are a solid foundation in understanding how things work, many opportunities to explore and manipulate materials, and opportunities for creative expression. How all this can be accomplished in the new world of standards is the balancing act in which many teachers now practice. "Developmentally Appropriate Practice in the Age of Testing" provides information to assist teachers dealing with this dilemma.

Each spring, the issue of grade retention creeps into the conversations of teachers and parents. Educators struggle to best address the needs of students who did not meet the standards or content expectations for that particular year. It is a challenge for teachers, parents, and the children who face another year in the same grade, which, research has consistently found, is not the best approach. Many countries do not retain students at all, while the United States retains over two million children each year. Is spending another year in the same grade the solution, or are there other ways educators can support struggling learners? Support for families, differentiated instruction, and outside services are successful strategies for children who do not achieve at the same level as their peers. Pamela Jane Powell's "Repeating Views on Grade Retention" will help answer some questions about this often misused educational practice.

We now know teaching is rocket science and does require committed individuals who are well prepared to deal with a variety of development levels and needs, as appropriate, intentional learning experiences are planned for all children. Good teaching does make a difference, as evidenced by the research noted in the first article in this edition, "$320,000 Kindergarten Teachers." Children deserve no less than adults who truly are well prepared and passionate about being with young children on a daily basis. Teaching cannot be viewed as a great profession for someone who wants their summers off. Teachers skilled in providing exemplary learning experiences for their children can make a real difference in the lives of their students.

In Hilary Seitz's "The Power of Documentation in the Early Childhood Classroom." Seitz describes the benefits of documentation and shares suggested ways to document learning. Teachers who take responsibility to educate others about the learning in their classroom will have successful partnerships with others, including family members and administrators.

When my colleague asked her 6-year-old granddaughter, Lily, the first week of school what was the best part of first grade, Lily replied, "Recess!" Lily knows she needs frequent breaks to learn effectively. Let's hope her teachers continue to provide those opportunities as she progresses through the educational system. In "Give Me a Break: The Argument for Recess" Barbie Norvell, Nancy Ratcliff, and Gilbert Hunt present striking data on the importance of daily recess for children and discuss the removal of critical items from the curriculum, such as recess, so there can be more time on task preparation for standardized testing. They encourage teachers to conduct their own action research to gather information that can be used to support recess in their school setting.

I often ask teachers what in their college course content addressed the purpose of and effective components of homework. Usually the response is, "Nothing." University faculty and school in-service coordinators must do a better job of helping teachers understand the characteristics of effective homework.

In Cathy Vatterott's "5 Hallmarks of Good Homework," she discusses the essential components. Homework can take many forms, and in the early years it can help children establish lifelong learning habits that will serve the students well later on. Marian Wright Edelman, president of the Children's Defense Fund, tells the story of her father asking her each day after school about her homework for the night. If she replied she didn't have any, he would say, "Well, assign yourself." Homework doesn't always have to be assigned by the teacher. It can be teacher assigned, but can also be family generated; inspired by upcoming family experiences, such as a trip to visit a relative in another state or child generated based on an interest in the spiders found crawling on the front porch. Homework is extending the learning that takes place in the school setting and allowing it to continue in the home environment.

This is a very long unit that includes articles on a number of critical issues related to helping children be successful learners. Be a thoughtful, intentional educator as you work to provide optimal opportunities for young children to thrive under your supervision.

Enhancing Development and Learning through Teacher-Child Relationships

KATHLEEN CRANLEY GALLAGHER, PHD AND KELLEY MAYER, PHD

From across the room, Miss Jilane notices that Maria has lost her toy to another toddler and is leaning toward the other child. She has seen Maria in these frustrating situations before and recognizes she may be about to bite her classmate. Calling her name gently, Jilane distracts her: "Maria, please help me with snack; I need a great snack helper. When we're done, you can play with that toy."

Tamara, the teacher, sits on a beanbag chair with Nick, a prekindergartner, reading a book about cars. They stop the story to talk about their own cars, with Tamara sharing what she likes about her truck and Nick explaining how his minivan has lots of room. They talk about what car Nick might get when he's "big" and what features it will have. They agree it will have to be a car that "is safe and goes fast."

Adam, the first-grade teacher, bends over a set of connecting blocks with Kwame. Tears are welling in Kwame's eyes, reflecting the frustration he feels trying to solve a math problem. Adam reassures Kwame that math can be hard work and proceeds to "think out loud" with him about how to solve the problem, regrouping the connecting blocks. "You don't have to do math alone, Kwame," Adam tells him. "It often helps to do it with another person. We can figure this out together."

How to be in a relationship may be the most important "skill" children ever learn.

Some researchers believe that children form ideas about relationships from their early experiences with their parents and apply these ideas to other relationships (Sroufe 2000). Others believe that children learn from teachers' modeling and imitate their social behavior (Baumrind 1973). It is likely that children use both of these strategies and more to learn about relationships. How to be in a relationship may be the most important "skill" children ever learn. While many teachers acknowledge their importance in helping children learn early academic and social skills, they sometimes underestimate the value of their personal relationships with children as supports for children's healthy development and learning. As the opening vignettes illustrate, teachers use their attunement to and knowledge of children to effectively scaffold children's development and learning.

This article reviews research on relationships between young children (birth to age 8) and their teachers, with the goal of offering research-proven strategies teachers can use to develop and sustain high-quality relationships with children at each stage of early childhood. This article considers the unique qualities and influences of teacher-child relationships for infants and toddlers, preschoolers, and primary-age children and provides ideas for how teachers can reflect on and enhance relationships in their daily classroom routines.

When teachers develop high-quality relationships with young children, they support problem solving, allowing the children to experience success without too much or too little assistance.

Early Relationships and Development

High-quality relationships in early childhood support the development of social, emotional, and cognitive skills (Goosens & van IJzendoorn 1990; Howes, Galinsky, & Kontos 1998). When children have secure relationships with their primary caregivers, they have better language skills (Sroufe 2000), more harmonious peer relationships (Howes, Hamilton, & Matheson 1994; Howes, Matheson, & Hamilton 1994), and fewer behavior problems (Rimm-Kaufman et al. 2002). In high-quality teacher-child relationships, teachers respond to children's needs appropriately and in a timely manner. Teachers are gentle and take frequent opportunities to interact face-to-face with children. When teachers develop high-quality relationships with young children, they support children's problem solving, allowing the children to experience success without too much or too little assistance (Bredekamp & Copple 1997).

Teachers in high-quality relationships with young children also support learning by assessing the children's instructional needs and offering support at each child's level. For example, when helping a young child comprehend a difficult story, the teacher may introduce key vocabulary words *before* the reading, helping to scaffold the child's understanding of the story while preventing the child from becoming too overwhelmed by the complexity of the language in the text. The teachers in the vignettes provide this kind of childspecific support—a delicate dance in which learning emerges in the context of the teacher-child relationship.

Relationships between teachers and children do not develop in isolation, however. They develop ecologically, influenced by many factors such as child and teacher characteristics, interactive processes, and contextual factors over time (Bronfenbrenner & Morris 1998). Teachers certainly set the tone for their relationships with children, but some children have a behavior style, or temperament, that challenges caregivers (Sturm 2004) and may make relationship building more difficult. Research suggests that children who respond to the environment with intense negative emotion, who are highly fearful, or who are very resistant to outside guidance are more likely to have relationships with teachers that are less close and higher in conflict (Birch & Ladd 1998). Children with disabilities, especially language-based disabilities that make communicating their needs more difficult, sometimes have difficulty building relationships (Mahoney & Perales 2003).

Culture and ethnicity are associated with differences in aspects of children's relationships with teachers. For example, some studies report that teachers feel closer to White and Hispanic children than to African American children (Saft & Pianta 2001; Hughes & Kwok 2007). Researchers speculate that ethnic match between teachers and students may be more important for relationships than ethnicity of the student (Saft & Pianta 2001), although few studies have included diverse samples of teachers to examine this issue (Saft & Pianta 2001). Based on the results of a recent study, in which both White and African American teachers reported more conflict in their relationships with children who were African American (Gallagher et al. 2006), more research is needed to understand how ethnicity is associated with relationships among children and teachers.

To enhance development and learning, it is important to know individual children and their families well and to "establish positive, personal relationships with children to foster the child's development and keep informed about the child's needs and potentials. Teachers listen to children and adapt their responses to children's differing needs, interests, styles, and abilities" (Bredekamp & Copple 1997, 17). Children have different needs, and their needs change as they develop. As their needs change, their relationships with teachers change as well. For example, in a study examining the stability of teacher-child relationships over the early childhood years from 10 to 56 months, most children established secure attachment relationships with their child care teacher (Howes & Hamilton 1992). When children were younger (18–24 months old), their relationships with teachers suffered when teacher turnover was frequent, but older toddlers (30-plus months) were less affected by turnover.

It is important to consider teacher-child relationships across development and schooling, paying particular attention to how such relationships function to sustain and enhance development at each age. Knowledge of individual children's needs at each developmental stage helps teachers understand how to best support children in their development and learning. The following sections highlight features of teacher-child relationships at different developmental periods and ways teachers and programs can enhance these relationships.

Teachers' Relationships with Infants and Toddlers

In infancy, social interaction forms the basis for the developing brain, supporting development of emotion regulation and attention (Shonkoff & Phillips 2000). Social relationships also teach infants and toddlers what they can expect from interacting with people. By crying, cooing, and smiling, infants express their needs and draw adult attention. Adults anticipate, sense, and interpret the infants' behaviors and then respond in a timely and appropriate manner. Through their positive affect, body language, and tone of voice, adults communicate warmth, positive regard, and safety. Infants, sensing comfort, safety, and security in the adult's presence, explore their environment and attempt new challenges.

John Bowlby ([1969] 1983) believed that children form cognitive schemas of their interactions with adults and use them to form ideas about self and relationships. For example, infants whose caregivers respond sensitively to their needs learn to expect that their needs will be met and their future interactions with adults will be positive. In these positive interactions, infants come to feel that they are "worthy" of these interactions and relationships. In contrast, infants whose needs are not met responsively, or are met inconsistently, learn that they cannot rely on others to care for them. These infants may become detached or aggressive in their relationships (Sroufe 2000).

The secure infant stays close to a trusted caregiver, watching newcomers with a healthy suspicion.

Before children are 6 months old, it may be difficult to tell the quality of teacher-child relationships by observing the child. But soon after a child begins to crawl, evidence of his relationship with a caregiver is reflected in several behaviors. The secure infant stays close to a trusted caregiver, watching newcomers with a healthy suspicion. Observation methods of examining teacher-infant relationships have been important in describing teacher behaviors that foster healthy relationships and influence children's development (Goosens & van IJzendoorn 1990; Howes & Smith 1995; Howes, Galinsky, & Kontos 1998). Sensitive teachers respond to children's cues and comfort distressed children (Howes & Smith 1995; Howes, Galinsky, & Kontos 1998). They provide multiple opportunities for creative play, engage toddlers in prolonged conversations, and frequently join in their play to encourage children's successful cognitive development. When children misbehave, sensitive teachers redirect and gently remind children of expectations; they assert their expectations for children's respectful social behavior while affirming their affection toward the child (Howes & Smith 1995; Howes, Galinsky, & Kontos 1998).

When teachers behave in a sensitive, responsive manner, children seek closeness and contact with them, share with them excitement and discovery in their play, and respond to teachers' suggestions and directions readily (Goosens & van IJzendoorn 1990; Howes & Smith 1995; Howes, Galinsky, & Kontos 1998). Children with close relationships with teachers have better relationships with other children (Howes, Matheson, & Hamilton 1994; Howes & Phillipsen 1998). In one study, toddlers who demonstrated a secure relationship with their teacher were, at 4 years of age, less aggressive with peers and more sociable and skilled in imaginative peer play (Howes, Hamilton, & Matheson 1994).

Implications for Infant/Toddler Teachers and Programs

Because secure attachment is so important to an infant's development, programs serving infants and toddlers must make supporting the development of relationships a priority (Bredekamp & Copple 1997). To that end, programs serving infants and toddlers must take care to maintain the lowest child-to-teacher ratios possible. However, low ratios alone are not sufficient for creating an environment that supports intimacy between teachers and young children (Lally, Torres, & Phelps 1994). Program environments should be touchable and comfortable. Spaces for infants and toddlers should be inviting and should contain interesting objects and textures to explore as well as interesting and attractive visual stimuli. The lighting should be soft, and there should be plenty of soft, comfortable seating or floor space where caregivers and children can interact with one another comfortably (Lally, Torres, & Phelps 1994). To provide for infants' and toddlers' need for continuity of care, each child should have the same primary caregiver for as long as possible.

Low child-to-teacher ratios help teachers provide one-on-one attention, and sufficient preparation time helps teachers plan for individual children's needs.

As in all teaching, but particularly with infants and toddlers, teachers need to attend to the individual needs of children in the context of a group (Lally, Torres, & Phelps 1994). In order to respond to infants' and toddlers' individual needs, teachers must be attuned to children's cues and be keen observers of child behavior. Likewise, programs must do what they can to ensure that teachers have the time to observe and interpret children's behavior. For example, low child-to-teacher ratios help teachers provide one-on-one attention, and sufficient preparation time helps teachers plan for individual children's needs.

Finally, each child lives in a unique family culture that a teacher must understand in order to develop a quality relationship with the child. Therefore, programs should support teachers' relationships with children's families by setting aside time for communication, conferencing, and home visits.

Teachers' Relationships with Preschoolers

As children enter preschool, they are typically ready for more complex relationships. Their language, motor, and cognitive abilities allow them to more easily initiate interactions and respond to other people. Preschoolers' readiness for new and more complex relationships is apparent in the classroom's stimulating environment and in their interests in the people and world around them.

Interactions between teachers and children are essential to the quality of the teacher-child relationship and to children's learning and development (Kontos & Wilcox-Herzog 1997a). When exploring interactions between teachers and children, researchers have observed key teacher behaviors that enhance relationships with children (Rimm-Kaufman et al. 2002) and support social and academic competence (Kontos & Wilcox-Herzog 1997a). Teachers who have high-quality relationships with children help children to focus their attention and interpret their emotions (Howes & Hamilton 1992). Sensitive and responsive teachers assess children's learning styles and use that knowledge to meet children's instructional and social needs (Hamre & Pianta 2005). The highest quality relationships between teachers and children are characterized by closeness (warmth and open communication) and low conflict (hostility and opposition) (Pianta, Hamre, & Stuhlman 2003).

Research emphasizes the importance of intentional, responsive teaching for children's learning in the context of play (Kontos & Wilcox-Herzog 1997b; Lobman 2006). Reflecting a complex set of practices, responsive teaching involves assessing children's individual needs, contextual needs, and cognitive and social competencies and responding in a timely and appropriate manner. Because different children require varying levels and qualities of teacher involvement, responsive teaching is a delicate, but not impossible, dance. Lobman (2006) elaborates on the complex processes of responsive teaching through the lens of theatrical improvisation. Using this lens in a case study, one teacher participated in preschool children's play, leading and responding to innovation and eventually leading to more complex, collaborative play. Lobman demonstrates that even subtle language differences within the realm of responsive teaching modifies the trajectory of children's engagement with the teacher, peers, objects, and ideas. Collectively, this evidence suggests that what teachers do and say matters highly in children's development and learning.

Close relationships with teachers have remarkable benefits for children. Children who develop close relationships with their teacher tend to explore the classroom environment (Coplan & Prakash 2003) and demonstrate more complex play than their peers who are not as close to their teacher. They are also sought out more by their playmates (Howes, Matheson, & Hamilton 1994). Finally, preschoolers with close teacher relationships have better school achievement, better social skills, and fewer behavior problems in first grade and throughout elementary school (Hamre & Pianta 2001; Pianta & Stuhlman 2004).

Implications for Preschool Teachers and Programs

Developmentally appropriate practice optimizes opportunities and strategies for developing teacher-child relationships (Bredekamp & Copple 1997). Children should begin the school day with a feeling of warmth and comfort as they transition from their family's care to their teacher's. Teachers who focus on their relationships with children take time to recognize children individually, personally greeting them and their families each morning and again at their departure. Acknowledging children's presence and welcoming them involves modeling very basic principles of respect and commitment to relationships.

Children enjoy knowing about their teachers' lives outside of school and develop empathy as they understand the different roles in people's lives.

Teachers can build positive relationships with children by spending time with them in individual and small group settings. To improve their relationships with children, teachers may engage in one-on-one activities such as shared story reading (Gallagher et al. 2006; Gallagher et al. under review). Story reading with individual children can stimulate meaningful conversations about topics such as the children's families, after-school experiences, and pets. The teacher should also feel comfortable sharing things that are important to her. Children enjoy knowing about their teachers' lives outside of school and develop empathy as they understand the different roles in people's lives. Becoming familiar with children's interests helps teachers meet their needs while also modeling for children how to care for another person.

When children experience conflict in relationships, teachers can encourage them to express their feelings through conversation or through writing and drawing. Having paper and writing materials in the quiet corner gives children a healthy outlet to express their anger or sadness (Mayer 2007). When a child uses negative behavior, the teacher should discuss the incident with the child in private and in the context of expectations based on respect. When teachers value relationships, they recognize that learning how to be in relationships is challenging and that children will learn acceptable social behavior over time.

Teachers' Relationships with Primary School Children

In the primary classroom, teachers usually are responsible for a larger group of children than in younger classrooms while at the same time focusing on academics and state standards (Barnett et al. 2005). Despite the greater responsibility to provide effective instruction in all content areas, teachers must continue to provide caring, supportive environments in which children feel emotionally supported and valued if children are going to benefit academically and socially from schooling (Hamre & Pianta 2001; Davis 2003; Pianta, Hamre, & Stuhlman 2003; Klem & Connell 2004; Koomen, van Leeuwen, & van der Leij 2004; La Paro, Rimm-Kaufman, & Pianta 2006).

Furthermore, emerging evidence suggests that teachers' support is even more important for children who are vulnerable to school failure (Henricsson & Rydell 2004; Hamre & Pianta 2005; Hughes, Gleason, & Zhang 2005; Picklo 2005; Hughes & Kwok 2007). Highstakes standards, larger class sizes, and decreased time for informal, relaxed engagement in primary grades mean teachers must work harder to build strong relationships with children.

Research demonstrates that classroom climate, specifically teachers' emotional and instructional support, is associated with teachers' relationships with children in the primary grades (Hamre & Pianta 2005). Teachers providing high levels of emotional support tend to be aware of the children's needs and interests, engage in conversations, and show positive affect toward children while also maintaining high yet attainable expectations for appropriate behavior. Teachers high in instructional support spend considerable time and effort on literacy instruction, give children evaluative feedback, encourage child responsibility, and offer conversational (not just didactic) instruction (Hamre & Pianta 2005).

In addition to teacher support in the classroom, relationships between teachers and individual children are associated with academic growth, social competence, and engagement in the primary grades. When kindergarten teachers' relationships with children were high in conflict, first grade teachers reported more behavioral problems and poorer social competence (Pianta & Stuhlman 2004). Subsequently, these children's relationships with their first grade teachers were associated with their social skills *and* academic achievement in first grade. Throughout research, children in close teacher-child relationships participated more in classroom activities (Ladd, Birch, & Buhs 1999), exhibited better work habits (Hamre & Pianta 2001; Baker 2006), and liked school more, while children with high conflict teacher-child relationships reported liking school less (Birch & Ladd 1998) and had poorer academic achievement (Hughes, Gleason, & Zhang 2005; Hughes & Kwok 2007). The quality of the teacher-child relationship also influences children's relationships with peers in the primary grades. When teachers reported less closeness and more conflict in their relationships with second-graders, these children showed more aggression with their classroom peers. When teachers reported closer, lower conflict relationships with second-graders, the children were more prosocial with classroom peers (Howes 2000).

Implications for Primary Teachers and Programs

The instructional methods teachers use are important for determining children's success in learning as well as their comfort and security when interacting with the teacher. Primary grade teachers need time for individual instruction with children (Ostrosky & Jung 2003). During this time, the teacher can observe and interact with the child while engaged in a learning activity. This helps teachers better assess children's needs. It also gives children opportunities to ask questions and express ideas in a safe space.

As with preschoolers, teachers can also build positive relationships with primary-age children through interactive storybook reading (Gallagher et al. 2006). Teachers can read aloud to children and encourage children's involvement in the story by engaging children in extended conversations about the text and making personal connections (Neuman, Copple, & Bredekamp 2000). These proven comprehension strategies help children process story information and allow teachers opportunities to become familiar with children's personal experiences.

Children can participate in family conferences as well, assessing achievements and setting goals.

Individual conferences between teachers and children provide opportunities for children to receive both emotional and instructional feedback from teachers. Involving the child's family in the conference can help the teacher build a relationship with the family as well as with the child. Children can participate in their conferences as well, assessing achievements and setting goals. This enables the children to feel care and support from the multiple adults responsible for their education and to own their own progress. Teachers can find opportunities to get to know children by having lunch with them or taking time to talk with them on the playground. Primary grade teachers can also get to know children better through participation in after-school activities and events. Attending such events allows teachers to see children immersed in their interactions with family members and peers, helping teachers to learn more about what is important to these children.

Summary

Research confirms that "children's development in all areas is influenced by their ability to establish and maintain a limited number of positive, consistent primary relationships with adults and other children. These primary relationships begin in the family but extend over time to include children's teachers and members of the community" (Bredekamp & Copple 1997, 15). To appropriately address children's needs, teachers and programs must put children's relationships at the forefront of planning and implementation of interactions and activities.

Putting relationships at the forefront involves recognizing the child, becoming familiar with the child and family, respecting the child's individuality, and committing to the ongoing process of being in the relationship (Gallagher & Mayer 2006). The beauty of working with young children is that while we, as teachers, practice building relationships, we also model relationship-building practices for them.

The privileges of caring for and educating children are not separate. We do both every day, building relationships with children and supporting their development and learning. Prospective parents would often ask, "Is your program child *care* or a pre*school?*" The response has always been, "We are both. We cannot care for children without educating them, and we cannot educate children without caring for them." We do both by building relationships.

References

Baker, J. 2006. Contributions of teacher-child relationships to positive school adjustment during elementary school. *Journal of School Psychology* 44 (3): 211–29.

Barnett, W. S., J. T. Hustedt, K. B. Robin, & K. L. Schulman. 2005. *2005 State preschool yearbook.* Third volume in the series The State of Preschool. New Brunswick, NJ: National Institute for Early Education Research (NIEER).

Baumrind, D. 1973. The development of instrumental competence through socialization. In *Minnesota symposia on child psychology: Volume 7,* ed. A. D. Pick, 3–46. Minneapolis: University of Minnesota Press.

Birch, S. H., & G. W. Ladd. 1998. Children's interpersonal behaviors and the teacher-child relationship. *Developmental Psychology* 34 (5): 934–46.

Bowlby, J. [1969] 1983. *Attachment.* Vol. 1 of *Attachment and loss.* New York: Basic Books.

Bredekamp, S., & C. Copple, eds. 1997. *Developmentally appropriate practice in early childhood programs.* Rev. ed. Washington, DC: NAEYC.

Bronfenbrenner, U., & P. Morris. 1998. The ecology of developmental processes. In *Theoretical models of human development,* ed. R. M. Lerner. New York: Wiley.

Coplan, R. J., & K. Prakash. 2003. Spending time with teacher: Characteristics of preschoolers who frequently elicit versus initiate interactions with teachers. *Early Childhood Research Quarterly* 18 (1): 143–58.

Davis, H. A. 2003. Conceptualizing the role and influence of student-teacher relationships on children's social and cognitive development. *Educational Psychologist* 38 (4): 207–34.

Gallagher, K. C., & K. L. Mayer. 2006. Teacher-child relationships at the forefront of effective practice. *Young Children* 61 (6): 44–49.

Gallagher, K. C., K. L. Mayer, P. Sylvester, M. P. Bundy, & P. Fedora. 2006. Teacher-child relationships and developing literacy and social-emotional skills in pre-kindergarten. Poster paper presented at the Annual Meeting of the American Educational Research Association, in San Francisco.

Gallagher, K. C., P. R. Sylvester, K. L. Mayer, & M. P. Bundy. Under review. Storytime in prekindergarten: Teacher-child story reading and associations with temperament, development, and teacher-child relationship. *Early Education and Development.*

Goosens, F. A., & M. H. van IJzendoorn. 1990. Quality of infants' attachments to professional caregivers: Relation to infant-parent attachment and day-care characteristics. *Child Development* 61: 832–37.

Hamre, B. K., & R. C. Pianta. 2001. Early teacher-child relationships and the trajectory of children's school outcomes through eighth grade. *Child Development* 72 (2): 625–38.

Hamre, B. K., & R. C. Pianta. 2005. Can instructional and emotional support in the firstgrade classroom make a difference for children at risk for school failure? *Child Development* 76 (5): 949–67.

Henricsson, L., & A.-M. Rydell. 2004. Elementary school children with behavior problems: Teacher-child relations and self-perception. A prospective study. *Merrill-Palmer Quarterly* 50 (2): 111–38.

Howes, C. 2000. Social-emotional classroom climate in child care, child-teacher relationships, and children's second grade peer relations. *Social Development* 9 (2): 191–204.

Howes, C., E. Galinsky, & S. Kontos. 1998. Child care caregiver sensitivity and attachment. *Social Development* 7 (1): 25–36.

Howes, C., & C. E. Hamilton. 1992. Children's relationships with child care teachers: Stability and concordance with parental attachments. *Child Development* 63: 867–78.

Howes, C., C. E. Hamilton, & C. C. Matheson. 1994. Children's relationships with peers: Differential associations with aspects of the teacher-child relationship. *Child Development* 65: 253–63.

Howes, C., C. C. Matheson, & C. E. Hamilton. 1994. Maternal, teacher, and child care history correlates of children's relationships with peers. *Child Development* 65: 264–73.

Howes, C., & L. Phillipsen. 1998. Continuity in children's relations with peers. *Social Development* 7 (3): 340–49.

Howes, C., & E. W. Smith. 1995. Relations among child care quality, teacher behavior, children's play activities, emotional security, and cognitive activity in child care. *Early Childhood Research Quarterly* 10 (4): 381–404.

Hughes, J., K. A. Gleason, & D. Zhang. 2005. Relationship influences on teachers' perceptions of academic competence in academically at-risk minority and majority first grade students. *Journal of School Psychology* 43 (4): 303–20.

Hughes, J., & O. Kwok. 2007. Influence of student-teacher and parent-teacher relationships on lower achieving readers' engagement and achievement in the primary grades. *Journal of Educational Psychology* 99 (1): 39–51.

Klem, A. M., & J. P. Connell. 2004. Relationships matter: Linking teacher support to student engagement and achievement. *Journal of School Health* 74 (7): 262–73.

Kontos, S., & A. Wilcox-Herzog. 1997a. Influences on children's competence in early childhood classrooms. *Early Childhood Research Quarterly* 12 (3): 247–62.

Kontos, S., & A. Wilcox-Herzog. 1997b. Teachers interactions with children: Why are they so important? *Young Children* 52 (2): 4–12.

Koomen, H., M. van Leeuwen, & A. van der Leij. 2004. Does well-being contribute to performance? Emotional security, teacher support and learning behaviour in kindergarten. *Infant and Child Development* 13: 253–75.

Ladd, G. W., S. H. Birch, & E. S. Buhs. 1999. Children's social and scholastic lives in kindergarten: Related spheres of influence? *Child Development* 70 (6): 1373–1400.

Lally, J. R., Y. L. Torres, & P. C. Phelps. 1994. Caring for infants and toddlers in groups: Necessary considerations for emotional, social, and cognitive development. *Zero to Three* 14 (5): 1–8.

La Paro, K. M., S. E. Rimm-Kaufman, & R. C. Pianta. 2006. Kindergarten to first grade: Classroom characteristics and the stability and change of children's classroom experiences. *Journal of Research in Childhood Education* 21 (2): 189–202.

Lobman, C. L. 2006. Improvisation: An analytic tool for examining teacher-child interactions in the early childhood classroom. *Early Childhood Research Quarterly* 21 (4): 455–70.

Mahoney, G., & F. Perales. 2003. Using relationship-focused intervention to enhance the social-emotional functioning of young children with autism spectrum disorders. *Topics in Early Childhood Special Education* 23 (2): 77–89.

Mayer, K. L. 2007. Emerging knowledge about emergent writing. *Young Children* 62 (1): 34–41.

Neuman, S. B., C. Copple, & S. Bredekamp. 2000. *Learning to read and write: Developmentally appropriate practices for young children.* Washington, DC: NAEYC.

Ostrosky, M. M., & E. Y. Jung. 2003. Building positive teacher-child relationships. In What Works Briefs. Champaign, IL: Center on the Social and Emotional Foundations for Early Learning. www.vanderbilt.edu/csefel/briefs/wwb12.html

Pianta, R. C., B. Hamre, & M. Stuhlman. 2003. Relationships between teachers and children. In *Educational psychology*, eds. W. M. Reynolds & G. E. Miller, 199–234. Vol. 7 of *Handbook of psychology*, ed. I. B. Weiner. Hoboken, NJ: Wiley.

Pianta, R. C., & M. W. Stuhlman. 2004. Teacher-child relationships and children's success in the first years of school. *School Psychology Review* 33 (3): 444–58.

Picklo, D. M. 2005. Behaviorally at-risk African American students: The importance of student-teacher relationships for school outcomes. Dissertation Abstracts International, Section A: Humanities and Social Sciences, ProQuest Information & Learning.

Rimm-Kaufman, S. E., D. M. Early, M. J. Cox, G. Saluja, R. C. Pianta, & C. Payne. 2002. Early behavioral attributes and teachers' sensitivity as predictors of competent behavior in the kindergarten classroom. *Applied Developmental Psychology* 23: 451–70.

Saft, E. W., & R. C. Pianta. 2001. Teachers' perceptions of their relationships with students: Effects of child age, gender, and ethnicity of teachers and children. *School Psychology Quarterly* 16 (2): 125–41.

Shonkoff, J. P., & D. A. Phillips, eds. 2000. *From neurons to neighborhoods: The science of early childhood development.* Report of the National Research Council. Washington DC: National Academies Press.

Sroufe, A. L. 2000. Early relationships and the development of children. *Infant Mental Health Journal* 21 (1–2): 67–74.

Sturm, L. 2004. Temperament in early childhood: A primer for the perplexed. *Zero to Three* 24 (4): 4–11.

Critical Thinking

1. What did the authors mean with the statement, "How to be in a relationship may be the most important 'skill' children ever learn."?

2. Write a paragraph for the newsletter at a preschool where you may potentially be employed addressing the important connection between education and care of young children. What role does the development of healthy relationships play in the care and education of young children?

KATHLEEN CRANLEY GALLAGHER, PhD, is an assistant professor in the School of Education at the University of North Carolina at Chapel Hill. Having worked with children and families in early education programs for 15 years, Kate's research and teaching now focus on children's social relationships with families, peers, and teachers. kcgallag@email.unc.edu. **KELLEY MAYER,** PhD, is an assistant professor at the College of Charleston, in South Carolina. Her research addresses associations between teacher-child relationships and children's early literacy development. Kelley was previously a literacy consultant and taught kindergarten in a public school. mayerk@cofc.edu. This Research in Review article was edited by journal research editor Sharon K. Ryan, EdD, associate professor of early childhood education, Graduate School of Education, Rutgers—The State University of New Jersey.

Promoting Emotional Competence in the Preschool Classroom

Hannah Nissen and Carol J. Hawkins

Beginning in the preschool years and continuing through the elementary years, successful and positive interactions with peers have been shown to be a central predictor of ongoing mental health and school success (Denham, 2001, 2006). As children become more skilled in interacting with others and managing emotions during interactions, they are better able to negotiate their ever-expanding social worlds. In recent years, the development of emotional competence also has received extensive attention in the literature on early childhood development and school readiness (Bracken & Fischel, 2007; Hyson, 2002; Knitzer & Lefkowitz, 2005; Raver & Knitzer, 2002).

Components of Emotional Competence

Emotional competence has been defined as having three specific components: emotional expressiveness, emotional knowledge, and emotional regulation (Denham et al., 2003). Each plays a key role in determining young children's ability to interact and form relationships with others (Denham, 2006).

Emotional expressiveness is central to emotional competence. Patterns of positive expression of emotion, such as happiness, aid in friendship development, while negative expressions of emotion, such as anger, interfere with peer relationships (Denham et al., 2003). Children often develop characteristic emotional responses, and these patterns of expressiveness either lead to positive interactions with agemates or serve as barriers to successful interactions.

Emotional knowledge involves identifying emotional expressions in others and responding to the emotional displays of others in acceptable ways. Children who comprehend the expressions of others or the emotions typically associated with social situations are more likely to respond in prosocial ways, and are regarded as more likeable by peers and teachers (Denham et al, 2003).

Emotional regulation, also a critical element of emotional competence, involves the ability to manage arousal and behavior during social interaction (Denham, 2006). Young children have limited resources for emotional regulation; both negative and positive emotions can overwhelm the child, often leading to disorganized thinking and problematic behavior (Ashiabi, 2000). For children who demonstrate difficulty in regulating emotion, their expression of emotion often seems aggressive or intense. This has the potential to interfere with these children's ability to interact with others in socially acceptable ways. Peers and adults are likely to have negative perceptions to such emotional responses.

The Importance of Emotional Competence

Research suggests that a child's state of emotional development impacts development in all domains. According to the National Association for the Education of Young Children (2004), development in physical, social, cognitive, and emotional domains all contribute to a young child's ability to adapt to school life. Emotional competence, especially, has been shown to link to social competence in profound ways (Denham et al., 2003).

Social, emotional, and cognitive learning are interconnected to a greater extent in younger children. Studies indicate that many young children struggle to develop the emotional and behavioral strategies necessary to succeed in school (Knitzer & Lefkowitz, 2005). Consequently, building emotional competence helps children form positive social relationships and positive self-esteem, and is critical for school readiness and ongoing academic success.

Children's ongoing emotional health is influenced by their growing ability to express, understand, and regulate various emotions (Denham et al., 2003). Researchers found that children who enter kindergarten lacking curiosity, persistence in learning situations, and an eagerness to learn are less successful, academically, at the end of the 1st grade (Hemmeter & Ostrosky, 2006). Thus, children's relationships with teachers and peers, their interest and motivation to participate in learning experiences, and their ability to learn can be influenced, negatively or positively, by their emotional development (Peth-Pierce, 2001; Raver & Knitzer, 2002).

Beyond children's home environments and interactions with parents and caregivers, the classroom context provides endless opportunities to foster emotional health and competence. Every encounter with a child provides an opportunity to support the development of emotional skills that will allow children to experience success within the classroom and other contexts. Throughout the day, children are involved in a variety of routine, planned, and spontaneous contexts. As they participate in classroom life, they both experience and express a variety of emotions—some in ways that suggest a positive course of development and others that may indicate deleterious effects on a child over time. Teachers play an important role in fostering healthy development through identification of behaviors that may interfere with emotionally healthy response patterns (Ashiabi, 2000). However, teachers are rarely trained in the assessment and promotion of emotional competence. This lack of educational preparation often causes teachers to overlook or minimize the implications of emotional competence.

Promoting Emotional Competence

Nurturing and individualized teacher-child relationships provide important contexts for the promotion of children's emotional health (Bagdi & Vacca, 2005). As they interact with children, teachers have opportunities to coach children regarding appropriate responses during peer interactions and classroom activities, and serve as role models of appropriate expression of emotions (Hyson, 2004). When teachers organize child-centered classroom environments, they are preparing an emotional climate that is positive and conducive to learning. Finally, as educators create learning communities in which children are valued, children experience psychological safety and security (Keogh, 2003) (see Box 1).

Nurturing and individualized teacher-child relationships provide important contexts for the promotion of children's emotional health.

The Teacher as Relationship Builder

According to theory rooted in principles of attachment, teacher-child relationships contribute in significant ways to a child's growing emotional competence (Howes, Hamilton, & Matheson, 1994). Nurturing relationships with teachers who are responsive to children's unique needs are necessary to foster healthy development in many areas, including empathy, self-regulation, and peer relationships (Shonkoff & Phillips, 2001). Children who are able to form secure relationships with their teachers are often able to use that relationship as a secure base from which to explore the classroom and participate in activities with others (Howes, Hamilton, & Matheson, 1994). Dependent and conflicting teacher-child relationships, however, may interfere with children's ability to participate positively in the school experience and negatively influence their learning and academic achievement (Coplan & Prakash, 2003).

Individualized relationships with children create an arena in which teachers model healthy emotional expression, as well as informally assess a child's emotional well-being. In the context of a trusting relationship, teachers begin to recognize children's characteristic emotional responses and ability to regulate these responses in various classroom scenarios. Teachers can ascertain children's knowledge about emotions, and plan for support as necessary.

Children's individual differences necessitate that the relationships teachers form with each child be specific and unique. Tailoring one's style of interaction to the characteristics, interests, and needs of each child will provide the context in which a relationship supportive of development can evolve. A child who is characteristically cautious, for example, may be best suited to a style of interaction that provides time for adapting and developing a level of comfort before engaging in interaction or activity. Such a child may enter the classroom each day standing in the doorway, cautiously observing the activity in the classroom. To match the child's style, the teacher could calmly approach the child and quietly greet him. Quiet conversation with the child might ensue, and the child could explore the arrival activities when he is ready. Pressuring the child to enter the classroom and participate may cause this child to experience discomfort and thus withdraw, as the child may feel psychologically threatened. Careful observations of children during arrival time, as they interact with peers and adults, and as they participate in classroom activities and routines, provide useful information to help teachers tailor their interactions to be respectful of children's individual behavioral styles.

As a child encounters new experiences or changes, the teacher should observe the child's responses and determine the extent to which the experiences cause stress. These observations allow the teacher to determine the level and forms of support the child may require to feel secure. A change in schedule, for instance, may be a source of stress for some children, as the element of predictability has been removed. Such a child may exhibit signs of distress, withdraw, or even display aggression. The trusted teacher can offer support as the child tries to adapt to the change, possibly by remaining near and providing a simple, age-appropriate explanation of the change. Helping the child reestablish a sense of predictability by describing what will happen next

---

Box 1
Promoting Emotional Competence

Teacher As Relationship Builder

- Observe children's abilities to regulate emotional responses
- Establish nurturing, individualized relationships with children
- Respond in ways that demonstrate the child is valued
- Tailor interactions to the characteristics and needs of each child

Teacher As Coach and Role Model

- Coach children in problem solving during activities and peer interactions
- Help children verbalize their frustrations and use language in solving problems
- Coach children in recognizing and naming their feelings
- Model appropriate expression of emotions

Teacher As Creator of Healthy Environments

- Establish a "good fit" between children's needs and characteristics and the expectations of the learning environment
- Provide appropriate choices and challenges
- Create soft spaces to serve as a retreat from stress
- Establish predictable routines
- Organize an environment that encourages autonomy and responsibility
- Provide blocks of time for free play
- Build understanding of emotions through intentional teaching
- Establish a climate of respect
- Believe that each child can succeed

also may be stabilizing. Furthermore, with this knowledge about the child in mind, the teacher can now plan for supports that may benefit this child in coping with future changes and unfamiliar experiences. Acknowledging the child's feelings, making advance preparation for change, encountering a new experience alongside the child, or modeling means for adapting to or approaching a new experience are effective strategies for bolstering children's emotional health. Anticipating children's needs and being responsive to those needs demonstrates that the child is valued, promotes a sense of psychological safety, and ultimately fosters children's emotional competence and well-being.

Teacher as Coach and Role Model

Much of emotional competence promotion is something that cannot be planned for; opportunities simply present themselves throughout the day (Hemmeter & Ostrosky, 2006). During daily routines and activities, one of the teacher's important roles is to carefully observe and reflect upon children's specific behaviors and responses. These observations help the teacher create an emotional profile of the child and serve to guide the practitioner in coaching children's behavior and responses, applying supportive strategies, and role-modeling.

When a child faces an upsetting or perplexing situation (e.g., a block structure that keeps falling) and gets angry (e.g., by kicking the blocks), the teacher has the opportunity to coach the child in problem-solving skills. By helping the child identify the problem, guiding the child in generating possible solutions, and co-playing with the child in trying out the new idea, a teacher serves as both a coach and a role model of appropriate behavior and emotional expression and regulation.

Other developmental challenges might present themselves throughout the day. Challenges can be small, like a stuck zipper that frustrates a child trying to fix it. In this situation, the teacher can work with the child to fix the zipper. At the end of the episode, the two can celebrate overcoming the challenge.

The challenge could be more complex, such as two children wanting to use the same item at the water table. A lack of communication skills often creates challenges for young children when they are in social encounters with peers. Children struggle to find the words to communicate their ideas and feelings in ways that are clearly understood.

Working through potential negative social situations requires expression of emotions in an acceptable manner. When children get into conflict, the helpful teacher assists them in becoming constructive problem solvers (Hyson, 2004). Ahn (2005a) states that teachers need to verbally guide children to express their feelings clearly and constructively. When the child approaches a peer, such statements as "use your words" are of limited value. Often, it is clear that children do not know what words to use. Coaching is necessary so that children will have confidence to use language to solve problems, and appropriately assert their rights. Children then will begin to realize that conflicts can be resolved verbally, rather than through aggression.

Teacher as Creator of Healthy Environments

The creation of emotionally healthy, nurturing classrooms requires careful organization of the physical environment, predictable routines, appropriate play activities, and a positive emotional climate (Hemmeter & Ostrosky, 2006). Thomas and Chess (1977) suggest that to support emotional competence, environmental expectations and demands should reflect the unique nature of the children in the classroom and establish a "good fit" with each child. The characteristics and behavioral style of each child must be respected and should be considered in planning both the physical and social environment within the classroom (Keogh, 2003). Attention to creating a "match" between the child's style and the environment ensures that children can interact with the environment in a positive and growth-promoting manner. For example, the choices that are available to the children affect the development of emotional regulation. By providing choices that match the needs of the children within the group, the teacher supports their emotional regulation. Environments that are either too stimulating or not stimulating enough can provide too much stress for a child. The child may respond to excessive stress by withdrawing, or, on the opposite end of the spectrum, by displaying aggression. In such a scenario, the mismatch between the child and the environment creates an obstacle to healthy peer interaction and learning-focused exploration.

In addition to appropriate choices, comfortable and soft spaces within classrooms also support children's emotional health. Such a place serves as a safe zone or a quiet area to which children can retreat from stress. This space is not to be associated with punishment, but rather should be considered a place to go when children seek some privacy, quiet, and comfort. It might be a quiet spot away from classroom traffic, furnished with pillows, a rug, and other soft surfaces.

Children often require a teacher's help to recognize when they need to go to this quiet place. Acknowledging and reflecting to the child a sense of what the child is experiencing and feeling bolsters knowledge about emotions and emotional expression. With practice, children learn to tune into their inner self-control and thus regain internal equilibrium and balance. The sensitive teacher remains nearby to observe and guide the process of emotional regulation as needed. When appropriate, the children return to the group and explore constructively once again.

Effective teachers establish routines throughout the classroom day (LaParo, Pianta, & Stuhlman, 2004). During carefully planned routines, and through organization of a child-centered environment, children learn what to expect, as well as what is expected of them. The predictability that results is psychologically stabilizing and preventive of difficult behavior (Hemmeter & Ostrosky, 2006). For example, a child learns through practice as he enters the classroom that he needs to store his belongings in his personalized cubby. If select activities have been organized in advance, the child comes to know that after he finishes hanging his coat, he may choose an available activity until the time for clean-up is signaled. Through thoughtfully constructed routines, children build a sense of responsibility and participate autonomously and positively in the classroom community.

The nature of the curriculum also has a significant impact on children's emotional competence. Children should have ample time for free play in which to experiment with appropriate releases of frustration and stress. During these times, children participate in activities that support emotional regulation and understanding. Lindsey and Colwell (2003) found that high levels of pretend play were associated with high emotional understanding in girls and boys, and with high emotional regulation and emotional competence in girls. Physical play was associated with boys' emotional competence with peers.

Classrooms that support healthy emotional development are characterized by a positive emotional climate and genuine respect for children's developmental characteristics, interests, and needs. Teachers hold developmentally appropriate expectations that guide the organization of the environment, the curriculum, and interactions with children. Effective teachers believe that children can succeed, provide opportunities for children to experience success, and recognize both their efforts and successes. In caring, child-centered classrooms such as these, children gain a sense of belonging, and learn about emotions. Teachers influence children's knowledge of emotion by discussing emotions during everyday interactions (Blair, Denham, Kochanoff, & Whipple, 2004). Building understanding of emotion-related words occurs through intentionally teaching children to label both negative and positive emotions, as well as understand the causes of emotion. Books are useful tools as teachers strive to help children identify emotion-related words, understand the causes of emotion, and manage emotions positively (Ahn, 2005b).

Conclusion

Early emotional competence—encompassing emotional regulation, expression, and knowledge—is strongly linked to children's mental health, influences children's social interactions and relationships, and affects school success. Teachers have critical roles in promoting emotional competence through forming nurturing and specific relationships with individual children, coaching children's emotional responses during social interactions and during activities and routines, modeling healthy emotional expression, building an understanding of emotions, and creating environments in which children feel valued and can thrive. Careful observation of children in classroom contexts allows educators to analyze current levels of emotional competence and plan for promotion of mental health. Such efforts are key to ensuring that children have the skills necessary to function effectively in a range of social and school contexts.

References

Ahn, H. (2005a). Child care teachers' strategies in children's socialization of emotion. *Early Childhood Development and Care, 175,* 49–61.

Ahn, H. (2005b). Teachers' discussions of emotion in child care centers. *Early Childhood Education Journal, 32,* 237–242.

Ashiabi, G. (2000). Promoting the emotional development of preschoolers. *Early Childhood Education Journal, 28,* 79–84.

Bagdi, A., & Vacca, J. (2005). Supporting early childhood social-emotional well being: The building blocks for early learning and school success. *Early Childhood Education Journal, 33,* 145–150.

Blair, K. A., Denham, S. A., Kochanoff, A., & Whipple, B. (2004). Playing it cool: Temperament, emotional regulation, and social behavior in preschoolers. *Journal of School Psychology, 42,* 419–443.

Bracken, St. S., & Fischel, J. E. (2007). Relationships between social skills, behavioral problems, and school readiness for Head Start children. *NHSA Dialog, 10,* 109–126.

Coplan, R. J., & Prakash, K. (2003). Spending time with teacher: Characteristics of preschoolers who frequently elicit versus initiate interactions with teachers. *Early Childhood Research Quarterly, 18,* 143–158.

Denham, S. A. (2001). Dealing with feelings: Foundations and consequences of young children's emotional competence. *Early Education and Development, 12,* 5–10.

Denham, S. A. (2006). Social-emotional competence as support for school readiness: What is it and how do we assess it? *Early Education and Development, 17,* 57–89.

Denham, S. A., Blair, K. A., DeMulder, E., Levitas, J., Sawyer, K., Auerbach-Major, S., & Queenan, P. (2003). Preschool emotional competence: Pathway to social competence? *Child Development. 74,* 238–256.

Hemmeter, M. L., & Ostrosky, M. (2006). Social and emotional foundations for early learning: A conceptual model for intervention. *School Psychology Review, 35,* 583–601.

Howes, C. Hamilton, C. E., & Matheson, C. C. (1994). Children's relationships with peers: Differential associations with aspects of the teacher-child relationship. *Child Development, 65,* 253–263.

Hyson, M. (2002). Emotional development and school readiness. *Young Children, 57,* 76–78.

Hyson, M. (2004). *The emotional development of young children.* New York: Teachers College Press.

Keogh, B. K. (2003). *Temperament in the classroom.* Baltimore: Brookes Publishing.

Knitzer, J., & Lefkowitz, J. (2005). *Resources to promote social and emotional health and school readiness in young children and families.* New York: National Center for Children in Poverty.

LaParo, K., Pianta, R., & Stuhlman, M. (2004). The classroom assessment scoring system: Findings from the prekindergarten year. *The Elementary School Journal, 104,* 409–426.

Lindsey, E., & Colwell, M. (2003). Preschoolers' emotional competence: Links to pretend and physical play. *Child Study Journal, 33,* 39–52.

National Association for the Education of Young Children. (2004). *Where we stand on school readiness.* Washington, DC: Author.

Peth-Pierce, R. (2001). *A good beginning: Sending America's children to school with the social and emotional competence they need to succeed.* Chapel Hill, NC: University of North Carolina.

Raver, C. C., & Knitzer, J. (2002). *Ready to enter: What research tells policymakers about strategies to promote social and emotional school readiness among three- and four-year-olds.* New York: National Center for Children in Poverty.

Shonkoff, J. R., & Phillips, D. (Eds.). (2001). *From neurons to neighborhoods: The science of early child development.* Washington, DC: National Academy Press.

Thomas, A., & Chess, S. (1977). *Temperament and development.* New York: Brunner/Mazel.

Critical Thinking

1. Describe the three ways teachers can promote emotional competence in children in their classroom.

2. Plan one classroom activity that will foster the emotional development of young children.

HANNAH NISSEN is Associate Professor, Early Childhood Education, Ohio University Zanesville. **CAROL J. HAWKINS** is Associate Professor, Human Ecology, Youngstown State University, Youngstown, Ohio.

From *Childhood Education*, vol. 86, no. 4, Summer 2010, pp. 255–259. Copyright © 2010 by the Association for Childhood Education International. Reprinted by permission of Hannah Nissen, Carol J. Hawkins, and the Association for Childhood Education International, 17904 Georgia Avenue, Suite 215, Olney, MD 20832.

Helping Young Boys Be Successful Learners in Today's Early Childhood Classrooms

NANCY GROPPER ET AL.

What has happened to pre-school and kindergarten classrooms? They were once places where play consumed much of the daily schedule; where children could move around at will, making their own decisions about which learning center or area to visit and what to do when they got there; where children had regular opportunities to have conversations with peers and adults.

The current academic focus of the Race to the Top education initiative, as well as that of its predecessor, No Child Left Behind, is in keeping with democratic ideals about success for all. However, the push-down approach to academics has transformed pre-school classrooms into environments that more closely resemble first or second grade. Many room arrangements and schedules are so focused on promoting academic learning that they do not attend to the developmental capacities and needs of young children, particularly young boys.

While it is not appropriate to suggest that early childhood teachers should ignore academic directives from their school administrators, it *is* critical to find ways to help educators address the needs of the *whole child,* a tenet central to sound early child-hood practice, thus coming to the aid of boys. Today, many 4- to 6-year-old boys attend early childhood programs where demanding academic seat work takes up most of the day (Sprung, Froschl, & Gropper 2010).

Research shows that boys, particularly African American and Latino boys, are more often labeled as having behavior problems and are often isolated, referred for evaluations, prescribed medication, and even suspended and expelled while still in preschool (Ferguson 2000; Smith 2002; US Department of Education 2003; Gilliam 2005; Barbarin & Crawford 2006; Mead 2006). To counteract these trends, school administrators should support principles suggested by Barbarin, for example, to "use instructional approaches that motivate and engage African American boys" and "support positive emotional development in African American boys" (2010, 85).

Early childhood teacher education is critical in enabling inservice and preservice teachers to better understand and meet boys' needs in the classroom (Sprung, Froschl, & Gropper 2010). Early childhood teacher educators who serve as course instructors and provide professional development activities can alert preservice and inservice teachers to the potentially damaging, albeit inadvertent, effects that young boys experience when their social-emotional and physical needs are ignored in favor of promoting academics. They can encourage teachers to reflect on how to infuse developmentally sound early childhood practices into their classrooms in spite of academic directives.

To assist in this effort, this article reviews the social-emotional development of boys, suggests ways to help teachers rethink the daily schedule, and encourages teachers to observe and record classroom behaviors as a way of identifying and better meeting boys' needs.

The Whole Child

The focus on child development that is largely missing from the preparation of educators probably contributes more to creating dysfunctional and under-performing schools than anything else.

—James Comer

Comer's words (2005, 758) tell us how far modern early childhood education has strayed from the principles developed by pioneering child development researchers such as John Dewey, Jean Piaget, and Lev Vygotsky (Bowman & Moore 2006, 17). Those researchers, along with visionary practitioners such as Lucy Sprague Mitchell, Caroline Pratt, and Maria Montessori, formulated theories of child development that encouraged educators to support children's physical, cognitive, and social-emotional growth by providing children with developmentally appropriate hands-on materials, manipulatives, indoor and outdoor play spaces, props for dramatic play, construction toys, and more.

In those same pioneering days, institutions of higher education began partnerships with nursery schools to prepare teachers to work with young children, leading to an increasing expectation that kindergarten teachers be professionally prepared. Even as early as the late 1800s, Normal Schools in New York, Kansas, Connecticut, and Michigan initiated kindergarten training. Thus, the field of early childhood education emerged and eventually extended into the primary grades (Lascarides & Hinitz 2000). The emphasis in early childhood teacher education courses at that time was on the whole child, which meant that teachers were trained to value and respect each individual child and to strive to meet his or her social-emotional, cognitive, *and* physical needs. There was wide acceptance that play could best convey to young children the skills that would prepare them for the more formal learning tasks required in the elementary grades.

The Effects of Academic Curriculum on Young Boys

In the quest to promote young children's academic achievement, far too many programs have veered away from a play-centered curriculum. Kindergartners spend an increasing amount of time in teacher-directed literacy and math activities in preparation for standardized testing in grade 3. This trend toward push-down curriculum—that is, increasingly academic, scripted, and standardized kindergarten and prekindergarten classrooms—is in direct opposition to a play-centered early childhood learning environment. The early learning standards movement and its corollary, high-stakes testing, have had an impact on early childhood education in ways that can have a detrimental effect on all children, and particularly on boys (Meisels & Atkins-Burnett 2006; Miller & Almon 2009).

Boys typically enter early childhood classrooms less developmentally mature than girls in terms of literacy and social-emotional skills. It is essential for early childhood settings to provide opportunities for all forms of play to help children acquire such skills naturally. Play not only provides a physical outlet for boys and helps to decrease instances of acting out (Baptiste 1995), but it also allows

boys to express themselves through dramatic play and to learn how to negotiate social-emotional challenges (Miller & Almon 2009). It is through imaginary scenarios that young children work through family situations, pretend to be firefighters or chefs, negotiate roles, and problem-solve other real-life situations.

Depriving boys in particular of dramatic play time limits their literacy development. As children mature, their dramatic play becomes more complex and, with skillful guidance from their teachers, can include assigned roles, written parts, and organized plays that display a rich use of language and literacy skills. Research bears out the positive effect that dramatic play has on comprehension and metalinguistic awareness, which are important precursors to reading and writing (Roskos & Christie 2000; Marcon 2002). Again, opportunities for this type of play are essential for boys who need lots of practice to build vocabulary and social skills.

Research bears out the positive effect that dramatic play has on comprehension and metalinguistic awareness, which are important precursors to reading and writing.

The building blocks of many gross motor and fine motor skills come from a play-centered environment in which children have experiences with painting, working with clay, assembling puzzles, and building with unit blocks, Legos, and other construction toys. Math, science, and social studies skills are woven into all parts of the curriculum through cooking, water and sand play, neighborhood walks, and field trips to museums and community sites. The Alliance for Childhood identifies 12 key modes of play—large motor, small motor, mastery, rule-based, construction, make-believe (or dramatic), symbolic, language, arts, sensory, rough and tumble, and risk-taking (Miller & Almon 2009). The Alliance encourages teachers to be aware of and use the modes to assess whether their classroom provides play-based opportunities for learning. (A classroom environment that provides opportunities for these 12 modes of play is exemplified in the Scenario 2 full-day schedule). Thus, a play-centered early childhood curriculum, guided by a skilled teacher with appropriate training, offers boys and girls alike a complex learning environment that can build up their skills in every area needed for later school success (Drew et al. 2006).

Unfortunately, many preschool and kindergarten classrooms no longer emphasize play in their daily schedules, instead focusing on academic skills. As reported in *Crisis in the Kindergarten* (Miller & Almon 2009), many experts believe that the pressure on children to meet inappropriate expectations causes stress and contributes to their anger and aggressive behavior. Because young boys have a great need for physical activity, a highly structured, teacher-directed learning environment that emphasizes seat work and worksheets is counter productive. This approach especially does not meet boys' physical, cognitive, and social-emotional development needs. The early childhood development concept of teaching the whole child is not compatible with an academies-focused learning environment for 4- to 6-year-old children (Miller & Almon 2009)

Social-Emotional Development: A Critical need for Boys

Many in the early childhood field believe that social-emotional skill development is key to a child's success in school. The Collaborative for Academic, Social, and Emotional Learning (CASEL) lists the attributes of social-emotional skills as the abilities to calm oneself when angry, initiate friendships, resolve conflicts respectfully, make ethical and safe choices, and contribute constructively to the community (CASEL 2007). Katz and McClellan say, "Socially competent young children are those who engage in satisfying interactions and activities with adults and peers and through such interactions improve their own competence" (1997, 17).

Social-emotional development is one of the eight general domains in the Head Start Child Outcomes Framework (Head Start 2000). The NAEYC Early Childhood Program Standard on Curriculum (Standard 2) (2008) includes interacting positively with others; recognizing and naming feelings; regulating one's emotions, behavior, and attention; developing a sense of competence and positive attitudes toward learning; resolving conflicts; and developing empathy as the vital social-emotional skills children need.

While the framework used to describe these essential skills may differ slightly from one source to another, early childhood educators agree that children's social-emotional development is important. The early childhood classroom traditionally has considered social-emotional skill development as a critical component of the curriculum, and as such, teachers have invested time interacting individually with each child, engaging in small group discussions, and supporting child-to-child interactions that foster these skills.

The early childhood classroom traditionally has considered social-emotional skill development as a critical component of the curriculum.

As discussed earlier, the push-down curriculum, with its teacher-directed—and in many cases, scripted—academic lessons, leaves little time for relationship building. But Raider-Roth (2005) stresses that vital relationships form the foundations for learning. Such relationships embody deep connections between the teacher and children, in which the teacher supports children's ideas, collaborates with them as they engage in learning activities, and establishes a sense of trust that enables them to take the risk of being wrong. One of Raider-Roth's students, an experienced kindergarten teacher, expressed her frustration during a graduate course on relational teaching: "I'm thinking, in the light of increasing standards-based work in the classroom and the need to justify every moment spent in the classroom with children, about how 'relationship' is being trivialized, marginalized" (2005, 167). This standards-based environment can begin to create a sense of failure and disengagement from school for young boys who have trouble sitting still for long periods of time, may not yet have developed impulse control, and are still developing the skills needed to learn to read and write.

If a child is reprimanded for not sitting still or finishing a worksheet, how does he build a sense of trust and comfort with being in school? If that child cannot meet the expectations of the classroom, which are beyond his developmental level, how can he feel positive about school? Take, for example, a kindergarten boy who is repeatedly reprimanded—in a gentle way—by his teacher for his restlessness during academic activities: when it is time for writer's workshop, he may refuse to try to write or even draw a picture, because he will not feel safe or confident.

Rethinking the Kindergarten Day

Imagine teaching a kindergarten class of 18 boys and 17 girls. More than 50 percent of the class consists of children of color. There is an age span of 18 months, from children who are 4 and 5 years old up to children who are about to turn 6. There is also a wide spectrum of social development represented.

Findings from studies of educators and families support the active involvement of adults in play with children and its subsequent positive effect on the behavior of boys.

Findings from studies of educators and families support the active involvement of adults in play with children (Nelson &Uba 2009) and its subsequent positive effect on the behavior of boys (Baptiste 1995). Now, however, "sand tables have been replaced by worksheets to a degree that's surprising even by the standards of a decade ago" (Paul 2010, 1). As mentioned earlier, No Child Left Behind and Race to the Top, though well intentioned, require that teachers get children test-ready by third grade. This means that playtime is limited in favor of the traditional reading, writing, and arithmetic. In addition, there are state-mandated curricula, and formal testing is done at the end of each school year (NAEYC & NAECS/SDE 2003; Meisels & Atkins-Burnett 2006; Solley 2007). Thus, kindergarten has steadily become, as many educators put it, "the new first grade" (Paul 2010, 1–2).

Two Contrasting Kindergarten Classroom Settings

Consider the following two examples of kindergarten classroom environments and daily schedules, each designed to prepare young children for the learning challenges and assessments to come. In the structured full-day kindergarten (see Scenario 1), the classroom contains an arrangement of tables with individual pencil and crayon boxes for each child and paste, scissors, and stamp pads at the center of each table. There is a library area, a puzzle rack, and one painting easel in the classroom. The small dramatic play area and the block shelf are not easily accessible in part because the daily routine rarely includes time for children to visit them. Stacks of workbooks, worksheets, preprimers, and primers cover most of the available shelf space, along with lined writing paper. Displayed on the wall are a list of rules, most of them suggested by the teacher, and the daily schedule.

In the example of the developmental full-day kindergarten (see Scenario 2), the classroom includes several areas or centers: art, blocks, construction, dramatic play, gross motor, literacy, manipulatives, math, science/discovery, computers, and tables where children explore the properties of light, water, and sand. The literacy area includes books, magazines, puppets, and a writing desk

---

Scenario 1: Sample Schedule for Structured Full-Day Kindergarten

8:30–8:45	**Arrival** (unpacking, homework in bin)
8:45–9:15	**Meeting** (attendance, calendar, weather, lunch choices)
9:15–10:00	**Readers' workshop**
10:00–10:15	**Snack**
10:15–11:00	**Writers' workshop**
11:00–11:45	**Math**
11:45–12:30	**Lunch and recess**
12:30–1:15	**Language arts**
1:15–1:30	**Read aloud**
1:30–2:15	**Specials**
2:15–2:45	**Social studies/Science/Friday choice time**
2:45–3:00	**Dismissal**

Scenario 2: Sample Schedule for Developmental Full-Day Kindergarten

7:00–8:30 Arrival
Puzzles, peg boards, books, and manipulative materials are available for the children to work with as they arrive. Books are available in the library area.

8:30–9:00 Outdoor or gross motor activity
Teachers actively participate and engage with the children rather than merely standing by.

9:00–9:20 Morning meeting and planning time

9:20–11:20 Center time
Children select the centers where they wish to work. Materials—such as blocks, paints, clay, wood, fabric, cardboard, packaging materials, musical instruments—are set out so that children can explore without interruption. Children act as researchers and document their findings graphically, orally, or in writing. Teachers work with individuals and small groups of children on literacy, math, and other skills. **Snack time** is included. The children choose when and where they will take a nutrition break. **Cleanup** concludes this time period.

11:30–12:00 Outdoor play
Vigorous outdoor play or fieldwork take place on the play yard.

12:00–12:20 Preparation for lunch
Teachers and children review the morning's activities, sing songs, and read stories and poetry. Children wash their hands and prepare for lunch.

12:20–1:00 Lunch
As children finish eating and move away from the tables, teachers may read stories to them or the children may play quiet games or look at books. They may listen to music as they brush their teeth, wash up, and prepare for quiet time.

1:00–2:00 Quiet time
Calming background music is played. Children do not have to actually sleep, but there needs to be a time when everyone is quiet and resting. Children can read books or engage in quiet play on their cots.

2:00–2:15 Afternoon snack

2:15–2:45 Outdoor/indoor centers and projects or group work

Music, learning activities, and project work take place either indoors or outdoors. Children engage in vigorous outdoor play.

2:45–3:00　　**Closing activities**
Teachers and children review the day, sing songs, and/or read stories and poetry. Children get ready to leave for the day.

with several kinds of paper, writing utensils, envelopes, scissors, stamp pads, stickers, and other materials used by children to write letters and signs for use in other areas of the classroom.

All of the tables, desks, and chairs are child size. In most of the areas, nonfiction trade books relevant to topics under investigation are displayed. The daily schedule and information on any special activities (like a field trip) are posted on the wall or on a bulletin board at the children's eye level, accompanied by children's drawings and actual classroom photographs (Seefeldt & Wasik 2006, 74). The guidelines take into consideration the fact that children are still acquiring interpersonal social skills and that the teacher's role is to guide them in learning how to get along with each other (Gartrell 2010).

Using Observation and Recording to Understand Boys

Drawing on best practice in the field, early childhood teachers are well positioned to address children's developmental needs. In addition to rethinking the daily schedule and infusing it with activities that better address boys' needs, teachers should observe and record children's behavior as a way of coming to know each child as an individual. This is particularly important in the social-emotional realm, where children's life experiences may, at times, impede their abilities to fully participate in the academic curriculum. In particular, emotional issues in boys' lives may translate into behavior that gets them into trouble, thus limiting their development and learning.

In particular, emotional issues in boys' lives may translate into behavior that gets them into trouble, thus limiting their development and learning.

Use of techniques such as note taking (Cohen et al. 2008), checklists, and sociograms (Almy & Genishi 1979) allows teachers to stand back and watch children while refraining from judgment about what is happening.

The information gathered can provide insights about an individual child that enable the teacher to adapt curriculum and materials to better meet that child's needs. This is particularly important for boys, who may run into difficulty when their socially or emotionally immature behaviors are dismissed as "acting out" or "being off task." Teachers who use the observation and recording strategies mentioned previously could view these instances as opportunities to look deeper into what boys' behaviors may suggest about their social-emotional needs and to build relationships with individual children.

In a graduate course taught by one of the authors, one student teacher's ongoing observation of a first grade boy yielded a good example of what can be learned through observation and note taking. Here is an excerpt from one set of her observation notes, describing Trey's behavior during a reading workshop:

He stared blankly at the [interactive whiteboard] with his head raised slightly. He flipped the pages of his journal in a deliberate manner, then turned to talk to two boys. He began to hit his face with his closed journal. When the teacher asked the class to write three prediction words, he slowly flipped his journal above his head and did not write anything.

At another time, the student teacher observed Trey draw a figure comprised of eyes, a nose, one arm, and an almost full set of pointed, shark-like teeth as the most prominent feature. Because she had a close relationship with Trey's mother, she knew that the mother's ex-boyfriend had recently been incarcerated for physically abusing the mother. This knowledge helped the student teacher to reflect on Trey's off-task behavior within a broader context. She was able to suggest that he have many opportunities to engage in expressive activities like drawing and painting, which he seemed to enjoy. Then these could be integrated into literacy activities so Trey would be able to accomplish academic tasks while simultaneously expressing his emotional turmoil in a constructive way.

Conclusion

Early childhood teacher educators and professional development providers are in a strong position to keep best practice alive. They can make preservice and inservice teachers aware of the risks of abandoning sound, research-based early childhood principles in an effort to meet current academic demands. These mandates put all children, but particularly boys, at risk for school failure as their school lives are just beginning. If boys' social-emotional needs are not addressed, they cannot be ready to learn.

It is therefore the responsibility of teacher educators and staff developers to share information about the research on boys, about the dangers of ignoring their need to engage in physical activity and to learn through play, and about the value of using observation and recording to identify the individual strengths and needs of boys, especially in the social-emotional domain. When active learning through play is the primary mode for interaction, children evidence notable strides in cognitive and linguistic domains (Rowen, Byrne, & Winter 1980; Miller & Almon 2009). With all this in mind, we pose the following reflection questions to teacher educators and professional development providers:

- What type of early childhood classroom is geared to meet the active learning styles that research shows to be most engaging for boys and beneficial for all young children?
- How can curriculum projects be planned to involve all children and address the specific needs of boys?
- What are some strategies for keeping the curriculum playful to meet all children's—especially boys'—social-emotional needs while still meeting current academic demands?
- How can teacher educators and professional development providers help preservice students address the requirements of a mandated curriculum while also implementing the whole child approach based on child development principles?

References

Almy, M., & C. Genishi. 1979. *Ways of studying children.* New York: Teachers College Press.

Baptiste, N. 1995. Adults need to play, too. *Early Childhood Education Journal:* 33–36.

Barbarin, O.A. 2010. Halting African American boys' progression from pre-K to prison: What families, schools, and communities can do! *American Journal of Orthopsychiatry* 80 (1): 81–88.

Barbarin, O., & G.M. Crawford. 2006. Acknowledging and reducing stigmatization of African American boys. *Young Children* 61 (6): 79–86.

Bowman, B., & E.K. Moore, eds. 2006. *School readiness and social-emotional development: Perspectives on cultural diversity.* Washington, DC: National Black Child Development Institute.

CASEL (Collaborative for Academic, Social, and Emotional Learning). 2007. *Background on social and emotional learning.* CASEL Briefs. www.casel.org/downloads/ SEL&CASELbackground.pdf

Cohen, D., V. Stern, N. Balaban, & N. Gropper. 2008. *Observing and recording the behavior of young children.* New York: Teachers College Press.

Comer, J. 2005. Child and adolescent development: The critical missing focus in school reform. *Phi Delta Kappan* 86 (10): 757–63.

Drew, W.F., J. Johnson, E. Ersay, J. Christie, L. Cohen, H. Sharapan, L. Plaster, N. Quan Ong, & S. Blandford. 2006. Block play and performance standards: Using unstructured materials to teach academic content. Presentation at the NAEYC Annual Conference, November 8, Atlanta, Georgia.

Ferguson, A. 2000. *Bad boys: Public school in the making of black masculinity.* Ann Arbor: University of Michigan Press.

Gartrell, D. 2010. Beyond rules to guidelines. *Exchange* 32 (4): 52–56.

Gilliam, W.S. 2005. *Prekindergarteners left behind: Expulsion rates in state prekindergarten systems.* Policy Brief, series no. 3. New York: Foundation for Child Development.

Head Start, 2000. *Head Start Child Outcomes Framework.* www.hsnrc.org/CDI/pdfs/UGCOF.pdf

Katz, L., & D. McClellan. 1997. *Fostering children's social competence: The teacher's role.* Research into Practice series. Washington, DC: NAEYC.

Lascarides, V.C., & B.F. Hinitz, 2000. *History of early childhood education.* New York: Falmer Press.

Marcon, R.A. 2002. Moving up the grades: Relationship between preschool model and later school success. *Early Childhood Research & Practice* 4 (1). http://ecrp.uiuc .edu/v4nl/marcon.html

Mead, S. 2006. *The evidence suggests otherwise: The truth about boys and girls.* Washington, DC: Education Sector.

Meisels, S.J., & S. Atkins-Burnett, 2006. Evaluating early childhood assessments: A differential analysis. In *The Blackwell Handbook of Early Childhood Development,* eds. K. McCartney & D. Phillips, 533–49. Oxford: Blackwell.

Miller, E., & J. Almon, 2009. *Crisis in the kindergarten: Why children need to play in school.* College Park, MD: Alliance for Childhood.

NAEYC, 2008. *Standard 2: Curriculum—A guide to the NAEYC Early Childhood Program Standard and related accreditation criteria.* Washington, DC: Author.

NAEYC & NAECS/SDE (National Association of Early Childhood Specialists in State Departments of Education). 2003. *Early childhood curriculum, assessment, and program evaluation.* www.naeyc.org/files/naeyc/file/ positions/pscape.pdf

Nelson, B.G., & G. Uba. 2009. Active adult play: Improving children's health and behavior while having fun. *Exchange* 31 (3): 62–65.

Paul, P. 2010. The littlest redshirts sit out kindergarten. *New York Times,* Sunday Styles: 1–2, August 22.

Raider-Roth, M.B. 2005. *Trusting what you know: The high stakes of classroom relationships.* San Francisco: Jossey-Bass.

Roskos, K., & J.F. Christie, eds. 2000. *Play and literacy in early childhood: Research from multiple perspectives.* Mahwah, NJ: Erlbaum.

Rowen, B., J. Byrne, & L. Winter. 1980. *The learning match: A developmental guide to teaching young children.* Englewood Cliffs, NJ: Prentice Hall.

Seefeldt, C., & B.A. Wasik. 2006. *Early education: Three- four-, and five-year-olds go to school,* 2d ed. Upper Saddle River, NJ: Pearson/Merrill/Prentice Hall.

Smith, R.A. 2002. Black boys: The litmus test for No Child Left Behind. *Education Week* 22 (9): 40, 43.

Solley, B.A. 2007. On standardized testing: An ACEI Position Paper. Olney, MD: Association for Childhood Education International. http://198.171.42.5/wp-content/uploads/standtesting.pdf

Sprung, B., M. Froschl, & N. Gropper, 2010. *Supporting boys' learning: Strategies for teacher practice, pre-K–grade 3.* New York: Teachers College Press.

US Department of Education, Office of Special Education Programs. 2003. *25th annual report to Congress.* Washington, DC: Author.

Critical Thinking

1. Develop a list of strategies you could share with teachers to make their classroom more user friendly for young boys.

2. Why is there such a disconnect between the push-down, academic, scripted curriculum in many kindergartens today and a child-centered learning environment for young children? How does this change affect boys the most?

NANCY GROPPER, EdD, is the interim associate dean for academic affairs at Bank Street Graduate School of Education. She is an early childhood educator with a long-standing interest in gender issues. ngropper@bankstreet.edu BLYTHE F. HINITZ, EdD, is a professor in the Department of Elementary and Early Childhood Education at The College of New Jersey; a member of the board of the World Organization for Early Childhood Education-U.S. National Committee (OMEP-USA), H-Education, and Professional Impact New Jersey; codirector of an anti-bullying research study with Indonesian colleagues; and a member of the Working Group that is acknowledged in *Supporting Boys' Learning* hinitz@tcnj.edu BARBARA SPRUNG, MS, is codirector of the Educational Equity Center at the Academy for Educational Development (EEC at AED), located in New York City. She has been developing programs and materials for teachers and parents on issues of equity in early childhood education since the 1970s. bsprung@aed .org MERLE FROSCHL, BA, is codirector of the Educational Equity Center at the Academy for Educational Development (EEC at AED), located in New York City. Merle has developed programs and materials that foster equality of opportunity, and she is a nationally known speaker on issues of gender equity. mfroschl@aed.org

Developmentally Appropriate Child Guidance: Helping Children Gain Self-Control

Will Mosier, EdD

Dealing with disruptive behavior in the classroom is one of the most difficult issues an early childhood educator faces. In trying to redirect or extinguish disruptive behavior, teachers need to use developmentally appropriate practices as laid out by the National Association for the Education of Young Children (NAEYC).

According to these practices, the purpose of child guidance, or discipline, is not to control young children but to help them learn to be cooperative. The most effective techniques help children learn how to accept responsibility for their actions and empower them to exercise self-control.

Discipline should not be punishing. Instead, it should provide children with learning experiences that nurture an understanding of social consciousness. Those learning experiences include participating in generating class rules, receiving positive reinforcement for pro-social behavior, experiencing the natural and logical consequences of their behavior, and observing adults in pro-social, person-to-person interactions. Ultimately, any child guidance technique must nurture each child's social, emotional, and cognitive development.

Discipline should not be punishing.

Involve Children in Creating Classroom Rules

An important initial step in ensuring a developmentally appropriate pro-social environment is to create a set of classroom rules in cooperation with all the children in your room on the first day of the school year. A cooperative approach is the key.

With 3-year-olds, you may need to propose two or three simple rules, explain the reasons behind them, and invite their cooperation. By the time they turn 4, most children will be able to propose rules and discuss them. Ideally, classroom rules are not teacher-dictated. They must evolve from ideas discussed with and agreed upon by the children.

By encouraging children to participate in setting rules, you are laying the foundation for a community of learners who follow rules, not because they will be punished by the teacher if they don't, but because they feel a part of that which they help to create. Using a democratic group process helps children to develop moral reasoning.

Creating rules helps clarify behavior expectations. If children are to know what behavior is expected, the guidelines must be stated as positive actions. Help children with wording that says what they are expected to do, not what they can't do.

For example, instead of a rule that says "No running," the rule would read "Running is an outside activity. I walk inside." Other examples:

"I touch people gently."

"I talk in a quiet tone of voice."

"When I finish with an activity, I put it back where I found it."

"I place trash in the wastebasket."

Once the rules have been established, create opportunities to practice them. During the first few weeks of the year, reinforce the class rules through role playing, singing songs, and reading children's books about the rules.

In addition, you must model the rules and socially competent behavior in general. Children best learn rules by seeing them practiced by the adults in their lives. Modeling pro-social behavior demonstrates how human beings should interact with one another. It reinforces behaviors that are respectful of others.

Use Positive Reinforcement

Make a commitment to verbally reinforcing the socially competent behavior you expect in young children. Use positive feedback to reinforce pro-social, productive behavior, and to minimize disruptive behavior.

To reinforce pro-social behavior, simply look for it. When it happens, use a three-part "I" message, as explained below, to reinforce it. When disruptive behavior occurs, use positive feedback to draw attention to classroom behavior that you would like to see. Avoid focusing on the disruptive behavior.

Reinforcing pro-social behavior should not be confused with praise. Praise can damage a child's self-esteem by making a child feel pressured into attaining arbitrary standards. Praise implies an objective value judgment. For example: "Josh, your painting is beautiful." If praise does not continue, Josh may perceive that his value, as a person, is diminishing. A young child may start to assume that a person's value is directly tied to an ability to produce a specific product.

A better alternative is recognition and encouragement. Encouragement is specific and focuses on the process the child used to produce the artwork or how the child is feeling at the moment. For example: "I like the effort you put into your picture" or "I see that you're happy with the red lines and green circles." In these examples, neither the child nor the product is labeled good or bad. The focus is on the process or behavior. When stated as positive affirmations, words of encouragement can help nurture self-esteem.

An encouragement system can also use tokens as positive feedback. For example, children could be offered tokens when displaying behavior you want to reinforce. The tokens are not used as rewards, and they are not redeemed for some tangible prize. Additionally, the tokens would never be taken away once given to a child.

This system encourages a child to repeat desired behavior and will tend to stimulate intrinsic motivation. When a child sees or hears a classmate being reinforced for a particular behavior, the attention given to the targeted behavior increases the odds that the disruptive child will be motivated to try the same behavior.

Examples of developmentally appropriate tokens are construction paper leaves that can be placed on a personalized paper tree, and paper ice cream scoops that can be stacked on a paper ice cream cone. Every child would have a tree trunk or ice cream cone on a designated bulletin board. Early in the year the children would cut out leaves or ice cream scoops and place them in a large container near the board. When a teacher observes a desired behavior, she states the behavior, how she feels about it, and invites the child to get a token. "Tyron, when I see you picking up those blocks, I feel so excited, I invite you to put a leaf on your tree!" Phrasing a message in this manner tends to encourage intrinsic motivation.

Use Natural and Logical Consequences, Not Punishment

Natural and logical consequences can effectively motivate self-control without inflicting the cognitive, social, and emotional damage caused by punishment. When appropriate, allow natural and logical consequences to redirect inappropriate or disruptive behavior. This will encourage self-direction and intrinsic motivation.

Assume, for example, that Melissa leaves her painting on the floor instead of putting it on the drying rack, and a minute later another child accidentally steps on the artwork and ruins it. Melissa ends up with a torn painting as a natural consequence.

Use logical consequences when natural consequences are not practical. If a child is throwing blocks, for example, a logical consequence would be to lose the privilege of playing in the block area for a set time. Children need the opportunity to connect their behavior and its consequences. Using logical consequences allows children to learn from their experience.

By contrast, punishment relies on arbitrary consequences. It imposes a penalty for wrongdoing. For example, "Steven, because you hit Johnny, you don't get to sit in my lap for story time." Loss of lap time here is an arbitrary consequence, unrelated to the hitting behavior.

Being punished for unacceptable behavior conditions young children to limit behavior out of fear and leads to lowered self-esteem. Experiencing logical consequences, on the other hand, allows children to see how to achieve desired goals and avoid undesired consequences.

Wanting attention is not a bad thing.

Inappropriate, disruptive behavior is typically motivated by the need to gain attention. Wanting attention is not a bad thing. The issue is how to gain it. Children need to learn that they can choose to satisfy needs in socially acceptable ways. Logical consequences help young children become self-correcting and self-directed.

Model Clear, Supportive Communication

Supporting a child's cognitive, emotional, and social development requires well-honed communication skills. When talking to young children about behavior, differentiate between the child and the behavior. It's the behavior that's "good" or "bad," not the child.

"I" Messages

Speaking in three-part "I" messages is an effective tool for keeping your focus on the child's behavior. This is a three-part, non-blaming statement that helps a young child hear which behaviors are not acceptable without damaging the child's social, emotional, or cognitive development. "I" messages can be used to address inappropriate or disruptive behavior as well as to reinforce socially competent and positive behavior.

Use this template for constructing "I" messages that encourage pro-social behavior: "When I see you _____ (identify acceptable behavior), it makes me feel _____ (identify your feelings about the behavior) that I want to _____ (identify what you want to do). For example: "Wow, Tara, when I see you turning the pages carefully as you read your book, I feel so happy I want to give you a high five."

To extinguish disruptive behavior, adapt the template as follows: "Tara, when I see you hit Mary, I get so sad that I am going to keep you with me until I think you understand about touching people gently."

Empathic Understanding

Empathy is the ability to identify with someone else's feelings. As early childhood educators, we are responsible for nurturing the development of emotional intelligence in young children. We need to reinforce behavior that is sensitive to the emotional needs of others.

An example of when to use this skill is when children are tattling. Children tattle as a passive-aggressive way to solicit adult attention. Assume, for example, that Takesha complains, "Johnny hit me." A developmentally appropriate response would be "You didn't like that, did you?"

This type of response does three things: 1) The focus remains on the child's feelings, rather than on the actions of another child. 2) It models words that help a child express what she is feeling. 3) It encourages the child to talk about how she feels, which helps her develop enhanced awareness of her feelings and pro-social ways to express them.

Attentive Listening

Children need to feel they are being listened to. To communicate that you are paying attention to a child, maintain eye contact, smile attentively, and use appropriate, gentle touch to convey that you have unconditional positive regard for the child. Use the same communication skills with children that you want others to use with you.

Common listening errors that adults make when interacting with young children are analyzing the child's words rather than focusing on the child's feelings, rushing the child through the expression of feelings, and interrupting the child's expressing of feelings. A teacher displaying impatience, for example, can stifle language development and discourage a child from sharing feelings. But a teacher who listens attentively helps children develop emotional intelligence.

Be Consistent

A critical factor for successfully implementing developmentally appropriate child guidance is consistency. You need to enforce rules consistently, even when it may be easier to look the other way.

Children need to know what is expected of them. They have difficulty adjusting to unexpected change. When they display disruptive behavior, keep in mind that it may have been conditioned into them since toddlerhood. It's unrealistic to assume that it will be extinguished in just one day. Behavior reinforced prior to the child's being exposed to your classroom will take time to reshape. Don't expect an overnight change.

You can change disruptive behavior by using a consistent, systematic process, such as the 12 levels of intervention.

Developing self-control is a process. Throughout the process early childhood educators must demonstrate considerable patience and be consistent in reinforcing productive, socially competent behavior.

References

Adams, S. K. 2005. *Promoting Positive Behavior: Guidance Strategies for Early Childhood Settings.* Columbus, Ohio: Pearson/Merrill/Prentice Hall.

American Academy of Pediatrics. 2007. Discipline for Young Children. Retrieved April 23, 2007, from American Academy of Pediatrics website, www.aap.org.

Bredekamp, S. and C. Copple (Eds.). 2009. *Developmentally Appropriate Practice in Early Childhood Programs, 3rd Edition.* Washington, D.C.: National Association for the Education of Young Children (NAEYC).

Cangelosi, J. S. 2000. *Classroom Management Strategies: Gaining and Maintaining Students' Cooperation,* 4th Edition. New York: John Wiley & Sons, Inc.

DiGiulio, R. 2000. *Positive Classroom Management,* 2nd Edition. Thousand Oaks, Calif.: Corwin Press, Inc.

Essa, E. 1999. *A Practical Guide to Solving Preschool Behavior Problems,* 4th Edition. New York: Delmar Publishers.

Feeney, S. and N. K. Freeman. 1999. *Ethics and the Early Childhood Educator: Using the NAEYC Code.* Washington, D.C: NAEYC.

Ferris-Miller, Darla. 2007. *Positive Child Guidance,* 5th Edition. Clifton Park, N. Y.: Thomson Delmar Learning.

Gartrell, D. 2004. *The Power of Guidance: Teaching Social-Emotional Skills in Early Childhood Classrooms.* Washington, D.C.: NAEYC.

Menke-Paciorek, K. 2002. *Taking Sides: Clashing Views on Controversial Issues in Early Childhood Education.* Guilford, Conn.: McGraw-Hill.

NAEYC, Division of Early Childhood of the Council for Exceptional Children, and National Board for Professional Teaching Standards. 1996. *Guidelines for Preparation of Early Childhood Professionals.* Washington, D.C.: NAEYC.

Mosier, W. (Ed.). 2005. *Exploring Emotional Intelligence with Young Children: An Annotated Bibliography of Books About Feelings.* Dayton, Ohio: Dayton Association for Young Children.

NAEYC. 1999. *NAEYC Position Statements.* Washington, D.C.: NAEYC.

NAEYC. 1998. *Accreditation Criteria and Procedures.* Washington, D.C.: NAEYC.

NAEYC. 1998. *Early Childhood Teacher Education Guidelines.* Washington, D.C.: NAEYC.

NAEYC. 1999. *The NAEYC Code of Ethical Conduct.* Washington, D.C.: NAEYC.

Rand, M. K. 2000. *Giving It Some Thought: Cases for Early Childhood Practice.* Washington, D.C.: NAEYC.

Critical Thinking

1. If possible, observe a preschool or primary grade classroom. What guidance techniques does the teacher use to manage behavior of the children?

2. From your previous work with young children, choose a situation and describe a successful guidance technique you used. Why do you think that was successful in that case? What else could you have done?

WILL MOSIER, EdD, is an associate professor in teacher education at Wright State University in Dayton, Ohio. He is a licensed independent marriage and family therapist in Dayton.

From *Texas Child Care Quarterly*, Spring 2009, pp. 2–5. Copyright © 2009 by Texas Child Care Quarterly. Reprinted by permission.

Kindergarten Dilemma: Hold Kids Back to Get Ahead?

Teachers and economists warn of the costs of 'redshirting' children.

STEPHANIE PAPPAS

As schools start back into session around the country, some parents of young children face a difficult question: Send their little ones to kindergarten as soon as they become age-eligible, or hold them back in hopes that an additional year of maturity will give them an academic boost?

This voluntary kindergarten delay, dubbed "redshirting" after the practice of benching college athletes for a season to prolong their eligibility, is a source of much national and personal debate. As kindergarten programs have become more rigorous, redshirting proponents argue, kids need to be older to handle the curriculum. For children whose birthdays fall just before the kindergarten age cut-off date, redshirting bumps them from one of the youngest in the class to one of the oldest. It's a tempting prospect for parents who don't want their child to be the least mature in the room (or the smallest in gym class).

But research on redshirting suggests that the benefits are tempered by the costs, from an extra year of childcare for parents to a year less in the workforce for kids. Even the size of the benefits is up for debate. For that reason, many education experts and economists are wary of redshirting.

"The trend seems to be to have kids start later without much thought to the cost versus the benefits," said Darren Lubotsky, an economist at University of Illinois at Urbana-Champaign, who has studied redshirting. "There might be some benefits, but there's a really big cost to kids starting later."

School Days Delayed

Benefits or not, kindergarteners are an increasingly older bunch these days. According to a 2008 paper published in the *Journal of Economic Perspectives,* 96 percent of 6-year-olds were enrolled in first grade 40 years ago. Now, 84 percent of 6-year-olds are in first grade. The missing 12 percent haven't dropped out—they're enrolled in kindergarten instead. About a quarter of the shift is due to state and school district policies that push age cut-off dates earlier in the year, the researchers reported. The rest is due to voluntary redshirting.

According to the National Center for Education Statistics (NCES), about 9 percent of kindergarteners were redshirted between 1993 and 1995. Data is currently being collected on this year's batch of kids, but won't be available for several more years. Based on a 2007 report, an NCES representative estimated that 14 percent of kids ages 5 to 6 were redshirted or had parents planning to delay their kindergarten entry.

Boys are more likely to be delayed than girls, as are white children and children in high-income families. Although studies show that minority parents are more concerned than white parents about their child's readiness, a lack of income often prevents minority parents from delaying their kids: Childcare is simply too expensive.

What redshirting means for individual kids is tough to determine. Some studies find that redshirted kids are academically on par with their classmates. Others detect a slight academic boost. A 2005 study by the RAND Corporation, for example, found that kids who delayed entry by a year scored 6 points higher than their classmates on standardized math tests and 5 points higher on reading tests, an effect that persisted to first grade.

"That's not surprising, because you *would* do better at age 6 than age 5," said Ashlesha Datar, the RAND economist who led the study. It's not that the 6-year-olds are smarter; they just have an extra year of life experience to draw on.

Higher-income kids who spent their year "off" in a good preschool got a bigger boost than low-income kids who got less stimulation, Datar reported, but delayed low-income kids did seem to learn slightly faster than non-delayed low-income kids.

"Over time, I think the effect of being in school becomes more dominant than your age effect," Datar told LiveScience. "So one might expect that these [redshirting] effects might fade off."

Looking Long-term

Indeed, many studies have found that redshirted kids lose their head start over time, some as early as third grade. The University of Illinois' Lubotsky looked at kids in kindergarten through eighth grade and found that older kids maintained a slight academic gain throughout elementary and middle school.

"The punch line of our paper is that they do better because they learn more before they started kindergarten, not because they learn more once they get to school," Lubotsky said.

Over the course of the study, the gap between older and younger kids began to close, the researchers found.

Poll: Should kids be held back a year before starting kindergarten?

"Kids who are older do a lot better at the beginning, but that doesn't mean they're going to do better throughout their educational career," Lubotsky said.

As with research on the early benefits of redshirting, research on long-term benefits is mixed. One 2006 study published in the *Quarterly Journal of Economics* looked at age at kindergarten entrance in an international sample of children and found the youngest kids in each grade lagged behind in test scores through eighth grade, though the gap shrank over time. The researchers also found that the oldest kids in each grade were about 10-percent more likely to go to a four-year college than younger peers.

Another study, this one published in 2010 in the journal *Economics of Education Review,* found very different results. In this study of American students, age at kindergarten entry had no effect on wages, employment, homeownership, household income, or marital status as an adult. The researchers also found no evidence for an effect of age on college enrollment.

TODAY: Discuss whether "redshirting" your kindergartener was the right decision

In fact, kids who entered kindergarten younger were about 1-percent *more likely* to graduate high school than older kids. That could be because older kindergarteners reach the age at which they can legally drop out of school earlier in their educational career than younger kindergarteners.

Making the Choice

For many parents, studies on thousands of kids mean little when they're contemplating sending their own child, with all of his or her individual strengths and weaknesses, to kindergarten. That's a reasonable response, according to Lubotsky.

"I wouldn't want parents to make a decision based on a single research study, because parents know more about their own kid," he said.

The important thing is that parents consider the costs of their choice as well as the potential benefits, he said. Delaying kindergarten means an extra year of childcare. And in a dozen years or so, that child's same-age peers will be going to college and entering the workforce while he or she is still in high school.

"If you hold your child back for a year, your child might do better in his or her grade," Lubotsky said. "But he's still going to be very behind all the kids who are the same age."

If questions arise about a child's social or academic readiness, parents should turn to a professional for advice, said Donald Easton-Brooks, a professor of education at the University of North Texas. In the absence of a diagnosable problem, most kids will do fine in public school, he said, especially if they've gone to preschool or had lots of opportunities to develop their social skills during play-dates.

"Teachers will tell you, 'I would much prefer children come into a classroom with good social skills and know nothing, because if they know how to behave in a classroom, I can teach them anything,'" Easton-Brooks said.

Critical Thinking

1. What are the economic costs for children starting kindergarten later than when they are age eligible to start?

2. What has been the increase in percentage of children being redshirted from 1993 to 2007? What do you think has contributed to that increase?

Want to Get Your Kids into College? Let Them Play

ERIKA CHRISTAKIS AND NICHOLAS CHRISTAKIS

Every day where we work, we see our young students struggling with the transition from home to school. They're all wonderful kids, but some can't share easily or listen in a group.

Some have impulse control problems and have trouble keeping their hands to themselves; others don't always see that actions have consequences; a few suffer terribly from separation anxiety.

We're not talking about preschool children. These are Harvard undergraduate students whom we teach and advise. They all know how to work, but some of them haven't learned how to play.

Parents, educators, psychologists, neuroscientists, and politicians generally fall into one of two camps when it comes to preparing very young children for school: play-based or skills-based.

These two kinds of curricula are often pitted against one another as a zero-sum game: If you want to protect your daughter's childhood, so the argument goes, choose a play-based program; but if you want her to get into Harvard, you'd better make sure you're brushing up on the ABC flashcards every night before bed.

We think it is quite the reverse. Or, in any case, if you want your child to succeed in college, the play-based curriculum is the way to go.

In fact, we wonder why play is not encouraged in educational periods later in the developmental life of young people—giving kids more practice as they get closer to the ages of our students.

Why do this? One of the best predictors of school success is the ability to control impulses. Children who can control their impulse to be the center of the universe, and—relatedly—who can assume the perspective of another person, are better equipped to learn.

Psychologists call this the "theory of mind": the ability to recognize that our own ideas, beliefs, and desires are distinct from those of the people around us. When a four-year-old destroys someone's carefully constructed block castle or a 20-year-old belligerently monopolizes the class discussion on a routine basis, we might conclude that they are unaware of the feelings of the people around them.

The beauty of a play-based curriculum is that very young children can routinely observe and learn from others' emotions and experiences. Skills-based curricula, on the other hand, are sometimes derisively known as "drill and kill" programs because most teachers understand that young children can't learn meaningfully in the social isolation required for such an approach.

How do these approaches look different in a classroom? Preschoolers in both kinds of programs might learn about hibernating squirrels, for example, but in the skills-based program, the child could be asked to fill out a worksheet, counting (or guessing) the number of nuts in a basket and coloring the squirrel's fur.

In a play-based curriculum, by contrast, a child might hear stories about squirrels and be asked why a squirrel accumulates nuts or has fur. The child might then collaborate with peers in the construction of a squirrel habitat, learning not only about number sense, measurement, and other principles needed for engineering, but also about how to listen to, and express, ideas.

The child filling out the worksheet is engaged in a more one-dimensional task, but the child in the play-based program interacts meaningfully with peers, materials, and ideas.

Programs centered around constructive, teacher-moderated play are very effective. For instance, one randomized, controlled trial had 4- and 5-year-olds engage in make-believe play with adults and found substantial and durable gains in the ability of children to show self-control and to delay gratification. Countless other studies support the association between dramatic play and self-regulation.

Through play, children learn to take turns, delay gratification, negotiate conflicts, solve problems, share goals, acquire flexibility, and live with disappointment. By allowing children to imagine walking in another person's shoes, imaginative play also seeds the development of empathy, a key ingredient for intellectual and social-emotional success.

The real "readiness" skills that make for an academically successful kindergartener or college student have as much to do with emotional intelligence as they do with academic preparation. Kindergartners need to know not just sight words and lower case letters, but how to search for meaning. The same is true of 18-year-olds.

As admissions officers at selective colleges like to say, an entire freshman class could be filled with students with perfect grades and test scores. But academic achievement in college requires readiness skills that transcend mere book learning. It requires the ability to engage actively with people and ideas. In short, it requires a deep connection with the world.

For a five year-old, this connection begins and ends with the creating, questioning, imitating, dreaming, and sharing that characterize play. When we deny young children play, we are denying them the right to understand the world. By the time they get to college, we will have denied them the opportunity to fix the world too.

Critical Thinking

1. How has playing around at something allowed you to learn a new skill? Observe a child playing with something and watch for the ah-ha moment of discovery when they figure something out through play?

2. What advice would you give to parents who are pushing their child into academics and limiting the amount of time for free-play?

Developmentally Appropriate Practice in the Age of Testing

New reports outline key principles for preK–3rd grade.

DAVID MCKAY WILSON

As the push to teach literacy and math skills reaches farther into preschool and kindergarten, educators are warning that teachers need to address young students' social, emotional, and physical needs as well as their cognitive development. Among their concerns:

- Teachers in preK–3rd grade increasingly focus on a narrow range of literacy and math skills, with studies showing some kindergarteners spend up to six times as much time on those topics and on testing and test prep than they do in free play or "choice time."

- Many schools have eliminated recess or physical education, depriving children of their need to move and develop their bodies.

- Instruction is often focused on "scripted" curricula, giving teachers little opportunity to create lessons in response to students' interests.

- Some state standards for literacy are too stiff, such as one state's standard that all students be able to read by the beginning of first grade.

In light of these concerns, several prominent early childhood organizations have issued reports on the importance of incorporating developmentally appropriate practice into elementary school classrooms, based on what research has confirmed about early learning.

The National Association for the Education of Young Children (NAEYC) is so concerned about the pressure to prepare students for third-grade standardized tests that it adopted a position statement in early 2009 on developmentally appropriate practice for educators in preK through third grade. In their report, "Developmentally Appropriate Practice in Early Childhood Programs: Serving Children from Birth Through Age 8," NAEYC researchers outlined 12 principles of child development that can be incorporated into classroom teaching (see "NAEYC's 12 Principles of Child Development").

The report urges educators to incorporate play into daily instruction, devise classroom tasks that are challenging yet attainable, and become attuned to the needs of each student so that materials can be adapted to a child's individual needs. It also urges educators in preK through third grade to learn from each other: While preschool educators can benefit from understanding the standards children are expected to meet by third grade, NAEYC believes primary-grade teachers can improve the quality of their instruction by learning more about children's developmental needs from early childhood educators.

The Alliance for Childhood's report, "Crisis in Kindergarten: Why Children Need to Play in School," cites nine new studies that focus on the role of play, child-initiated learning, highly structured curricula, and standardized testing. One study found that the preponderance of time in 254 New York City and Los Angeles kindergartens was spent on literacy and math. Teachers reported that the curricula didn't have room for dramatic play, blocks, or artistic activities, and that school administrators didn't value such activities. A report from the American Academy of Pediatrics, however, concluded that play was essential for healthy brain development. And a cross-national study of 1,500 young children in 10 countries found that children's language at age seven improved when teachers let them choose their activities rather than teaching them in didactic lessons.

"The studies showed that teachers were spending two to three hours a day hammering in their lessons, with little time for play," says Joan Almon, executive director of the Alliance for Childhood. "The brain is eager to learn at this age, but the kids are more eager to learn from things they can touch and feel."

Charging that "developmental psychology and education have grown apart," the FPG Child Development Institute in Chapel Hill, N.C., is also advocating for more professional development and coursework for teachers in the science of child development. The institute's researchers emphasize the importance of four foundations of learning: self-regulation, representation, memory, and attachment (see "Four Foundations of Learning").

"The ability to focus, pay attention, and work with others is very predictive of long-term success in school," says Carol

NAEYC's 12 Principles of Child Development

- All domains of development and learning—physical, social and emotional, and cognitive—are related.
- Children follow well-documented sequences to build knowledge.
- Children develop and learn at varying rates.
- Learning develops from the dynamic interaction of biological maturation and experience.
- Early childhood experiences can have profound effects, and optimal periods exist for certain types of development and learning.
- Development proceeds toward greater complexity and self-regulation.
- Children thrive with secure, consistent relationships with responsive adults.
- Multiple social and cultural contexts influence learning and development.
- Children learn in a variety of ways, so teachers need a range of strategies.
- Play helps develop self-regulation, language, cognition, and social competence.
- Children advance when challenged just beyond their current level of mastery.
- Children's experiences shape their motivation, which in turn affects their learning.

Four Foundations of Learning

Teachers of children from preK to age eight should focus as much on self-regulation, representational thought, memory, and attachment as they do on basic skills, say researchers at the University of North Carolina's School of Education.

These four issues serve as the foundation for young children's development, according to Sharon Ritchie, a senior scientist at FPG Child Development Institute and coauthor of the report, "Using Developmental Science to Transform Children's Early School Experiences." She offers the following examples:

- *Self-regulation* is often developed through play. For example, when kindergartners play "restaurant," they must regulate their behavior to stay in the role of customer, waiter, cashier, or store manager. As children grow older, their play follows more complex rules, as when third-graders act out a story they have read.
- Secure *attachment* relationships help young children feel comfortable exploring the world to learn. Teachers can nurture good relationships by helping students express their feelings and resolve conflicts.
- *Representational thought* is the ability to use an expression—be it a word, gesture, or drawing—to depict an idea. Teachers need to help children find ways to express their own ideas before guiding them to new understanding.
- *Memory* is a crucial part of learning. Strategies to help strengthen students' memory include encouraging students to talk about what they have just learned or, as they grow older, reflecting on what they do when they need to remember something. Teachers can also structure their classes to help children remember the most important items taught that day.

Copple, coeditor of the NAEYC report. "Those things are typically emphasized in preschool, but they are important for older children as well."

Responsiveness and Engagement

Developmentally appropriate practice is based on the recognition that child development generally occurs in a predictable sequence of stages. While children may develop at different rates, each stage of development lays the groundwork for the acquisition of new skills and abilities in the next phase. Research has long indicated that children do best when they are supported to achieve goals just beyond their current level of mastery.

In crafting their report, NAEYC researchers reviewed recent educational research, interviewed scores of experts, and observed classrooms. They note the crucial connection between children's social and emotional life and their academic competence. Children make the biggest strides, the authors found, when they are able to cement secure, consistent relationships with responsive adults.

For classroom teachers, they say, being responsive means being able to adapt the curriculum to address their students' needs and interests and to allow children to discuss their experiences, feelings, and ideas. That can be difficult when teachers are following the highly regimented lesson plans now mandated in many classrooms.

Developing an enthusiasm for learning is especially important in the primary grades. Even students who have excelled in preK or kindergarten can find first or second grade so trying that they turn off to learning. Such disengagement has become so widespread that Sharon Ritchie, a senior scientist at FPG Child Development Institute, has worked with educators on a dropout-prevention project that focuses on children in preK through third grade.

"You can walk into a classroom and see kids who by third grade are done with school," she says. "They are angry and feel school is not a fair place or a place that sees them as the individual that they are."

Some of that disengagement, Ritchie says, is rooted in the way students in second or third grade are taught. She found that students in preK classes spent 136 minutes a day involved in hands-on projects. That dropped to 16 minutes by kindergarten and 12 minutes a day by second and third grade.

She encourages teachers to use hands-on activities in kindergarten and the early primary grades to allow students to experience learning through inquiry. In a first-grade lesson on evaporation, for instance, Ritchie suggests that the teacher ask the children to describe where they think rain comes from and have them draw pictures depicting their theories. Based on that information, the children can discuss their hypotheses and begin to investigate what actually happens. For example, they might observe an ice cube at room temperature as it melts and then evaporates. Older children could deepen their inquiry through library research or designing and performing their own experiments.

Teachers also need to listen to what interests their young students. Patricia Lambert, principal of the Barnard Early Childhood Center in New Rochelle, N.Y., says listening to students can spark engaging lessons. At her school, which serves children from preK through second grade, teachers are encouraged to weave district-mandated outcomes into lessons that teach but do not drill. "Our goal by the end of kindergarten is to have children count from zero to 20," she says. If the children are learning about sharks, she adds, "we may use a model of a shark, and count the shark's teeth."

"I'm all for exposing preschool children to numbers and letters," Lambert says, "but we introduce by listening to what the children are interested in and then gently imposing these concepts on their interests."

Learning through Play

Young children do much of their learning through play, says Robert Pianta, dean of the Curry School of Education at the University of Virginia, but adults need to guide their play to help them learn. "It's a misinterpretation to think that letting students loose for extended periods of time is going to automatically yield learning gains," he says. "This is particularly true for students struggling to self-regulate and communicate."

Teachers must intentionally engage with their students, shaping play in a way that's enjoyable, while providing the child with the information and skills to allow playful exploration to produce learning. With blocks, for example, a teacher can talk about shapes, sizes, and colors to help the student bring those concepts to life.

That intentional engagement, says Sharon Kagan, the Marx Professor of Early Childhood and Family Policy at Columbia's Teachers College, should be subtle and keyed to a child's particular needs. If a boy is having trouble using scissors, then scissors, paste, and other art supplies should be set up for him at a table. "The teacher shouldn't push the child to the table, but needs to provide encouragement," she says. "Then the teacher can watch and monitor and guide."

Other advocates, however, note that some of the richest learning for children comes through child-initiated or child-directed play. The Alliance for Childhood report recommends at least three daily play periods of an hour or longer in a full-day, six-hour kindergarten program, with at least one hour spent playing outdoors.

Let's Get Physical

At a time when some schools are cutting recess and physical education classes in favor of academic instruction, researchers say these districts are depriving children of essential school-based activities that prepare them for learning. The NAEYC report, for example, recommends that children play outside every day, have regular physical education classes, and have ample opportunities to use their large muscles for balancing, running, jumping, and other vigorous activities.

A recent study in *Pediatrics* detailed the benefits of recess for third-graders. Dr. Romina Barros, pediatrician at Albert Einstein College of Medicine in New York City, surveyed about 11,000 eight-year-olds and found that 30 percent had little or no recess. Those who had at least 15 minutes of recess exhibited better classroom behavior than those who didn't have a break.

The study shows that giving children a break from their studies helps them with self-regulation, a key predictor of long-term success in school. On the playground, children learn how to resolve conflicts, control their actions in a game, and take turns. They also get to use some of that natural energy that spills out of some children in the classroom and can be seen as disruptive.

"You can't move forward with another half-hour of math if you see the kids are bouncing out of their skins," says Alice Keane, a first-grade teacher at Lake Bluff Elementary School in Shorewood, Wis. "We might take what we call a 'wiggle walk' around the school because the kids in the class have too many wiggles. It's amazing how more receptive the children are after they've moved around."

Critical Thinking

1. Name the four foundations of learning discussed in the article and describe their importance in the overall learning of young children.

2. How would you respond to the following questions during a job interview for a kindergarten teaching position? What do you believe is the role of play in the learning of young children? Describe the types of learning experiences you would provide in your classroom on a daily basis.

DAVID MCKAY WILSON is a freelance education journalist who lives in New York State.

Acknowledging Learning through Play in the Primary Grades

On the first day of the new school year, Micah walks into his 2nd-grade classroom. He considers the rows of freshly polished desks, the neatly stacked workbooks, and the newly sharpened pencils on the shelf. Looking perplexed, he turns to his teacher and asks, "But where are the toys?"

JEANETTA G. RILEY AND ROSE B. JONES

Younger children are expected to be playful, and play generally is an acceptable activity in preschool classrooms (Wiltz & Fein, 2006). However, once children enter the primary grades (i.e., kindergarten through 3rd grade), time for play is often dramatically reduced (Bergen, 2002), leaving children like Micah wondering what happened to the toys.

Actually, Micah was one of the fortunate children. He had known the joy of learning through play during his kindergarten and 1st-grade years. For many children, textbooks and worksheets take over their lives beginning in kindergarten. Too often, parents, administrators, and teachers see the primary years as a time to get down to business and begin the *real* work involved in learning; play is considered a frill or add-on that has no place in the academic setting. Nevertheless, as Elkind (2007) proposes, "Play is not a luxury but rather a crucial dynamic of healthy physical, intellectual, and social-emotional development at all age levels" (p. 4). Furthermore, according to Copple and Bredekamp (2009), play is developmentally appropriate for primary-age children and can provide them with opportunities that enrich the learning experience.

Over a decade ago, Sandra J. Stone (1995) encouraged primary-grade teachers to incorporate play into their classrooms. Stone described the many ways children develop through their play and suggested that primary-age children have a need to play. Therefore, rather than educators giving into the thinking that play has no place in the primary grades, Stone urged teachers to design classrooms that encourage play. Unfortunately, even after these many years, play continues to be a misunderstood aspect of primary-grade children's development and learning.

For educators who do see value in the play of primary-age children, the pressures of standardized testing and mandated instructional programs may compel them to forgo time for play. Primary-grade teachers who believe that play is an avenue for learning may be required to defend the inclusion of play in their classrooms. The authors of this article explore the learning that can occur when primary-age children are allowed to play, and they provide primary-grade teachers with information to support developing a playful environment for learning.

Criteria of Play

While various meanings are applied to play, researchers have found certain characteristics that are typical of play. According to Brewer (2007), play involves the following criteria: 1) intrinsic motivation to participate, 2) active involvement of players, 3) nonliteral meanings of the activity, 4) focus on participation rather than outcome, 5) meaning of activities and objects supplied by players, and 6) flexibility of rules. Activities that meet these characteristics are often found in settings for younger children; however, once children enter the primary grades, time set aside for play in the classroom tends to completely disappear.

Time for Play

According to Bergen (2002), little play research has been conducted in primary classrooms, possibly because there are so few primary classrooms in which children actually play or where children are allowed to engage in playful, learning activities. Teachers may feel pressured to focus on academic achievement and the preparation of children for testing and meeting curricular standards, using strategies that do not include play. Although primary-grade teachers may feel pressured to prepare children for the inevitable testing, they should not overlook the "proper balance between spontaneous play and other activities" (Monighan Nourot, Scales, Van Hoorn, & Almy, 1987, p. 146).

Unfortunately, many teachers feel they no longer have the professional autonomy that once was a cornerstone of teaching (Mihans, 2008). Often, teachers no longer have the authority to make many of the instructional decisions that they believe will benefit their students. These decisions are made for the teachers, through mandated use of scripted instructional materials and programs, many of which require an overabundance of teacher-directed activities (National Kindergarten Alliance, n.d.). When every moment of the instructional day is preplanned, it is difficult for primary-grade teachers who believe that children's play is an important part of the learning environment to justify the inclusion of play in the schedule. Nevertheless, the learning that takes place when children play must not be overlooked, and teachers can be advocates for the use of developmentally appropriate practices that include free play during the primary grades.

Play as an Avenue for Learning

The focus of highly structured instructional materials that have children sit and listen or engage in paper/pencil work tends to be basic factual learning (Brewer, 2007). For deeper levels of learning (Brooks & Brooks, 1993), active involvement is needed. Additionally, education should focus on all aspects of a child's development: social, emotional, physical, and cognitive. Requiring primary-grade children to sit and listen to the teacher, to complete the work provided by the teacher, and to do their "own" work without disturbing others overlooks the natural development of children and the social context conducive to learning.

Almost 30 years ago, David Elkind (1981) wrote that society, including schools, rushes children toward adulthood at the expense of their childhood. Adults within the school environment often pressure children to conform to standards that are not child-friendly. McEachron (2001) writes, "When children are not allowed to be children, stress is sure to follow" (p. 82). The brain's ability to perform well is reduced when a child is under stress. Recent research into how the brain functions helps substantiate this idea (Jensen, 2006).

Classroom environments can be altered to decrease children's stress levels. Play is an important avenue to providing a relaxed classroom environment (National Kindergarten Alliance, n.d.). Teachers can create environments that are more playful and less stressful by allowing children to make choices about their activities. Wolk (2007) suggests that allowing students to make decisions about what and how they learn helps them to find the enjoyment that can come from learning. Furthermore, when children are given the freedom to make decisions, such as during play, they develop confidence in their growing abilities. This emerging confidence in young children plays a role in developing positive self-efficacy.

Self-Efficacy through Play

Self-efficacy is the belief that people can influence what happens in life through the actions they take; people with a strong sense of self-efficacy tend to believe they are capable of having at least some control over what happens as they make decisions and take action on those decisions (Bandura, Barbaranelli, Caprara, & Pastorelli, 1996). This belief begins to develop in children as they are allowed to make choices and to do things for themselves. When children play, they develop the sense that they can have control over themselves and their environment (National Kindergarten Alliance, n.d.).

Wassermann (2000) uses the term "can-do" attitude to explain the self-efficacy that children can gain through play. During play, children make choices and see the outcomes of those choices within the safety of the play setting. In this way, they experience the cause and effect of their actions and learn to regulate their behaviors. If children are constantly told what to do and how to do it, they miss the opportunities to practice controlling their own actions. When children are allowed to make choices about the activities that they will pursue, they are more likely to learn to make wise choices.

Children construct their knowledge as they choose activities, discuss their ideas, and work together to solve problems that arise during play. Early childhood education is based on theories that learning is an active, social endeavor. Such theorists as Dewey, Piaget, and Vygotsky believed that interaction is a key to learning (Mooney, 2000). The conversations that occur during interactive play awaken children to diverse ideas. By hearing and discussing different ideas, children see situations in new ways, thus deepening their understanding of concepts.

Literacy Skills through Play

Children's early experiences with language and literacy are key to their later learning (Hart & Risley, 1995; Montie, Xiang, & Schweinhart, 2006). Play allows for the practice of literacy skills. A critical part of literacy learning is language development. Very young children begin their path to later literacy learning as they hear and use language in their environment (Hart & Risley, 1995). Language provides the means for children to create play scenarios. Davidson (2006) suggests that "playing pretend pushes children to stretch their language skills in a number of ways" (p. 37), such as determining the specific words and tone to use within the play scenario. Moreover, language allows children to interact with others, helping them to learn the expectations of their sociocultural environment (Mooney, 2000). As children play together, they develop their understanding of language and how it allows them to interact with people in their environment.

Although primary-age children tend to demonstrate a wealth of language abilities, they continue to develop oral language skills, which, in turn, helps them learn to read and write (Brewer, 2007). By the end of the primary grades, children are expected to be proficient readers and writers. As with very young children, primary-age children need time to hear new vocabulary and experiment with the language in order to build their understanding of the ways language works. Children's engagement in playful activities allows them to practice language skills with peers. Primary-grade teachers can encourage children in their enjoyment of and involvement with literacy by placing appropriate literacy materials into play centers. One study found that when kindergarten teachers included more literacy materials in all centers, the children engaged in a variety of literacy activities (Saracho, 2001). Centers can include materials for children to read, a variety of writing implements, and various sizes and colors of paper. Other materials that can be included in centers to encourage literacy play are magnetic letters to spell words, signs to read, word games, flannel boards with flannel cut-outs of book characters, and tape players with blank cassettes for children to record their own stories. Placing literacy materials within children's easy access encourages them as they develop literacy skills.

Mathematics and Science Learning through Play

Piaget believed that learning occurs when children are curious and interact with the materials in their environment (Mooney, 2000). Children's curiosity leads them to choose activities that have meaning for them and about which they want to know more. Through exploring their environment with their curious natures, children build their knowledge of the world around them.

Primary-age children are typically in transition between what Piaget called the preoperational stage and the concrete operational stage (Piaget & Inhelder, 1969). During this transition phase, the materials available for children to use can assist in their initial understandings of mathematical and scientific concepts (Gallenstein, 2003). For example, playing with puzzles helps children understand spatial concepts, and play with pattern blocks helps children make discoveries about geometric shapes (e.g., three triangles placed together make the shape of one trapezoid). Exploring with magnets allows children to experiment with magnetic force and begin to understand that metals have different properties. When primary-grade children have these types of materials available to choose from, they gain the ability to understand abstract mathematical and scientific concepts that they can use throughout their lives (Elkind, 2007).

Social Skills through Play

A vital task for educators is helping children to develop the social skills necessary to live in society and effectively associate with other people. Sitting quietly and working alone on a task does not allow children to develop a genuine understanding of social skills; internalizing accepted social behaviors requires interaction. Play is a natural way for children to interact. Much of the research conducted on children's play describes the social processes that develop (e.g., Boulton, 2005; Gagnon & Nagle, 2004; Pellegrini, Blatchford, Kato, & Baines, 2004). Children learn important social expectations as they play with each other. The social skills that are often practiced when children play together are numerous; for example, opportunities for cooperating, taking turns, sharing, listening, and negotiating exist within the play context (Spodek & Saracho, 1998). Primary-age children may take on roles during sociodramatic play in which they play out their own life experiences (e.g., "I'm the mommy. You're the baby, and you have to stay in the car with Daddy while I go into the store."). The negotiation of who takes what role during play and how that person must act within the play scenario provides children practice with conflict-resolution skills and with understanding various points of view (Monighan-Nourot, 2006).

Furthermore, the social aspect of play allows primary-age children to practice specific skills that are usually required in primary curricula. Sociodramatic play offers many opportunities

for learning. For instance, children learn the value of specific coins and bills within the context of playing store. Children learn new vocabulary and measuring skills as they "build" a cardboard spaceship to take them to the moon, and a pretend restaurant leads to reading and writing skills when children create menus.

Additionally, many children of primary-grade age have advanced to playing games with rules (Piaget & Inhelder, 1969). Children who play board games practice such skills as adding, subtracting, reading words, and analyzing possibilities. Primary-age children may re-create rules for games that already have established rules (e.g., chase or board games). For example, in a simple spinner counting game in which the rule is for each person to have one turn before the next person spins, the children may decide to allow each person two spins before passing the turn to the next person. The conversations that emerge as children invent game rules provide opportunities for them to express their ideas, analyze and discuss various options for the game, and negotiate with each other (e.g., "If you'll play with me, I'll let you go first").

Conclusion

The beginning scenario illustrates that children like Micah often enter into primary classrooms where the tools of play are missing, and this will continue unless advocates for play work diligently to change the status quo and provide an environment in which play and playful learning experiences are woven back into the classrooms for the children. As Frost, Wortham, and Reifel (2001) note, "The shift in focus from make-believe play of the preschooler to the growing frequency of playing organized games of the school-age child should transition gradually, with continual attention to providing play materials and equipment for cognitive, social, and language development through the primary grades" (p. 434). This type of play-based learning within a curriculum focuses more "on imaginative expression of ideas and open-ended experimentation" (Frost, Wortham, & Reifel, 2001, p. 300), both of which allow children to learn to think critically and solve problems strategically.

Learning and play do not have to be contradictory; learning can occur during times of play. When children transition into the primary grades, they should not have to leave their childhoods behind. Appropriate instructional practices are as necessary in the elementary grades as they are in the preschool years. By examining the learning that takes place when children are allowed to make choices, encouraged to explore new materials and ideas, and given freedom to interact with one another, primary-grade teachers can better advocate for play as appropriate and effective for children's learning and development.

References

Bandura, A., Barbaranelli, C., Caprara, G. V., & Pastorelli, C. (1996). Multifaceted impact of self-efficacy beliefs on academic functioning. *Child Development, 67*(3), 1206–1222.

Bergen, D. (2002). The role of pretend play in children's cognitive development. *Early Childhood Research and Practice, 4*(1). Retrieved December 29, 2008, from http://ecrp.uiuc.edu/v4n1/bergen.html.

Boulton, M. J. (2005). Predicting changes in children's self-perceptions from playground social activities and interactions. *British Journal of Developmental Psychology, 23*(2), 209–226.

Brewer, J. A. (2007). *Introduction to early childhood education: Preschool through primary grades.* Boston: Pearson Education.

Brooks, J. G., & Brooks, M. G. (1993). *In search of understanding: The case for constructivist classrooms.* Alexandria, VA: Association for Supervision and Curriculum Development.

Copple, C., & Bredekamp, S. (Eds.). (2009). *Developmentally appropriate practice in early childhood programs: Serving children birth through age 8* (3rd ed.). Washington, DC: National Association for the Education of Young Children.

Davidson, J. I. F. (2006). Language and play: Natural partners. In D. P. Fromberg & D. Bergen (Eds.), *Play from birth to twelve: Contexts, perspectives, and meanings* (pp. 31–40). New York: Routledge.

Elkind, D. (1981). *The hurried child: Growing up too fast too soon.* Reading, MA: Addison-Wesley.

Elkind, D. (2007). *The power of play: How spontaneous, imaginative activities lead to happier, healthier children.* Cambridge, MA: Da Capo Press.

Frost, J. L., Wortham, S. C., & Reifel, S. (2001). *Play and child development.* Upper Saddle River, NJ: Merrill/Prentice Hall.

Gagnon, S. G., & Nagle, R. J. (2004). Relationships between peer interactive play and social competence in at-risk preschool children. *Psychology in the Schools, 41*(2), 173–189.

Gallenstein, N. L. (2003). *Creative construction of mathematics and science concepts in early childhood.* Olney, MD: Association for Childhood Education International.

Hart, B., & Risley, T. R. (1995). *Meaningful differences in the everyday experience of young American children.* Baltimore: Paul H. Brookes.

Jensen, E. (2006). *Enriching the brain: How to maximize every learner's potential.* San Francisco: Jossey-Bass.

McEachron, G. (2001). Mediating stress: Personal growth for student teachers. In B. H. Stanford & K. Yamamoto (Eds.), *Children and stress: Understanding and helping* (pp. 77–93). Olney, MD: Association for Childhood Education International.

Mihans, R. (2008). Can teachers lead teachers? *Phi Delta Kappan, 89*(10), 762–765.

Monighan-Nourot, P. (2006). Sociodramatic play pretending together. In D. P. Fromberg & D. Bergen (Eds.), *Play from birth to twelve: Contexts, perspectives, and meanings* (pp. 87–101). New York: Routledge.

Monighan-Nourot, P., Scales, B., Van Hoorn, J., & Almy, M. (1987). *Looking at children's play: A bridge between theory and practice.* New York: Teachers College Press.

Montie, J. E., Xiang, Z., & Schweinhart, L. J. (2006). Preschool experience in ten countries: Cognitive and language performance at age seven. *Early Childhood Research Quarterly, 21*(3), 313–331.

Mooney, C. G. (2000). *Theories of childhood: An introduction to Dewey, Montessori, Erikson, Piaget and Vygotsky.* St. Paul, MN: Redleaf Press.

National Kindergarten Alliance, (n.d.). *Childhood: A time for play.* Retrieved December 27, 2008, from www.nkateach.org/NKA/research.html

Pellegrini, A. D., Blatchford, P., Kato, K., & Baines, E. (2004). A short-term longitudinal study of children's playground games in primary school: Implications for adjustment to school and social adjustment in the USA and the UK. *Social Development, 13*(1), 107–123.

Piaget, J., & Inhelder, B. (1969). *The psychology of the child.* New York: Basic Books.

Saracho, O. N. (2001). Exploring young children's literacy development through play. *Early Childhood Development and Care, 167*(1), 103–114.

Spodek, B., & Saracho, O. N. (1998). The challenge of educational play. In D. Bergen (Ed.), *Readings from play as a medium for learning and development* (pp. 11–28). Olney, MD: Association for Childhood Education International.

Stone, S. J. (1995). Wanted: Advocates for play in the primary grades. *Young Children, 50*(6), 45–54.

Wassermann, S. (2000). *Serious players in the primary classroom.* New York: Teachers College Press.

Wiltz, N. W., & Fein, G. G. (2006). Play as children see it. In D. P. Fromberg & D. Bergen (Eds.), *Play from birth to twelve: Contexts, perspectives, and meanings* (pp. 127–140). New York: Routledge.

Wolk, S. (2007). Why go to school? *Phi Delta Kappan, 88*(9), 648–658.

Critical Thinking

1. How has play become what many consider a "four letter word" in schools today? What steps can educators take to prevent that from happening?

2. Expand on Elkind's quote in the article that, "Play is not a luxury but rather a crucial dynamic of healthy physical, intellectual, and social-emotional development at all age levels." What did he mean by that statement?

JEANETTA G. RILEY is Assistant Professor, Department of Early Childhood and Elementary Education, Murray State University, Murray, Kentucky. **ROSE B. JONES** is Assistant Professor, Early Childhood Education/Literacy, The University of Southern Mississippi, Hattiesburg.

Repeating Views on Grade Retention

PAMELA JANE POWELL

The call for accountability in U.S. schools is gaining intensity. The emergence of No Child Left Behind (NCLB), the high dropout rate, and media reports of declining test scores fuel claims that children are not achieving, and that schools do not do enough to ensure that achievement. The resulting rhetoric pits grade retention against social promotion, as if they were the only options. What is wrong with this tired view of schooling? Is grade retention really a viable intervention that can ensure a child's academic achievement? If not, what are the alternatives?

What School Looks Like

Children come to school to learn. In kindergarten, they begin to acquire the skills needed to move up the educational ladder. At the end of kindergarten, those children who have the requisite skills move on to 1st grade, and this pattern continues as the child progresses through the grades. This structure seems logical, linear, and commonsensical. However, this entrenched line of thinking has shallow roots, as we examine the history of education and the research that has been conducted in regard to this movement, or lack of movement, upward through the age-graded system.

The age-graded system, which segregates students by age, is the most common structure for schools in the United States. It was introduced by Horace Mann, who brought the model from Prussia and implemented it in the mid 1800s at the Quincy Grammar School in Boston, Massachusetts. Textbooks became associated with curricula for grade levels and that, it seems, laid the groundwork for a rudimentary standards movement. Children were promoted to higher grade levels on the basis of their mastery of the affiliated skills.

This model is the only one that most people in the United States have ever known. In fact, because most people have known this system from the inside out, they feel comfortable making judgments about the system. Politicians, parents, and the media often rate schools poorly and offer much advice for improving the quality of schools. Consequently, students are trundled through the system as if they are products on an assembly line. Yet, the reality is far more complicated.

All Things Are Not Equal

First, let us analyze how children are typically admitted to school in any given year. If the cut-off date (by birthdate) is September 1st, for example, then children can enter the grade if they have their fifth birthday at any time from September 1st of the previous year to August 31st of the school entry year. Given that this span of a year accounts for a huge percentage of a kindergartner's lifetime, when progress and development are marked in months, not by years, you begin to realize the vast differences that may exist among these 5-year-olds. Also realize that many children are overage for grade, including children who are academically redshirted or those who have been held back in grade. This further divides a classroom chronologically.

Chronology is but one factor. Consider the different domains—cognitive, affective, physical, and social—that reside within each child. All of these factors impact the child and his ability to operate within a school setting.

> **Consider the different domains—cognitive, affective, physical, and social—that reside within each child. All of these factors impact the child and his ability to operate within a school setting.**

Now, contemplate language development. Again taking into consideration the age differences within any given classroom, the stages of language development also will be varied. Children's expressive vocabulary, ability to articulate needs and ideas, and aptitude to converse socially are uneven. Add to this the reality that most children in the United States are asked to perform academically and socially in English, which may not be their first language. These English language learners are learning a new language, may be adjusting to a new culture, and are trying to become attuned to school.

A class of 24 kindergartners further separates when we take into consideration that some children will have developmental delays, some will have learning differences, and some will have separation anxiety and/or other issues that inhibit their abilities to engage in the school experience.

The accountability movement has thrust incredible responsibility on teachers and students to perform in spite of this diversity. While accountability is necessary, the *way* in which accountability is measured and what is done with this information can be disturbing.

High-stakes tests in the United States often determine whether students will be promoted or graduate. Many states have instituted policies prohibiting children from promotion if they do not achieve a minimum score on an achievement test. It seems intuitive that if students have not mastered content, they should not be able to move forward. Holding children back in grade, it is thought, will allow them time to mature and/or acquire the needed skills and knowledge to provide a foundation for success. Again, the reality is more complicated.

Holding Children Back: Grade Retention

Children who are held back and denied the ability to be promoted with their peers—being retained in grade—are most commonly kept back due to academic or socioemotional reasons. A significant proportion of these children are male, young for grade, small for age, of color, and/or living in poverty conditions.

Researchers have studied grade retention since the early part of the 20th century. Keyes (1911) conducted a longitudinal study that examined "accelerates," students who were promoted, and "arrests," those who were retained. This seven-year study suggested that 21% of the repeaters did better after repeating the grade and 39% did worse. Interestingly, he also noted that "arrest is most likely to follow too early or too late entrance to school" (Keyes, 1911, p. 62). His research indicated that almost 25% of pupils were retained at some point during grades 1 through 9. He also cited a tendency for students to leave school after the 8th grade, rather than risk repeating a grade.

In an early experimental study, Klene and Branson (1929) examined students who were potential repeaters and then assigned to promotion or retention based on chronological age, mental age, and gender. They concluded that promoted students benefited more than those who were retained.

In 1933, Caswell looked at the current retention research of the time in his study titled *Non-Promotion in Elementary Schools*. He concluded that "non-promotion is a type of failure that tends to deaden, disillusion and defeat the child" (p. 81).

Arthur (1936) studied the achievement of 60 grade-1 pupils who repeated a grade, using a pre- and post-test design. She determined that "the average repeater of the group studied learned no more in two years than did the average non-repeater of the same mental age in one year" (p. 205), echoing the results of Klene and Branson (1929).

Goodlad (1954) conducted a comparative study of the effects of promotion and non-promotion on social and personal adjustment. He found that the children who were not promoted did not thrive as well as their promoted counterparts when compared with their own class groups.

In 1975, Jackson "provided the first systematic, comprehensive overview of the research evidence on the effects of grade retention" (Jimerson, 2001, p. 421). Jackson concluded that

"there is no reliable body of evidence to indicate that grade retention is more beneficial than grade promotion for students with serious academic or adjustment difficulties" (1975, p. 627). Still, the practice continued.

Holmes and Matthews (1984) conducted another seminal piece of research examining the effects of retention on elementary and junior high school students' achievement and socioemotional outcomes. They concluded that promoted students fared better than their retained counterparts, stating that "those who continue to retain pupils do so despite cumulative research evidence showing that the potential for negative effects consistently outweighs positive outcomes" (Holmes & Matthews, 1984, p. 232). Five years later, Holmes added 19 more studies to the original meta-analysis conducted by Holmes and Matthews. Out of a total of 63 empirical studies, only nine yielded positive results (Holmes, 1989). Despite yet another admonition regarding the practice and a track record of over 50 years of inconclusive research at that time, grade retention continued.

In his subsequent meta-analysis, Jimerson (2001) explained that the previous review and meta-analyses indicate an "absence of empirical evidence" to support the practice of retention. Jimerson's study summarized much of the research regarding retention executed in the 20th century.

While research regarding the efficacy of grade retention has provided mixed results, the existing theory regarding grade retention is that it is probably ineffective as a strategy to improve academic achievement or increase personal adjustment (Holmes, 1989; Holmes & Matthews, 1984; Jackson, 1975; Jimerson, 2001). This option has been researched for almost a century, and few clear-cut benefits are evident (Holmes, 1989; Holmes & Matthews, 1984; Jackson, 1975; Jimerson, 2001). Yet, the practice persists.

Grade Retention and Dropout

One of the most reported consequences of student retention is its correlation with subsequent dropout. Children who are retained have a higher incidence of dropout (Grissom & Shepard, 1989; Roderick, 1994; Rumberger, 1995). Anderson, Whipple, and Jimerson (2002) found "retention to be one of the most powerful predictors of high school dropout, with retained students 2 to 11 times more likely to drop out of high school than promoted students" (Anderson, Whipple, & Jimerson, 2002, p. 2). In fact, Rumberger (1995) indicates that retention is the strongest predictor of subsequent dropout.

Shepard and Smith (1989) also state that "large-scale surveys of dropouts and graduates reveal that substantially more dropouts than graduates have at some time in their career been retained in grade" (p. 215). Roderick (1994) concluded that "repeating a grade from kindergarten to sixth grade was associated with a substantial increase in the odds of dropping out" (p. 729). In addition, the National Center for Education Statistics (NCES) reported in 1995 that individuals who are retained are almost twice as likely to drop out than those who have never been retained. Males were two-thirds more likely to be retained than females, and retention rates increased from 1992 to 1995.

Similarly, Frymier (1997) reported that those that have been retained in grade are about twice as likely to drop out as those who were never retained. Additionally, those who were retained had more difficulty in every risk area examined in his descriptive, comparative study. Jimerson and Ferguson (2007) again examined the efficacy of the practice of grade retention and noted, "The association of grade retention and high school dropout is disconcerting and seems to be the most common deleterious outcome during adolescence" (p. 334). This leads to a critical question—of the over six million students who dropped out in 2007 (Center for Labor Market Studies, 2009), how many were retained in grade? This outcome associated with the practice of grade retention has far-reaching ramifications, both for the individual and society.

If Not Retention, Then What?

There is no question that interventions (other than grade retention) are needed to help all children succeed in school. We need fresh alternatives and new ways of thinking about children.

Consider the following: Children do not develop neatly in all domains and, especially, not simultaneously. The complexity of the individual is incalculable, and children in any given classroom may vary by age and by ability across domains. All children will not and should not be on the same page at the same time, and children should be *met* where they *are*, not where we think they *should be*.

Such issues as language development affect learning, and teachers should expect skill and knowledge acquisition to differ from child to child. By recognizing that children may be highly skilled and knowledgeable in one area and have gaps in another, and still believing that each child can succeed, teachers may capitalize on the strengths of each child and scaffold learning.

Furthermore, learning in the early childhood years is vastly different than in later years, and children may make leaps in their development, because learning does not only occur incrementally. As has been often stated, schools must be ready for children just as much as children should be ready for school.

Finally, it is important to look at viable interventions. The system of grade retention intervention, at a cost of approximately $18 billion per year (Xia & Glennie, 2005), does not guarantee subsequent school success and has been linked to later high school dropout. Surely, other interventions could promote success and prevent some of the negative consequences of grade retention, and perhaps at a fraction of the cost.

Such alternatives can include greater early assessment and interventions in the early childhood years prior to schooling and substantive interventions in the early grades. Flexible time lines can be employed for skill, language, and knowledge acquisition with enrichment programs for all children, to enhance their experiences and provide rich language opportunities. Furthermore, we should ditch the deficit model of learning and instead provide opportunities for mastery and success while honoring development, which may be uneven across domains, and look at multiple options for schooling, such as multiage classrooms (Stone, 2009), in order to implement true systemic change.

Leaving Children Behind

The act of grade retention may keep children behind. Decades of research have been inconclusive regarding the benefits of the practice, with much of the research pointing to its detriments. It is time to employ the whole world of a child when helping him learn and succeed. The family, the school, and the community can assist in uncovering and maximizing the potential of every child.

References

Anderson, G., Whipple, A., & Jimerson, S. (2002, November). Grade retention: Achievement and mental health outcomes. *Communiqué, 31*(3), handout pages 1–3.

Arthur, G. (1936). A study of the achievement of sixty grade 1 repeaters as compared with that of non-repeaters of the same mental age. *The Journal of Experimental Education, 5*(2), 203–205.

Caswell, H. L. (1933). *Non-promotion in elementary schools.* Nashville, TN: George Peabody College for Teachers.

Center for Labor Market Studies. (2009). *Left behind: The nation's dropout crisis.* Retrieved from www.clms.neu.edu/publication/documents/CLMS_2009_Dropout_Report.pdf

Frymier, J. (1997). Characteristics of students retained in grade. *The High School Journal, 80*(3), 184–192.

Goodlad, J. (1954). Some effects of promotion and non-promotion upon the social and personal adjustment of children. *Journal of Experimental Education, 22,* 301–328.

Grissom, J.B., & Shepard, L. A. (1989). Repeating and dropping out of school. In L. A. Shepard & M. L. Smith (Eds.), *Flunking grades: Research and policies on retention* (pp. 34–63). London: Falmer Press.

Holmes, C. T. (1989). Grade level retention effects: A meta-analysis of research studies. In L. A. Shepard & M. L. Smith (Eds.), *Flunking grades: Research and policies on retention* (pp. 16–33). London: Falmer Press.

Holmes, C. T., & Matthews, K. M. (1984). The effects of nonpromotion on elementary and junior high pupils: A meta-analysis. *Review of Educational Research, 54*(2), 225–236.

Jackson, G. (1975). The research evidence on the effects of grade retention. *Review of Educational Research, 45,* 613–635.

Jimerson, S. (2001). Meta-analysis of grade retention research: Implications for practice in the 21st century. *School Psychology Review, (30)3,* 420–437.

Jimerson, S. R., & Ferguson, P. (2007). A longitudinal study of grade retention: Academic and behavioral outcomes of retained students through adolescence. *School Psychology Quarterly, 22*(3), 314–339.

Keyes, C. (1911). *Progress through the grades of city schools.* New York: AMS Press.

Klene, V., & Branson, E. (1929). Trial promotion versus failure. *Educational Research Bulletin, 8,* 6–11.

National Center for Education Statistics. (1995). *Dropout rates in the United States: Grade retention.* Retrieved from http://nces.ed.gov/pubs/dp95/97473–5.asp

Roderick, M. (1994). Grade retention and school dropout: Investigating the association. *American Educational Research Journal, 31*(4), 729–759.

Rumberger, R. W. (1995). Dropping out of middle school: Analysis of students and schools. *American Educational Research Journal, 32*(3), 583–625.

Shepard, L. A., & Smith, M. L. (1989). *Flunking grades: Research and policies on retention.* London: Falmer Press.

Stone, S. (2009). Multiage in the era of NCLB. *Center for Evaluation and Education Policy: Education Policy Brief, 7*(1), 5.

Xia, C, & Glennie, E. (2005). *Grade retention: The gap between research and practice.* Durham, NC: Duke University, Center for Child and Family Policy, Terry Sanford Institute of Public Policy.

Critical Thinking

1. What would you say to a friend who told you retention was recommended for her daughter for the next year, and your friend isn't sure what she should do. She asked if you knew of any research on the topic. Write your response.

2. Develop a list of some possible solutions, other than grade retention, to assist struggling learners.

PAMELA JANE POWELL is Assistant Professor, Department of Teaching and Learning, Northern Arizona University, Flagstaff, Arizona.

The Power of Documentation in the Early Childhood Classroom

A parent eyes something on the wall in the hallway near her child's classroom. She stops and looks across the entire wall, as if trying to determine where to start. She moves to the left a bit and scans the bulletin board posted farther down. At one point she nods as if in agreement and mouths a yes. Another parent approaches and turns to see what is on the wall. He too is mesmerized by the documentation of what one child discovered about pussy willows by using an I-scope lens.

HILARY SEITZ

Early childhood educators might ask, "What is documentation?" or "Is this documentation?" They sometimes wonder, "Can my bulletin board be documentation?"

What Is Documentation?

Knowing what is documentation is the first stage of understanding the process. Katz and Chard offer this explanation: "Documentation typically includes samples of a child's work at several different stages of completion: photographs showing work in progress; comments written by the teacher or other adults working with the children; transcriptions of children's discussions, comments, and explanations of intentions about the activity; and comments made by parents" (1996, 2).

Effective Communication

An effective piece of documentation tells the story and the purpose of an event, experience, or development. It is a product that draws others into the experience—evidence or artifacts that describe a situation, tell a story, and help the viewer to understand the purpose of the action.

When used effectively, consistently, and thoughtfully, documentation can also drive curriculum and collaboration in the early childhood classroom setting.

Formats That Work

A bulletin board can be a form of documentation, but there are any number of other possible formats, including a presentation board containing documentation artifacts and/or evidence (documentation panels), class books, portfolios, slide shows, movies, and other creative products.

The format that documentation takes can be as varied as the creator's mind permits. Because documentation should provide evidence of a process with a purpose, whatever the format, it should fully explain the process, highlighting various aspects of the experience or event.

Audience and Purposes

Successful documentation formats reflect the intended audience and purposes. In addition, the format selected will depend on the individual preparing the documentation and how the children are involved in the experience.

For example, if one teacher wants to highlight for families and administrators how the class is meeting a particular math or science standard, she would use examples of children participating in experiences that align with the standard. As evidence, she might include photographs of children measuring plant stems with a ruler, children's comments about measuring the stems, background information about how the children learned about measurement (or plants), and the specific learning standard the children are meeting by participating in this experience. To best combine all of these elements, the teacher may choose a documentation panel as the format to help the audience understand how children are learning.

If children in the class are the intended audience, however, and the purpose of the documentation is to help children reflect on their math and science learning and connect them to future lessons, then the teacher would select different artifacts and evidence. A documentation panel could again be appropriate, but different artifacts and evidence might include a web of children's ideas: for instance, why an elephant should not live at the Alaska Zoo, children's comments about the elephant, and questions for further exploration, such as, "Where should an elephant live?" Add related photographs and work samples.

Again, an explanation about where the learning began and where it is intended to go will help any audience better

Documentation Artifacts and Evidence

- Teacher's description and overview of an event/experience/skill development, such as photographs and descriptions of a field trip
- Photographs of children at work—for example, conducting a science experiment
- Samples of children's work, like a writing sample from the beginning of the year
- Children's comments, such as "All the rocks have sparkles in them," in writing or as recorded by the teacher
- Teacher or parent comments about a classroom event—for instance, "It was really fun helping the children measure the ingredients for playdough"
- Teacher transcriptions of conversations during small group time when children are exploring a new topic, such as why snow melts indoors
- Important items or observations relating to an event/experience/development, such as "Johnny can now write his own name on his work"

Possible Topics to Document

- Individual child growth and development, such as language development progression
- Expected behaviors (at group time, in using a certain toy, while eating together)
- Curriculum ideas or events (field trips, presentations, special activities, celebrations)
- Curriculum projects, such as learning about plant life cycles
- Families and relationships (different types of family structures and characteristics of the families in the classroom community)
- Evidence of meeting learning standards (by posting work samples)
- Questions and answers of the children, teachers, and families about such topics as classroom routines (like how to wash your hands)

understand the documentation. In both cases, the quality of the end product will depend on the teacher's understanding of children, the curriculum, and the standards, along with his or her effective use of technology and observation.

What Should We Document?

A variety of experiences and topics are appropriate to document, but documentation should always tell a complete story. To stay on track, carefully select one topic and explore it to the fullest rather than trying to do a little of everything. For example, if the class is learning about plants (and studying plant parts, how to grow particular plants, types of plants, and so on), it would be best to document fully just one aspect of children's learning.

To stay on track, carefully select one topic and explore it to the fullest rather than trying to do a little of everything.

Choosing a Focus

The teacher might choose to document only the children's study of plant parts, for example, and could start by providing a learning spark, such as a new plant in the classroom (Seitz 2006). As children comment on the plant parts, the teacher can create a web to record what they know and to help them formulate questions. The children might also draw and label the various plant parts.

Presenting the Topic and Learning

The teacher can combine all of these pieces to make a documentation panel. This panel would illustrate the children's knowledge and understanding more thoroughly than a panel displaying every child's worksheet on plant parts, all of their water-color paintings of a plant, and every brainstormed list of vegetable plants. Offering specific examples of how children came to their understandings about just one aspect of a lesson—in this case, plant parts—achieves more than offering an overview of several experiences.

Showing Developmental Progress

One important and common topic for documentation is individual child growth and development. As previous examples have shown, the documenter is a researcher first, collecting as much information as possible to paint a picture of progress and outcomes. Documenting individual growth requires a great deal of research, as the teacher must observe each child in a variety of areas of development (such as social-emotional, cognitive, language, and motor) over a substantial length of time. Only then can the teacher create a documentation piece that tells an accurate story about each child.

The documenter is a researcher first, collecting as much information as possible to paint a picture of progress and outcomes.

A teacher should be careful to avoid displaying private or confidential information in public forums. There are times when documentation may be more appropriately shared in other, more private venues, such as a portfolio.

Portfolios used for individual assessment of children make a particularly good format for documenting developmental progress. Teachers select several domains to research. They then collect evidence of a child's interaction with other children (photographs and written observations), record the child's reflections about their friendships and cognitive abilities in interviews or group discussions, collect work samples, and tie the documentation together by writing a narrative describing the child's abilities (not deficits) in the selected domains. Even though the portfolio focuses on a child's abilities, teachers may want to consider sharing the documentation/portfolio in a private setting, such as a parent/child/teacher conference, so that parents do not feel compelled to compare their child to others in the class.

Why Should We Document?

There are several important reasons for using documentation in early childhood classrooms.

Showing Accountability

Accountability is one reason for documentation. Teachers are accountable to administrators, families, community members, and others, and documentation helps to provide evidence of children's learning. In addition, documentation can improve relationships, teaching, and learning. Use of this tool helps educators get to know and understand children, and it allows them to reflect on the effectiveness of their teaching practices (Kroeger & Cardy 2006).

Extending the Learning

Consider the following example of how one thoughtful teacher could use documentation to prolong and extend an unexpected learning opportunity. A group of children finds some miscellaneous nuts and bolts on a playground, and their teacher, noting their curiosity, carefully observes their responses and listens to and documents their conversations (by using written notes, photographs, and video). She listens to learn what the children know about the items and what they wonder, such as "Where do these come from?" Then she facilitates a conversation with the children to learn more about their ideas and theories behind the purpose of the nuts and bolts and how they came to be on the playground.

Later the teacher incorporates the initial comments, the photographs, and the conversations in a documentation source (panel, notebook, PowerPoint, or other creative product). The children and teacher revisit the encounter through the documentation and reflect on the experience, which helps the children continue their conversation and drives forward their interest. This back-and-forth examination of the documentation helps the teacher and children negotiate a curriculum that is based on the children's interests (Seitz 2006).

Making Learning Visible

When expected to provide evidence that children are meeting learning standards, documentation is a natural way to make learning visible. Helm, Beneke, and Steinheimer (1998) call this idea "windows on learning," meaning that documenting offers an insight into children's development and learning. Moreover, they observe, "When teachers document children's learning in a variety of ways, they can be more confident about the value of their teaching" (1998, 24).

How Should We Document?

The documentation process is best done in collaboration with other teachers, parents, and, in some cases, children soon after the experience. The information and product become richer when two or more teachers, children, and parents work together to understand an event. Collaboration also helps build a classroom community, which is important because it engages teachers, parents, and children in thinking about the process of learning.

> **The documentation process is best done in collaboration with other teachers, parents, and, in some cases, children soon after the experience.**

When two or more people discuss an event, each brings a different perspective and a new level of depth. The photo below [not provided] shows two teachers discussing a possible change to the classroom environment. They have discussed aspects that are necessary and that work and things they would like to change based on the children's needs, such as repositioning the furniture. Together they share how they have observed young children using the space. This environment plan would look very different if just one individual had created it. Carlina Rinaldi discusses this notion of working together and building community: "To feel a sense of belonging, to be part of a larger endeavor, to share meanings—these are rights of everyone involved in the educational process, whether teachers, children, or parents . . . working in groups is essential" (1998, 114).

Stages of the Documenter

First and foremost, documentation is a process that is learned, facilitated, and created in stages. I would even go so far as to say that documenters go through their own stages as they learn more about documenting and using documentation to support their ideas. Many early childhood educators already document children's development and learning in many ways, and most communicate a variety of messages in diverse formats to families (Brown-DuPaul, Keyes, & Segatti 2001).

There are six stages that most early childhood educators, including college students and practicing teachers, move through both individually and collaboratively (see "Stages of Documenter Experience"). Educators who collaborate to learn more about documentation tend to have more positive experiences than those who work on their own.

Stages of Documenter Experience

Stage	Experience	Value
1. Deciding to document	Documenters ask, "What should I document?" They collect artwork from every child but at first tend to create busy bulletin boards with too much information. Concerned with equity, many include every item rather than being selective.	Documenters show pride in the children's work.
2. Exploring technology use	Documenters explore how to use equipment and photographs from various events and experiences. Most of the photos are displayed on bulletin boards or inserted in photo albums. The video clips are placed in slideshows or movies and shown to children and parents.	Documenters work hard to learn more about technology. They show pride in the children's actions by displaying photos and video clips.
3. Focusing on children's engagement	Documenters learn to photograph specific things and events with the intent of capturing a piece of the story of children engaged in learning.	Documenters become technologically competent and able to focus on important learning events and experiences.
4. Gathering information	Documenters title the photographs, events, and experiences and begin to write descriptions that tell the story of children's learning.	Documenters begin to connect children's actions and experiences.
5. Connecting and telling stories	Documenters combine work samples, photographs, descriptions, and miscellaneous information in support of the entire learning event. They tell the whole story with a beginning, middle, and an end, using supporting artifacts.	Documenters continue to use documentation artifacts to connect children's actions and experiences to curriculum and learning standards.
6. Documenting decision making	Documenters frame questions, reflect, assess, build theories, and meet learning standards, all with the support of documentation.	Documenters become reflective practitioners who document meaningful actions/events, explain why they are important, and push themselves and others to continue thinking about these experiences.

Conclusion

Documentation can be a rewarding process when educators understand the value associated with collecting evidence and producing a summary presentation, whether in a bulletin board, panel, video, or other format. To become a documenter, one must first understand what to observe and what to do with the information collected. It takes time and practice to learn which experiences support effective documentation and how to collect artifacts and evidence.

Next, as documenters learn why the information is important, they begin to understand the value of documentation for different audiences and come to recognize why certain aspects of child development are important to assess. In addition, documenters learn that administrators and parents value this information, yet it also has value to the children and the teacher in planning authentic curriculum that meets children's needs.

Often the documentation provides insights into children's thinking and helps drive the future curriculum.

Finally, the documenter learns how best to interpret and display the information gathered. Often the documentation provides insights into children's thinking and helps drive the future curriculum. Deepening children's learning is the ultimate reward of documentation.

References

Brown-DuPaul, J., T. Keyes, & L. Segatti. 2001. Using documentation panels to communicate with families. *Childhood Education* 77 (4): 209–13.

Helm, J.H., S. Beneke, & K. Steinheimer. 1998. *Windows on learning: Documenting young children's work.* New York: Teachers College Press.

Katz, L.G., & S.C. Chard. 1996. The contribution of documentation to the quality of early childhood education. ED 393608. www.eric-digests.org/1996-4/quality.htm.

Kroeger, J., & T. Cardy. 2006. Documentation: A hard-to-reach place. *Early Childhood Education Journal* 33 (6): 389–98.

Rinaldi, C. 1998. Projected curriculum construction through documentation—*Progettazione.* In *The hundred languages of children: The Reggio Emilia approach—Advanced reflections,* 2nd ed., eds. C. Edwards, L. Gandini, & G. Forman, 114. Greenwich, CT: Ablex.

Seitz, H. 2006. The plan: Building on children's interests. *Young Children* 61 (2): 36–41.

Further Resources

Chard, S.C. 1998. *The Project Approach: Making curriculum come alive.* New York: Scholastic.

Curtis, D., & M. Carter. 2000. *The art of awareness: How observation can transform your teaching.* St. Paul, MN: Redleaf.

Edwards, C., L. Gandini, & G. Forman, eds. 1998. *The hundred languages of children: The Reggio Emilia approach—Advanced reflections.* 2nd ed. Greenwich, CT: Ablex.

Fraser, S., & C. Gestwicki. 2002. *Authentic childhood: Exploring Reggio Emilia in the classroom.* Albany, NY: Delmar/Thomson Learning.

Fu, V.R., A.J. Stremmel, & L.T. Hill. 2002. *Teaching and learning: Collaborative exploration of the Reggio Emilia approach.* Upper Saddle River, NJ: Merrill.

Gandini, L., & C.P. Edwards, eds. 2001. *Bambini: The Italian approach to infant/toddler care.* New York: Teachers College Press.

Hill, L.T., A.J. Stremmel, & V.R. Fu. 2005. *Teaching as inquiry: Rethinking curriculum in early childhood education.* Boston: Pearson/Allyn & Bacon.

Jones, E., & J. Nimmo. 1994. *Emergent curriculum.* Washington, DC: NAEYC.

Katz, L.G., & S.C. Chard. 2000. *Engaging children's minds: The project approach,* 2nd ed. Greenwich, CT: Ablex.

Oken-Wright, P. 2001. Documentation: Both mirror and light. *Innovations in Early Education: The International Reggio Exchange* 8 (4): 5–15.

Reed, A.J., & V.E. Bergemann. 2005. *A guide to observation, participation, and reflection in the classroom.* 5th ed. Boston: McGraw-Hill.

Shores, E.F., & C. Grace. 2005. *The portfolio book: A step-by-step guide for teachers.* Upper Saddle River, NJ: Pearson.

Wurm, J. 2005. *Working the Reggio way: A beginner's guide for American teachers.* St. Paul, MN: Redleaf.

Critical Thinking

1. Why is it important to adapt the documentation you provide for your audience, such as administrators, families, or the children?

2. Observe in a local school setting and look for signs of documentation that are listed in the article. What did you see that documents or tells the story of the learning occurring in that setting?

HILARY SEITZ, PhD, is the early childhood coordinator in the Department of Teaching and Learning at the University of Alaska in Anchorage. Her wide range of early childhood experiences includes teaching in child care centers, a public preschool, and elementary schools. hilary@uaa.alaska.edu.

From *Young Children*, March 2008, pp. 88–92. Copyright © 2008 by National Association for the Education of Young Children. Reprinted by permission.

When School Lunch Doesn't Make the Grade

Is your child's cafeteria failing to provide healthy, nutritious food?

ELIZABETH FOY LARSEN

Deep-fried popcorn chicken, tiny taters, bread, barbecue sauce, ketchup, milk. That high-fat, high-sodium, low-fiber menu is a typical lunch at a typical American elementary school. We know about it because Mrs. Q., a grade-school teacher, decided to eat her school's lunch every day for an entire school year and report anonymously to the world on her blog, "Fed Up With Lunch: The School Lunch Project" (fedupwithschoollunch. blogspot.com). What she discovered about our kids' midday meals is sobering if not surprising: Menu mainstays routinely feature fatty items such as pizza, french fries, hot dogs, and a mystery pork product called "ribicue." She's eaten beef with fake grill marks and lots of sweetened fruit cups.

Mrs. Q. didn't know when she started documenting each meal that she would become a prominent voice on a hot-button issue that has galvanized not only high-profile chefs such as Jamie Oliver and Rachael Ray but also First Lady Michelle Obama. "I'm normally not subversive in any way," Mrs. Q. says of her unexpected though anonymous celebrity status—we promised not to reveal her identity when we interviewed her. "But if you're a parent you may not have a clue about what your kids are really eating. Lunches at my school are like overly packaged TV dinners gone bad."

It doesn't have to be this way. At Galtier Magnet Elementary School, in St. Paul, Minnesota, menus include whole-grain bread and pasta, along with unsweetened applesauce for dessert. There's also a salad bar stocked with greens, carrots, peas, and grape tomatoes. A sauce station offers seasonings—low-fat ranch dressing, soy sauce, Louisiana hot sauce. Many of the kids in St. Paul still eat tacos and macaroni and cheese, but the cafeteria makes lower-fat versions of both. They also get edamame and chicken stew, which add vital nutrients into their diet.

While even detractors acknowledge that the quality of most American school lunches has steadily improved over the past 15 years, everyone from nutritionists and public-health experts to the First Lady—not to mention a growing number of extremely frustrated parents—believes that our children's school lunches are still overprocessed affairs laden with unhealthy preservatives, sodium, sugar, and trans fat. Nutritional quality varies widely from district to district, but according to the USDA a typical school lunch far exceeds the recommended 500 milligrams of sodium; some districts, in fact, serve lunches with more than 1,000 milligrams. The USDA also reports that less than a third of schools stay below the recommended standard for fat content in their meals. "School lunches hardly resemble real food—they serve items such as chicken nuggets, which are highly processed, with additives and preservatives, and list more than 30 ingredients instead of just chicken," says Marion Nestle, PhD, professor of nutrition food studies and public health at New York University. Nuggets are only one example of how schools rely on too many foods that are heavily processed and high in sugar, sodium, and chemicals. The problem isn't simply that kids are eating unhealthy foods for lunch. The cafeteria's offerings also give a seal of approval: "Kids associate school with education; therefore they get the wrong impression that these kinds of foods are healthy," says Dr. Nestle.

Nearly 17 percent of kids between the ages of 2 and 19 are obese.

Don't Just Get Angry...Do Somethink

Be realistic

In an ideal world, schools would serve more organic food, but most experts say that the current economic climate means that we need to set doable goals. Focus on requesting more fresh fruits and veggies, and adding whole-grain bread products.

Say no to Junk

According to the Center for Science in the Public Interest, the notion that schools need to sell junk food to raise revenue is a myth. USDA studies have shown the average school uses revenue from NSLP meals to offset the costs of producing à la carte options

Say yes to Tastings

Kids love events with food. Hold a fruit festival where parent volunteers offer pears, papayas, and more. Or get students invested in what's being studied in class. If they're learning about the Middle East, try a tasting with hummus and tabbouleh.

Go to the Cafeteria

Everyone from lunch reformers to cafeteria managers insists that the best way to be informed is to experience it yourself. Reading weekly menus is no substitute for seeing, smelling, and tasting the food—as well as checking out the ambience.

Get Kids Growing

Plant a school garden, connect with a local farm, or just plant pots of herbs for the classroom windowsill. "When children grow food themselves, they want to eat it," says the founder of the fresh and local food movement in the United States, chef Alice Waters.

Recess Before Lunch

Researchers at Central Washington University, in Ellensburg, found that when recess was scheduled before lunch, students consumed significantly more food and nutrients than when play was after lunch.

And we're not just talking about the stuff on the hot-lunch menu. Provided through the National School Lunch Program (NSLP) to children who qualify for free or reduced-price lunches and breakfasts (and also offered to students who can pay full price), it meets the Dietary Guidelines for Americans. While NSLP meals—eaten by more than 31 million children, over half of all American students—need to be improved, the worst food lurks in what's called à la carte service. That's where any kid can buy anything from cake to pizza or brand-name junk food. These heavily marketed choices are essentially unregulated. (Hard candy and gum are not allowed to be sold but chocolate bars are, for example.) "We offer many choices in the school library but no pornography," says Janet Poppendieck, PhD, author of *Free for All: Fixing School Food in America*. "We should offer an array of meals in school, but nothing unhealthy."

Meals Gone Bad—and Good

That disconnect shocked Lolli Leeson, a wellness educator and parent, when she volunteered in her kids' lunchroom in Marble- head, Massachusetts. After 15 minutes, the students were allowed to throw out their lunch and buy junk food, such as cookies, candy, and chips, from the à la carte menu. "The kids were taught a bit about nutrition in the classroom, but the school was being hypocritical in not modeling it in the lunchroom," she says.

We take it for granted that these are the foods that kids want to eat. But most experts disagree. Sam Kass, Mrs. Obama's food-initiative coordinator, has been spending a lot of time visiting schools and hosting children at the White House garden as part of Mrs. Obama's Let's Move! campaign. "When the First Lady planted and harvested the garden with kids and then cooked a meal with them, those kids ate salad like it was going out of style—like it was french fries—and they ate peas like they were the best thing they had ever tasted," says Kass.

The food kids eat for lunch around the world is evidence that what we think of as kid-friendly is more nurture than nature. In France, menus include beet salad, pumpkin soup, and veal stew. Korean students eat kimchi and stir-fried beef with carrots.

In fact, the successes at Galtier Magnet School, where 80 percent of all the elementary students eat what's prepared at school, and at other districts throughout the country, prove that it is possible to serve meals that are healthy, appeal to kids' taste buds, and offer important lessons about the value of good nutrition—instead of being based on children's whims. "We don't allow kids to not learn about Shakespeare," says chef Ann Cooper, aka "The Renegade Lunch Lady," who overhauled the Berkeley, California, and Boulder, Colorado, school-lunch programs. "Why would we allow kids to decide that they don't want to eat green food?" The urgency over what our kids are eating is due to some scary facts: Children born in the year 2000 have more than a 30 percent chance of developing diabetes during their lifetime, according to a study published in *The Journal of the American Medical Association,* and the Centers for Disease Control and Prevention (CDC) reports that 16.9 percent of children between the ages of 2 and 19 are already obese.

Lunch Lessons

At its core, the National School Lunch Program is a noble institution. Started in 1946 by President Truman to provide lunches to school-age children, the program was founded on the principle that keeping children healthy is vital to America's prosperity. But even that basic mandate has become a complicated issue. Take milk, for example: Chocolate milk, for decades a school-cafeteria staple, has double the sugar content of unflavored milk, and some school districts, including Washington, D.C., have banned it while others are trying to reposition the drink as a dessert and limit when it's offered. (For example, Chicago schools serve it only on Friday.) But flavored milk's defenders can be found among the ranks of parents who fear that their children will miss out on crucial vitamin D and calcium because they won't drink the unsweetened variety. The dairy industry, naturally, is also supportive: "It's important to know that flavored milk provides the same nine essential nutrients as white milk, while contributing only 2 percent of the added sugar in a child's diet. There are more valuable places to look if you're trying to reduce sugar, like sports drinks, sodas, and other empty-calorie beverages," says Ann Marie Krautheim, RD, a spokesperson for the National Dairy Council.

Paying the Tab

It's unfair to place all the blame on the schools, especially in these budget-strapped times where lunch programs are under pressure to break even. As Mrs. Obama told a national meeting of school-nutrition professionals back in the spring: "If you asked the average person to do what you do every day, and that is to prepare a meal for hundreds of hungry kids for just $2.68 a child—with only $1 to $1.25 of that money going to the food itself—they would look at you like you were crazy. That's sad, but that's less than what many folks spend on a cup of coffee in the morning." When districts do want to make changes, even what seem like small tweaks start to add up; switching to 100 percent whole-wheat bread (which contains more protein, fiber, vitamins, and minerals than white bread) costs Seattle Public Schools an extra $20,000 each year.

Both Dr. Nestle and Dr. Poppendieck recommend making school lunches free to all students. Doing so, they argue, will allow schools to put money spent on administering the current tiered system into improving the actual meals. With less pressure to lure paying students into the lunch line, food-service departments could concentrate on healthier foods.

But many of those sweeping changes aren't in the cards yet. In fact, President Obama's plan to reauthorize the Child Nutrition Act has been scaled back to call for only six additional cents per meal. Although the funding increase is not enough to ensure that every American child will eat like the students in St. Paul, experts agree that the attention school lunches are getting in the media and the halls of Washington, D.C., should make it easier for parents to change their communities' school lunches.

What should those changes be? Margo Wootan, the nutrition-policy expert at the Center for Science in the Public Interest (CSPI), along with other advocates, says the first priority should be to increase the amount of fruits and vegetables offered at every meal. They would also like school-nutrition services to set maximum calorie targets rather than minimums—a practice that was started when the goal was to fight malnutrition. Switching to whole grains and low- or non-fat milk, getting rid of products that contain trans fat, and limiting sodium are the other goals rounding out their wish list.

Moms Make a Move

As anyone who has gone up against a school-lunch program knows, change can take years. That's why even if your child is just a toddler, it's not too early to start pushing for better food. When Weston, Connecticut, mom Amy Kalafa realized what was being served in her children's lunchroom, she made *Two Angry Moms,* a documentary

---

Freshly Picked

First Lady Michelle Obama has set an ambitious goal: to end the childhood-obesity epidemic within a generation. To do so she's advocating for better food labeling, encouraging increased physical activity, engineering access to nutritious food for all Americans, and demanding healthy food for our nation's schools. As she told us in June when *Parents* visited the White House, "The school piece remains a critical part [of the campaign], because millions of kids are getting two meals a day at school." The plan: fighting against the conventional wisdom that children won't eat food that's good for them by encouraging everything from school gardens to partnerships between local chefs and lunchroom staff.

about what's wrong with school lunches and how parents can improve them.

Kalafa's film follows the efforts of Susan Rubin, a mom who had been working for more than a decade to improve the lunches in her children's schools in Westchester County, New York. The film takes viewers through Rubin's successful crusade to get items such as neon-green slushies, supersize cookies, and greasy fries off the menu.

The CDC reports that junk food is rampant in the schools.

Since making the film, Kalafa has seen improvements across the country, including chicken served on the bone, hearty soups, and vegetarian options. Change is possible. The CDC reports that while junk food is rampant in schools, the percentage of schools in which children are not permitted to buy it is increasing. But even though the government is advocating for change, parents still need to push for improvements at the district level. "Go into any school that has joined the school-lunch revolution and you will see kids eating unprocessed food, helping themselves from salad bars, and actually eating the meals, all within the typical 20-minute lunch period," says Dr. Nestle. "Teachers in these schools swear that the kids behave and learn better, do not bounce off the walls after lunch, and show fewer signs of learning disorders. Can we teach schools to care about what students eat? Of course we can."

Critical Thinking

1. Check out the website for two or three local schools and print off the lunch menus. Do you see similar food served at these schools? How would the lunches rate if you used the criteria in the article to assess the nutritional value?

2. What can families do to help their children make healthy choices?

From *Parents*, September 2010, pp. 219–222. Copyright © 2010 by Meredith Corporation. Reprinted by permission.

Give Me a Break
The Argument for Recess

Barbie Norvell, Nancy Ratcliff, and Gilbert Hunt

The authors recently had an opportunity to talk with a group of early childhood teachers who shared some of the stress they were experiencing. Over and over, we heard accounts of how the curriculum and daily routines of the students and teachers were being affected by the need for students to reach annual yearly progress (AYP) expectations on standardized tests. These teachers clearly understood that high standards were important, and it was clear that these teachers agreed that all children could and must learn; however, the learning environments in their classrooms seemed to have changed negatively. Nichols and Berliner (2007) have suggested that high-stakes testing does have a negative impact on both teachers and students. These authors discuss a phenomenon called Campbell's Law, which states that the greater the social consequences associated with a quantitative indicator (in this case, standardized test scores and AYP), the more likely it is the indicator will become corrupted and result in the corruption of the process it was intended to monitor (in this case, school improvement and student learning).

One of the changes that has taken place in many schools has been the increase in engaged time on topics that are to be assessed on high-stakes tests (sometimes referred to as time on task). Obviously, common sense dictates that if we want children to learn a skill, they need time to practice that skill. However, as Woolfolk (2008) and others have noted, spending more time engaged on a task does not guarantee an increase in learning. Furthermore, some of what Nichols and Berliner (2007) call "collateral damage" to the curriculum can take place when important activities are removed from the daily routine in order to increase time spent practicing skills or learning information that will be assessed on a high-stakes test.

Educator Joe Frost has long argued that the emphasis on high-stakes testing has had a negative effect on all schooling for young children. Frost, Wortham, and Reifel (2007) discuss the important relationship between children's play and their total development. Many schools have totally dropped free play (e.g., recess breaks), because it was thought that such an activity took up valuable time needed to prepare children for high-stakes tests (Sindelar, 2002). The Association for Childhood Education International (ACEI), the National Association for the Education of Young Children (NAEYC), the National Association

of Early Childhood Specialists in State Departments of Education (NAECS/SDE), and the National Association of Elementary School Principals (NAESP) are a few of the national and international organizations emphasizing the importance of free play through recess breaks. Nevertheless, more and more school districts are electing to eliminate recess breaks, citing safety and behavior issues, along with time on task, as key reasons (Sindelar, 2002; Villaire, 2001).

Despite numerous arguments, no research clearly supports eliminating recess breaks (Jarrett, 2003). NAEYC and other related professional associations have long advocated for more appropriate scheduling, including times for breaks. NAEYC's *Developmentally Appropriate Practice in Early Childhood Programs* (Bredekamp & Copple, 1997) provides teachers of young children with specific guidelines for creating optimal learning environments. Examples of appropriate practices for creating a classroom environment and schedule for 3- to 5-year-olds include the following:

- The environment is designed to support young children's physiological needs for activity and fresh air.
- The daily schedule provides for alternating periods of active and quiet time.
- Teachers plan extended periods of time for children to participate in play projects.
- Opportunities for children to move freely and use large muscles are strategically planned.

Despite numerous arguments, no research clearly supports eliminating recess breaks.

These examples of developmentally appropriate practices clearly can be used to support the inclusion of recess breaks in the daily routine of young children. Additionally, the authors include specific references for teachers of 6- to 8-year-olds. Bredekamp and Copple recommend that teachers of primary-age children plan alternating periods of physical activity and quiet time, although they are not as specific as when making recommendations for 3- to 5-year-old students. Although these guidelines have been widely distributed and well-known for several years, administrators and politicians tend to overlook such research and guidelines.

Research evidence also abounds showing that play is beneficial to cognitive development. Jarrett (2002) explains that recess breaks provide the brain with opportunities to create chemicals crucial for the formation of long-term memory. Pellegrini and Bohn (2005) build on Jarrett's argument by connecting it to Piagetian theory, which suggests that cognitive imbalance (disequilibration) through peer interaction facilitates cognitive development more than interactions between adults and children. Cognitive imbalance, Pellegrini and Bohn argue, is more likely to occur when children are allowed opportunities to exchange ideas with one another in natural contexts, such as they do in a free play, recess break setting.

Research Project

A research project (Norvell, 2006) was carried out in a public school, 1st-grade setting to determine if the students' performance on a literacy task was affected by the timing of when students were given a 15-minute recess, free activity break. Specifically, the children's spelling and writing productivity, story retelling ability, and story comprehension processes were assessed to see if the timing of recess breaks made a difference in the quality and quantity of the children's work. That is, did recess breaks immediately before their literacy lesson (as opposed to immediately after their lesson) have any effect on the students' performance on the given literacy tasks? It is interesting to note that the project had to be completed in only three weeks, because the school district had discontinued recess breaks and would not dedicate more than that time to a non-academic endeavor such as free play (recess breaks) for 1st-grade students.

The project began by randomly assigning 16 children to each of two groups; one group had recess breaks immediately prior to instruction, and one had recess breaks immediately after instruction. The children came from the three 1st-grade classrooms located in a rural school populated with highly diverse students. All 32 students were administered the Peabody Picture Vocabulary Test (PPVT-IIIA) to determine basic language ability. The results of this test were used prior to the investigation in order to ensure that the two groups were equal, and to provide baseline information needed to ensure that all of the material taught and any directions needed to complete the assigned tasks would be understood by the students.

Each of the 14 lessons taught consisted of one folktale read aloud to the students and one open-ended question, which was verbally asked. The students could respond to the question in written form, in pictorial form, or both. Some examples of the questions asked were, "What was your favorite part of the story?"; "What did King Midas learn about loving gold?"; "Why did Rumpelstiltskin want the queen's child?"; and "Why was the little owl considered to be good luck?" After reading the story (each of which lasted about five minutes), the teacher reviewed the events of the story to help students with comprehension. The students then had 10 minutes to respond to the question on a blank sheet of paper.

After all data were collected, writing samples were evaluated for productivity as determined by total word count, conventional word count (i.e., number of correctly spelled words), and total sentence count. A retelling rubric was adapted for use (Moss, 1997) to evaluate students' responses for content, clarity, and structure, with scores ranging from the lowest level (providing poor or irrelevant information) to the highest level (able to sequence the events in correct order and summarize most of the material). The data analysis provided a statistical difference between the two groups. The students who had recess breaks prior to their literacy lesson performed better than their peers who had recess breaks after instruction and assessment took place.

Implications for Young Children

Although this research project does not provide definitive evidence of the positive effects of recess breaks, it does provide evidence of the need for further investigation. Early childhood professionals have a number of ways to use information from this project to design their own investigations. Such investigations would contribute evidence that would help to clarify how recess breaks would be most beneficial to the education process. Numerous questions could be explored in early childhood settings, such as:

- How often should recess breaks occur?
- What is the optimal duration for recess break?
- At what times throughout the school day would recess breaks be most beneficial?
- Which activities provide the maximum benefit during recess break?
- Should recess break activities be free choice only, or should some type of structured games and/or physical exercise be included?
- Do breaks need to be outdoors, or can indoor breaks be just as effective?
- Are breaks more advantageous for boys or girls, or do they benefit equally?
- What types of activities do children choose during recess breaks time?
- How do groups having recess breaks perform on standardized tests compared to those not having recess breaks?
- How do groups having recess breaks compare to those not having recess in regard to attention on task?
- How do groups having recess breaks compare to those not having recess breaks in regard to adjustment to school?

These are some of the questions that need to be answered to convince administrators and politicians that recess breaks do, in fact, have a positive effect on children's ability to achieve at high levels.

One of the first things early childhood teachers can do to support and encourage the inclusion of recess breaks in schools is to become more knowledgeable regarding the research focusing on the importance and effectiveness of recess breaks. The

Internet provides a plethora of resources that can be used to educate oneself on the benefits of recess breaks. For example, a variety of articles, press releases, and position statements from professional associations provide summaries of findings, along with resources for additional reading. Vito Perrone, in his classic *A Letter to Teachers* (1991), explained how important it is for teachers to become students of teaching and learning. Obviously, this implies reading and discussing professional literature, but it goes much further. We are suggesting that teachers should engage in inquiry in their own classrooms to determine what is most beneficial for their children's growth and development. In this case, turn the classroom into a laboratory where one can collect information on the impact that recess breaks have on student performance; this type of inquiry, or action research, can be both informative and engaging.

"Action research" is a term that is widely used today and can take many different forms. Specifically, action research refers to any question investigated by a teacher to determine ideas that will inform and possibly change future practice. The investigation, or research, occurs in the teacher's own classroom and focuses on questions that deal with educational matters (Ferrance, 2000). For example, in a district that requires a 120-minute literacy block with no planned breaks each morning, a 1st-grade teacher noted instances of children behaving in a disruptive manner after an hour of instructional time. The teacher believed the children were acting disruptively because they were not able to deal with the amount of time they were being asked to spend on literacy tasks. The teacher provided a short (5 to 10 minutes) break, when the children sang, participated in creative movement experiences, or engaged in some other type of physical movement activity. The teacher then noted the number of disruptive behaviors that occurred. Fewer instances of disruptive behavior were noted over several weeks; the teacher then had data to take to administrators to support a change in the schedule.

Teachers should join with parents to advocate for recess breaks as a vital part of the school curriculum. Teachers need to educate the parents/families in their schools, sharing the information they have gleaned about the importance of recess breaks and how recess breaks are slowly being sacrificed in an effort to meet state requirements. Approximately "40% of the nation's 16,000 school districts have either modified, deleted, or are considering deleting recess breaks" (cited in NAECS/SDE, 2002, p. 2). Many families have no idea that recess breaks are being greatly reduced or even eliminated from the school day. It is necessary for teachers to become active participants of the parent/teacher associations in their schools. Families should be encouraged to join with the teachers to demand the establishment of school district policies that require recess breaks as part of the curriculum. In an increasing number of school districts across the United States, vocal parents have been quite successful in getting the school board policies they want. Remember, school board officials and elected officials will typically listen to groups of parents.

Early childhood professionals also have an ethical, moral obligation to become strong advocates for the rights of young children to have recess breaks during the school day. Adults take coffee breaks throughout the day; yet, young children, who are most in need of periodic breaks, get few or none. We often hear teachers say, "What can I do?" Alone, you may not be able to do much, but you can be the impetus needed to bring about change in your school or district. Involve the community in efforts to save recess breaks. Invite a reporter from the local newspaper or television station into your classroom to share the action research you are conducting. "The Demise of Recess Breaks: A Trio of Local Moms Fights Back With a Little Book," an article posted on OrlandaSentinel.com (Postal, 2008), demonstrates how the press was used to widely publicize efforts to reinstate recess breaks in Florida schools. The three mothers cited in the article used a self-published and downloadable book in their attempt to bring attention to children's need for recess breaks. Actual photographs of a beautiful, well-furnished, empty playground were used to emphasize the tragic waste of both physical and financial resources. This little book attempts to bring to light two important issues. Not only are children being deprived of the opportunity to use this wonderful playground, but taxpayer dollars used to build the playground are going unused. Early childhood professionals could use similar strategies to share results of the action research being conducted in their own classrooms. Teachers can write a short article explaining the results of the action research projects, post it on the school or district website, and/or submit it to the local newspaper.

Summary

A research project was conducted to determine if 1st-grade students would perform better if they took a recess break before a literacy lesson instead of waiting to go to recess after the lesson. Once the data were collected and analyzed, it was found that students perform better if they have a recess break before their literacy lesson. Early childhood professionals are encouraged to do their own action research in order to convince parents, board members, and elected officials that children, like adults, need to take a reasonable number of breaks during the day. This article argues a point that many early childhood educators have understood since the days of Friedrich Froebel: Children learn better when they are given time to play and talk together.

References

Bredekamp, S., & Copple, C. (1997). *Developmentally appropriate practice.* Washington, DC: National Association for the Education of Young Children.

Ferrance, E. (2000). *Action research.* (Themes in Education Series.) Providence, RI: The Northeast and Islands Regional Educational Laboratory at Brown University.

Frost, J.L., Wortham, S.C., & Reifel, S. (2007). *Play and child development* (3rd ed.). Englewood Cliffs, NJ: Prentice Hall.

Jarrett, O. S. (2003). Recess in the elementary school: What does the research say? *ERIC Digest.* Retrieved June 7, 2008, from www.ericdigest.org/2003-2/recess.html.

Moss, B. (1997). A qualitative assessment of . . . retelling of expository text. *Reading Research and Instruction,* 37, 1–13.

National Association of Early Childhood Specialists in State Departments of Education. (2002). *Recess and the importance of play: A position statement on young children*. Retrieved June 9, 2008, from http://naecs.crc.edu/position/recessplay.html.

Nichols, S. L., & Berliner, D. C. (2007). *Collateral damage: How high-stakes testing corrupts America's schools*. Cambridge, MA: Harvard Education Press.

Norvell, B. N. (2006). *An examination of the effects of recess on first graders' use of written symbol representations*. Unpublished doctoral dissertation, Auburn University, Auburn, Alabama.

Pellegrini, A., & Bohn, C. (2005). The role of recess in children's cognitive performance and school adjustment. *Educational Researcher, 34*(1), 13–19.

Perrone, V. (1991). *A letter to teachers: Reflections on schooling and the art of teaching*. San Francisco: Jossey-Bass.

Postal, L. (2008, April 21). The demise of recess: A trio of local moms fights back with a little book. *Orlando Sentinel. Retrieved* June 7, 2007, *from* http://blogs.orlandosentinel.com/news_education_edblog/2008/04/recess.html#more.

Sindelar, R. (2002). *Recess: Is it needed in the 21st century?* ERIC clearinghouse/http://eruceece.org/faq/recess.html.

Villaire, T. (2001). The decline of physical activity: Why are so many kids out of shape? *Our Children, 26,* 7.

Woolfolk, A. (2008). *Educational psychology: Active learning edition* (10th ed.). Boston: Pearson Allyn & Bacon.

Critical Thinking

1. Your local school board allows five minutes each for citizens' comments at every school board meeting. Write out your comments you will present to the board related to their agenda item to vote on eliminating recess from the elementary school day.

2. Ask three parents of children in elementary school about the recess breaks allowed their children during a typical school day. Are the parents aware of the time their children spend in recess? What role can families play in providing for appropriate recess breaks for their children?

BARBIE NORVELL is Assistant Professor, Early Childhood Education, Spadoni College of Education, **NANCY RATCLIFF** is Assistant Dean and Director of Curriculum & Instruction, Spadoni College of Education, and **GILBERT HUNT** is Singleton Chaired Professor and Research Scholar, School of Teacher Education, Coastal Carolina University, Conway, South Carolina.

5 Hallmarks of Good Homework

Homework shouldn't be about rote learning. The best kind deepens student understanding and builds essential skills.

CATHY VATTEROTT

For tonight's homework, Write the 10 spelling words 3 times each. Write definitions of the 15 science vocabulary words. Do the math problems on page 27, problems 1–20 on dividing fractions.

Check any homework hotline, and you're likely to find similar homework assignments, which look an awful lot like those we remember from school. But do these tasks really reinforce learning? Do they focus on rote learning—or on deeper understandings?

The Fundamental Five

The best homework tasks exhibit five characteristics. First, the task has a clear academic purpose, such as practice, checking for understanding, or applying knowledge or skills. Second, the task efficiently demonstrates student learning. Third, the task promotes ownership by offering choices and being personally relevant. Fourth, the task instills a sense of competence—the student can successfully complete it without help. Last, the task is aesthetically pleasing—it appears enjoyable and interesting (Vatterott, 2009).

Hallmark 1: Purpose

Let's start by examining how purposeful tonight's homework assignments are and whether there are better alternatives.

The purpose of the spelling homework—"Write the 10 spelling words 3 times each"—might be to practice spelling words correctly—a rote memory task. Many teachers believe that writing is a good method, especially if they learned well that way when they were students. But not all students remember by writing. Our goal is to give students methods that are purposeful for *them*, methods that work for *their* learning styles.

The goal is to give students methods that are purposeful for *them*, methods that work for *their* learning style.

A better way might be to allow students to design their own task:

> Create your own method to practice spelling words or choose one of the following: Write or type the words three times, spell them out loud, use Scrabble tiles to spell them, trace them with your finger, or create a puzzle using the words.

The teacher could also make the task more meaningful by having students connect the spellings to a spelling rule (such as "*i* before *e,* except after *c*").

The second assignment is to "Write definitions of the 15 science vocabulary words." Although the words may have been discussed in class, they're probably new; students are often expected to learn new words to prepare for reading or a class discussion.

But does writing definitions really help us learn what words mean? Writing definitions is a low-level rote task—students best learn the meanings of new words by using them in context. A better task might be one of the following:

> Show that you know the meaning of the science vocabulary words by using them in sentences or in a story.

> For each vocabulary word, read the three sentences below it. Choose the sentence that uses the word correctly.

A more thoughtful way to understand and remember what words mean is to assign the vocabulary words as an application task *after* the lesson. For instance, one middle school teacher has students build and launch rockets. After they launch their rockets, the students add the definitions of such words as *force, speed, acceleration,* and *momentum* to their notebooks. At that point, the definitions have meaning and connect to the students' experience (Vatterott, 2007).

The third homework assignment—"Do the math problems on page 27"—is more complicated because we don't know whether the purpose of the assignment is to check for understanding of dividing fractions or to practice dividing fractions.

Let's assume the purpose is to practice dividing fractions. The math teacher demonstrates how to divide fractions and monitors the students while they do practice problems in class. Because students can successfully complete the problems immediately after instruction, the teacher assumes that the students understand the concept. The teacher then assigns 20 problems as practice for homework. However, when some of the students get home, they realize that they did not fully understand how to do the problems—and what the teacher thought was practice turns out to be new learning. The students struggle or, worse, do the 20 problems the wrong way.

Ideally, homework should provide feedback to teachers about student understanding, enabling teachers to adjust instruction and, when necessary, reteach concepts *before* assigning practice. Assigning practice prematurely can cause student frustration and confusion.

Practice is more effective when distributed in small doses over several days or weeks (Marzano, Pickering, & Pollock, 2001). That is, distributed practice is more effective than mass practice. A student may need to practice a math operation 50 times to master it—but not all in one night! Instead of the traditional 20–30 problems each night, a better math assignment is two-tiered—for example, three questions or problems to check for understanding of today's lesson and 10 questions or problems to practice previous learning

> **"Too often we give children answers to remember rather than problems to solve."**
>
> —Roger Lewin

Hallmark 2: Efficiency

Some traditional tasks may be inefficient—either because they show no evidence of learning or because they take an inordinate amount of time to complete but yield little "bang for the buck." Both students and parents tend to view tasks that don't appear to require thinking as busywork.

Projects that require nonacademic skills (such as cutting, gluing, or drawing) are often inefficient. Teachers assign projects like dioramas, models, and poster displays with all the best intentions—they see them as a fun, creative way for students to show what they have learned. But unless a rubric clearly spells out the content requirements, projects may reveal little about students' content knowledge and much more about their artistic talents (Bennett & Kalish, 2006). Even content-rich projects can be inefficient in terms of time spent. Teachers often don't realize how many hours these projects take and how tedious they may be for both student and parent.

There are more efficient ways to accomplish the same goal and better demonstrate student learning. Instead of creating a diorama of life during the Reconstruction after the U.S. Civil War, students could write a diary entry as though they were living in the time, discussing daily life, race relations, and laws that affected them. Instead of building a model of the solar system, students could create a poster to show the planets' temperature extremes, periods of rotation in Earth time, and the importance of inertia and gravity to the motion of the planets. Students could create a video that they post on YouTube or a game to demonstrate their knowledge of the steps in a process, such as how the digestive system works, how a bill becomes a law, or how to solve an algebra problem (Vatterott, 2007).

Hallmark 3: Ownership

As a teacher once said, "I never heard of a student not doing *his* work; it's *our* work he's not doing." When we customize tasks to fit student learning styles and interests, the task becomes theirs, not ours. The goal of ownership is to create a personal relationship between the student and the content (Vatterott, 2009).

One of the easiest ways to promote ownership is through individual research. For instance, if the class is studying the history of Europe, students could write a report about the country of their choice. They could choose a topic they want to learn more about. Even though for all reports students would use the same rubric—which would focus on facts about government, economy, culture, or geography—students could write a traditional research paper, create a PowerPoint presentation, or design a travel brochure.

Instead of having students write out multiplication tables, a more meaningful assignment would ask, "What is the best way for you to practice your multiplication tables?" Some students may learn better by reciting them, creating a table, or setting them to music. Thinking about how they learn best makes the learning more relevant.

When students practice reading (and grow to enjoy reading for pleasure), choice of what, when, and how much to read is especially important. Typical assignments dictate what, as well as how much: "Twenty minutes each night, two chapters from the novel each night, or 30 pages from your textbook each night." Forcing students into those requirements may have the adverse effect of students actually reading less than they would if they were not "on the clock" (Kohn, 2006).

When teachers tell students how much to read, students often just read to an assigned page number and stop. A California mother wrote,

> Our children are now expected to read 20 minutes a night and record such on their homework sheet. What parents are discovering (surprise) is that those kids who used to sit down and read for pleasure . . . are now setting the timer, choosing the easiest books, and stopping when the timer dings. . . . Reading has become a chore, like brushing your teeth. (Kohn, 2006, pp. 176–177)

Then comes the tedious task of judging whether the students met the requirement. The reading log is the typical proof: "Each night, write down the author, title, and number of pages you read, how much time you spent reading, and the date. Have your parent sign the log each night." Whew! Not only are reading logs time-consuming, but also focusing on documenting takes a lot of the joy out of reading (Bennett & Kalish, 2006).

This might be a better approach:

Try to read an average of 30 minutes each night. Once a week, estimate how much time you've spent reading. Write a short paragraph about what you've been reading.

If we want to promote ownership and encourage students to enjoy reading, we must go beyond the assigned reading list. One student who usually enjoyed reading lamented, "I just want to read something that *I want* to read!" We should broaden what "counts" as reading to include such nontraditional sources as blogs, websites, and magazines. Instead of worrying about whether students did the reading, we should be focusing on whether the reading did them any good.

Hallmark 4: Competence

If all students are to feel competent in completing homework, we must abandon a one-size-fits-all approach. Homework that students can't do without help is *not* good homework; students are discouraged when they are unable to complete homework on their own (Darling-Hammond & Hill-Lynch, 2006; Stiggins, 2007). To ensure homework is doable, teachers must differentiate assignments so they are at the appropriate level of difficulty for individual students (Tomlinson, 2008).

Struggling students may require fewer questions, less complex problems with fewer steps, or less reading. Some students may be given abbreviated reading assignments, adapted reading packets, or simplified directions. One of the simplest ways to help struggling students is to require less writing, with fewer blanks to fill in, or answers that the student can circle instead of writing out. Although some students may *create* a graphic organizer, others may be *given* a graphic organizer. Teachers might give some students word banks, copies of their notes, or hint sheets. English language learners may benefit from assignments containing pictures that give clues to meaning in assignments with difficult vocabulary and may find it easier to complete work in their native language first.

The *amount* of work is a huge obstacle to feelings of competence for some students. A task that takes the average student 15 minutes to complete could take another student an hour. It doesn't make sense for slower students to have to spend more time on homework than other students do—instead, teachers should simply give them less work (Goldberg, 2007).

A simple means of differentiating is to make homework *time-based* instead of *task-based*. Instead of assigning all students 20 questions to answer, assign all students to complete what they can in a specified amount of time: "Answer as many questions as you can in 30 minutes; work longer if you like." In one 5th grade classroom, the rule is "50 minutes is 50 minutes." Students are not expected to work more than 50 minutes each night. If students have homework in math, science, and reading and they spend 50 minutes on science and math, parents simply write a note saying, "Rhonda spent her 50 minutes on science and math and had no time for reading tonight" (Vatterott,

2009). Teachers who are uncomfortable with this method might want to prioritize subjects ("Do the reading first, then math, then science") or ask students to spend a little time on each subject ("Spend at least 10 minutes on each subject. You do not need to work more than 50 minutes total"). A better solution may be to limit homework to one or two subjects each night.

A simple means of differentiating is to make homework time-based instead of task-based.

Teachers must also take care to adequately explain assignments—preferably in writing—and structure them so students know how to complete them (Darling-Hammond & Hill-Lynch, 2006). "Read Chapter 4" is an inadequate direction at any grade level. Reading to acquire information or think critically about the content requires a scaffolded task. Teachers may rely on worksheets, but when students can simply fill in the blanks, they aren't necessarily demonstrating understanding of the content. A more meaningful scaffold would focus on broader concepts and would include graphic organizers, big-picture questions, or reflective tasks, such as the following:

List the four most important ideas in Chapter 4.

Keep a journal. After each chapter section, write a reaction to what you read.

During your reading, place sticky notes on the parts you have questions about.

During your reading, place sticky notes on the parts you found most interesting to discuss in class.

When we want students to focus on the main ideas of a novel or short story, high-interest and high-emotion questions such as these work well:

Which characters best typify the following virtues: honor, integrity, strength? What did they do that shows that virtue?

Which characters best typify the following vices: greed, jealousy, arrogance? What did they do that shows that vice?

With which character do you most identify and why?

How does the story relate to life today? (Vatterott, 2007)

Teachers need to adequately structure complex tasks. For example, if the assignment is for 4th graders to research and write a report about a time period or an important person, do all 4th graders know how to do research? Students not only need a rubric that details what they must include in the report, but they also need instructions on how to find resources, steps to follow in organizing the process, and suggested websites. Long-term projects require monitoring, with intermittent due dates for outlines and rough drafts.

If the homework assignment is to "Study for the test," does that mean memorize facts, review concepts, or learn new material not covered in class? And how do students know what it means? Although a study guide or take-home test that shows students exactly what they need to know is helpful, they don't necessarily have to write or complete anything to study. Teachers should encourage students to create their own best method of reviewing the information, suggesting possible options, such as organizing notes into an outline, writing test questions for themselves, putting important information on note cards, or studying with a partner.

Hallmark 5: Aesthetic Appeal

Every day, students make decisions about whether to do a homework assignment on the basis of their first impressions. The way homework *looks* is important. Five-page worksheets or endless lists of definitions or math problems look boring and tedious. As a gourmet cook would say, "Presentation is everything." Wise teachers have learned that students at all levels are more motivated to complete assignments that are visually uncluttered. Less information on the page, plenty of room to write answers, and the use of graphics or clip art make tasks look inviting and interesting (Vatterott, 2009).

In an effort to create appealing tasks, teachers sometimes compromise learning. A word search may look like fun, but it has little value in reinforcing spelling and can be a torturous task. A better task would be for students to create their own pattern of content-related words, as in Scrabble. Likewise, crossword puzzles are fun, but students may benefit little from matching definitions with words when the focus is on solving the puzzle. A better task would be for the students to find connections between the concepts that the words represent. For example, students might group words as "feeling words" or "action words," as nouns or verbs, or as words with one or two syllables.

Free to Learn

Meaningful homework should be purposeful, efficient, personalized, doable, and inviting. Most important, students must be able to freely communicate with teachers when they struggle with homework, knowing they can admit that they don't understand a task—and can do so without penalty.

References

Bennett, S., & Kalish, N. (2006). *The case against homework: How homework is hurting our children and what we can do about it.* New York: Crown.

Darling-Hammond, L., & Ifill-Lynch, O. (2006). If they'd only do their work! *Educational Leadership, 63(5),* 8–13.

Goldberg, K. (2007, April). *The homework trap.* Paper presented at the annual meeting of the American Educational Research Association, Chicago.

Kohn, A. (2006). *The homework myth: Why our kids get too much of a bad thing.* Cambridge, MA: Da Capo Press.

Marzano, R. J., Pickering, D. J., & Pollock, J. E. (2001). *Classroom instruction that works: Research-based strategies for increasing student achievement.* Alexandria, VA: ASCD.

Stiggins, R. (2007). Assessment through the student's eyes. *Educational Leadership, 64(8),* 22–26.

Tomlinson, C. A. (2008). The goals of differentiation. *Educational Leadership, 66(3),* 26–31.

Vatterott, C. (2007). *Becoming a middle level teacher: Student focused teaching of early adolescents.* New York: McGraw-Hill.

Vatterott, C. (2009). *Rethinking homework: Best practices that support diverse needs.* Alexandria, VA: ASCD.

Critical Thinking

1. List and describe the five essential characteristics of effective homework activities.

2. Discuss the following quote from the article; "The goal is to give students methods that are purposeful for them, methods that work for their learning style." Why is this important for the learning experiences the students will encounter as they continue their education?

CATHY VATTEROTT is an associate professor of education at the University of Missouri-St. Louis. She is the author of *Rethinking Homework: Best Practices That Support Diverse Needs* (ASCD, 2009); vatterott@umsl.edu.

UNIT 6
Curricular Issues

Unit Selections

Learning Outcomes

After reading this Unit, you will be able to:

• Identify the key components of various curriculum models teachers might consider using in their classroom.

• Develop a rationale for the benefits of extended experiences in the out-of-doors.

• Describe how engaging in constructive play can benefit children's learning.

• Plan to incorporate appropriate calendar activities into large-group time.

• Explain the importance of physical education and the link between physical fitness and academic performance.

Student Website
www.mhhe.com/cls

Internet References

Action for Healthy Kids
www.actionforhealthykids.org
Awesome Library for Teachers
www.awesomelibrary.org/teacher.html
The Educators' Network
www.theeducatorsnetwork.com
Free Resources for Educational Excellence
http://free.ed.gov/
Grade Level Reading Lists
www.gradelevelreadinglists.org
Idea Box
www.theideabox.com
International Reading Association
www.reading.org

Kid Fit
www.kid-fit.com
The Perpetual Preschool
www.perpetualpreschool.com
Phi Delta Kappa
www.pdkintl.org
Teacher Quick Source
www.teacherquicksource.com
Teachers Helping Teachers
www.pacificnet.net/~mandel
Technology Help
www.apples4theteacher.com

Increasingly, preschool teachers are becoming aware of the tremendous responsibility to plan learning experiences that are aligned with state and national standards to allow children to develop a lifelong love of learning along with the necessary skills they will need to be successful. There are typically two camps into which teachers fall as they begin to plan for the young children in their classroom. First are those who use a generic curriculum model that may be used at thousands of preschool programs across the country and is regimented down to the day and time of day for presentation to the children. Second, are those teachers who choose to develop curriculum based on standards and input from the children, to develop an emergent child-centered curriculum that does not follow a set approach. Both approaches can lead to outstanding learning experiences for young children and the selection of the appropriate approach depends on teachers being confident in their beliefs of how young children best learn. "Preschool Curricula: Finding One That Fits" by Vivian Baxter and Karen Petty describes some of the more popular preschool curriculum models available for teachers.

"Constructive Play: A Value-Added Strategy for Meeting Early Learning Standards" helps teachers address early learning standards by providing constructive play experiences. Standards help guide teachers as they plan appropriate activities that will allow their students to gain the necessary skills to continue to learn as they move through school. It is the responsibility of any teacher of young children to be very familiar with standards. If you are unaware of where to start, try your state Department of Education, many of which have standards for programs serving preschool children. Become familiar with the standards and incorporate them into your planning.

There is a major difference between eating frozen dinners every night vs. meals that have been prepared using the freshest local ingredients. The same holds true for planning curriculum. The "generic one-curriculum-package for all classrooms" approach allows for little, if any, local flavor. Curriculum that is jointly developed by the teachers and children brings the best of the children's interest coupled with what is happening in their world for meaningful, authentic learning. Teachers who carefully observe and listen to their children and know the events of their local community will find plenty of possibilities for topics of investigation. Young children are most interested in authentic curriculum that is meaningful to their lives. We wouldn't want to eat frozen dinners every night for the rest of our lives; neither would we want to teach from a prepackaged curriculum that does not meet the needs of our students at all. Get out there and choose some local flavor and spice up the teaching and learning experience in your classroom. One of the most successful investigative projects I have observed was developed by a teacher who involved her class of kindergarteners in the design and building of her house. Her husband, a general contractor, was overseeing the construction, and the teacher involved the children in many classroom activities that made use of the materials used in the construction of the house. Measuring standards were addressed by using construction materials such as wood scraps, fine motor experiences were available

using parts of pipes and wires left over and sequencing concepts were acquired through a series of pictures of the actual house construction. The children were excited to participate in the house building process, and videos, narratives of the process, and two trips to the site added to their involvement and engagement in the project.

This unit includes a focus on the importance of getting children outside to play. Clare Lowell wrote "Beyond *The Lorax?*: The Greening of the American Curriculum" as another way of reaching educators and parents about the importance of getting children out of doors. Richard Louv's popular book, *Last Child in the Woods: Saving our Children from Nature-Deficit Disorder* first explored the concept of children growing up nature deficit and not familiar with the great outdoors. Children today spend hours inside playing video games when their parents spent hours outside playing games and riding bikes. Resist the pressure to keep children inside on beautiful weather days and take them outside for learning experiences not available in the classroom. I recently stopped by a preschool program that had relocated to another building, and the staff was lamenting the fact that the air conditioning in the gymnasium was not working. It was an absolutely beautiful day with a perfect breeze blowing, and the teachers had the children running around inside the hot gymnasium. The situation provided an opportunity for teacher reflection on the use of outside space.

In "Calendar Time for Young Children: Good Intentions Gone Awry," the traditional calendar time, where children sit for long periods of time as phrases, dates, or songs that are often meaningless to young children are repeated, is in desperate need of updating. Learning experiences should be meaningful and applicable to the lives of children. Children simply parroting back to the teacher the full date including day of the week, month, date, and year has little application to young children. They instead could benefit from tracking the weather, counting the number of days until important events, or using vocabulary that will be relevant to their daily lives.

This unit ends with a passionate argument against the elimination of physical education; which is happening all over the country. "Why We Should Not Cut P.E." provides data to support keeping physical education and describes the many lifelong benefits children gain from participating in physical education experiences. These are different from recess, which children also need, but organized physical education time, taught by a certified physical educator, allows children to strength and use all of the muscles in their body. A first step for all teachers is to call it physical education, not gym. Physical education takes place in a gymnasium or gym, but when we refer to education centered on physical education of the total body as gym we cheapen it and make it less important.

A number of the articles in Unit 6 provide opportunities for the reader to reflect on the authentic learning experiences, available for children. How can they investigate, explore, and create while studying a particular area of interest? Make children work for their learning or as noted early childhood author Lilian Katz says, "Engage their minds." As a teacher of young children, acquaint yourself with the importance of firsthand experiences. Teachers often confuse firsthand and hands-on experiences but they are very different. Firsthand experiences are those where the children have a personal encounter with an event, place, or activity. Firsthand experiences include having the local fire department stop by with their truck for a visit to your school, looking for life at the end of a small pond, or touring a local business. After children have these firsthand experiences, they are then able to incorporate them into their play, investigating and exploring in the classroom. Hands-on experiences allow the children to actually use their hands and body to manipulate materials as they learn about the activity such as making a batch of play-dough, building a garage with the blocks, or investigating bubbles in the water table.

This unit is full of articles addressing different curriculum areas. Active child involvement leads to enhanced learning. Suggestions for project-based activities in literacy, movement, and technology are also included. Again, the theme runs deep. Hands on = Minds on!

Professional organizations, researchers and educators are reaching out to teachers of young children with a clear message that what they do in classrooms with young children is extremely important for children's future development and learning capabilities. Of course, the early childhood community will continue to support a hands-on experiential learning environment, but teachers must be clear in their objectives and have standards that will lead to future school success firmly in mind. Only when we are able to effectively communicate to others the importance of what we do and receive proper recognition and support for our work, will the education of young children be held in high regard. We are working toward that goal, but need adults who care for and educate young children to view their job as building a strong foundation for children's future learning. Think of early childhood education as the extremely strong and stable foundation for a building that is expected to provide many decades of active service to thousands of people. If we view our profession in that light, we can see the importance of our jobs. Bring passion and energy to what you do with young children and their families and you will be rewarded ten times over. Enjoy your work, for it is so important.

Preschool Curricula: Finding One That Fits

VIVIAN BAXTER AND KAREN PETTY

What are your beliefs about how children should be educated? Do you think play is important? Is play more important than academics? Do you believe children should be allowed to explore and construct on their own with little instruction, or do you believe that they should be "taught" everything?

Knowing your values and beliefs about education can make you a more effective and efficient teacher.

Knowing your values and beliefs about education can make you a more effective and efficient teacher. It can also help you explain your program to parents.

With information, you will be able to find a curriculum that fits your values and beliefs.

This article offers a brief look at different preschool curriculum models. Within each model, there will be an overview and an explanation of the child's role and the teacher's role. With information, you will be able to find a curriculum that fits your values and beliefs.

Direct Instruction

Overview. The direct instruction model is academically based and teacher-centered. It is a highly structured instructional approach, designed to help at-risk students accelerate their learning (American Federation of Teachers 1998).

The main feature of the DI approach is the classroom scripts: The teacher presents activities, and the children respond to them. Classroom activities are continuous academic lessons that elicit positive reinforcements with correct responses (Schweinhart and Weikart 1998). The wording is designed to ensure consistency across the lessons and to guarantee that all students will comprehend the information presented (Association for Direct Instruction 2007).

The preschool design is to provide intensive academic instruction in reading, language, and math for at-risk students. The DI model is based on the premises that teachers can increase the amount of children's learning in the classroom by carefully planning the details of the student's interaction with their environment, and that the rate and the quality of children's learning is a function of environmental events (Jensen 2005).

Child's role. The child in a DI classroom is a recipient of learning instead of a participant in learning. Children are expected to meet the demands of the workload and work at a fast pace. Correct verbal responses are required, proper replies are expected, and children are questioned until appropriate answers are given. Children are grouped by ability as a means of allowing teachers to maintain the pace and the progress of the scripted material (Jensen 2005).

Teacher's role. The teacher is an authoritative figure, meaning that it is the teacher who plans and carries out the activities. It is the teacher who is responsible for determining what is being learned each day. The teacher works at a fast pace, giving lessons on various levels of difficulty at different times of the day. To motivate children and to keep them motivated, the teacher uses a system of rewards and praise (Jensen 2005).

Developmental-Interaction/ Bank Street

Overview. This is a child-centered approach focused on individual development. It stresses the importance of the whole child, and it recognizes the importance of both the cognitive and social parts of development.

The educational emphasis is the child's developmental progress toward competence (being capable in thought and action/movement), individuality (letting the child be unique and accepting that uniqueness), socialization (helping children learn to control their impulses and govern their own actions), and integration (helping children merge personal and impersonal experiences) (Goffin and Wilson 2001).

Developmental-interaction schools empower children to deal effectively with their environments. The school is an active community, connected to the community around it, so it is not just an isolated place for learning (Roopnarine and Johnson 2005).

This model uses a play-based approach to early childhood education with goals of nurturing the ego development and overall mental health of the child (Frost et al. 2008).

Child's role. The child is a curious being actively engaged in the social and physical environment through sensorial exploration and experimentation (Jensen 2005; Roopnarine and Johnson 2005).

Teacher's role. The teacher is an observer (to watch the children and observe their progress), questioner (to ask questions to help children develop language skills), and planner (to plan opportunities for experiences that meet the needs of every child as an individual). The teacher facilitates and guides the children through activities that are initiated by the child and promotes play as a source of learning (Jensen 2005).

High/Scope

Overview. The High/Scope curriculum is play-based (Frost et al. 2008) and views children as active learners who create their own knowledge of the world (Samuelsson et al. 2006; High/Scope Educational Research Foundation 2007). Active learning means that the children have direct hands-on experiences with people, objects, events, and ideas, and they construct their own knowledge with these experiences (Epstein 2007).

Children take the first steps in the learning process by making choices and following through on their plans. After the children have made their plans, they experiment with their ideas. Teachers support the children in their endeavors by asking questions, providing the background support, guiding the planning process, and commenting on the children's progress (Frost et al. 2008; Samuelsson et al. 2006; Schweinhart and Weikart 1998; Walsh and Petty 2006). After the children have had time to experiment with their plans and ideas, they share and discuss their findings with their teachers and peers (Samuelsson et al. 2006).

Child's role. The child in a High/Scope classroom is an active learner, experimenter, and explorer. Children develop a sense of self as they interact with significant people in their environment.

Teacher's role. The teacher follows the children and their interests and does not impose ideas and beliefs on them. The teacher shares control with the child by following the child's lead in activities and play and by interacting on the child's level of understanding, and encouraging the child to achieve success (Jensen 2005). In this way, teachers are also active learners because they do not have a precise script. Instead, they listen closely to the child and then actively work with the child to extend activities to more challenging levels (Roopnarine and Johnson 2005).

Montessori

Overview. The Montessori method is a developmental, child-centered, hands-on approach to education. Although play was not central to Maria Montessori's view of education and development, some aspects of the curriculum are related to play. Children are allowed to choose materials and "play" with them. As children grow and develop, they no longer "play" with materials but instead prepare for lessons that refine the senses and create order (Frost et al. 2008).

In a Montessori classroom, children have the freedom to explore and construct knowledge by their participation in learning and by making their own choices and experiences. Montessori believed children have the power to teach themselves and the ability to develop freely if their minds are not oppressed by adults who may limit them (Tzuo 2007).

The classroom or environment contains a few essential materials to promote self-discovery and social development. Children learn to respect the work of others as they wait to use materials their peers are using (Walsh and Petty 2006).

Montessori classrooms are filled with children of mixed ages on the belief that children of different ages help one another. The younger

children see what the older ones are working on and ask for explanations. Montessori believed that there are many things that the teacher cannot "convey to a child of three, but that a child of five can do with the utmost ease" (1995, 226). She also felt that "a child of three will take an interest in what a five-year-old is doing, since it is not far removed from their own powers," therefore making the older children heroes and teachers and the younger children their admirers (1995, 226).

Child's role. The children in a Montessori classroom are active learners who construct their own knowledge and understanding of the world and have the ability to control their focus and actions. Children are given freedom within a carefully prepared environment and have the opportunity for active involvement to develop according to their own developmental timetables and tendencies.

Teacher's role. The teacher or *directress* facilitates as opposed to teaching directly. The main responsibility of the directress is to prepare the environment to meet the needs of the children and to be an observer of the children's development (Jensen 2005). Teachers refrain from interfering with children while they are absorbed in their work and do not prevent the children's free expansion. The directress does, however, intervene in the negative behaviors of children and guides them toward the right track (Tzuo 2007).

Waldorf

Overview. The Waldorf education model seeks to educate the whole child: the head, heart, and hands (Chauncey 2006; Walsh and Petty 2006). This means that young children are working to develop their physical bodies and their will through activities that are hands-on instead of academic (Roopnarine and Johnson 2005).

The Waldorf model supports children in an aesthetic environment where creative play and artistic activities are frequent. This allows the children to learn about their world through movement (Walsh and Petty 2006).

A Waldorf classroom is designed to be an extension of the home (Roopnarine and Johnson 2005) on the belief that children relate what they learn to their own experiences and therefore are then deeply engaged and can readily integrate what they learn (Chauncey 2006).

This model is also concerned with the moral education of children, emphasizing that improving a child's sense of morality is of high importance as part of a child's well-being and development of educational abilities (Woodward 2005).

Waldorf classrooms are of mixed ages to promote a family-like atmosphere so that children become much like siblings. The younger children watch and imitate the older children, and the older children look out for and nurture the younger children (Roopnarine and Johnson 2005).

Child's role. The child learns through imaginary play, oral language, and hands-on experiences (Edwards 2002).

Teacher's role. The teacher provides language and literacy-rich experiences through stories, songs, and poems (Roopnarine and Johnson 2005).

Reggio Emilia

Overview. Reggio Emilia is a play-based approach centered on the child, the family, and the community. Families are made to feel welcome, and in return parents get an environment that supports their children's relational, aesthetic, and intellectual needs (New 2007).

Overview of Preschool Curriculum Models

Name	Teacher-Centered vs. Child-Centered	Approach	Child Groupings	Child's Role	Teacher's Role
Direct Instruction	teacher	provides intensive instruction in reading, language, and math, often for at-risk students	by ability	receives the learning	determines and presents the learning activities
Developmental Interaction/ Bank Street	child	focuses on the whole child as an individual with emphasis on intellectual and social-emotional skills	by age	actively engages in the social and physical environment	observes and guides children through learning
High/Scope	child	provides hands-on experiences to allow children to construct knowledge on their own	by age	actively experiments and explores	follows the children's lead and actively works to extend learning
Montessori	child	provides a carefully prepared environment in which children become actively involved and learn according to their own timetables	mixed ages	participates in learning by making choices and respecting others	prepares the environment to meet children's needs and facilitates learning
Waldorf	child	seeks to educate the whole child through a balance of head, heart, and hands in a family-like environment	mixed ages	learns through imaginary play and oral language	provides literacy-rich experiences
Reggio Emilia	child and family	provides play experiences and collaborative projects focusing on relationships with others	mixed ages	follows natural curiosity and engages in creative expression	learns alongside children and collaborates with other teachers to nurture and guide learning

Based on "Preschool curricula: Finding one that fits" by Vivian Baxter and Karen Petty, *Texas Child Care*, Fall 2008.

In Reggio, play is considered essential and one of the "hundred languages." What or how the children play is not the main focus, rather it is the relationships that occur within the play experiences that are given greater attention. Teachers listen closely to children's conversation and work with them as equals in the development of learning activities and projects in the classroom (Fraser 2007). Reggio classrooms are designed to promote all areas of development, not just play.

Children spend much of their time in small or large groups collaborating on projects and play activities (Frost et al. 2008). Projects are at the center of the Reggio curriculum, but the teacher does not plan them in advance. Instead, the projects and the teacher follow the direction of the children's understanding and knowledge—giving rise to an "emergent curriculum." This approach also places a heavy emphasis on art as a means for children to express themselves (Judd 2007).

Child's role. The child's role or image in the Reggio classroom is that of being resourceful, curious, imaginative, and inventive (Gilman 2007). In the Reggio classroom, children are viewed as citizens of the community with the right to be taken seriously, respected for their intelligence and feelings, and valued for their lives (Goffin and Wilson 2001).

Teacher's role. The teacher is a nurturer, guide, and facilitator. Teachers work as a team to provide materials for open-ended discovery and problem solving and listen to and observe the children. By these methods, teachers are able to uncover children's thoughts, theories, and curiosities (Gilman 2007). Teachers encourage the children to explore and extend their own ideas and theories but do not give immediate answers (Judd 2007).

Mixed Methods

Many preschools have developed their own curriculum based on trial and error over time. These preschools have pulled ideas from various methods and theorists such as Montessori, Piaget, Vygotsky, and Gesell. Their idea is to reach the whole child. They reason that it is necessary to pull from different theorists because using just one theory may reach only part of the child. These approaches can be based on play or academics or they can be mixture of both.

Many religion-sponsored schools use a faith-based curriculum that emphasizes religious principles and may be combined with one or more of the approaches above.

Know Yourself

As a preschool educator, it is important to know how you want to teach. Do you want to guide education as you follow the child, or do you want to be in the front of the room "teaching" what the children are to learn? Whatever your beliefs, it is important to know them so you can find a school with the same educational beliefs. Knowing what kind of teacher you want to be and which curriculum fits you can help you to be the most effective and efficient teacher you can be.

References

American Federation of Teachers. 1998. Direct instruction. In *Six Promising School Wide Reform Programs.* www.aft.org/pubs-reports/downloads/teachers/six.pdf.

Association for Direct Instruction. 2007. General FAQ's. http://adihome.org/index.php?option=com_content&task=view&id=12&Itemid=31.

Chauncey, B. 2006. The Waldorf model and public school reform. *ENCOUNTER: Education for Meaning and Social Justice* 19(3): 39–44.

Edwards, C. P. 2002. Three approaches from Europe: Waldorf, Montessori, and Reggio Emilia. *Early Childhood Research and Practice* 4 (1), http://ecrp.uiuc.edu/v4n1/edwards.html.

Epstein, A. S. 2007. All about High/Scope FAQ's. *High/Scope Educational Research Foundation.* www.highscope.org/Content.asp?ContentId=291.

Fraser, S. 2007. Play in other languages. *Theory into Practice* 46(1): 14–22.

Frost, Joe L., Sue C. Wortham, and Stuart Reifel. 2008. *Play and Child Development* (3rd ed.). Upper Saddle River, NJ: Pearson.

Gilman, S. 2007. Including the child with special needs: Learning from Reggio Emilia. *Theory into Practice* 46(1): 23–31.

Goffin, Stacie G. and Catherine G. Wilson. 2001. *Curriculum Models and Early Childhood Education* (2nd ed.). Upper Saddle River, NJ: Merrill Prentice Hall.

High/Scope Educational Research Foundation. 2007. *Active Learning.* www.highscope.org/Content.asp?ContentId=217.

Jensen, M. K. 2005. Development of the early childhood curricular beliefs inventory: An instrument to identify preservice teachers' early childhood curricular orientation. PhD dissertation, Florida State University. *Dissertation Abstracts International,* publ. nr. AAT 3156224, DAI-A 65/12 (Jun 2005): 4458.

Judd, J. 2007. The conversation: Reggio Emilia preschools. *The Times Educational Supplement* 4764: 24.

Montessori, Maria. 1995. *The Absorbent Mind.* New York: Henry Holt and Company.

New, R. S. 2007. Reggio Emilia as cultural activity theory into practice. *Theory into Practice* 46(1): 5–13.

Roopnarine, Jaipaul L., and James E. Johnson. 2005. *Approaches to Early Childhood Education* (4th ed). Upper Saddle River, NJ: Merrill Prentice Hall.

Samuelsson, I. P., S. Sheridan, and P. Williams. 2006. Five preschool curricula—Comparative perspective. *International Journal of Early Childhood* 38(1): 11–30.

Schweinhart, L. J., and D. P. Weikart. 1998. Why curriculum matters in early childhood education. *Education Leadership* 55(6): 57–60.

Tzuo, P. W. 2007. The tension between teacher control and children's freedom in a child-centered classroom: Resolving the practical dilemma through a closer look at related theories. *Early Childhood Education Journal* 33(1): 33–39.

Walsh, B. A., and K. Petty. 2006. Frequency of six early childhood education approaches: A 10-year content analysis of early childhood education journal. *Early Childhood Education Journal.* 34(5): 301–305.

Woodward, J. 2005. Head, heart and hands: Waldorf education. *Journal of Curriculum and Pedagogy* 2(2): 84–85.

Critical Thinking

1. Many teachers use an eclectic teaching model; one that incorporates components from a variety of different curriculum models. Using the seven different approaches described in the article, choose the key components from each one that you would consider adopting to form the basis of your curriculum. Why did you choose those specific components?

2. Why is it important for teachers to know how their values and beliefs affect the education they provide for young children?

VIVIAN BAXTER is a doctoral student in child development at Texas Woman's University in Denton. She has a master's degree emphasizing Montessori education and has been working in Montessori education since 2003. KAREN PETTY is an associate professor in the Department of Family Sciences at Texas Woman's University. Her interests lie in furthering the professional development of doctoral students, especially in the area of publications in peer-reviewed journals.

From *Texas Child Care Quarterly*, Fall 2008, pp. 34–39. Copyright © 2008 by Texas Child Care Quarterly. Reprinted by permission.

Beyond *The Lorax?*

The Greening of the American Curriculum

Getting children outside to play and stay in touch with nature is important for their health and for developing environmental awareness.

CLARE LOWELL

There is a classic *Peanuts* cartoon that features little yellow-haired Sally, ensconced in a bean-bag chair, watching TV, telling big brother Charlie Brown that he should check out the enthralling program she's watching on the tube. "You should watch this," she urges. "They're showing pictures of huge snowflakes falling gently on this beautiful snow covered meadow . . ."

Charlie Brown looks at the TV and tells her, "You can see the same thing right now if you go outside," pointing out the window. The final frame shows Sally—clearly appalled and momentarily distracted from her TV viewing—exclaiming in horror, "OUTSIDE?!"

It might be funnier if it weren't so scarily true: Our children are growing up without nature—clearly preferring their electronic diversions to the real thing.

What Sally didn't know at the time is that, not only is there a name for her affliction, it's a syndrome that is virtually dominating the younger generation. "Videophilia," defined as the new human tendency to focus on sedentary activities involving electronic media,[1] has virtually supplanted the need for "biophilia," or the urge to affiliate with other forms of life. This particular theory is bolstered by research that supports the positive reaction of people to natural landscapes. The quality of this exposure affects human health and child development at an almost cellular level.[2]

As recently as a generation ago, playtime usually meant outdoor play and activity that put children in touch with nature and encouraged direct involvement with their physical environment. Now chat rooms, video games, and indoor playdates occupy much of their playtime. Playrooms as opposed to playgrounds; virtual nature as opposed to the real thing.

Caring about Nature

It's not too much of a stretch to say that, if children don't care about nature today, they won't care about conserving it tomorrow when they're adults. And, if one doesn't care about something, there will be no investment in protecting it. In addition, with most of the populace living in urban areas, people will be even more disconnected from the natural world. Considering the looming environmental issues that await this generation (climate change, population/human consumption, carbon footprints, etc.), this creates a downright depressing, if not apocalyptic, view of the future.

It's not too much of a stretch to say that, if children don't care about nature today, they won't care about conserving it tomorrow when they're adults.

Richard Louv's recent bestseller, *Last Child in the Woods: Saving Our Children from Nature-Deficit Disorder,* discusses the "criminalization of natural play," in which communities, more concerned with property values and lawsuits, have outlawed unstructured outdoor nature play.[3] From public government to community associations, rules govern and restrict children in everything from building tree houses to erecting basketball hoops. When climbing a tree on public land can be actionable as an illegal activity designed to "injure" the landscape, children move indoors to recreate, electronically, what they are missing in real life. As recently as this past summer, teenagers who turned public land in Greenwich, Connecticut, into a Wiffle® ball field were threatened with litigation and unending complaints by locals who wanted them out. In the words of one Wiffle®-ball athlete, "People think we should be home playing 'Grand Theft Auto'."[4]

Whether this can be attributed to a shrinkage of open space (thereby encouraging overuse of the accessible natural areas) or the overstructuring of childhood, a generation of American children is being raised indoors. From 1977 to 2003, the proportion of 9- to 12-year-olds who engage in outside activities such as hiking, walking, fishing, beach play, and gardening has declined by 50%. In addition, children's free play time in a typical week has declined by a total of nine hours over a 25-year period.[5]

While this physical restriction of childhood may be an unintended outgrowth of an urban society, there may be correspondingly unintended consequences as a result. As nature deficit grows, so does the increase of childhood disorders such as Attention Deficit Hyperactivity Disorder (ADHD) and obesity.[6] In a series of studies designed to explore potential new treatments for ADHD, the inclusion of after-school and weekend activities centered on natural outdoor environments may be widely effective in reducing symptoms of the disorder. The advantages of these relatively simplistic approaches are many: They are widely accessible, inexpensive, non-stigmatizing, and free of side effects.[7]

And, lest one think that children in rural areas are immune from the urban blight of constricted space and diminished play, studies demonstrate otherwise. While adults may delight in idyllic country life images of open fields, green pastures, and limitless opportunity for play, nothing could be further from the reality of today's youth. Images of *Lassie* aside, most rural children are in the same sedentary boat as their urban counterparts: inside, in front of a screen. Statistics reflect this, with 16.5% of rural kids qualifying as obese, compared with 14.4% of urban kids (according to a 2003 National Survey of Children's Health). In many ways, they are more disadvantaged than their suburban counterparts because their homes may not be near areas suitable for play and often lack a support system for activity. According to David Hartley, director of the Maine Rural Health Center, children living in isolated communities tend to have fewer places to walk and play. In addition, they also suffer from decreased opportunities to buy healthy foods (a situation often referred to as "nutritional isolation"), an ironic twist on the fresh-air-and-good-food misconception most Americans have of country life.[8]

In addition to a high-fat, high-calorie daily menu, other factors contribute to this situation. American homes have become high-def, Web-enabled, TiVo-driven entertainment meccas that offer 24-hour-a-day diversion from anything that would get a kid out of his or her rocker lounge chair. After a full day at a school desk, the American child comes home to spend, on average, three or more sedentary hours in front of some kind of screen. What's worse, school budgets have slashed physical education programs in cost-cutting moves that have resulted in plummeting participation in daily physical education—down to 25% from 42% 17 years ago.[9]

Vision for Environmental Education

So what's a school board/principal/teacher to do? Throw away our old classroom science kits and take the kids out to play? Close.

Recent proposals, such as the Vision for Environmental Education in Ontario, Canada, promote innovative programs and partnerships with community-based environmental organizations as well as outdoor education centers. In doing so, the Canadian Ministry of Education is offering a vision for environmental education that provides a context for applying knowledge and skills to real-world situations through an integrated approach. Their science curriculum embraces education for sustainability as well as outdoor education. Consequently, students are afforded opportunities for experiential learning that foster connections to local places, develop a greater understanding of ecosystems, and supply a unique context for learning.[10]

Closer to home, the Open Spaces program of the Urban Resources Initiative (under the aegis of Yale University) is on the same track. Open Spaces balances classroom learning on key ecological concepts with outdoor experiences that bring these ideas to life. Whether students are identifying trees and habitats in a schoolyard or connecting human history to the environment, this program opens kids' eyes to nature in the city and teaches them how to protect urban resources.[11]

Regardless of the worldwide location—be it New Haven or New South Wales—the objectives of enlightened environmental education policies are predictably consistent: to create eco-schools in coordination with a holistic, participatory approach through a combination of learning and action. Raising awareness through inspiring and motivating students is integral to comprehensive program design.

The Lorax

Which brings us to *The Lorax*. Theodore Seuss Geisel, a.k.a. "Dr. Seuss," created this celebrated story almost 40 years ago, but its prescient message is as timely today as though it were written during the last election cycle. In it, Dr. Seuss introduces the "Once-ler," who cuts down the beautiful truffula trees so that he can use their bright-colored, silky tufts to knit "thneeds." The blissful world of happy "Brown Barba-loots," who play in the shade of the trees and eat their fruits, is destroyed by the factory built by the Once-ler and the Super Axe Hacker, who cuts down four trees at a time. Enter the Lorax, who speaks up in defense of the trees, animals, air, and water that the Once-ler is destroying in pursuit of bigger and bigger profits. Finally, when the last truffula tree is cut down, production of the thneeds ends. Closed factories, polluted air, polluted water, and an uninhabitable wasteland are all that remains. The Lorax can no longer live there, but he leaves a small pile of rocks on which the word "UNLESS" is inscribed.

What's left, ultimately, is one last truffula seed and the hope that the forest will come back, bringing with it the Lorax and all of his friends.

The basic message of *The Lorax* deals with ecosystems and the interrelatedness of all parts—living and non-living—as a viable, functioning unit. Environmental impact is told from a simplistic yet environmentally accurate viewpoint, demonstrating the conflict between natural resources and man-made production.

This fable of reckless deforestation and its dire ecological consequence was an outgrowth of the environmental reform movement of the 1960s, which peaked with the nation's first Earth Day on April 22, 1970. Issues of the day were presented in a means that allowed children to equate the ideas in the story with real, present-day situations.[12]

For years, teachers have used *The Lorax* to help students understand the need for conservation as well as the effects of lifestyle changes that will result from the thoughtless devastation of the natural world.

And yet, there is an environmental movement that goes beyond the obvious message. The interrelatedness of environmental education and the reconnection of children with nature are at the heart of both. Perhaps the message should be, "Heal the globe, and you heal yourself."

Conservation will fail unless it is better connected to people, and people start out as children who need to revere their connection to nature from a personal, rather than intellectual, viewpoint. And so we must bridge the rhetoric/reality gap between conservation for its own sake and conservation for the sake of the health and well-being of our children.

Dr. Seuss rhymes aside, how do we cast as wide a net as possible in capturing the imagination of children in inspiring them to become an active part of their ecological environment? Is it something that can be legislated, or is it an intangible passion that can only be appreciated through firsthand experience? Actually, research suggests both.

No Child Left Inside

To address the problems voiced here, the No Child Left Inside Coalition—a broad-based organization of more than 200 member groups throughout the U.S.—has focused its efforts on legislation that would authorize new funding for states to provide high-quality, environmental instruction. The No Child Left Inside Act (NCLI) would provide subsidies to support outdoor learning activities both at school and in non-formal environmental education centers, teacher training, and the creation of state environmental literacy plans.[13]

The intersection between healthy people and a healthy environment is critical to the future of youngsters everywhere, yet the movement to reconnect children with nature is still in its infancy. The retreat indoors is not only limiting to the next generation, it's downright dangerous. Public health workers already see the effects in fatter, sicker children whose life expectancy is alarmingly shorter than that of their parents. As the American Public Health Association notes in its publication, *The Nation's Health*, "The future . . . is in the hands of today's children, many of whom are more likely to view nature through the screen of a television rather than the netted screen of a camping tent."[14]

"Which brings us back to little Sally Brown, still in her bean-bag chair, still watching nature on TV. Take note, little yellow-haired girl: Get up, put on your mittens, and go out and play in the snow. Your future depends on it.

Notes

1. Patricia A. Zaradic and Oliver R.W. Pergams, "Videophilia: Implications for Childhood Development and Conservation," *Journal of Developmental Processes,* Spring 2007, pp. 130–47.
2. Edward O. Wilson, *Biophilia* (Cambridge, Mass.: Harvard University Press, 1984).
3. Richard Louv, *Last Child in the Woods* (New York: Workman, 2008).
4. Peter Applebome. "Build a Wiffle Ball Field in Greenwich, and Lawyers Will Come," *New York Times,* 10 July 2008, pp. A1, A15.
5. Sandra L. Hofferth and John F. Sandberg, "How Children Spend Their Time," *Journal of Marriage and Family,* May 2001, pp. 295–308.
6. Frederick J. Zimmerman, Dimitri A. Christakis, and Andrew N. Meltzoff, "Television and DVD/Video Viewing in Children Younger than 2 Years," *Archives of Pediatrics and Adolescent Medicine,* May 2007, pp. 473–79.
7. Frances E. Kuo and Andrea F. Taylor, "A Potential Natural Treatment for Attention-Deficit/Hyperactivity Disorder: Evidence from a National Study," *American Journal of Public Health,* September 2004, pp. 1580–86, www.pubmedcentral.nih.gov.
8. Bryan Walsh, "It's Not Just Genetics," *Time,* 23 June 2008, pp. 70–80.

9. Jeffrey Kluger, "How America's Children Packed on the Pounds," *Time,* 23 June 2008, pp. 66–69.

10. Roberta Bondar, *Shaping Our Schools, Shaping Our Future: Environmental Education in Ontario Schools* (Toronto: Working Group on Environmental Education, 2007), www.edu .gov.on.ca/curriculum-council/shapingSchools.pdf.

11. Pegnataro, Justin, "Open Spaces as Learning Places," Urban Resources Initiative, 2005, www.yale.edu/uri/programs/osalp .html.

12. Christine Moseley, "The Continuing Adventures of the Truffula Tree Company," *Science Scope,* May 1995, pp. 22–25.

13. Chesapeake Bay Foundation, "No Child Left Inside," 2008, www.cbf.org, search on title.

14. Kim Krisberg, "Movement to Reconnect Kids with Nature Growing Nationwide: Working to Improve Children's Health," *The Nation's Health,* October 2007.

Critical Thinking

1. If you live somewhere, other than in a college or university residence hall, observe children in your neighborhood engaged in outside play. If you live in a residence hall with limited access to children, find a location where you can observe young children at play. What is the most common form of play you observe? What affects the outside play of the children?

2. Develop a list of outside activities you could implement with a group of children ages 4–6 to get them more interested in nature.

CLARE LOWELL is an assistant professor of education at Marymount Manhattan College in New York City.

Constructive Play

A Value-Added Strategy for Meeting Early Learning Standards

Walter F. Drew et al.

This was one of the children's first days using turkey basters in water play. We try to add only one new thing at a time. The children started hooking the funnel to the turkey baster and found ways to fill the baster and squirt out water. They were so excited to discover they had made a fountain. They named it Water Spout. We had read the book *I Wish that I Had Duck Feet*, and the children remembered the water spout in the story.

—Trisha McCunn, Preschool Teacher

Constructive play involves building and making things no one has ever seen before. As young children fiddle with, sort, and arrange materials, ideas and imagination begin to flow. Questions arise naturally. They wonder: What will happen if I put this here? How tall will it go? Where did the bubble come from? In this way, constructive play serves to focus the minds of children through their fingertips and leads them to invent and discover new possibilities, to fulfill their sense of purpose.

Play in a Standards-oriented World

In many early childhood programs across the country, time for play is dwindling away. The field of early childhood education is in the midst of a major shift in orientation toward a standards base. Early learning standards specify what young children should know and be able to do in academic areas such as science, literacy, and mathematics. These standards have rapidly become an integral part of state systems of early childhood education. All the states plus the District of Columbia have approved early learning standards for preschoolers. As a structural element of education reform, early learning standards shape the content of instructional curriculum, set the goals of professional development, and establish the focus of outcomes assessment. Standards are increasingly seen as a powerful lever for improving preschool instruction and children's school readiness.

This rise of state early learning standards has alarmed many early childhood educators, especially advocates of play-based approaches to teaching and learning. Play has long had a central role in early childhood education, where it has been viewed as an effective means for promoting all aspects of child development. Many early childhood teachers are concerned that the standards movement and its narrowing of educational goals are pushing aside classroom learning through play in favor of more didactic forms of instruction.

Reconciling Play and Standards

In this article, we take a more positive, pragmatic approach and propose to reconcile constructive play with the standards movement. Recognizing that standards have become an integral part of early education, we believe that mature forms of play, such as the examples presented in which children are focused and intentional, can be effective strategies for helping children learn academic skills stressed in state standards (Kagan & Lowenstein 2004; Van Thiel & Putnam-Franklin 2004; Christie & Roskos 2006). Mature play is mindful make-believe and reasonably self-regulated.

Our proposals are based on field research, observations, interviews, and vignettes focused on constructive play that uses a variety of open-ended materials to promote learning and development. We share educators' stories, experiences, and ideas around principles of constructive play and include specific suggestions for practice.

Three Principles for Using Constructive Play to Meet Early Learning Standards

We identify three key principles that explain why developmentally appropriate constructive play is an ideal instructional strategy for meeting early learning standards. These principles are derived from our own experiences as play researchers and teacher educators.

1. During the preschool years, constructive play merges with exploration and make-believe play and becomes a mature form of play that allows children to strengthen inquiry skills and build conceptual understanding.

Constructive play is organized, goal-oriented play in which children use play materials to create or build something (Johnson, Christie, & Wardle 2005). It often begins during the toddler years and becomes increasingly complex with age. Constructive play involves open-ended exploration, gradually becoming more functional in nature, then evolving to make-believe transformations. Four- and 5-year-olds often switch back and forth between constructive and dramatic play, and it can be difficult to distinguish between the two forms of play. According to Bodrova and Leong (2004), the type of mature play that promotes learning and development has three critical components: imaginary situations, explicit roles, and implicit rules.

Mature play has three critical components: imaginary situations, explicit roles, and implicit rules.

We typically think of constructive play as building with blocks and other three-dimensional materials. Building a road or castle with wooden blocks, shaping a ball out of clay, constructing a spaceship with recycled materials, and putting a puzzle together are all examples of constructive play. But how is the water play, described at the beginning of this article, constructive play (see "Water Play" below)?

Trisha McCunn, a teacher of 3- to 5-year-olds at Lollipop Pre-School in rural Iowa, uses *Exploring Water with Young Children,* the Young Scientist series, and records observations of the children:

> The children discovered that a little squeeze of a water-filled baster made the water bubble, but with a big squeeze the water shot up with great force. They had made water play rules, and one was that the water had to stay in the water table. For today, we decided to set aside the rule because the water could be wiped up. Everyone wiped up water most of the afternoon, but how exciting it was to make a fountain in preschool.

> When I added clear plastic hoses, the children discovered that if they pushed the hose into the water and stuck their thumbs or fingers on the top end, they could make a bubble go up and down inside by moving the hose up or down like a steering wheel. One boy exclaimed, "Look, I'm driving a car!" He drove the car for 20 minutes, pretending the moving air bubble was the road and imagining he was following it.

For Ms. McCunn and the children in her class, constructive play is a form of hands-on inquiry, a way of meeting early learning standards. She knows the children have an innate need to understand their worlds, physically explore, and manipulate materials, and she values the exploring, inventing, and discovering they do together.

Inquiry is a way of looking at the world, according to Parker (2007), a questioning stance we take when we seek to learn something we don't yet know. And when we are truly into inquiring about something, whatever it may be, we drive ourselves to learn more and more because we seek answers to our own questions. This definition captures the very heart of inquiry-based learning and aptly relates what the children in

Trish's class are doing. Believing that all children have the desire and capacity to explore and better understand their worlds is the foundation of constructive play and inquiry-based teaching in early childhood.

Trisha McCunn provided the kinds of simple constructive play materials that appeal to the children's natural desire to question and find out things for themselves. She set the stage in a way that encouraged children to construct new knowledge and thus initiated the learning process.

According to Chouinard (2007), humans' ability to seek out information from one another seems to give us a particular evolutionary advantage and allows us to learn efficiently. Chouinard's research also substantiates the belief that children need to take an active role in the questioning and information-gathering process. When children are actively involved, they remember the information they gather better than information simply given to them. Children build knowledge through active questioning and information gathering combined with hands-on experiences and direct personal-social interactions. This process of active learning and acquisition of knowledge occurs during play with materials, play with ideas, and play with others.

Vygotsky and other well-known theorists have stressed the importance of play in the learning process of young children (Bodrova & Leong 2004). Play provides an intrinsically motivating context in which children come together to understand their world. Constructive play, with its emphasis on hands-on inquiry, is ideally suited for helping children learn the academic skills and concepts found in states' early learning standards (see "Connections between Arizona Early Learning Standards and Constructive Play").

2. Teachers who are knowledgeable about the purposeful use of materials, the process of constructive play, and intentional strategies for interacting with children succeed in helping children develop essential concepts and skills in all content areas.

Making things is an activity that is key to successful learning for young children. They combine the dexterity of their little fingers with the power of their brains to develop a knack for representation and the capacity for creative visual symbolizing. It is interesting to consider this as the ability to imagine the future. The ability to physically construct new connections between thoughts and objects is the act of innovation and change. Teachers who understand and encourage this process of learning help children develop a very important talent.

By taking known elements and creating new connections, children demonstrate the lifelong process of accommodation and improvisation. In this regard, current research emphasizes the importance of school readiness factors covering all developmental domains and including active approaches to learning (Bowman & Moore 2006). Child-focused inquiry learning that involves constructive play with an array of three-dimensional materials, fosters positive learning, such as enthusiasm, resilience, creativity, decision making, and persistence in completing tasks (Day 2006).

For optimal learning to occur through play, children need support, time, and open-ended materials that stimulate the brain to think imaginatively. The materials teachers choose to bring into the classroom reveal the choices they have made about knowledge and what they think is important for children to learn, including the content of applicable learning standards.

Pauline Baker, a cooperating early childhood resource teacher in the Tucson Unified School District, supports the constructive play of 4-, 5-, and 6-year-olds who come to her studio.

> I pick up interesting materials all the time . . . sticks, stones, wire, wood, and use them all with the children.

> I organize materials by color and keep them in baskets, bins, boxes, and lettuce trays. Some materials are organized by "circleness," both man-made and nature-made.

Water Play

. . . is about physical science, the study of fluid dynamics. Understanding how the water spout works involves design technology, which is part of the construction of simple systems. It requires a different kind of knowledge than constructing with blocks.

If children have a goal in mind in relation to water flow, they are motivated to learn about forces of gravity, water pressure, and fluids in motion to be successful at what they are doing.

When teachers encourage children to explore and think about what they are doing and talk and plan together, there is potential for skill development in a lot of areas . . . language, science, social competence, as well as positive dispositions toward learning and learning how to learn.

—Ingrid Chalufour, Young Scientist Series Author

Connections between Arizona Early Learning Standards and Constructive Play

Early Learning Standards (Arizona)	Constructive Play, Research Supported
Language and Literacy	
Strand 2: Pre-Reading Processes, **Concept 5:** Vocabulary Development—The child understands and uses increasingly complex vocabulary.	Research by Cohen (2006) shows that children learn new vocabulary words as they socially interact with partners and in groups during constructive play.
Strand 2: Pre-Reading Processes, **Concept 1:** Print Awareness—The child knows that print carries meaning.	Literacy-enriched play centers contain theme-related reading and writing materials. For example, a block center might contain pencils, pens, materials for making signs, storage labels (for large blocks, Legos), and so on. Research indicates that when children play in print-enriched settings, they often learn to read play-related print (Neuman & Roskos 1993; Vukelich 1994).
Strand 3: Pre-Writing Processes, **Concept 1:** Written Expression—The child uses writing materials to communicate ideas.	Research by Pickett (1998) shows that adding writing materials to block centers results in a large increase in emergent writing, including making signs to identify function and ownership, regulate behavior, and communicate messages.
Mathematics	
Strand 4: Geometry and Measurement, **Concept 1:** Spatial Relationships and Geometry—The child demonstrates an understanding of spatial relationships and recognizes attributes of common shapes.	Recent research by Miyakawa, Kamii, and Nagahiro (2005) confirms that block building can help children learn important spatial relationships.
Social-Emotional	
Strand 2: Social Interactions with Others, **Concept 2:** Cooperation—The child demonstrates the ability to give and take during social interactions.	Creasey, Jarvis, and Berk (1998) contend that a two-way relationship exists between group play and social development: the social environment influences children's play, and play acts as an important context in which children acquire social skills and social knowledge needed to engage in group play. Children learn attitudes and skills needed for this play from their parents, teachers, and other children. At the same time, play with others has a key role in social development by providing a context in which children can acquire many important social skills, such as turn taking, sharing, and cooperation, as well as the ability to understand other people's thoughts, perceptions, and emotions.
Strand 4: Approaches to Learning, **Concept 5:** Problem-solving—The child demonstrates the ability to seek solutions to problems.	Bruner (1972) proposes that play contributes to children's ability to solve problems by increasing their behavioral options and suggests that block play encourages inventive thinking and logical reasoning while constructing three-dimensional patterns. Copely and Oto (2006) find that young children demonstrate considerable problem-solving knowledge during block play.

Source: Arizona Early Learning Standards, www.azed.gov/earlychildhood/downloads/EarlyLearningStandards.pdf.

Quality early childhood programs reflect the knowledge of teachers, like Ms. Baker, who understand their roles during children's constructive play and learning and routinely allocate ample time for children to choose and engage in a wide variety of play-related activities, including constructive play with different types of blocks and other open-ended materials (Drew & Rankin 2004).

By age 4, children begin to move from sorting, lining up, stacking, and pushing blocks to constructing and symbolically representing a tree house, for instance, as in the classroom description. As children practice building, their constructions become more detailed, more complex, more coordinated, and balanced.

In addition, constructions are more likely to be used in dramatic pretense. Children may use foam blocks to make a forest of trees, while using other materials to represent people and animals that have adventures in the forest. Constructive play becomes more popular with age, accounting for more than 50 percent of play activity in preschool settings (Rubin, Fein, & Vandenberg 1983).

Linda Vinson, a pre-K teacher of children with disabilities in Brevard County, Florida, offers a variety of materials to the children in her class.

The eight 2- to 4½-year-olds in my class are socially and emotionally developmentally delayed. At the beginning of the year they did not know how to play. I put something in their hands to get them started.

Gradually, I've offered more open-ended and natural materials to help the children express their thinking through words and actions and gain a sense of competence. Now the children have wooden blocks, foam rectangles, purple cylinders, stretchy fabric scraps, soft wire, cardboard tubes, colorful plastic caps, and mat board, all collected from our local reusable resource center. The materials are arranged in straw baskets that add a homelike atmosphere to my classroom.

> Yesterday, after reading the Three Little Pigs, we talked about the wolf and the forest and the different houses the pigs built. The children retold the story, using stuffed animals and puppets. Afterwards, they went to the shelves of materials and began building. Kevin made a tree house of foam rectangles. He built it up and knocked it down 15 or 20 times—each time confidently building it a little higher, laughing as it toppled, and exclaiming, "I can build anything all the way to the sky!"

In construction play activities, children do both science and mathematics.

Linda Vinson's account of the children's play shows the opportunity for conceptual understanding in the area of structural engineering as Kevin makes his tree house. He explores the forces of gravity, compression, tension, and the relationship between the characteristics of materials and successful design to achieve balance, stability, and even aesthetic sensibility. During construction play, Kevin discovers the science of quantity (arithmetic) and shape (geometry) in the making and testing of different design patterns. In short, in construction play activities, children do both science and mathematics. Ms. Vinson is aware of the value-added benefits that come from joyful play—like Kevin's feeling a sense of personal power, competence, and a positive disposition about himself and learning.

3. Professional development experiences that feature hands-on constructive play with open-ended materials help early childhood educators extend and deepen their understanding of constructive play as a developmentally appropriate practice for meeting early learning standards.

Providing professional development opportunities that supply rich, hands-on play experiences using a variety and abundance of open-ended materials, time for reflection on those experiences, and guidance in applying new insights to teaching practice is a powerful strategy for helping teachers develop deeper understandings of developmentally appropriate practice and the essential role of constructive play in quality early childhood programs. Adults who engage in active inquiry and construct knowledge through creative exploration with materials are more positively disposed to encouraging children to do the same. In this way teachers come to understand and appreciate how play helps children develop character virtues, such as tenacity, flexibility, creativity, courage, and resilience—all are characteristics practiced in constructive play, by child and adult.

The adults' hands-on experience is consistent with recommended developmentally appropriate practices for young children. Just as with children, constructive play stimulates an inner dialogue between the teacher and the materials. Ideas, feelings, questions, and relationships begin to take form. The teacher becomes the protagonist—exploring, assuming control through objects, creatively inventing, and becoming the empowered initiator of inquiry and self-discovery.

In *The Ambiguity of Play,* play scholar Brian Sutton-Smith describes play not only as about learning important concepts and skills but also as about playing with interpreting one's own feelings and thoughts instead of primarily representing the external world. He says, "What is adaptive about play, therefore, may be not only the skills that are a part of it but also the willful belief in acting out one's own capacity for the future" (2001, 198). Teachers and children who are most likely to

succeed are the ones who believe in possibilities—optimists, creative thinkers, people who have flexibility along with a sense of power and control. Adult constructive play helps to inform teachers of the kinds of insights, issues, and feelings children experience during their play. Teachers discover new ways of thinking about play and compelling new insight into children's learning. Constructive play becomes an effective self-reflective professional practice that stimulates the creativity of teachers to construct new play strategies to meet early learning standards.

In *Teaching Adults Revisited: Active Learning for Early Childhood Educators,* Betty Jones reminds us that, "Wherever they are in their educational journey, teachers of young children need to tell their stories, hear other stories, and practice reflective thinking about children's development—over and over again" (2007, ix).

Conclusion

Professional development activities in which teachers play together using construction materials can foster a deeper understanding of how to employ materials and engage young children in positive constructive play. Play can be a bridge to school readiness and academic success for all children. Three key principles in using constructive play to meet early learning standards are interrelated in this way.

Players are active agents in learning, imagining, and creating together. This kind of mature or quality play involves imaginary situations, explicit roles, and implicit rules and is recognizable by its persistence and tendency to become more elaborate over time.

Social interaction and shared imaginings often emerge in the context of constructive play, adding values over and above the benefits of reaching academic standards. These extra benefits include creativity, imagination, problem solving, eagerness to learn, ability to cooperate and stay on task, and learning how to self-regulate and be more responsible overall for one's own learning and development in general.

Finally, setting up and supporting positive constructive play in the early educational setting rests on teachers' creativity, sound judgments, and wise decisions. Although constructive play involves objects, good teachers do not focus on these per se but instead on the actions that take place and especially on the children playing. Learningful play, or "play learning" as it is called by some (Pramling-Samuelsson 2007), occurs when children have teachers who are empathic, playful, and intentional. Open-ended, fluid, and natural materials for creative constructive play are important. In addition, teachers must guide exploration and play, helping children as needed, stepping in and out at the right times, and scaffolding in appropriate ways during constructive play episodes.

Constructive play must connect to other kinds of play and activities and be networked with different aspects of the curriculum to maximize its value. To be sure, for the benefit of young children, we must see clearly the value-added connection between constructive play and meeting early learning standards. The challenges are great, as is the reward. Teachers will be helping to restore play to its proper place in early education.

References

Bodrova, E., & D. Leong. 2004. Observing play: What we see when we look at it through "Vygotsky's eyes"? *Play, Policy and Practice Connections* 8 (1–2).

Bowman, D., & E.K. Moore, eds. 2006. *School readiness and social-emotional development: Perspectives on cultural diversity.* Washington, DC: National Black Child Development Institute.

Bruner, J. 1972. The nature and uses of immaturity. *American Psychologist* 27: 687–708.

Chouinard, M.N. 2007. Children's questions: A mechanism for cognitive development. Serial no. 286. *Monographs of the Society for Research in Child Development* 73 (1).

Christie, J., & K. Roskos. 2006. Standards, science, and the role of play in early literacy education. In *Play = learning: How play motivates and enhances children's cognitive and social-emotional growth,* eds. D. Singer, R. Golinkoff, & K. Hirsh-Pasek, 57–73. Oxford, UK: Oxford University Press.

Cohen, L. 2006. Young children's discourse strategies during pretend block play: A sociocultural approach. PhD diss., Fordham University, New York.

Copely, J., & M. Oto. 2006. An investigation of the problem-solving knowledge of a young child during block construction. www.west.asu.edu/cmw/pme/resrepweb/PME-rr-copley.htm.

Creasey, G., P. Jarvis, & L. Berk. 1998. Play and social competence. In *Multiple perspectives on play in early childhood education,* eds. O. Sara-cho & B. Spodek, 116–43. Albany: State University of New York Press.

Day, C.B. 2006. Leveraging diversity to benefit children's social-emotional development and school readiness. In *School readiness and social-emotional development: Perspectives on cultural diversity,* eds. D. Bowman & E.K. Moore, 23–32. Washington, DC: National Black Child Development Institute.

Drew, W., & B. Rankin. 2004. Promoting creativity for life using open-ended materials. *Young Children* 59 (4): 38–45.

Johnson, J., J. Christie, & F. Wardle. 2005. *Play, development, and early education.* New York: Allyn & Bacon.

Jones, E. 2007. *Teaching adults revisited: Active learning for early childhood educators.* Washington, DC: NAEYC.

Kagan, S.L., & A.E. Lowenstein. 2004. School readiness and children's play: Contemporary oxymoron or compatible option? In *Children's play: The roots of reading,* eds. E. Zigler, D. Singer, & S. Bishop-Josef, 59–76. Washington, DC: Zero to Three Press.

Miyakawa, Y., C. Kamii, & M. Nagahiro. 2005. The development of logico-mathematical thinking at ages 1–3 in play with blocks and an incline. *Journal of Research in Child Development* 19: 292–301.

Neuman, S., & K. Roskos. 1993. Access to print for children of poverty: Differential effects of adult mediation and literacy-enriched play settings on environmental and functional print tasks. *American Educational Research Journal* 30: 95–122.

Parker, D. 2007. *Planning for inquiry: It's not an oxymoron!* Urbana, IL: National Council of Teachers of English.

Pickett, L. 1998. Literacy learning during block play. *Journal of Research in Childhood Education* 12: 225–30.

Pramling-Samuelsson, I. 2007. A research-based approach to preschool pedagogy: Play and learning integrated. *Play, Policy, and Practice Connections* (Newsletter of the Play, Policy, & Practice Interest Forum of NAEYC) 10 (2): 7–9.

Rubin, K., G. Fein, & B. Vandenberg. 1983. Play. In *Socialization, personality, and social development,* vol. 4, *Handbook of child psychology,* ed. E. Hetherington, series ed. P. Mussen, 693–774. New York: Wiley.

Sutton-Smith, B. 2001. *The ambiguity of play.* Cambridge, MA: Harvard University Press.

Van Thiel, L., & S. Putnam-Franklin. 2004. Standards and guidelines: Keeping play in professional practice and planning. *Play, Policy, and Practice Connections* 8 (2): 16–19.

Vukelich, C. 1994. Effects of play interventions on young children's reading of environmental print. *Early Childhood Research Quarterly* 9 (2): 153–70.

Critical Thinking

1. Describe the importance of incorporating constructive play experiences in your preschool classroom.
2. Choose three other materials you could add to clay so children could have the opportunity to construct. What do you think children will do with the materials you chose?

WALTER F. DREW, EdD, is executive director of the Institute for Self-Active Education and cofounder of the Reusable Resources Association. He chairs the Play Committee for the Early Childhood Association of Florida and is creator of Dr. Drew's Discovery Blocks. drdrew@cfl.rr.com. **JAMES CHRISTIE,** PhD, is a professor of curriculum and instruction at Arizona State University in Phoenix. He is past president of the Association for the Study of Play and a member of the board of directors of Playing for Keeps. jchristie@asu.edu. **JAMES E. JOHNSON,** PhD, is professor-in-charge of early childhood education at Penn State University in University Park. He is the current series editor of *Play and Cultural Studies* and the former president of the Association for the Study of Play. **ALICE M. MECKLEY,** PhD, professor in early childhood education at Millersville University, Pennsylvania, researches the social play of young children. She is a member of the NAEYC Play, Policy, and Practice Interest Forum's Research Group and TASP (The Association for the Study of Play). Alice.Meckley@millersville.edu. **MARCIA L. NELL,** PhD, is assistant professor in the Elementary and Early Childhood Department at Millersville University. Marcia has been a public school teacher for 25 years in kindergarten through second grade classrooms.

From *Young Children*, July 2008, pp. 38–44. Copyright © 2008 by National Association for the Education of Young Children. Reprinted by permission.

Calendar Time for Young Children
Good Intentions Gone Awry

SALLEE J. BENEKE, MICHAELENE M. OSTROSKY, AND LILIAN G. KATZ

Why do the children struggle to answer Ms. Kelsey correctly, when they have participated in this routine for months? What is the long-term impact on children when they engage regularly in an activity they do not fully understand? Here is a fresh look at calendar time in light of what we know about child development and best practices.

Young Children's Development of a Sense of Time

Adults use calendars to mark and measure time, such as scheduling appointments, remembering birthdays, and anticipating upcoming special events (spring break, a basketball tournament). However, if we look at the development of children's understanding of time (sometimes referred to as *temporal understanding*), there is little evidence that calendar activities that mark extended periods of time (a month, a week) are meaningful for children below first grade (Friedman 2000). However, there *are* some temporal concepts that preschoolers can grasp in the context of their daily activities—concepts such as *later, before,* and *after.*

Barriers to Meaningful Participation

To participate meaningfully in calendar activities, young children must understand that time is sequential. The sequences include yesterday, today, and tomorrow; morning, afternoon, and evening; Sunday, Monday, Tuesday, and so on. Children also must be able to conceptualize *before* and *after* and think about future and past events. Three-year-olds typically "have established object permanence and can recall past events, even though they do not understand the meaning of the words 'yesterday,' 'today,' or 'tomorrow'" (CTB/McGraw-Hill 2002, 9). Thus, young children can talk about things that have happened or will happen, but they cannot yet understand or talk about these events in terms of units of time (days, weeks) or sequence. This child development knowledge draws into question the usefulness of calendar activities for children under age 6.

Heather, a student teacher, watches as Ms. Kelsey begins calendar time with the 4-year-olds seated in a semicircle on the rug. "What day is it today?" Ms. Kelsey asks, gesturing toward the large calendar on an easel next to her. When no one responds, she asks, "Well, what day was it yesterday?" The children show little enthusiasm for the exercise, but finally Mindy offers, "Yesterday was Friday!" Ms. Kelsey says, "No, it wasn't Friday, Mindy. Does someone else know what day it was yesterday?" Terrance suggests, "Wednesday?" to which Ms. Kelsey responds, "Right! And if it was Wednesday yesterday, then what day is it today?" Several wrong guesses later, the correct answer emerges.

Ms. Kelsey then asks Terrance to cross out the corresponding date on the calendar. When he hesitates, she prompts, "Just look at the date we crossed out yesterday." Terrance still seems confused, so Ms. Kelsey points to a box and says, "That's the one for today." Although the children are quite restless and appear indifferent to the solution to the date problem, Ms. Kelsey succeeds in getting them to say in unison, "Today is Thursday, February 15th."

Shortly after large group time, Heather meets with her faculty supervisor, who suggests that when helping the children get ready to go home, Heather might casually ask them what day it will be when they get home. She also suggests that when a child gives the correct answer, Heather should ask, "Are you sure?"

Later, following this advice, Heather finds that about a third of the children do not know what day it will be when they get home. Among those who get the day right, about half are unsure of their answer. Heather wonders about the calendar activity. After all, it is February, and calendar time has been part of the children's daily routine since September.

Young children can talk about things that have happened or will happen, but they cannot yet understand or talk about these events in terms of units of time or sequence.

Distance in Time

Calendar use requires children to understand not only concepts such as *before* and *after* but also the relative lengths of time or distance of past or future events from the present (Friedman 2000). For example, how far away is October 30 when today is October 5? How long is the weekend? Preschoolers cannot usually judge such distances or lengths of time. A 4-year-old who learns that there will be a field trip in five days will not judge the temporal distance of this event any differently than if he were told it is in eight days. In fact, it is difficult for preschoolers to judge length of time within a given day (with hours as the unit of time), such as "in two hours" versus "in four hours." Perhaps this is the reason children on a car trip repeatedly ask, "How long until we get there?"

According to Friedman (2000), the ability to judge the relative time from a past event or until a future event in terms of the calendar year is not in place until sometime between 7 and 10 years of age. The following anecdote about 6-year-olds' attempts to understand time concepts associated with birthdays and age illustrate Friedman's point.

As Joey's grandparents arrive for his birthday, Joey runs to greet them, saying, "I can't believe I'm gonna be 6." "So, you're going to be 6. Six what?" his grandmother asks. Joey responds, "It's my birthday. I'm gonna be 6." "Yes, I know," she replies, "but six what? You're not six books." At that point Joey's 9-year-old brother whispers in his ear, "You're gonna be 6 years old, dummy!" and Joey says, "I'm gonna be 6 years old."

Three days later, as Joey's friends assemble for the traditional noisy birthday party, a discussion begins about who is already 6 and who is not. Marta states, "Well, I'm 6½." Joey asks her, "Six-and-a-half what?" Marta responds, "I don't know." Another child says to 6½-year-old Marta, "Wait a minute. When were you a baby?" She hesitates and then answers, "I don't know, maybe 10 years ago."

True understanding of dates and the calendar comes with maturity. Given the above information on the level of thinking required to grasp the time concepts of the calendar and the developmental abilities of young children, teachers may want to reconsider the calendar routine and their expectations for young children's comprehension.

Teaching Using the Calendar—or Not?

Early childhood educators may use the calendar to teach concepts other than time, including numeracy, vocabulary (month, year, weekend), sequencing (yesterday, today, tomorrow), and patterning (Monday, Tuesday, Wednesday). Additionally, as children attend to the visual calendar, teachers may hope they will learn numeral recognition and one-to-one correspondence. Early childhood specialists have cited numbers, spatial reasoning, patterning, logical relations, measurement, and early algebra as key components of young children's mathematical

growth (for example, Greenes 1999; NCTM 2000). However, most 4-year-olds are not ready to grasp the complex concepts involved in dates (Etheridge & King 2005).

Math Concepts

Learning experiences that center on mathematical concepts should not only be enjoyable and meaningful but also direct children's thinking toward, and focus it on, important mathematical ideas (Trafton, Reys, & Wasman 2001). Giving preschool children opportunities to explore and experiment individually with math concepts, using concrete materials with a responsive adult to question and guide learning, is likely to be more meaningful and beneficial than having young children participate in a whole group discussion of such concepts centered on the calendar.

For example, a teacher can help children notice patterns in the environment and in their work and explain the process of patterning both at circle time and individually. A teacher might join a child who is stringing beads and say, "I think I will make a pattern with my beads. My pattern is blue, yellow, red; blue, yellow, red. What kind of pattern can you make with your beads?" These approaches can help children build their own patterning abilities.

Other Knowledge and Skills

Many teachers use calendar time to teach skills unrelated to math, such as colors, letters, emergent writing, and social skills. While each of these concepts and skills is important for young children to learn, the calendar routine is not the most useful format for teaching them. For example, it is difficult for teachers to individualize instruction to meet the diverse needs of young learners during a large group activity such as calendar time.

Better Alternatives at Group Time

If focusing on the calendar is not an appropriate way to introduce young children to time concepts, numeracy, and the other concepts mentioned above, then what are some better ways?

The following evidence-based practices are likely to be more effective than calendar activities in presenting time concepts to young children.

Picture Schedules

Although young children have difficulty judging the length of time between events (for example, how long the time between snack and outside play will be), they can understand a sequence of events (for example, snack comes after circle time). Young children generally have a strong sense of narrative and the way a story progresses. Pictures illustrating the schedule of class activities are often recommended for children with particular disabilities. Similarly, a poster with illustrations or photos of the day's activities in sequence can be helpful for all young children.

A poster with illustrations or photos of the day's activities in sequence can be helpful for all young children.

Classroom Journal

Using a digital camera, the teacher can take frequent photographs of classroom events, projects, or field trips, then invite the children to help select photos for a classroom journal. Attach the photos to a dated page (one photo per page or multiple photos on a page) or tuck them into a plastic sleeve. Post or display them in a designated place—on a wall or bulletin board or in a binder—to clearly reflect the sequence of activities: "On Tuesday, we went to the park, we made pancakes, and we read *Pancakes, Pancakes!* by Eric Carle." As the children add new pictures chronicling recent events, they can revisit and discuss past shared events.

Along these same lines, the teacher can collect samples of children's work in a notebook as a visual record of shared events. Children can take turns contributing work to this community notebook. When teachers encourage children to tell peers or their families the story of their project, the children strengthen their understanding of the way an event unfolds, with the various activities taking place in a time sequence.

Documentation Displays

Displaying documentation of shared class events can lead to meaningful discussions that involve time-linked vocabulary. For example, when looking at a documentation display about the class construction of a giant papiermâché butterfly, one child said, "See, there's the butterfly we made that other time." Her teacher responded, "Yes, we made the giant butterfly two weeks ago. Here [pointing to a photograph on the display] is a picture of the frame we built the first day, and the picture next to it shows you adding the papiermâché on the second day."

Linear Representations

Linear representations also can help children begin to understand and conceptualize that a day is a unit of time and talk about it with increasing clarity. For example, to count the number of days they have been in kindergarten, children can add a link to a paper chain each day, or number a pattern of colored Post-it notes and place them on the classroom wall, or add a Unifix cube to a stack of cubes. The teacher can emphasize time-linked vocabulary, such as *before, after, later, earlier*, as the children add the new link. Unlike calendars, linear representations do not require the left-to-right orientation.

Games

Games are another way for children to begin to get a feel for the length of various units of time and the vocabulary associated with them. For example, children might guess how many seconds it takes to walk from one side of the playground to the other, and the teacher or another child can time it with a watch. Or a teacher might ask the children to guess how many minutes it will take for a snowball to melt indoors and then time it with a clock. They might guess how many hours it will be until story time, tally the hours as they pass, and then compare the result with their estimate. These experiences with units of time (seconds, minutes, hours) can lead to discussions about points in time during the school day and the relative distance in the future of these points in time. For example, the teacher might say, "We are going to the library at nine o'clock, and we will go outside at ten o'clock. Where are we going first?"

Project Work

Project work, in which children actively engage in ongoing investigations of events and phenomena around them, is another way to give children opportunities to acquire many concepts and skills related to time (Helm & Beneke, 2003). In project work, calendar concepts are useful rather than ritualistic in nature. Project work lends itself to planning future events and keeping a record of events that happen over time. For example, in a mixed-age preschool, the children investigated eggs. They incubated mallard duck eggs, and each day they added to a tally of days until the ducklings would hatch. As children plan for investigation and reflect on what they have learned and when they learned it in the meaningful context of a project, they naturally begin to develop a sense of the relative lengths of time in the past and future.

> **Project work lends itself to planning future events and keeping a record of events that happen over time.**

Intellectual Development and Calendar Time

A teacher's actions can enhance or inhibit young children's learning. Communication, classroom support, activities, and interactions all play a part. If young children participate frequently in activities they do not really understand, they may lose confidence in their intellectual powers. In this case, some children may eventually give up hope of understanding many of the ideas teachers present to them. Certainly all children will experience some degree of not fully understanding activities at some point. However, in such cases it is helpful for the teacher to reassure learners that fuller understanding will come and that it often takes practice to master a concept, and to indicate in other ways that feeling "out of it" happens to us all sometimes and will be overcome. "Curriculum goals must be both challenging and achievable for all children . . . one size does not fit all. Children will learn best if curriculum content connects with what they already know and have experienced, while introducing them to important new ideas and skills" (Hyson 2000, 61).

In a joint position statement on best practices in early childhood mathematics learning, NAEYC and the National Council of Teachers of Mathematics (NCTM) (2002) stated,

> It is vital for young children to develop confidence in their ability to understand and use mathematics—in other words, to see mathematics as within their reach. In addition, positive experiences with using mathematics

to solve problems help children to develop dispositions such as curiosity, imagination, flexibility, inventiveness, and persistence that contribute to their future success in and out of school. (p. 5)

Lengthy daily calendar sessions in which a teacher expresses the expectation that young children will understand the workings of a calendar run counter to this position. Teachers who intend to keep calendar a part of their daily classroom routine will be more effective if they develop ways to incorporate the calendar that require little time and reflect young children's limited development of time concepts.

Conclusion

As teachers reflect on their practice, they may experience an inner conflict in terms of what they believe about children's development and how and what they teach. Understanding how children learn should enable teachers to focus on calendar-related constructs such as patterning, sorting, and seriating during more natural and appropriate routines. In fact, many teachers will likely realize they already address these fundamental concepts during other parts of the classroom day.

As we return to the opening vignette, considering the information in this article, the discussion Ms. Kelsey has with her class might look something like this:

As Heather watches, Ms. Kelsey addresses the 4-year-olds seated on the rug in front of her: "It's time for us to add another link to our chain. Who would like to attach the link that stands for today?" Mindy volunteers, and Ms. Kelsey says, "Wonderful! Pick someone for your partner, and you two can take care of that." Mindy holds out her hand to Ginelle, and Ginelle joins her in attaching the latest link.

"Now, let's look at our picture chart. Who can tell me what we are going to do after circle time?" Terrance offers, "We're going to the library." Ms. Kelsey responds, "Right! Does anyone remember what are we going to do after that?" Althea enthusiastically states, "We're going out for recess!" Ms. Kelsey cheerfully responds, "Yes, that's right, Althea."

Ms. Kelsey then says, "Mindy and Ginelle have added a link for today to the paper chain. How far does the chain reach, now?" Ginelle responds, "It's almost to the window. It's really getting long." Many of the children voice their agreement.

Not long after circle time, Heather's faculty supervisor suggests that when she helps the children get ready to go home, she might ask them what they are going to tell their parents they did that day at school. Most of the children plan to tell their parents about the day's sequence of activities, and when Heather prompts them with, "Are you sure?" several children refer to the picture chart to verify their statements.

References

CTB/McGraw-Hill. 2002. *Pre-kindergarten standards: Guidelines for teaching and learning.* Executive summary. www.ctb.com/media/articles/pdfs/resources/PreKstandards_summary.pdf

Etheridge, E.A., & J.R. King. 2005. Calendar math in preschool and primary classrooms: Questioning the curriculum. *Early Childhood Education Journal* 32 (5): 291–96.

Freidman, W.J. 2000. The development of children's knowledge of the times of future events. *Child Development* 71 (4): 913–32.

Greenes, C. 1999. The Boston University-Chelsea project. In *Mathematics in the early years,* ed. J.V. Copley, 151–55. Washington, DC: NAEYC.

Helm, J.H., & S. Beneke. 2003. *The power of projects.* New York: Teachers College Press.

Hyson, M. 2000. "Is it okay to have calendar time?" Look up to the star—Look within yourself. *Young Children* 55 (6): 34–36.

NAEYC & NCTM (National Council of Teachers of Mathematics). 2002. Early childhood mathematics: Promoting good beginnings. A joint position statement of NAEYC and NCTM.www.naeyc.org/about/positions/mathematics.asp

NCTM (National Council of Teachers of Mathematics). 2000. *Principles and standards for school mathematics.* Reston, VA: Author.

Trafton, P., B.J. Reys, & D.G. Wasman. 2001. Standards-based mathematics curriculum materials: A phrase in search of a definition. *Phi Delta Kappan* 8 (3): 259–64.

Critical Thinking

1. If possible, arrange with a teacher to observe a group in a program serving children from preschool age through third grade where specific reference to calendar is discussed. What did you observe during the discussion on the calendar? How did it conflict or coincide with what Beneke, Ostrosky, and Katz discuss in the article?

2. Develop a plan for incorporating appropriate experiences that provide children with a sense of the passing of time and numeracy.

SALLEE J. BENEKE is the author and coauthor of several books on the project approach. She is a doctoral student in the Department of Special Education at the University of Illinois and provides professional development for school districts and child care centers. **MICHAELENE M. OSTROSKY**, PHD, is on faculty in the Department of Special Education at the University of Illinois at Urbana-Champaign. She collaborates with other faculty in the Center on Social and Emotional Foundations for Early Learning and is involved with The Autism Program in Illinois. Micki is involved in research on social interaction interventions, naturalistic language interventions, social-emotional competence, challenging behavior, and transitions. ostrosky@uiuc.edu. **LILIAN G. KATZ,** PHD, is codirector of the Clearinghouse on Early Childhood and Parenting and professor emerita at the University of Illinois, Urbana-Champaign. Lilian served as vice president and president of NAEYC in the 1990s. She has lectured in more than 60 countries and served as visiting professor in a half dozen countries.

Why We Should Not Cut P. E.

Eliminate physical education to increase time for reading and math, the theory goes, and achievement will rise. But the evidence says otherwise.

STEWART G. TROST AND HANS VAN DER MARS

Thinking of cutting physical education? Think again. Even as we bemoan children's sedentary lifestyles, we often sacrifice school-based physical education in the name of providing more time for academics. In 2006, only 3.8 percent of elementary schools, 7.9 percent of middle schools, and 2.1 percent of high schools offered students daily physical education or its equivalent for the entire school year (Lee, Burgeson, Fulton, & Spain, 2007).

We believe this marked reduction in school-based physical activity risks students' health and can't be justified on educational or ethical grounds. We'll get to the educational grounds in a moment. As to the ethical reasons for keeping physical activity part of our young people's school days, consider the fact that childhood obesity is now one of the most serious health issues facing U.S. children (Ogden et al., 2006).

School-based physical education programs engage students in regular physical activity and help them acquire skills and habits necessary to pursue an active lifestyle. Such programs are directly relevant to preventing obesity. Yet they are increasingly on the chopping block.

The Assumption: Time in the Gym Lowers Test Scores

No Child Left Behind (NCLB) has contributed to this trend. By linking federal funding to schools' adequate yearly progress in reading and mathematics, NCLB has created an environment in which such classes as physical education, music, and art are viewed as nonessential and secondary to the academic mission of the school.

According to a national study conducted by the Center on Education Policy in 2007, since the passing of NCLB in 2002, 62 percent of elementary schools and 20 percent of middle schools have significantly increased the instructional time they allocate to reading/language arts and math. To accommodate such increases, 44 percent of school districts reported cutting time in such areas as social studies, art, music, physical education, and recess. On average, schools reduced the time allotted to these subjects by more than 30 minutes per day.

But is the assumption that eliminating physical education improves academic performance sound? Not according to the evidence. A comprehensive review of the research shows that academic performance remains unaffected by variations in time allocated to physical education. In fact, in studies that did show physical activity had an effect, increasing instructional time for physical education resulted in *improvements* in academic performance.

Is the assumption that eliminating physical education improves academic performance sound? Not according to the evidence.

The Evidence: P. E. Does Not Hurt—and May Help

In study after study, researchers have concluded that devoting more instructional time to physical education or another in-school physical activity program does not harm academics. Five prominent studies show that students' achievement levels remained unchanged when schools increased or reduced instructional time for physical education.

- Researchers in Australia studied 350 5th graders in seven schools throughout the country. They increased instructional time for physical education for some students by 210 minutes per week. After 14 weeks, there were no significant differences in math or reading skills between students who received additional physical education instruction and those who completed the standard three 30-minute periods of physical education per week (Dwyer, Coonan, Leitch, Hetzel, & Baghurst, 1983).

- A study in California investigated the effect on academic achievement of an intensive two-year program in seven schools that more than doubled the amount of time elementary students spent in physical education. Neither overall academic achievement nor achievement in language arts and reading were adversely affected (Sallis et al., 1999).

- A study of 214 6th graders in Michigan found that students enrolled in physical education had grades and standardized test scores similar to those of students who were not taking physical education, despite receiving nearly an hour less of daily instruction in core academic subjects (Coe, Pivarnik, Womack, Reeves, & Malina, 2006).

- A study involving 287 4th and 5th graders in British Columbia evaluated the effects of daily classroom physical activity sessions on academic performance. Ten elementary schools participated. Although students who attended schools implementing this program spent approximately 50 more minutes per week in physical activity, their standardized test scores in mathematics, reading, and language arts were equivalent to those of students in control schools (Ahamed et al., 2007).

- A study involving more than 500 Virginia elementary schools examined the effect of *decreasing* time for physical education, music, and art on academic performance. Reducing or eliminating the time students spent in these content areas did not increase academic achievement (Wilkins et al., 2003).

- In addition, three major studies indicate that when students participate in physical education, achievement is positively affected for some groups.

- A Canadian study examined the effects on 546 elementary students' academic performance of one additional hour per day of physical education. Students in grades 2 through 6 who received additional physical education earned better grades in French, mathematics, English, and science than did students who received the standard one period per week (Shephard, 1996).

- Studying 311 4th grade students in two schools, Tremarche, Robinson, and Graham (2007) found that students who received 56 or more hours of physical education per school year scored significantly higher on Massachusetts' standardized tests in English and language arts than did comparable students who received 28 hours of physical education per year. There were no significant differences on mathematics scores.

- A longitudinal study by the Centers for Disease Control and Prevention followed two national samples involving 5,316 students from kindergarten to 5th grade. Girls who participated in physical education for 70 or more minutes per week had significantly higher achievement scores in mathematics and reading than did girls who were enrolled in physical education for 35 or fewer minutes per week. Among boys, greater exposure to physical education was neither positively nor negatively associated with academic achievement (Carlson et al., 2008).

The evidence is clear. Decreasing time for physical education does not significantly improve academic performance. Consequently, in an education climate that demands evidence-based instructional practices, the policy of reducing or eliminating school-based physical activity programs cannot be justified.

The Link between Physical Fitness and Academic Performance

The case for sacrificing physical education is further eroded by studies reporting a significant positive relationship between physical fitness and academic performance. In a nutshell, physically active, fit youth are more likely to have better grades and test scores than their inactive counterparts.

Physically active, fit youth are more likely to have better grades and test scores than their inactive counterparts.

National health surveys involving large representative samples of children and teens from the United States, Australia, Iceland, Hong Kong, and the United Kingdom have reported statistically significant positive correlations between physical activity and academic performance (Trost, 2007). One study analyzed data from nearly 12,000 U.S. high school students. Students who reported participating in school-based physical activities or playing sports with their parents were 20 percent more likely than their sedentary peers to earn an *A* in math or English (Nelson & Gordon-Larsen, 2006).

An analysis of fitness testing results from more than 800,000 students in California revealed a significant positive correlation between physical fitness achievement and performance on state achievement tests in reading and mathematics (Grissom, 2005). And in a study conducted in Illinois, children who performed well on two measures of physical fitness tended to score higher on state reading and math exams than low physical performers, regardless of gender or socioeconomic status (Castelli, Hillman, Buck, & Erwin, 2007).

Although the relationship between physical activity and academic performance requires more research, available evidence suggests that the academic mission of schools may be better served by providing *more* opportunities for physical activity. In fact, controlled studies strongly suggest that engaging in physical activity throughout the school day makes students more focused and ready to learn.

The academic mission of schools may be better served by providing *more* opportunities for physical activity.

Research has shown that aerobic exercise can improve memory and executive functioning in school-age youth, especially those who are overweight (Buck, Hillman, & Castelli, 2008; Davis et al., 2007). Drawing on a meta-analysis of more than 40 studies that looked at how engaging in regular physical training affects cognition, Sibley and Etnier (2003) concluded that regular physical activity significantly improves multiple categories of cognitive function in children and adolescents. Researchers found improvements in perceptual skills, IQ, scores on verbal and mathematics tests, concentration, memory, achievement (as measured by a combination of standardized test scores and grades), and academic readiness.

Giving students breaks for physical activity throughout the school day can significantly increase on-task behavior. A study conducted in North Carolina evaluated the effects of a classroom-based program that, for 12 weeks, gave students daily 10-minute breaks for organized physical activity. Researchers observed students in grades K through 5 for 30 minutes before and after each break. On average, the activity breaks increased on-task behavior by 8 percent. Among students who tended to be least focused in class, the breaks improved on-task behavior by 20 percent (Mahar et al., 2006).

Researchers don't understand well the physiological mechanisms responsible for enhancements in cognition related to physical activity. However, emerging evidence from neuroscience suggests that regular physical activity promotes the growth of new brain cells, stimulates formation of blood vessels in the brain, and enhances synaptic activity or communication among brain cells (Hillman, Erickson, & Kramer, 2008).

What We Can Safely Conclude

The research on the relationship between physical education and academic performance does have limitations. For one, the majority of studies have been conducted at the elementary school level; we need additional studies in middle and high schools. In addition, most studies use the *amount* of time spent in physical education as the key independent variable, without considering the *quality* of instruction. Studies of the effects of in-school physical activity on cognitive functioning also often lack what researchers call ecological validity (transferability of findings). For example, research findings may not transfer to school physical education settings if a study was conducted in a lab or if the type, amount, or intensity of physical activity in the study differed greatly from a typical session in a school gymnasium.

Perhaps most important, we know too little about the effect of in-school physical education on academic performance among students at the highest risk for obesity, including low-income children and those from black, Latino, American Indian, and Pacific Islander backgrounds.

Notwithstanding these limitations, we believe the evidence is sufficiently robust to enable us to draw the following conclusions:

- Decreasing (or eliminating) the time allotted for physical education in favor of traditional academic subjects does not lead to improved academic performance.
- Increasing the number of minutes students spend per week in physical education will not impede their academic achievement.
- Increasing the amount of time students spend in physical education may make small positive contributions to academic achievement, particularly for girls.
- Regular physical activity and physical fitness are associated with higher levels of academic performance.
- Physical activity is beneficial to general cognitive functioning.

Implications for Policymakers

Keeping in mind that overweight and obesity are compromising the health of one-third of U.S. students, we see three clear implications of these conclusions.

Conclusion 1: Policymakers must stop trying to justify cuts to physical education on the grounds that such cuts will strengthen school achievement or, ultimately, the economy.

To be sure, a strong academic education contributes to the future economic health of our society. However, the nation's economic and public health are linked in a delicate balance. It is indefensible to support an education system based primarily on promoting economic productivity in people who will likely be too unhealthy to enjoy whatever benefits come their way

Conclusion 2: Policymakers, school administrators, and teachers should stop arguing over whether physical education is essential.

Physical education is now crucial for promoting and increasing physical activity for children and youth. Considering the amount of time students spend in school and the generally accepted mandate of schools to model wholesome life choices, the negative effect of keeping students sedentary all day seems obvious. Although school physical education programs cannot single-handedly reverse the trend of weight gain in youth, they can create conditions that help students learn the importance of leading physically active lives—and encourage them to lead such lives.

Conclusion 3: School administrators must aggressively make room for physical education.

Administrators may feel hamstrung because of the current climate, but they can promote healthier schools by recognizing the barriers to out-of-school physical activity that exist for many students, working with physical education staff to maximize opportunities for physical activity for all students, and monitoring what goes on in physical education classes.

Those who help shape the education of children can no longer ignore the evidence about physical activity and academics, as well as the serious negative health consequences of further reducing physical education. Physical activity is crucial to shaping future generations of healthy people. It has a legitimate claim to part of the school day.

References

Ahamed, Y., Macdonald, H., Reed, K., Naylor, P. J., Liu-Ambrose, T., & McKay, H. (2007). School-based physical activity does not compromise children's academic performance. *Medicine and Science in Sports and Exercise, 39*(2), 371–376.

Buck, S. M., Hillman, C. H., & Castelli, D. M. (2008). The relation of aerobic fitness to stroop task performance in preadolescent children. *Medicine and Science in Sports and Exercise, 40*(1), 166–172.

Carlson, S. A., Fulton, J. E., Lee, S. M., Maynard, M., Brown, D. R., Kohl, III, H. W., & Dietz, W. H. (2008). Physical education and academic achievement in elementary school: Data from the early childhood longitudinal study. *American Journal of Public Health, 98*(4), 721–727.

Castelli, D. M., Hillman, C. H., Buck, S. M., & Erwin, H. E. (2007). Physical fitness and academic achievement in third- and fifth-grade students. *Journal of Sport and Exercise Psychology, 29*(2), 239–252.

Center on Education Policy. (2007). *Choices, changes, and challenges: Curriculum and instruction in the NCLB era.* Washington, DC: Author.

Coe, D. P., Pivarnik, J. M., Womack, C. J., Reeves, M. J., & Malina, R. M. (2006). Effect of physical education and activity levels on academic achievement in children. *Medicine and Science in Sports and Exercise, 38*(8), 1515–1519.

Davis, C. L., Tomporowski, P. D., Boyle, C. A., Waller, J. L., Miller, P. H., Naglieri, J. A., & Gregoski, M. (2007). Effects of aerobic exercise on overweight children's cognitive functioning: A randomized controlled trial. *Research Quarterly for Exercise and Sport, 78*(5), 510–519.

Dwyer, T., Coonan, W. E., Leitch, D. R., Hetzel, B. S., & Baghurst, R. A. (1983). An investigation of the effects of daily physical activity on the health of primary school students in South Australia. *International Journal of Epidemiology, 12*(3), 308–313.

Grissom, J. B. (2005). Physical fitness and academic achievement. *Journal of Exercise Physiology Online, 8*(1), 11–25.

Hillman, C. H., Erickson, K. I., & Kramer, A. F (2008). Be smart, exercise your heart: Exercise effects on brain and cognition. *National Review of Neuroscience, 9*(1), 58–65.

Lee, S. M., Burgeson, C. R., Fulton, J. E., & Spain, C. G. (2007). Physical education and physical activity: Results from the School Health Policies and Programs Study 2006. *Journal of School Health, 77*(8), 435–463.

Mahar, M. T., Murphy, S. K., Rowe, D. A., Golden, J., Shields, A. T., & Raedeke, T. D. (2006). Effects of a classroom-based program on physical activity and on-task behavior. *Medicine and Science in Sports and Exercise, 38,* 2086–2094.

Nelson, M. C., & Gordon-Larsen, P. (2006). Physical activity and sedentary behavior patterns are associated with selected adolescent health risk behaviors. *Pediatrics, 117,* 1281–1290.

Ogden, C. L., Carroll, M. D., Curtin, L. R., McDowell, M. A., Tabak, C. J., & Flegal, K. M. (2006). Prevalence of overweight and obesity in the United States, 1999–2004. *Journal of the American Medical Association, 295*(13), 1549–1555.

Sallis, J. F., McKenzie, T. L., Kolody, B., Lewis, M., Marshall, S., & Rosengard, P. (1999). Effects of health-related physical education on academic achievement: Project SPARK. *Research Quarterly for Exercise and Sport, 70*(2), 127–134.

Shephard, R. J. (1996). Habitual physical activity and academic performance. *Nutrition Reviews, 54*(4), S32–S36.

Sibley, B. A., & Etnier, J. L. (2003). The relationship between physical activity and cognition in children: A meta-analysis. *Pediatric Exercise Science, 15,* 243–256.

Tremarche, P., Robinson, E., & Graham, L. (2007). Physical education and its effects on elementary testing results. *Physical Educator, 64*(2), 58–64.

Trost, S. G. (2007). *Active education: Physical education, physical activity and academic performance* (Research Brief). San Diego, CA: Robert Wood Johnson Foundation Active Living Research. Available: www.activelivingresearch.com/alr/alr/files/Active_Ed.pdf.

Wilkins, J. L., Graham, G., Parker, S., Westfall, S., Fraser, R. G., & Tembo, M. (2003). Time in the arts and physical education and school achievement. *Journal of Curriculum Studies, 35,* 721–734.

Critical Thinking

1. Write a letter to the principal at the school your first grade child attends opposing the principal's decision to cut physical education down to once a month so more time can be devoted to academics. Make sure you incorporate the data included in the article in your letter.

2. Develop a list of five key points you can share with parents who are concerned about the lack of physical education in the school their children attend.

STEWART G. TROST is Associate Professor in the Department of Nutrition and Exercise Sciences at Oregon State University in Corvallis; stewart.trost@oregonstate.edu. HANS VAN DER MARS is Professor in the College of Teacher Education and Leadership at Arizona State University in Mesa; hans.vandermars@asu.edu.

From *Educational Leadership,* December 2009/January 2010, pp. 60–65. Copyright © 2010 by ASCD. Reprinted by permission. The Association for Supervision and Curriculum Development is a worldwide community of educators advocating sound policies and sharing best practices to achieve the success of each learner. To learn more, visit ASCD at www.ascd.org

Test-Your-Knowledge Form

We encourage you to photocopy and use this page as a tool to assess how the articles in *Annual Editions* expand on the information in your textbook. By reflecting on the articles you will gain enhanced text information. You can also access this useful form on a product's book support website at www.mhhe.com/cls

NAME: DATE:

_____

TITLE AND NUMBER OF ARTICLE:

_____

BRIEFLY STATE THE MAIN IDEA OF THIS ARTICLE:

_____

LIST THREE IMPORTANT FACTS THAT THE AUTHOR USES TO SUPPORT THE MAIN IDEA:

_____

WHAT INFORMATION OR IDEAS DISCUSSED IN THIS ARTICLE ARE ALSO DISCUSSED IN YOUR TEXTBOOK OR OTHER READINGS THAT YOU HAVE DONE? LIST THE TEXTBOOK CHAPTERS AND PAGE NUMBERS:

_____

LIST ANY EXAMPLES OF BIAS OR FAULTY REASONING THAT YOU FOUND IN THE ARTICLE:

_____

LIST ANY NEW TERMS/CONCEPTS THAT WERE DISCUSSED IN THE ARTICLE, AND WRITE A SHORT DEFINITION:

NOTES

NOTES

NOTES

NOTES

NOTES

NOTES

NOTES